Writing in Response

Writing in Response

Matthew Parfitt

Boston University, College of General Studies

BEDFORD/ST. MARTIN'S
Boston • New York

For Bedford/St. Martin's

Executive Editor: John E. Sullivan III
Senior Production Editor: Lori Chong Roncka
Assistant Production Editor: Katherine Caruana
Assistant Production Manager: Joe Ford
Senior Marketing Manager: Molly Parke
Editorial Assistant: Alyssa Demirjian
Production Assistant: Elise Keller
Copy Editor: Linda McLatchie
Indexer: Mary White
Photo Researcher: Linda Finigan
Permissions Manager: Kalina K. Ingham
Senior Art Directors: Donna Lee Dennison and Anna Palchik
Text Design and Illustration: Brian Salisbury
Cover Design: Sara Gates and Marine Miller
Composition: Graphic World Inc.
Printing and Binding: RR Donnelley and Sons

President: Joan E. Feinberg
Editorial Director: Denise B. Wydra
Editor in Chief: Karen S. Henry
Director of Marketing: Karen R. Soeltz
Director of Production: Susan W. Brown
Associate Director, Editorial Production: Elise S. Kaiser
Managing Editor: Elizabeth M. Schaaf

Library of Congress Control Number: 2011939733

Manufactured in the United States of America.
6   5   4   3   2   1
f   e   d   c   b   a

For information, write:
Bedford/St. Martin's, 75 Arlington Street, Boston, MA 02116   (617-399-4000)

ISBN: 978-0-312-40393-5

Preface for Instructors

Some years ago, I realized that my students were having a hard time getting a purchase on the smooth surfaces of the academic readings I assigned. Since they didn't have the repertoire of reading skills that this kind of prose demands, the students weren't able to read closely or write thoughtful responses to these texts. To provide them with the analytical tools they needed, I developed materials that have become *Writing in Response*. This book is a short rhetoric designed for first-year composition courses, especially those that include a focus on academic writing. Academic writing typically means writing about texts because the academy functions through dialogue, through conversations that take place mostly in writing — yet many students have never written a serious, thoughtful response to a text, especially a nonfiction text. Frequently, students have very little sense of how scholarship proceeds. They need to learn how they can participate in these conversations by responding to what they read, by approaching their reading as itself a kind of writing.

In addition to offering concrete strategies for academic reading and writing, *Writing in Response* strives to shed light on the conventions of academic discourse, in particular the relationship between the genres of student writing and the genres of academic writing — between what students are expected to do as writers and what faculty scholars do as writers. The book places a strong emphasis on reading and rereading, not just repetitively but actively, so that note-taking flows smoothly into extended prose writing. An equally important theme is the notion that academic writing addresses a genuine *problem* of some kind, whether it is a practical problem or a "knowledge problem" (a purely intellectual problem). This essential element in student writing frequently takes a backseat to the notion of a thesis, but a thesis has no purpose or motive unless it somehow speaks to a need. Too often, student essays read merely like a perfunctory performance of academic prose — or certain qualities of it — if the writer lacks a clear sense of what the problem is and why it matters. This accounts for the book's introduction of the exploratory essay, a less common form of academic writing (not to be confused with personal writing), yet a powerful way to encourage more complex, deeper thinking.

Writing in Response presumes a deep connection between reading and writing and so begins with an extensive discussion of active reading. It continues with further strategies for critical reading as well as for reflection and response, aiming to give students the tools they need to work seriously with texts, particularly challenging ones. The book models practices that help students view the composing process as dialogic, nonlinear, and recursive. It presents a method of composition that includes engagement with other texts, has overlapping phases, and embeds revision as an essential component. With a model of reading and writing that is accessible yet grounded in theory, students learn to connect the texts they read to the texts they write in response.

The process of making those connections necessarily involves informal as well as formal writing. Here, "informal writing" is envisioned both as a product, an end in itself, and as a crucial phase in composing a formal essay. The kind of writing encouraged by many composition instructors today reflects the more exploratory, personal, and even experimental style of recent academic prose, and this development represents a return to the possibilities of the essay as it was first conceived. *Writing in Response* carries an emphasis on craftsmanship and creativity through to the tasks of composing a final paper. Informal writing is presented as much more than just drafting, prewriting, or brainstorming — writing that serves no purpose except as a stage on the way to a finished product — but instead as the occasion for real thinking and learning. Such writing is vital to this book's purpose: *Writing in Response* aims to restore to college composition the pleasures and rewards of exploring, imagining, questioning, reflecting, and speculating.

Throughout *Writing in Response*, samples of student writing (showing both work-in-progress and finished products) are included as illustrations, yet the emphasis is on broadly applicable principles, concepts, and strategies rather than on rules and formulas; therefore, these samples are provided in order to give students ways of imagining what *they* might do as college writers, showing possibilities for how they might carry out their *own* plans. "Try This" activities appear in each chapter, giving students the opportunity to practice skills and strategies as they learn them. These activities are invitations to exercise the responsiveness, flexibility, and creativity that are central to this book's purpose. Most ask for a fairly substantial piece of work, suitable for an evening's homework. Checklists and guidelines throughout provide practical references. These cover such topics as evaluating evidence and developing an argument. *Writing in Response* also discusses style, emphasizing the principles of plain style best suited for academic writing. The book

includes strategies for managing the research process — finding, evaluating, and using varied sources purposefully and documenting them appropriately. Throughout,
student and professional readings provide engaging models and topics, with a cluster of five professional essays in the final part.

Organization

The organization of *Writing in Response* falls into five parts: (1) responsive reading,
(2) composing and revising, (3) issues of style, (4) research and documentation, and
(5) readings.

Writing in Response assumes that the writing process begins in active reading: students should be writing as they read — though this writing may be in the
form of only marginalia and journal notes — so that they begin to generate ideas,
to formulate a response, well before they sit down to draft a full-length essay. If
writing begins with reading notes and then progresses smoothly into low-stakes
informal writing and from there into drafting, students should never have the
numbing experience of sitting in front of a blank computer screen with nothing
to say. In addition, their writing will begin and end as a response, as an original
statement that is anchored in a text or in multiple texts, a statement that makes
a contribution to a scholarly conversation. The structure of the book thus mirrors the incremental nature of the writing process — reading, informal writing,
and formal writing — yet it emphasizes reflection and revision rather than lin-
earity. The discussions in each chapter show how the process is recursive and
seamless, an arc of interpretation that begins in attentive listening and ends in
thoughtful discourse.

Part 1, "Responsive Reading," offers students three chapters on general concepts and specific strategies for reading actively and initiating a response to a text.
These chapters aim to show students how, starting from their own knowledge and
experience, they can arrive at insights, formulate arguments, and enter scholarly
conversations, thereby making essay-writing a more exciting and satisfying undertaking.

Part 2, "Composing and Revising," presents three chapters that offer varied
practical strategies for structuring an essay, shaping paragraphs (the building blocks
of an argument), and revising for organization and meaning.

Part 3, "Attending to Style," includes two chapters on crafting and revising prose at the sentence level, asking students to consider not only meaning and grammar but also stylistic elegance for vigorous and compelling writing.

Part 4, "Research and Documentation," consists of two chapters providing instruction in conducting academic research. The chapters guide students in finding, evaluating, incorporating, and documenting sources in MLA, APA, and *Chicago* formats.

Part 5, "Readings," includes five professional essays to provide good models of thinking while offering possibilities for student response.

You Get More Digital Choices for *Writing in Response*

Writing in Response doesn't stop with a book. Online, you'll find both free and affordable premium resources to help students get even more out of the book and your course. You'll also find convenient instructor resources, such as downloadable sample syllabi, classroom activities, and even a nationwide community of teachers. To learn more about or order any of the products below, contact your Bedford/St. Martin's sales representative, e-mail sales support (sales_support@bfwpub.com), or visit the Web site at bedfordstmartins.com/parfitt/catalog.

Student Site for *Writing in Response*

bedfordstmartins.com/writinginresponse

Send students to free and open resources, choose flexible premium resources to supplement your print text, or upgrade to an expanding collection of innovative digital content.

Free and open resources for *Writing in Response* provide students with easy-to-access reference materials, visual tutorials, and support for working with sources.

- Five free videos of real writers from *VideoCentral*
- Three free tutorials from *ix visual exercises* by Cheryl Ball and Kristin Arola

- *TopLinks* and *AuthorLinks* with reliable online sources
- *Research and Documentation Online* by Diana Hacker
- *Bedford Bibliographer*: a tool for collecting source information and making a bibliography in MLA, APA, and *Chicago* styles

VideoCentral is a growing collection of videos for the writing class that captures real-world, academic, and student writers talking about how and why they write. Writer and teacher Peter Berkow interviewed hundreds of people — from Michael Moore to Cynthia Selfe — to produce fifty brief videos about topics such as revising and getting feedback. *VideoCentral* can be packaged with *Writing in Response* at a significant discount. An activation code is required. To order *VideoCentral* packaged with the print book, use ISBN 978-1-4576-1320-3.

Re:Writing Plus gathers all of Bedford/St. Martin's premium digital content for composition into one online collection. It includes hundreds of model documents, the first ever peer review game, and *VideoCentral. Re:Writing Plus* can be purchased separately or packaged with the print book at a significant discount. An activation code is required. To order *Re:Writing Plus* packaged with the print book, use ISBN 978-1-4576-1319-7.

E-book Options

bedfordstmartins.com/parfitt/catalog

Bedford/St. Martin's e-books let students do more and pay less. For about half the price of a print book, the e-book for *Writing in Response* offers the complete text of the print book combined with convenient digital tools such as highlighting, note-taking, and a search function.

More Options for Students

Add more value to your text by choosing one of the following resources, free when packaged with *Writing in Response*. To learn more about package options or any of the products below, contact your Bedford/St. Martin's sales representative or visit the Web site at bedfordstmartins.com/parfitt/catalog.

i-series

Add more value to your text by choosing one of the following tutorial series, free when packaged with *Writing in Response*. This popular series presents multimedia tutorials in a flexible format — because there are things you can't do in a book. To learn more about package options or any of the products below, contact your Bedford/St. Martin's sales representative or visit bedfordstmartins.com.

ix: visualizing composition 2.0 (available online) helps students put into practice key rhetorical and visual concepts. To order *ix: visualizing composition* packaged with the print book, use ISBN 978-1-4576-1317-3.

i-claim: visualizing argument (available on CD-ROM) offers a new way to see argument — with six tutorials, an illustrated glossary, and more than seventy multimedia arguments. To order *i-claim: visualizing argument* packaged with the print book, use ISBN 978-1-4576-1316-6.

i-cite: visualizing sources (available online as part of *Re:Writing Plus*) brings research to life through an animated introduction, four tutorials, and hands-on source practice. To order *i-cite: visualizing sources* packaged with the print book, use ISBN 978-1-4576-1315-9.

Portfolio Keeping, Second Edition, by Nedra Reynolds and Rich Rice, provides all the information students need to use the portfolio method successfully in a writing course. *Portfolio Teaching*, a companion guide for instructors, provides the practical information instructors and writing program administrators need to use the portfolio method successfully in a writing course. To order *Portfolio Keeping* packaged with the print book, use ISBN 978-1-4576-1516-0.

Oral Presentations in the Composition Course: A Brief Guide, by Matthew Duncan and Gustav W. Friedrich, offers students the advice they need to plan, prepare, and present their work effectively. With sections on analyzing audiences, choosing effective language, using visual aids, collaborating on group presentations, and dealing with the fear of public speaking, this booklet offers help for students' most common challenges in developing oral presentations. To order *Oral Presentations in the Composition Course* packaged with the print book, use ISBN 978-1-4576-1515-3.

Instructor Resources

bedfordstmartins.com/parfitt/catalog

You have a lot to do in your course. Bedford/St. Martin's wants to make it easy for you to find the support you need — and to get it quickly.

Resources for Teaching Writing in Response is available as a PDF that can be downloaded from the Bedford/St. Martin's online catalog. The manual includes a variety of sample syllabi (for first-year writing for single-semester, two-semester, and quarter-system courses, as well as upper-division writing and courses linked to other disciplines). It provides an overview of teaching exploratory writing. The manual addresses every step of the process of critical reading and academic writing discussed in the text, with overviews of each chapter of the student edition. *Resources for Teaching Writing in Response* also offers additional classroom and homework activities for each chapter; a section on how to integrate the readings in Part 5; hints for choosing and using additional readings; and a list of suggested supplementary readings.

Teaching Central offers the entire list of Bedford/St. Martin's print and online professional resources in one place. You'll find landmark reference works, sourcebooks on pedagogical issues, award-winning collections, and practical advice for the classroom — all free for instructors.

Bedford Bits collects creative ideas for teaching a range of composition topics in an easily searchable blog format. A community of teachers — leading scholars, authors, and editors — discuss revision, research, grammar and style, technology, peer review, and much more. Take, use, adapt, and share the ideas. Then, come back to the site to comment or offer your own suggestion.

Bedford Coursepacks for the most common course management systems — Blackboard, WebCT, Angel, and Desire2Learn — allow you to easily download Bedford/St. Martin's digital materials for your course.

A Great Package Option

Writing in Response can be combined with any Bedford/St. Martin's reader at a discount. For details, see bedfordstmartins.com/parfitt/catalog.

Acknowledgments

I am grateful for the suggestions from reviewers who provided feedback at several stages in the development of this project. They include Thomas Amorose, Seattle Pacific University; Reine Bouton, Southeastern Louisiana University; Jeffrey Cain, Sacred Heart University; Joan R. Griffin, Metropolitan State College–Denver; Jane Hoogestraat, Missouri State University; Kathleen Lawson, Oakland University; Jennifer Lee, University of Pittsburgh; Karen Bishop Morris, Purdue University Calumet; Cary Moskovitz, Duke University; Rolf Norgaard, University of Colorado, Boulder; Irvin Peckham, Louisiana State University; Nedra Reynolds, University of Rhode Island; Judith Rodby, California State University, Chico; Mary Sauer, Indiana University–Purdue University Indianapolis; Marti Singer, Georgia State University; Donna M. Souder, Colorado State University–Pueblo; Laura H. Thomas, University of Colorado, Boulder; Greg Van Belle, Edmonds Community College; and Michael Wallwork, Oakland University. I am also grateful to several reviewers who have chosen to remain anonymous.

Barbara Fister made a number of recommendations for the section on research and documentation, and Ellen Kuhl Repetto assisted with the documentation examples. I am grateful for their assistance.

I would also like to thank the people at Bedford/St. Martin's who fostered this project. They include Joan Feinberg, president; Denise Wydra, editorial director; Karen Henry, editor in chief; Steve Scipione and Leasa Burton, senior executive editors; John Sullivan, executive editor; Alicia Young and Shannon Walsh, associate editors; Alyssa Demirjian, editorial assistant; Molly Parke, senior marketing manager; Sue Brown, director of production; Elizabeth Schaaf, managing editor; Elise Kaiser, associate director of production; Katherine Caruana, assistant production editor; Lori Roncka, senior production editor; Donna Dennison and Anna Palchik, senior art directors; Brian Salisbury, text designer and illustrator; Sara Gates and Marine Miller, designers; Kalina Ingham, permissions manager; Martha Friedman, photo editor; and Elaine Kosta and Linda Finigan, permissions editors.

I am particularly grateful to John Sullivan for his expert guidance, steady support, and infinite patience from the start of this project to its end. His help has been invaluable; had I been in less good-natured and capable hands, the writing of this book would certainly have been far more difficult and less enjoyable.

I am also grateful to my past and present students at Boston University for all that they have taught me. In particular, I would like to thank those students who helped me with this project directly, often by writing extracurricular pieces or patiently conversing with me about some aspect of their experience as writers: Gretchen Baker, Brendan Barrett, Zach Benabid, Amal Benaissa, Ben Dauskewicz, Amy Dipolitto, Joseph Christian Greer, Sergio Herrera, Tiffany Massood, Zach Peikon, Yona Porat, Adam Romines, Nathan Selsky, and Dessa Shuckerow. I owe a great debt to my friend and colleague Professor Dawn Skorczewski, director of University Writing at Brandeis University, for her encouragement, guidance, and inspiration throughout the writing of this book. Professor Stephen Dilks of the University of Missouri, Kansas City, taught me to appreciate the radial diagram as a reading strategy, among other things. Dr. Tom Casserly, associate university librarian at Boston University, generously and expertly answered my questions pertaining to undergraduate research. Professor Tina Loo of the Department of History at the University of British Columbia, Professor David Greven of the English Department at Connecticut College, and Professor Dave Hunt of the Department of Criminology, Social Justice, and Social Work at Augusta State University kindly allowed me to quote assignments of their devising. I am grateful to my dean, Linda Wells, for granting me a leave of absence so that I could complete this book. I would like to thank Deanne Harper for her support. And I owe my partner, Jeff Welch, immeasurable thanks for his support and patience throughout the writing of this project. Finally, I would like to express my deep gratitude to my parents, Mary and Tony Parfitt, for encouraging and supporting me in every endeavor.

About the Author

Matthew Parfitt (Ph.D., Boston College) is an associate professor of Rhetoric and chair of the Division of Rhetoric at Boston University's College of General Studies. In 2002 he received the Peyton Richter Award for interdisciplinary teaching. He is coeditor of *Conflicts and Crises in the Composition Classroom — And What Instructors Can Do About Them* (2003) and *Cultural Conversations: The Presence of the Past* (2001).

Brief Contents

Contents

3 Further Strategies for Active Reading

Part Two   Composing and Revising   91

4   Writing to Discover and Develop Ideas   93

5   Developing an Argument   110

6 Organizing the Essay   150

Part Four Research and Documentation

9 Conducting Research

Part Five Readings   381

Writing in Response to Reading

"What Does the Professor Want?"

> "In many ways writing is the act of saying *I*, of imposing oneself upon other people, of saying *listen to me, see it my way, change your mind.*"
>
> **JOAN DIDION**

Subject: Hi!
Date: Monday, Oct. 15, 2012 3:40 PM
From: Sam Piotrowski <sammyp@bu.edu>
To: Rachel Piotrowski <rpiotrowski87@ hotmail.com>

Hey sis: What's up? College is still great. Classes still pretty interesting. And I'm pressing my nose to the grindstone as Dad would say. The only downer is English — which is weird because in high school that was always a personal best. Got As and Bs without even trying. But my prof gave me a C on my first paper, even though I worked really hard on it, and Julio (remember my roommate Julio, smart kid with green hair?) said it was an A, guaranteed.

Honestly, I can't figure out the problem. The course is Writing about Literature — which is something I've done before. Plenty. And I have to give Prof. Hughes credit: he gives a good lecture. I almost always stay awake. I used the five-paragraph structure that Mrs. Kelly taught back in sophomore year, so I know it was organized. I stayed away from saying anything too controversial because I didn't want to be wrong; just made three really strong points.

I used the thesaurus and found some great words to use, like "stentorian" and "pusillanimous." Impressive, no? I also included a classy quotation about narrative by someone named Robert Coover. I opened the essay with it, along with a dictionary definition of "narrative."

So far, my prof hasn't explained the C. I did make some grammar mistakes. Maybe I'll go see him tomorrow. Anyway, I won't let this thing eat away at me! I'm sure I'll do better on the next paper, which is due at midterms.

See ya! Sam

This book is for Sam. He'll soon learn that some of his notions about what Professor Hughes hoped to find in his essay were misplaced, and those misconceptions are the chief reason he earned a C — not because he was poorly prepared in high school or because he lacks brains or writing talent, but because his expectations for the assignment were different from his professor's. And eventually he'll begin to understand what Professor Hughes and his other instructors do hope to find in his papers, and he may even begin to understand *why* they want these things. Assuming that Sam does speak to Professor Hughes and that Professor Hughes explains to him where he went wrong and how he can do better next time, the C grade might prove to be a blessing. Some students spend months, even years, trying to figure out through trial and error what professors want in a paper. One of the aims of this book is to explain what professors want, and why. The other is to provide strategies and exercises to help you not just meet expectations but surpass them — and get the most you can out of the experience.

So this book is also for students who, unlike Sam, might do fairly well on their papers right from the start but would find the process of writing college essays more rewarding, enjoyable, and worthwhile if they were armed with certain concepts and strategies. After all, the point of writing in college is not ultimately to get good grades but to learn, and essay assignments afford an exceptional opportunity to develop ideas of your own and share them with your instructor and perhaps your classmates. Over the long run, many students find that this kind of learning is the most meaningful and exciting they do. One premise of this book is that it should be — and certainly can be.

When college professors read student essays, their expectations are often quite different from those of high school teachers. This difference, which professors sometimes take for granted and fail to explain, can be one of the great obstacles that students face when they begin writing at the college level. The mere fact that a difference exists may become clear early in the freshman year, as it did for Sam, but *what* the difference is and *why* it exists can remain a mystery for years. Some students complete their entire undergraduate program without being quite sure what professors are looking for in their writing or how to go about actually producing it. For them, writing can feel like a game of chance, with grades awarded randomly and unpredictably, or as if there's a secret to it that no one is willing to share. Some students do seem to catch on at some point and do consistently well — though even they may have trouble saying exactly what it is they've grasped and how it relates to their educational goals.

It would be nice if there were a simple one-sentence answer to the question "What do professors want from student writing?" There isn't. But while there may be no foolproof recipe for success, certain concepts and strategies can help anyone be more successful in pursuit not only of grades but also of the more lasting rewards that grades are meant to stand for: meaningful learning, the satisfaction of expressing ideas effectively, a proud sense of accomplishment and craftsmanship. These concepts and strategies can be learned without great difficulty. Nevertheless, "a smooth sea never made a skilled mariner," as the saying goes. Most of the time, good writing takes hard work, and there's no getting around it. But while misdirected effort leads to frustration and disappointment, even very hard work can be deeply satisfying when the rewards, both short- and long-term, repay the cost.

We mentioned concepts and strategies that can help you be a successful college writer. The chief aim of this introductory chapter is to clarify **concepts**[1] — the ideas that underlie the professors' expectations for college writing. Most of the rest of the book is devoted to **strategies** — tools and techniques to help you meet these expectations. Three of the ten chapters in this book discuss reading and note-taking. This might seem odd in a book about writing, but, for reasons that we will explain shortly, reading and note-taking — of a particularly careful and thoughtful kind — play so essential a role in the process of college writing that it makes sense to devote a good deal of time and attention to them.

---

[1] Terms in **boldface** are explained in the glossary at the back of the book.

⊙Try This Exploring the Culture of Education

Option 1. An "ethnography" is a description of a culture or subculture, with particular emphasis on the rules or norms that define the culture. In two or three pages, describe the culture, social and academic, of your high school. Then, in one or two additional pages, describe as best you can the social and academic culture of college, based on your experience so far. Finally, write two or three paragraphs to compare the two cultures and draw conclusions: How are they similar? How are they different? And how did your expectations of the culture of college compare to your actual experience so far?

Option 2. Visit your college or university Web site and review some of the pages that describe its academic programs. What do these descriptions reveal about the culture of higher education in general and of your college in particular? What goals and expectations does your college have for its students? How might a student's work as a writer contribute to meeting these goals and expectations? In a two- to three-page essay, write up your conclusions.

The Values of the Academy

College is not simply a continuation of high school. As an institution of learning, college is different in kind. The function of a college or university in society is not only to educate but also to create new knowledge: to conduct research that advances our understanding of the world — both the natural world and the human world, both past and present — and to develop new technologies and methods that help to make the world better. Most large universities devote a sizable portion of their resources to research, aided by grants from governments, nonprofit foundations, and businesses. Colleges and universities (collectively known as "the academy") exist both to pass on knowledge and to advance it, and this mission shapes the expectations that professors bring to their students' writing.

The habits of mind and values that are necessary for good **research** and **scholarship** — for making discoveries and producing insights — are ones that professors aim to instill in their students; they include a willingness to question conventional wisdom, a capacity to imagine fresh hypotheses, the patience to gather information and sift it with care, and the ability to reason strictly from data to a conclusion. You may have entered college with the idea that higher education will train you to work in your chosen profession and give you the credentials necessary to land a good job. It probably will, but much of what you'll be taught has little to do with job training. Many colleges require every student to take a certain number of liberal arts courses in order to acquire some familiarity with subjects such as literature, history, and philosophy — knowledge that all educated persons should possess, whatever their profession. But the purpose of a college education extends beyond even this kind of core learning (after all, you could acquire it through correspondence courses); more important, it seeks to impart certain skills and values: the ability to attend, to reason and to judge, to think for oneself and to think with others, to examine the basis of belief, to ask questions, to distinguish sound reasoning from flawed, to draw conclusions and communicate them persuasively. Though you are likely planning a career outside the academy — perhaps in business, communications, law, medicine, engineering, or social work — such skills and habits of mind will help you be a more thoughtful, insightful, and useful member of your profession, serving you well no matter where you work. Moreover, they will help you be a better citizen and a wiser leader.

College, then, does not expect you simply to take in more knowledge of the same kind that you acquired in high school. You will learn new things, of course, but you will be expected to take a different approach to your learning. In high school, knowledge tends to be treated as **fact**, as truth that reasonable people accept because the best authorities on the subject maintain that it is true. But in college, knowledge tends to be treated as **current belief**, as what reasonable people today believe because there are good reasons to believe it — even though new reasons might well come along that would force us to revise our views. As one writer put it, "What is treated in high school as eternal and unchangeable fact that human beings have discovered in their continual and relentless progress toward total knowledge will be treated in college as belief that may perhaps be well supported at the present but that could turn out to be wrong."[2] Why is this? The simple answer goes back to the university's role, which is not only to pass along knowledge but also to create it. Teacher-researchers at the college level are aware that if our knowledge is to advance, we must constantly be willing to question the conventional wisdom. We must be willing to reexamine the evidence behind a claim rather than accepting it blindly. At the same time, knowledge can move forward only by building out from what we already

---

[2] Jack W. Meiland, *How to Get the Best Out of College* (New York: Mentor/New American Library, 1981), 14.

know. So scholars strive to combine a healthy *respect* for existing knowledge with a healthy *skepticism* of it. The history of learning is a history of revision — of mastering knowledge in order to improve on it.

Professors consider their students to be members of the university — researchers and thinkers like themselves, if only at the beginning stage — so they expect students to demonstrate these intellectual skills and values in their writing and speaking. If this may seem a little daunting at first, it can also be tremendously exciting: you are being invited to enter into a genuine conversation about ideas, to reexamine everything you thought you knew, and to share your ideas with teachers who take them seriously enough to scrutinize them in the same way they would scrutinize the ideas of fellow scholars.

Academic Discourse

Unfortunately, professors who have been working in colleges or universities for many years — and since it takes five to ten years to complete a PhD, most have been — sometimes take their values and habits of mind for granted and may not always perceive the need to explain them fully or to describe their expectations for what an essay or a research paper should sound like or look like or do. (And even if they recognize this need, they may not find the space to explain it in an already packed syllabus.) Just as there is a certain **culture** that typically prevails in other American institutions such as churches or the military or high schools — social rituals, ways of speaking, unwritten rules of behavior, and so on — so there is a culture of higher learning. It is far from being uniform; just like other cultures, it varies by region, discipline, age group, and other factors. Nevertheless, its members share a certain common stock of ideas and assumptions, as well as certain ways of speaking and writing. As in any culture, members of the academy often take its ways for granted, forgetting or never realizing their differences from the outside world.

The conventional way of speaking and writing in the academy is often called **academic discourse**. Although each discipline has technical terms and concepts of its own, the term "academic discourse" refers to ways of speaking and writing that are found widely throughout the academy, a set of conventions that have grown up over the years in order to facilitate scholarly work. You already know something about academic discourse because your high school teachers probably expected your writing to reflect at least some of its conventions. For example, academic discourse is typically more formal and precise than ordinary speech. When writing a lab report, you would not write, "I saw this ugly squishy thing through the microscope." More likely, you'd write something like, "The microscope revealed a formless, semiliquid object." Academic discourse is typically more exact and less subjectively impressionistic than casual conversation.

Academic literacy, or a familiarity with academic discourse that enables a person to understand it and speak it, distinguishes insiders from outsiders, members of the academic community from everyone else, just as any type of cultural literacy tends to do. Although you're not expected to become fluent in the discourse of higher education overnight, as a member of the academic community you will need to begin to speak the local language in order to communicate effectively. Some students are understandably reluctant to adopt this language, fearing they may sound stuffy or pretentious. Granted, some academic discourse certainly *is* stuffy and pretentious, but as we will see, it need not be. In essence, it reflects the "ethos" or culture of the academy, and while it is impossible to describe that culture fully in just a few sentences, two practices stand out so prominently that they are nearly definitive. First, academic discourse reflects the speaker's awareness of the work of other specialists who have already contributed to our understanding of the subject under discussion. Second, it reflects the need to proceed cautiously and to follow strict reasoning.

Scholars proceed cautiously because they know that reliable conclusions must be based on evidence and that the evidence is always incomplete. Jumping to unsupportable conclusions would be pointless. But this does not prevent scholars from drawing conclusions at all: over time, they build up reliable, well-tested theories, but such theories are rarely, if ever, the work of just one or two individuals. Thus, scholars avoid making excessively grand claims and tend to **qualify** their statements in words that show their claims are provisional, based on the limited data available so far.

Likewise, scholars carefully try to avoid errors in reasoning that would make their conclusions worthless. Since their arguments must stand up to careful scrutiny, scholars must reason strictly from the evidence, avoiding personal bias, overgeneralization, emotional appeal, careless use of language, self-contradiction, and other fallacies. Typically, articles and books by scholars are reviewed by other scholars in the same field before being published. If reviewers find errors or holes in an argument, the author may need to revise or start over.

Thus, academic discourse reflects a set of assumptions about how scholarly work proceeds, how knowledge gets made. We can readily see how the work of academic writers embodies the values of the academy by examining a single paragraph from Frans de Waal's essay "Are We in Anthropodenial?" (reprinted on p. 432). In paragraph 7 de Waal, a biologist who studies primates, seeks to question whether biologists take their avoidance of "anthropomorphism" — the misattribution of human qualities to animals — too far.

> Modern opposition to anthropomorphism can be traced to Lloyd Morgan, a British psychologist, who dampened enthusiasm for liberal interpretations of animal behavior by formulating, in 1894, the perhaps most quoted statement in all of psychology: "In no case may we interpret an action as the outcome of the exercise of a higher psychical faculty, if it can be interpreted as the outcome of the exercise of one which stands lower on the psychological scale."* Generations of psychologists have repeated Morgan's Canon, taking it to mean that the safest assumption about animals is that they are blind actors in a play that only we understand. Yet Morgan himself never meant it this way: he didn't believe that animals are necessarily simpleminded. Taken aback by the one-sided appeals to his canon, he later added a rider according to which there is really nothing wrong with complex interpretations if an animal species has provided independent signs of high intelligence. Morgan thus encouraged scientists to consider a wide array of hypotheses in the case of mentally more advanced animals.
>
> * Morgan (1894).
>
> Morgan, C. L. (1894). *An Introduction to Comparative Psychology.* London: Scott.

To reexamine the basis of conventional views about the importance of avoiding anthropomorphism, de Waal takes us back to the origins of this view in the work of Lloyd Morgan. He quotes the actual words that Morgan used, and he provides an endnote and a bibliographical entry to attribute the quotation to its source. Like any scholar, de Waal would not expect readers to take it on faith that the quotation appears exactly as it stands here or that in its original context it means what de Waal claims it means. The citation information enables readers to find the source and examine it for themselves. De Waal then explains why conventional ideas about anthropomorphism deserve to be examined more closely. He brings forward little-known information that could change the way scientists think about "Morgan's Canon" and what it might mean for their own work. This matters, he suggests, because if scientists continue to accept this notion unquestioningly, it might become an obstacle, preventing scientists from understanding primates and other animals as fully as they might. And this unquestioning acceptance might inhibit our understanding of how humans resemble these animals, affecting even the way that we think about what it means to be human.

→ **Try** **This** **Learning the Values of the Academy**

Working with the following passage from paragraphs 40–42 of Jane Tompkins's "At the Buffalo Bill Museum, June 1988" (reprinted on p. 413), consider how it embodies the intellectual values of the academy. How does the essay embody the values described in this chapter? What other values, or aspects of these same values, can you infer from it? Write up your conclusions in a short essay of your own, and share them with your classmates.

This is where my visit ended, but it had a sequel. When I left the Buffalo Bill Historical Center, I was full of moral outrage, an indignation so intense it made me almost sick, though it was pleasurable too, as such emotions usually are. But the outrage was undermined by the knowledge that I knew nothing about Buffalo Bill, nothing of his life, nothing of the circumstances that led him to be involved in such violent events. And I began to wonder if my reaction wasn't in some way an image, however small, of the violence I had been objecting to. So when I got home I began to read about Buffalo Bill, and a whole new world opened up. I came to love Buffalo Bill.

• • •

"I have seen him the very personification of grace and beauty . . . dashing over the free wild prairie and riding his horse as though he and the noble animal were bounding with one life and one motion." That is the sort of thing people wrote about Buffalo Bill. They said "he was the handsomest man I ever saw." They said "there was never another man lived as popular as he was." They said "there wasn't a man, woman or child that he knew or ever met that he didn't speak to." They said "he was handsome as a god, a good rider and a crack shot." They said "he gave lots of money away. Nobody ever went hungry around him." They said "he was above the average, physically and every other way."

These are quotes from people who knew [Buffalo Bill] Cody, collected by one of his two most responsible biographers, Nellie Snyder Yost. She puts them in the last chapter, and by the time you get there they all ring true.

Why Do College Instructors Assign Writing?

To understand what you need to accomplish in a college essay or paper, it helps to have a clear sense of why professors give writing assignments. If they simply wanted to make sure that you had read the textbook carefully or listened attentively to lectures, they could give a multiple-choice test — which takes much less time and effort to grade than an essay. But most tests only require you to regurgitate content that the course fed to you in some form. They ask you to behave a little like a sponge: you absorb knowledge and, when asked, squeeze it out again, in pretty much the same form that you took it in. This kind of learning certainly has its value: much of what a doctor or an engineer or any expert needs to know has to be learned by rote memorization, and tests are a necessary means of making sure that students have mastered the material. But this kind of learning is not necessarily the deepest or richest kind. It doesn't compel learners to *think* carefully about ideas or *do* anything with them. True expertise requires much more than just an ability to recite memorized facts and definitions: in the real world, we need to *use* knowledge, to apply old ideas in new situations, to solve problems, to analyze data and draw conclusions, to see patterns, to make predictions, to make connections between concepts, to assess the merits of a hypothesis, and in a host of other ways to *think* creatively with what we know. These skills define true expertise just as much as — or even more than — the possession of a body of information. So professors typically ask students to write essays in order to give them the opportunity not only to practice such skills but also to get to know key concepts well enough to be able to use them in the real world.

For this reason, essay assignments typically expect a different kind of work from you than exams and tests do. An essay assignment often poses a problem to which there is no single right answer and no tidy solution. Problems of this kind require us to do the kind of deeper analytic, synthetic, evaluative, and creative thinking just described; they compel us to become actively involved in our learning in a way that exams rarely do. Very often, an essay assignment requires each student to develop an original argument in support of the student's own solution or approach or perspective on a problem.

Let's look at some representative college writing assignments. All of these are taken from actual introductory college courses.

A *"Close Reading" Essay on* Paradise Lost (Humanities): Choose a short passage (10–15 lines) from Book I of *Paradise Lost* that in your view stands as a "microcosm" of the work as a whole. Analyze it in terms of form (imagery, style, figurative language) and content (meaning, literal truth), and discuss the ways in which form and content are related to each other in the passage. Provide a very specific analysis of the passage, but also communicate your sense of the ways in which the passage reflects, contains, and synthesizes issues and qualities of the work as a whole. Length: 5–7 pages. Format: MLA.

Analysis of a News Story (Sociology): Write an essay that uses one or more of the sociological concepts we have learned this semester to analyze an article from a newsmagazine such as *Time, Newsweek,* or *U.S. News and World Report.* Choose your article with care, and decide on one or more appropriate sociological concept(s) that can help the reader understand the sociological dimension of the story. In your essay, you must explain the sociological concept, explain the article, and apply the sociological concept to the article. Length: 5–6 pages. Format: *Chicago* style.

Inferences about Eighteenth-Century Society (History): Choose one chapter from Christopher Moore's *Louisbourg Portraits: Life in an Eighteenth-Century Garrison Town.* Write an essay that explains what the life of the individual in question tells us about eighteenth-century society (e.g., social relations, class, race, gender). Do not draw on outside sources for this assignment. Instead, use the selected chapter and your knowledge of concepts from lectures and discussions to generalize from the particular. Length: 6–8 pages, double-spaced. Include a title page with your name and the name of your TA on it. Format: *Chicago* style.

All three assignments ask students to work carefully with a text and to use concepts from the course to draw conclusions of their own. The first assignment is from a humanities course: students have been reading and discussing the seventeenth-century English poet John Milton's *Paradise Lost* for several weeks. The instructor wants her students to work closely with just a few lines from the poem, but she wants them to demonstrate that they comprehend the major themes and issues of the poem as a whole, by relating the lines to the rest of the poem. She also wants them to practice for themselves the kind of literary analysis that she has been demonstrating in her lectures and discussions. The most interesting papers, and likely the most successful, will be those that work with a passage that hasn't been discussed in class at any length and thus offer original insights into the poem.

The second assignment also requires students to work with a text, but this is not a literary analysis; here, the instructor wants his students to demonstrate that they not only understand sociological concepts in an abstract way but also can *work* with these concepts and show how they apply to and help us understand real-world situations. A successful essay will demonstrate a strong grasp of the concepts and use them in a precise way, but it will also show some creativity and insight in working with the news story, probing details that a casual reader might overlook and noticing patterns that reveal the sociological background.

The third assignment, for a history course, also asks students to work with a text. In this case, the professor wants students to make generalizations based on a particular example — a single individual described in one of the chapters of *Louisbourg Portraits*. Students will need to apply the knowledge of eighteenth-century society that they have gathered from lectures and other texts as they develop their argument. But their argument will need to be supported by specific details from the text. Like professional historians, students will need to pay careful attention to the clues — the telling details — in the source text in order to make inferences about the society of that time. Because students are working with just one life, this assignment will involve some guesswork, and they might not be quite certain that their inferences are valid. But making this kind of educated guess based on evidence from documents is the only means historians have of drawing conclusions about the past. While the assignment does require students to do the sort of work that professional historians do, it also requires students to develop analytical skills that are widely applicable.

When you write an essay, it is more important to demonstrate your thinking skills than to be precisely "right," in the sense of repeating an answer that has already been defined as correct, as you might do on an exam. And essays give you the opportunity to show your professor what you, as a unique individual, can do with the concepts that he or she has been teaching, to explain the distinct meaning and interest that they have for you. Think of an instructor sitting down to read thirty or more essays on basically the same subject. For both your sake and the instructor's, it's a good idea to make your essay interesting. As a colleague of mine used to say, with only slight exaggeration, "It's more important to be interesting than to be right." While a frivolous argument made just for the sake of being clever wouldn't pass muster in most college courses (and probably wouldn't be very interesting), my colleague wanted to address a different and more common problem with freshman writing: the fact that the arguments are often *too* correct — too familiar, too superficial, too simplistic, too dull. By encouraging students to find something *interesting* to say, she wasn't inviting them to develop arguments that were outlandish or implausible. Instead, she was asking them to be willing to take risks, to think deeply enough about a problem to develop ideas of their own, ones that, if not absolutely new and original, were at least fresh and engaging.

With most assignments, a strong essay makes a clear and convincing argument for an original insight. There are two sides to writing this kind of essay: the thinking side and the communicating side. When professors assign an essay, they typically have both sides in mind: providing the opportunity for you to learn on your own as you figure out what you're going to say, and providing the opportunity to share your thinking with your professor. As a rule, these two sides emerge in the writing process as two different phases: in the early stages, you focus mostly on **writing to learn**, figuring out

> **➔ Try**
> **This**   **Exploring Key Terms**
>
> Look up the following terms in a good diction- ary: *opinion, argument, hypothesis, thesis, the- ory*. Choose two and write a brief essay or journal entry explaining the difference between the two words.

your ideas and finding something to say; in the later stages, you focus more on **writing to communicate**, finding a way of arranging and expressing your ideas that will make sense to, and persuade, the reader. Writing to learn tends to be inward-looking: it involves your own struggle to figure things out in a way that makes sense to you. Writing to communicate is outward-looking: now that you have some ideas, you're concerned with expressing them effectively to someone who cannot see inside your mind and has no way of understanding your ideas except through the words you put onto the page. These twin goals of the writing process — the writer's need to understand and the reader's need to understand — are equally important and will receive roughly equal emphasis in the chapters that follow. Early chapters emphasize writing to learn, and later chapters emphasize writing to communicate. Both phases are essential to a successful paper.

Critical Thinking

Instructors often use the phrase **critical thinking** in connection with writing assignments. This umbrella term refers to the creative ways of using knowledge that we have just described: applying ideas, analyzing ideas (or taking them apart), synthesizing ideas (or putting them together), and evaluating ideas. When used in ordinary speech, the word "critical" often has a negative connotation (for example, "Helen was critical of my taste in clothes"). But it has another meaning that carries none of this negative sense. Deriving from the Greek word for "judgment," it means in this sense "involving careful and exact observation and judgment." College writing instructors often speak of critical reading, critical writing, and critical thinking — all terms that imply attention to detail, careful reasoning, and a mental attitude that seeks out the rational basis for claims rather than accepting them merely on authority. Richard Rodriguez, author of a well-known intellectual autobiography entitled *Hunger of Memory* (1982), recalls his precocious reading habits as a grade school student. By the time he entered high school, he had read hundreds of difficult books that most students would not encounter until college. "But I was not a good reader," he writes. "Merely bookish, I lacked a point of view when I read. Rather, I read in order to acquire a point of view."[3] Now an adult, Rodriguez recognizes that he had formerly been too passive and diffident a reader, too ready to accept what he read at face value, and unable to enter into any sort of dialogue with texts because he lacked ideas of his own. To be able to have a conversation with texts is essential to critical reading and writing. It requires no great fund of learning or special expertise; all it really requires is curiosity, a readiness to pose questions and to wonder, and a degree of confidence in your right to do so. These are precious skills, yet ones that everyone possesses to some degree. They are certainly the keys to critical thinking. Criticism, then, can refer not to the business of finding fault but to the business of analyzing a text closely, entering into a conversation with it, and bringing an independent mind to bear. The result might be a judgment of some kind — positive or negative — but it might equally be a new insight or perspective that emerges from this encounter between a curious mind and a text.

Reading is the principal means by which college writers inform their thinking and develop new ideas. For this reason, three chapters in this book are concerned with reading strategies. The act of reading and the act of scholarly writing are so deeply intertwined as to be almost inseparable. Reading at the college level is never just a passive act of absorbing information; it involves an active dialogue that, like a good conversation, gives birth to new ideas, new ways of seeing, and — as these thoughts find their way into words — new texts. As the nineteenth-century philosopher and essayist Ralph Waldo Emerson wrote in "The American Scholar" (1837), "One must be an inventor to read well. . . . There is then creative reading as well as creative writing."[4] Reading, thinking, crafting an argument, and revising are not entirely separable activities. To read is to think, to think is to reason and imagine arguments, to make an argument is to revise old ideas, and to revise is to read — creatively.

---

[3] Richard Rodriguez, *Hunger of Memory* (New York: Random House/Dial, 2005), 68.
[4] Ralph Waldo Emerson, "The American Scholar," in *Little Masterpieces: Ralph Waldo Emerson,* ed. Bliss Perry (New York: Doubleday, Page, 1901), 160, http://www.archive.org/details/historyselfrelia00emer.

College professors are interested in your ideas, but students sometimes confuse ideas with **opinions**. By definition, an opinion is a judgment that rests on insufficient grounds, on data and reasoning that are not adequate to raise the opinion to the level of a hypothesis or theory. Of course, we all have opinions about all kinds of matters — social, political, theological, and so on — that we've never studied in great depth, and as the cliché reminds us, we're all entitled to our opinions. Many questions are intrinsically undecidable and are necessarily "matters of opinion." But opinions, in the strict sense, do not play a major role in academic writing. Instead, most academic writing presents an informed argument and works with and against informed arguments made by others on the same subject. An argument may or may not be *true*, and its claims may or may not be proven. But every argument aims to stand on sufficient grounds.

But even an uncertain argument is better than no argument at all — a point that Sam seems to have misunderstood. Judging from what he tells his sister in his e-mail, his essay apparently did little more than echo back ideas the professor had

➔ Try This   Thinking Critically about a Text

Earlier in this chapter, we looked at a paragraph from Frans de Waal's "Are We in Anthropodenial?" Now read the rest of de Waal's essay (p. 432), and choose one of the following options.

Option 1. Identify at least two other passages that seem to you to embody the values of the academy, as described on pages 4–6. De Waal is a scientist (specifically, a primatologist), and although he is writing for a general audience here rather than strictly for fellow scientists, his writing exhibits some of the characteristics of academic discourse. Identify at least two or three passages or sentences that, in your view, reveal these characteristics. In a notebook, explain what each passage reveals and how it does so. Be prepared to discuss your conclusions in class.

Option 2. Using one of the three sample writing assignments from this introduction (pp. 10–11) as a general guide, write an assignment for de Waal's essay that requires students to engage in critical thinking. It might be a formal essay assignment or a short, informal homework or even an in-class assignment. But it should ask students to analyze the text, not merely repeat what they learned from it.

already discussed in class. The essay used a rather simplistic structure in a formulaic way; it used words that Sam didn't really understand or need; and it incorporated material, like the quotation and the dictionary definition, designed to produce the *appearance* of scholarship rather than to say anything substantial or interesting or new. These devices did little to support Sam's own argument — if indeed he *had* an argument of his own. But when Sam does start writing the kind of essays his professors hope to read, he may well find that the work is much more exciting, creative, and satisfying than writing used to be. The process will take more time, and he may still experience the occasional midnight agony when up against a deadline, but he'll be involved in and committed to this work time after time. As another student, Zach Benabid, remarked: "The way I write papers [in college] is completely different from high school. In the past, I'd try to write the final draft right away. Now, when I revise a paper, I *butcher* it; it's a completely different paper. I'm not satisfied or confident in the paper unless I go through seven drafts."

As Zach suggests, there is no simple formula for producing college-level essays. The five-paragraph model that you might have learned in high school will no longer suffice, and a rapid, last-minute writing process will no longer work. The remainder of this book offers some strategies for developing ideas about your reading and for expressing these ideas in essay form.

"Live the Questions"

In *Letters to a Young Poet* (1903), the celebrated Austrian poet Rainer Maria Rilke writes to an unnamed younger poet, offering guidance and advice as the youth embarks on a lifelong journey that will demand enormous dedication and hard work. Rilke tells him that he will need patience, that he should not expect to find quick, easy solutions for his doubts and questions. To obtain answers, he will need to "live the questions."

> I would like to beg you, dear Sir, as well as I can, to have patience with everything unresolved in your heart and to try to love *the questions themselves* as if they were locked rooms or books written in a very foreign language. Don't search for the answers, which could not be given to you now, because you would not be able to live them. And the point is, to live everything. *Live* the questions now. Perhaps then,

someday far in the future, you will gradually, without even noticing it, live your way into the answer.[5]

The situation of the young poet might seem very different from that of the average college student. In many respects, it is: student writers are under pressure to meet deadlines, to study for exams, to fulfill the exacting requirements of an instructor's assignments, to earn good grades — and to balance all this with a satisfactory personal life. How different from the poet who can afford the time to "gradually, without even noticing it, live [his or her] way into the answer"!

But looked at from another point of view, Rilke's advice may be pertinent after all. In the end, all those readings, lectures, exams, and assignments must add up to something; they cannot be perfectly disconnected from one another, each an end in itself. In fact, any thoughtful student notices threads that run from one assignment to another, one course to another; together, these threads compose an education. And let's not forget that the point of college studies is to be found not merely in a grade or diploma but in the way it changes us, making us more informed, understanding, and wise. At the center of a liberal education are fundamental questions: Who am I? What is the good life? What kind of world do I live in? How did we get here?

In the thick of reading and writing to complete an assignment, we need to remind ourselves of these questions from time to time. And we need to remember to reflect on the meaning of readings and lectures for our actual lives, our actual selves. To "live the questions" means taking the questions into our lives and making them truly our own — pondering them at any time of day, not only when we're studying but also when we're exercising or commuting or relaxing or talking with friends. It means taking the work seriously and letting it enter the parts of our lives that are not strictly given over to work.

We cannot really respond to a writer unless we are willing to "live the questions," to make connections between what a writer says and all the other things we know or think or wonder about. Responding to a reading means allowing our questions to surface and be taken seriously. It means developing a connection between schoolwork and the thinking that you do outside of school. Over the long term, this habit will help you make the most of your education. But in the short term, it will also help you write more interesting and satisfying essays.

---

[5] Rainer Maria Rilke, *Letters to a Young Poet,* trans. Stephen Mitchell (New York: Random House/ Vintage, 1986), 34.

✅ Checklist for Understanding Academic Discourse

☐ Begin learning the discourse conventions of higher education.

☐ Understand your assignment.
- Make an appointment with your instructor if aspects of the assignment confuse you.

☐ Understand that writing involves rewriting.
- Write to discover what you want to say.
- As you begin to discover what you want to say, focus next on writing to communicate your ideas.
- All good writers revise. Make revision a step in your process.

☐ Demonstrate critical thinking skills in your writing.
- Seek to say something interesting and original.
- Be prepared to take risks.

part 1

Responsive
Reading

chapter 1

Reading with a Purpose

In the academic world, reading is part of the writing process. To respond to a text in a meaningful way, a writer must first listen carefully to what the text is saying. In the case of academic writing, this usually means tracing the main argument — which is something more than just the general topic or main themes — and grasping it

> **"** Read not to contradict and confute, nor to believe and take for granted . . . but to weigh and consider. **"**
>
> **FRANCIS BACON**

firmly enough to be able to assess its strengths and weaknesses. Sometimes this poses few difficulties and the argument is sufficiently clear after only one reading, but frequently understanding the main argument requires concentration, effort, and several passes through the text. And even when a text is fairly straightforward, reading it at least twice usually pays dividends if you're planning to write about it.

Academic texts — including the kind that college professors assign to first-year students — are often demanding, so attentive, thoughtful reading plays a fundamental role in college writing. Good academic essays — not just student essays but nearly all academic essays — result from a thinking process that begins in a dialogue with texts. Such dialogues require **active reading** and rereading — a kind of reading that draws on nearly all your mental faculties, including questioning, analyzing, reasoning, weighing, drawing inferences, and more. This kind of reading isn't something you do hastily at the start of the writing process and then put behind you. The dialogue continues throughout the writing process, and, as experienced writers know, the best way to get started, or to get moving again when stuck, is always reading.

For any text that you'll be writing about, expect to read it several times. This means that initially you can hold off making judgments or worrying too much about your own response and just concentrate on making good sense of the author's argument. You will develop well-thought-out ideas later: the first task is to get the clearest and most complete understanding possible of what the text has to say. This is no small matter: the problem readers often have with difficult or lengthy academic texts is not a failure to understand anything at all about them, but rather a failure to gather up all the pieces of the jigsaw puzzle, fit them together, and clearly see the big picture, the main point. But neglecting this task means that their response, however inventive and well argued, inevitably ends up being somewhat irrelevant and pointless.

Unfortunately, careful reading is an aspect of the writing process that students frequently neglect. Under pressure to meet a deadline, you might be tempted to cut corners, and rereading may seem a time-consuming task that can be hurried a bit. But doing so can thwart all your efforts from the starting gate. As noted in the Introduction, one of the main causes of disappointing essays is thin, simplistic ideas that are weakly supported by evidence. Having a clear understanding and full appreciation of another writer's ideas — even if you ultimately disagree with them — is the first step toward developing rich, interesting, strongly supported ideas of your own, whether you are working on a research paper or an analytical essay involving just one or two assigned readings.

This chapter concerns some fundamentals of reading with a purpose — that is, reading with the ultimate goal of coming up with something interesting and valid to say. Chapter 2 offers basic strategies for active reading, and Chapter 3 offers several additional strategies for working closely with arguments, strategies that you can use where appropriate but probably will not use routinely.

First, to better understand this concept of "active reading," let's consider what any sort of reading really involves.

Making Sense

Physically, a text is made up of ink marks on a page or dots on a screen: letters, punctuation marks, numerals, spaces. As children, we learn to decipher the code and recognize words that the marks represent. But reading means much more than this: it involves perceiving how a series of isolated letters and words make sense as meaningful phrases and sentences, and tracing a sequence of meanings as they accumulate across a whole page, a chapter, a book. It's what you're doing right now: continually putting together the sentence you are now reading with everything you've read so far, in order to make sense of the whole, developing and revising your sense of the whole as you go.

So it is not only the writer's job to "make sense" but also the reader's. When we're reading something that's easy or familiar, we are barely aware of this need to put together the meaning of the text — in a sense, to "compose" it. But when we're faced with difficult or unfamiliar writing, even if written clearly, making sense of the text is a job that calls for great powers of concentration and tenacity.

The ancient Greek philosopher Socrates famously distrusted the written word because he believed it weakened the memory and because the absence of the writer allowed the text to be misunderstood. Indeed, the capacity of most people to remember exactly what they've heard does appear to be much weaker today than it was in Socrates' time, and certainly texts are often misinterpreted. But the modern world relies utterly on writing — from the constitutions that undergird our legal systems to the Twitter feeds that tell us the latest news — so we must deal with the fact that the absence of the writer defines the task that both readers and writers face: both must "make sense" without the benefit of a present speaker who can clarify, correct, or revise. Writing is communication at a distance — but unlike talking on the telephone or through a microphone, it normally takes place across time as well as space. Although this spatial and temporal distance complicates communication through the written word, it also accounts for its tremendous power. "Thanks to writing, man and only man has a world and not just a situation," wrote the French philosopher Paul Ricoeur.[1] Writing makes it possible to know how women lived in China a thousand years ago, who won yesterday's hockey game in Philadelphia, how to roast a Thanksgiving turkey, how many moons circle Jupiter, and, of course, what Socrates had to say about writing. (If Socrates' student Plato had not written down his teacher's ideas, we would probably know little about them today.) By reading, we come to know the world and to have a world.

What's the point of all this? It reminds us that reading is never simply the passive act of absorbing information. Making sense of a text does not mean simply figuring out what the author meant; for a text to make real sense, it has to make sense *to you*: you have to recognize the words and phrases, and the text's meanings have to

---

[1] Paul Ricoeur, *Interpretation Theory: Discourse and the Surplus of Meaning* (Fort Worth: Texas Christian University Press, 1976), 36.

● **Try This**   **Reading Closely**

Read the essay "At the Buffalo Bill Museum, June 1988," by Jane Tompkins (p. 413). Pay special attention to the last two paragraphs. In a notebook, write one or two pages that explain your understanding or "reading" of these paragraphs. What sense do you make of the last sentence: "Genocide matters, and it starts at home"? Compare your reading of these paragraphs with that of other students in your class. Does it differ? How and why? Write one or two more pages in your notebook discussing your answer to these questions.

"fit" somehow with other things you know, even if the subject is all quite new to you. Usually we do not know the author personally, but we recognize the world that he or she describes, at least partially. The late English novelist Angela Carter observed, "Reading a book is like rewriting it for yourself. You bring to a novel, anything you read, all your experience of the world. You bring your history and you read it in your own terms."[2] The practical consequence is that reading well means understanding that the reader is an active player in the game of making meaning. Readers can never know *exactly* what the author intended; all they have to go by are the marks on the page. Your reading of a text will differ a little from mine, but this doesn't mean that all interpretations are equally valid. A reader cannot simply invent a text's meaning and make it mean anything at all. Readers have a dual responsibility: they must strive to work out the author's meaning, and at the same time they must work out its meaning for themselves. This is the basis of the dialogue that generates ideas for writing.

Academic Reading: Reading with a Purpose

We read with many different purposes — to be informed, edified, entertained, stirred, provoked, persuaded. Much of our reading rewards us on several levels at the same time. In college, of course, the principal purpose for reading is to learn, and so the way you read *should* differ from the way you would read a book for entertainment. As you have probably already discovered, reading to learn often requires more effort than reading for pleasure, more focused concentration, and more active involve-

---

[2] Angela Carter, "The Company of Angela Carter: An Interview," *Marxism Today,* January 1985, 21, http://www.amielandmelburn.org.uk/collections/mt/index_frame.htm.

ment. After all, you did not choose these texts for yourself, the subject matter tends to be unfamiliar, and you can't just skim past difficult or tedious passages. Reading in order to complete a writing assignment is even more demanding: not only must you fully grasp the text's meaning, but you must also work out what you have to say about it and perhaps also how it fits into a larger project.

Close reading (reading slowly, with careful attention to the text) is a fundamental skill required not only in the academy but also in many professions. Good academic writing presents fresh and interesting ideas that are based on solid research and sound reasoning. While research can take many forms (chemists conduct experiments in laboratories, anthropologists observe human culture in locations far and near, archaeologists dig through the remains of lost civilizations, historians study documents in archives, and so on), nearly every kind of research involves reading at some point — not just casual reading but a careful analysis of arguments made by others concerning the problem under investigation. To produce new and worthwhile ideas, researchers must become familiar with the work that has already been done on the problem; otherwise, they risk merely duplicating existing work and pointlessly retracing another's steps. So even researchers in the field and in the lab must do a good deal of reading before they can get started. Moreover, it takes expertise to understand the meaning and importance of whatever might be found in the course of research, and this expertise can be developed only by reading extensively. So the ability to say something fresh and interesting depends to a great extent on careful reading — even in fields that rely heavily on experiment and observation. Reading is the starting point: reading the work of others gives researchers the questions and insights that make it possible to say something new and useful.

Close reading is important beyond the walls of the university as well. Nonacademic research projects — such as the kind that journalists do to write magazine or newspaper articles, that lawyers do to build a case, that architects and engineers do to create new structures — also require this kind of responsive and creative reading. In both academic and nonacademic arenas, researchers must do more than simply summarize the work of others: their research must be informed by what they read, but it must produce something new as well.

So it's no accident that when reading student essays, professors usually look for signs that students have read the assigned texts attentively and fully grasped the arguments. If you fail to show that you've read the text carefully, your argument will not be based on the kind of evidence your instructor probably expects.

Reading with a purpose, then, means reading with the aim of responding, rather than reading simply to take in a writer's ideas. Like professional researchers, student writers must become familiar with the work of others and then bring something fresh to the conversation. Reading with a purpose is reading as a means to an end, rather than as an end in itself, and it bridges reading and writing — a kind of reading that is itself almost a kind of writing, certainly the first step in the process of academic writing. So academic reading is always a special kind of reading, different from reading a novel for pleasure or reading the newspaper casually over breakfast or surfing randomly across Web pages. Whether you are writing an ambitious research paper or simply a brief response to a single text, reading with a purpose means reading with questions always in mind: "How does this argument work? How strongly supported are the author's claims? What does this argument mean to me? How would I respond? What questions does it raise? What further problems does it imply?" This kind of reading launches a kind of dialogue with the text, as you struggle to figure out where you stand in relation to the writer's argument, or to work out how you might respond to it.

But as we suggested above, the first step is to make sense of that argument fully and precisely. The crucial difference between reading with a purpose well and reading with a purpose poorly is chiefly a matter of recognizing and respecting the author's purpose. In the case of academic writing, this usually means recognizing and respecting the author's argument and the context or situation in which it was made.

Context

Earlier we noted that readers have a dual responsibility: they must try to work out *the author's* meaning and, at the same time, work out what the text means *for them* as individuals. An important aspect of working out the author's meaning involves taking into account the historical or cultural situation in which the author was writing — that is, its *context.* The beliefs and values of one culture can be quite different from another's; this may be true even of assumptions so deeply held that individuals in that culture may be unaware of them. And beliefs, values, and assumptions change through time, as well, so that a way of seeing and understanding the world in one century can seem quite foreign to readers in a later century. Arthur Miller's 1953 play *The Crucible* shows how fervently many citizens in seventeenth-century New England feared witchcraft. Indirectly, Miller was condemning the "witch hunts" in his own time (the 1950s) for Communist sympathizers; the mentalities of both periods might seem unintelligible to members of an audience today—unless they strive to see the world through others' eyes and to understand the real fear that gripped people in both those periods as a result of their beliefs. A Japanese writer of two centuries ago might bring to the subject of class relations very different assumptions than those of many readers today. A contemporary Brazilian writer might see issues involved in environmental policy quite differently from the way many Americans see them. Ideally, readers should try to learn as much as they can about the thinking of the writer's time period and culture in order to avoid misapprehensions. When this is impractical, readers should at least make allowances for historical and cultural differences, recognizing that what's strange or puzzling about a text may reflect a different way of thinking and opening their imaginations to a different way of seeing the world. Often, these differences have much to teach us; they help us recognize our own assumptions and put them in perspective. And readers cannot adequately assess an argument without recognizing the cultural or historical differences that might explain the author's point of view.

Books usually contain clues about the time and place in which they were written. Here is some guidance on where to look.

- The copyright page at the front of the book usually includes the date and place of earliest publication.
- A preface or introductory chapter may explain the author's purpose or offer useful information about the circumstances in which the text was written.
- When reprinted in anthologies or textbooks, essays or chapters often include short introductions or "headnotes" that provide background information and a sense of historical and cultural context. The headnotes may also tell you something about the author's career and work. See page 383 for an example.

This kind of information is helpful when available, but readers can gather important clues about context from another source: the body of the text itself. Typically, an academic writer will reveal a good deal about the context of his or her argument in the first paragraph or two, describing (though sometimes very briefly) an existing controversy or question that he or she intends to address. For example, in "Are We in Anthropodenial?" Frans de Waal outlines the context of his argument in the first paragraph, just before he announces his main purpose or thesis. (De Waal coined the term "anthropodenial" to name the tendency of many scientists to exaggerate the difference between humans and nonhumans, especially when considering the motives behind their behaviors.

"Anthropomorphism" names the opposite tendency: to attribute human motives to nonhuman animals.)

> The human hunter anticipates the moves of his prey by attributing intentions and taking an anthropomorphic stance when it comes to what animals feel, think, or want. Somehow, this stance is highly effective in getting to know and predict animals. The reason it is in disrepute in certain scientific circles has a lot to do with the theme of this book, which is how we see ourselves in relation to nature. It is not, I will argue, because anthropomorphism interferes with science, but because it acknowledges continuity between humans and animals. In the Western tradition, this attitude is okay for children, but not for grown-ups. (pp. 432–33)

In five compact sentences, de Waal explains that the anthropomorphic stance of the hunter, despite its usefulness in predicting animal behavior, "is in disrepute in certain scientific circles," and he hints that he wants not only to suggest *why* it is so ill favored but also to argue that this attitude should be reexamined. The essay was published as part of a book intended for general readers as well as specialists, and thus de Waal relates this specific question of method (the role that anthropomorphism should or should not play in making inferences about the meaning of animal behavior) to a broad theme of interest to scientists and nonscientists alike, namely "how we see ourselves in relation to nature." But he is also addressing his fellow scientists and hoping they will be persuaded by his arguments. Part of the implied context of this argument, then, is a long history of practice in scientific circles, one that carefully avoids any trace of anthropomorphism in the study of animals. De Waal alludes to this long history by referring to anthropomorphism's "disrepute" in scientific circles and to "the Western tradition" that holds this attitude to be inappropriate for grown-ups. This practice of avoiding, even fearing, anthropomorphism is one that de Waal hopes to reexamine and perhaps even change.

Scholarly essays, like de Waal's, invariably make an argument that relates to a *problem* — often a controversial, unresolved, or problematic aspect of a larger project (here, the larger project being the study of animals, and the problematic aspect being the strict avoidance of anthropomorphism). The writer typically aims to contribute something useful to a conversation that is already in progress. (Occasionally, a writer may hope to launch a completely new conversation, but even then, the writer often refers to a recognized problem or context that helps explain why this new conversation is needed.) Recognizing this context — the problem that warrants the argument — helps us understand the author's purpose, but we may have to read carefully to find it, and we may need to make some inferences or even do some quick research to understand it fully when we do.

> → **Guidelines**   **Analyzing Rhetorical Context**
>
> Whenever you read a piece of academic writing, look in the first two or three paragraphs for answers to the following questions. (Occasionally the answers may appear later in the essay.)
>
> - Whom is the writer primarily addressing? Who is the expected audience?
> - When was the text written? Where? What do you know about the political and social realities of that time and place?
> - How will the argument contribute to an existing conversation? What is that conversation about? Why does this conversation matter?
> - What is the author's purpose?

Your Own Contexts

When assigned as a reading in a college course, an article like de Waal's has another context — the goals of the *course* — and while this context does not normally conflict with the author's purpose, it is not quite identical with it either. If you were reading de Waal's article in a biology course, it might be paired with one or two other readings that present very different perspectives on the question of anthropomorphism. The instructor might expect you to see it as one position statement in a larger debate. In a writing course, the purpose for reading it might be quite different: to illustrate certain features of scientific discourse, perhaps, or to show how an academic argument can be structured. You thus need to recognize not only the author's purpose but also the instructor's purpose in assigning it.

Finally, working out a text's meaning involves a third context: the reader's. Not only do writers produce texts in a particular historical and cultural situation, but readers read them in some situation that influences the way the text gets used and even understood. If you read Charles Dickens's *Oliver Twist* (1838) on your own over a vacation, you would likely read it differently than if you were to read it for a nineteenth-century British literature course. There, you might be asked to compare it to other novels by Dickens and to novels by other authors; you might be encouraged to think about its relation to British social problems and political struggles of the nineteenth century; you might read critical essays on the novel by scholars who read it from a Marxist perspective, or a feminist perspective, or a biographical perspective, and these articles might

---

> ⊖ **Guidelines**   **Analyzing the Purpose of Reading**
>
> As you read a text, consider these questions:
>
> - What was the instructor's purpose in assigning this text?
> - How does this argument relate to the topic or questions currently being considered in the course?
> - How does the text's particular topic or question relate to the overall goals and themes of the course?
> - How does the reading relate to others that have been assigned?
> - What is the importance of the text in the course? (Is it required reading? Are you spending a lot of class time on it? Does your instructor refer to it frequently? Will it play a major role in assignments or in exams?)

influence your own thinking about the novel. And of course, you would probably be concerned with the exam or paper that you'd have to write. But if you read *Oliver Twist* on your own, over summer vacation, you might be more likely simply to enjoy the plot and the characters and to think about the novel in relation to your own life. This is not a bad thing — indeed, it is essential — but the course might lead you to think about the book differently. For example, you might pay closer attention to the possible interpretations of other readers and find yourself justifying your own reading in preparation for any questions that might be raised about it. Reading with these considerations in mind — reading with a purpose — can give you a deeper appreciation and understanding of the book than you would likely get from reading it on your own on vacation.

Identifying the Genre of a Text

In addition to context, readers must recognize and respect a text's **genre** in order to understand it well. The word "genre" (from the French word for "kind" or "sort") refers to the literary category to which a text belongs. The novel — a lengthy fictional narrative or story in prose — is one genre. The essay — generally a brief, nonfiction composition that discusses a limited subject — is another genre. There are countless genres and subgenres — tragic plays, romance novels, cookbooks, mystery novels, comic books, scholarly articles, textbooks — and their existence allows readers to

> **→ Guidelines** | **Analyzing Your Motives for Reading**
>
> The following questions can help you focus on your motives for reading a particular text.
>
> - What do you personally hope to learn?
> - What particular interests and ideas do you bring to the reading?
> - How does the reading relate to your goals for your education? To your particular interests and concerns? To your own experience, academic or general?
> - How will the reading help you in your coursework?

know roughly what to expect from a text before they begin reading. We read a cookbook differently from a short story, and we read an essay differently from a scholarly article or textbook. College courses assign texts from a wide variety of genres; understanding something about the differences among them can help you adopt an appropriate reading strategy. Table 1.1 provides a simplified overview of genres (certainly not all the texts you read will fit into these few categories), but it shows that genre greatly influences how you read.

Genres are really sets of assumptions that writers and readers share concerning the nature and purpose of a text. Having an awareness of genre will prevent you from reading a scholarly article as though it were simply a source of information, or an essay as though it were simply a newspaper report.

Clearing Space to Concentrate

In today's "wired" world, we need to be more deliberate about clearing a space for attentive reading than we did just a few years ago. It takes a positive effort now to set aside thirty minutes or an hour to concentrate on a task without the distraction or temptation of text messages, phone calls, e-mail, TV, chat roulette, and who-knows-what's-next. But it's worth the effort because we read so much better and, in fact, more *efficiently* when we fully immerse ourselves in it — not for just a minute or two at a time, but for an extended period (thirty minutes or an hour at a time). We'd all like to believe that we're capable multitaskers, but research suggests that, like driving, reading requires the mind's full attention. (A recent study found that heavy

Table 1.1 Types of Sources and Their Characteristics

Genre	Typical Focus	Typical Author	Typical Audience	Reading Strategy
Textbook (such as this one)	Widely accepted facts and theories	A scholar in the discipline	Undergraduate students	Read chiefly for information
Article from a scholarly journal (such as *The New England Journal of Medicine*)	Specific problem or question in the discipline	Specialist in a particular discipline	Other specialists in that discipline	Read for thesis; weigh the argument
Classic text or "great book" (such as *Moby Dick*)	Human experience	Major author or thinker from the past	Educated general reader	Read for themes and perspectives
Contemporary nonfiction essay (from a periodical such as *The New Yorker*)	Human experience; social, political, and cultural issues	Professional writer, scholar, or journalist	General reader	Read for insight into the subject
Contemporary poetry and fiction (such as *The Girl with the Dragon Tattoo*)	Human experience	Professional writer	General reader	Read for themes and perspectives
Journalistic essay (from a periodical such as *Time* magazine)	Topical issues; social and political problems	Professional journalist	General reader	Read for argument and information

multitaskers actually perform worse than the average person, even though they feel more confident of their ability.[3])

If you find it difficult to stay focused for thirty minutes at a time, try just ten minutes or even five. With practice, you will gradually be able to increase the length

---

[3] Eyal Ophir et al., "Cognitive Control in Media Multitaskers," *Proceedings of the National Academy of Sciences* 106 (2009): 37.

of your sessions. (Use a timer. If your phone has a timer, for now use it *only* as a timer!) Even if you find that ten minutes or so is your limit, you can schedule several sessions an hour with short breaks in between and get the work done more efficiently than if you allow distractions and interruptions.

The right space for reading is also important — with good lighting and a good chair that encourages an upright posture. Not surprisingly, many students discover (sooner or later) that the library affords a better space than home or a dorm room and that in the library they can do better work and do it more quickly, thanks to the freedom from distractions.

Some Sources of Difficulty

Unfortunately, you will occasionally come across an academic text that is hard to understand simply because it is badly written. But more often, academic texts are difficult because they discuss difficult ideas — those that are subtle, complex, and finely nuanced. Such texts unavoidably make demands on the reader's attention and patience. For students, the difficulty can be even greater because course readings often include texts that were originally intended not for undergraduates or even general readers but for other specialists in the author's field, who speak the language of the discipline and are familiar with all its terms, concepts, assumptions, and problems. When writing for fellow specialists, scholars do not have to explain the whole context and background of their research, as they might for the general reader; instead, they explore problems and explain their insights in all their complexity and richness, without compromise. Although such texts can be bewildering and frustrating at first, it would be a mistake to conclude that such writing is simply "too difficult." Even if some passages remain a little puzzling, you can still learn a tremendous amount from them, especially with a little persistence and a good reading strategy.

A few other sources of difficulty are worth noting, having to do with **diction**, **sentence structure**, and **tone**. Academic writers sometimes use familiar words in unfamiliar ways, and words that have one meaning in ordinary speech may have another meaning in a scholarly context. (For example, a scholar of eighteenth-century British literature might use the word "sublime" in a technical sense. In ordinary speech, it usually means "very beautiful," but a literary critic might use it, as did Edmund Burke and some other eighteenth- and nineteenth-century theorists, to refer specifically to the aspect of things that provokes an *irrational* response in the beholder; by contrast, the critic might use the word "beautiful" to refer to the aspect that provokes a *rational* response.) Stay alert for familiar words that are being used in specialized senses. In many cases, a good college-level or unabridged dictionary will explain these alternative meanings; occasionally, you might need to refer to a specialized dictionary (see p. 299).

Complicated ideas often require complicated and lengthy sentence structures. This type of writing is necessary when a good deal of qualification is needed to convey ideas precisely, but it requires readers to hold one idea in their heads while other ideas gather round to modify, expand, limit, and revise it. Paraphrasing or mapping long sentences in a notebook may help to clarify or untangle them.

Finally, look out for shifts in tone that may affect the text's meaning. Academic writers, no less than other writers, employ humor, annoyance, skepticism, gravity, sarcasm — the whole spectrum of intonations — to express ideas and persuade readers. But because difficult texts demand so much of us, especially the first time we read them, we may miss subtle shifts in tone. Since we cannot literally hear the author's voice, we must detect such shifts purely from written clues. For example, Jane Tompkins tells us in "At the Buffalo Bill Museum, June 1988" (p. 413) that the slide show about the Plains Indians has been "discontinued" and adds, "It occurred to me then that that was the message the museum was sending, if I could read it, that that was the bottom line. Discontinued, no reason given." In this passage, her tone shifts from one of earnest inquiry to one that could be described as irony tinged with bitterness. She wants the reader to consider how the termination of the slide show may be taken as a symbol for the termination of an entire people and its culture, and how the whole Plains Indian Museum, instead of preserving that people and that culture, stands for their demise. The clue to the shift in tone is the fact that the section ends with a short, blunt sentence fragment that throws great emphasis on the repeated word "discontinued." But if we were to miss Tompkins's ironic tone here, we might never see the connection between the word "discontinued" here and the "genocide" of which she speaks in the essay's last paragraph.

Identifying Arguments

Throughout this book, we use the word **argument** in a particular sense, referring not to a debate that ends with a winner and a loser but to a kind of logical structure. The *Oxford English Dictionary* defines "argument" in this sense as "a connected series of statements or reasons intended to establish a position." The way that statements and reasons are connected, the way that evidence supports claims and one claim supports another, makes it possible to speak of the *structure* of an argument, even the "architecture" of an argument.

In any free society, and especially in a liberal democracy such as the United States, *argument* in this sense plays an essential and conspicuous role. Barring physical force, the only way to get citizens to do something or believe something is through persuasion. Candidates for political office must persuade voters to support their platforms. Once elected, politicians must persuade one another to support legislation. In the judicial system, lawyers must persuade judges and juries to convict or release the accused, or to rule in favor of a client. The health of the political and judicial systems depends greatly on citizens' ability to distinguish between a strong argument and a weak one.

Moreover, arguments in the form of advertisements drive the economy. Many corporations live or die by their ability to persuade consumers to buy their products. Every advertisement presents an argument of some kind, whether bold or subtle, aimed at convincing members of the audience to spend money on the company's product — or at least to give the company a few seconds of their attention. Americans are bombarded with advertisements, thousands a day according to some estimates.[4] A century ago, advertisers would pitch their products with slogans that now seem obvious and crude ("Dooley's Yeast Powder. The Best. Try It"). Today, most advertisers use more subtle and indirect approaches, hoping to create positive associations with the product in the viewer's mind or to sell an idea that will ultimately lead to some sort of behavior.

Let's take a look at an advertisement and examine its argument. Figure 1.1 shows an advertisement from the U.S. Department of Health and Human Services. This apparently simple ad is not selling a product, but it *is* selling something: a preventive measure, the idea that adolescent alcoholism can be avoided if parents discuss drinking with their children before they reach middle school. Presumably, many parents fail to do so because they believe grade-school children are still too innocent to discuss such a subject. The ad aims to overcome this reservation.

The visual is disarmingly simple: a snaggle-toothed, freckle-faced boy smiles directly, guilelessly, at the viewer. Resting his chin in his hand, he seems composed and self-confident. Otherwise, he isn't very remarkable — he has a familiar-looking sort of

---

[4] "The Harder Hard Sell," *The Economist,* 24 June 2004, http://www.economist.com/node/2787854?Story_ID=2787854. Also, Louise Story, "Anywhere the Eye Can See, It's Likely to See an Ad," *New York Times,* 15 January 2007, http://www.nytimes.com/2007/01/15/business/media/15everywhere.html.

My name is Peter,
and in eight years I'll be an alcoholic.

I'll start drinking in middle school, just at parties. But my parents won't start talking to me about it until high school. And by then, I'll already be in some trouble. The thing is my parents won't even see it coming.

START TALKING BEFORE THEY START DRINKING
Kids who drink before age 15 are 5 times more likely to have alcohol problems when they're adults.
To learn more, go to www.stopalcoholabuse.gov or call 1.800.729.6686

Figure 1.1 This straightforward ad contains a complex argument.

face, the kind we might associate with a Norman Rockwell or Winslow Homer painting. That's the point: he could be almost anyone's child.

The image, of course, makes a jarring contrast with the text, which tells us that the boy will become an alcoholic. But the text is less straightforward than it seems at first. In childish script and using first-person narrative, it begins simply with "My name is Peter." But when we read the rest of the text, it is as though we are being led into a future when the boy's innocence has been lost. In a sense, the ad gives us two contrasting "nows" — the now of the image and the now of the text. It tells of a missed opportunity that led to disaster, a tragedy. But the "now" of the text isn't *really* a now. It's a future that's preventable. The text uses the future tense (it might have used the past tense): what "will" happen but hasn't happened yet. So we read it as an opportunity to act before it's too late.

Toward the bottom of the ad, the bold all-caps type takes a very different, more authoritative tone. But this section of the ad only underscores the argument and adds some notes. The argument is really made in the contrast between the image and the superimposed text: parents should discuss alcohol consumption with their children sooner than they might have thought necessary, even at the age of the boy in the pic-

Figure 1.2 **The Freedmen's Memorial (1876),** by Thomas Ball, in Lincoln Park, Washington, D.C.

ture (which cleverly is unspecified, as the point is that parents should speak to children not at some particular age but as early as possible).

Political speeches, legal speeches, and commercials exist in order to persuade, but other kinds of texts also make arguments, though argument may not be their only purpose. Films and novels often make arguments. For example, the film *Avatar* might be said to argue that our modern, industrial civilization's objectification and exploitation of the natural world cannot be reconciled with the longer-term need to live harmoniously with it. Sculptures and paintings make arguments — for example, about what we should consider good or noble or beautiful. In arguments like these, the claim being made is implied rather than stated. But the argument exists nevertheless, and it may be powerful.

For instance, in Figure 1.2, a photograph of the Freedmen's Memorial in Washington, D.C., a nameless slave stoops at the feet of Abraham Lincoln, apparently paying tribute to him. Lincoln is emancipating him, signing a proclamation with his right hand and sweeping his left hand over the slave's head. The figures are slightly larger than life and stand on a column about seven feet high. The sculpture makes an argument about the historical significance of the Emancipation Proclamation, certainly, but in doing so, it makes other claims as well. For example, Lincoln stands upright, as though solely responsible for the emancipation of slaves. The slave, though finally free, still kneels at the feet of a powerful white man. Of course, viewers can draw their own conclusions, but the sculpture — created by Thomas Ball only a decade after the end of the Civil War — does appear to invite the viewer to remember the emancipation of slaves in ways that today would make many of us uneasy.

We can even speak of the argument of a piece of music, such as a movement in a symphony, even if the piece has no words. Here the term would refer to the way that a composer varies and develops musical ideas — themes and phrases — such that the piece has a structure something like that of a written text. And just as music listeners or viewers of visual works of art must often look for an implied argument, so readers of texts sometimes encounter arguments that remain unstated. At times, a text that seems to be simply telling a story is actually making an argument. Consider the following example, the first paragraph of Jane Tompkins's essay "At the Buffalo Bill Museum, June 1988."

> The video at the entrance to the Buffalo Bill Historical Center says that Buffalo Bill was the most famous American of his time, that by 1900 more than a billion words had been written about him, and that he had a progressive vision of the West. Buffalo Bill had worked as a cattle driver, a wagoneer, a Pony Express rider, a buffalo hunter for the railroad, a hunting guide, an army scout and sometime Indian fighter; he wrote dime novels about himself and an autobiography by the age of thirty-four, by which time he was already famous; and then he began another set of careers, first as an actor, performing on the urban stage in wintertime melodramatic representations of what he actually earned a living at in the summer (scouting and leading hunting expeditions), and finally becoming the impresario of his great Wild West show, a form of entertainment he invented and carried on as actor, director, and all-around idea man for thirty years. Toward the end of his life he founded the town of Cody, Wyoming, to which he gave, among other things, two hundred thousand dollars. Strangely enough, it was as a progressive civic leader that Bill Cody wanted to be remembered. "I don't want to die," the video at the entrance quotes him as saying, "and have people say — oh, there goes another old showman. . . . I would like people to say — this is the man who opened Wyoming to the best of civilization." (p. 413)

At first, the paragraph might seem to be merely an assemblage of biographical facts. But Tompkins selects these facts carefully so that together they do make an implied claim. The argument is no less present and no less important for being a little hidden. It all leads up to the word "civilization," which becomes the starting point for a further exploration in which more arguments are made, and these lead to profound, sometimes troubling questions about the meaning of Buffalo Bill's legacy in American culture. This opening paragraph, however, shows the reader that Buffalo Bill (William Cody) was not just some sort of cartoon figure or mascot, not just "another old showman" who gave his nickname to a football team. He was a real person of exceptional talent, intelligence, and munificence — a figure of true historical impor-

> ### ➔ Try This   Analyzing an Advertisement
>
> Find an ad, either in a magazine or from television. Study it closely (no detail is insignificant). What claim does the advertisement make? What evidence (implied or stated) does the ad offer for this claim? In your notebook, write out the argument of the ad as fully and accurately as you can. Now, assess this argument. In your view, is the argument rational or irrational? Logical or emotional? Some combination? Neither?

tance, someone who made a difference to this country and is worth serious consideration. The collection of data suggests that his influence on our culture justifies the Buffalo Bill Historical Center, that the center is right to bring him to our attention — though whether his life is a matter for *celebration* may be a more difficult question.

Reading Critically

We said earlier that readers must first listen carefully to what the text is saying, but we have also spoken of the importance of entering into a dialogue with the text: at some point, readers must go beyond just listening if they want to develop a response. Even if readers primarily listen first and figure out their ideas about the text later, both of these activities are part of what we mean by "reading critically." The difference is really a matter of emphasis, since it's impossible to separate them *completely*: it is impossible *not* to reflect, weigh, and even react as you read, even for the first time. (The eighteenth-century Irish statesman Edmund Burke once observed, "To read without reflecting is like eating without digesting.") "Listening" carefully to what the author has to say produces an understanding of the text that inevitably reflects something of your own priorities, interests, and even personality. As such, it becomes the basis of your response.

So good readers take into account the context in which the piece was written and its genre. They attempt to look at the question through the writer's eyes, and they strive to give some thought to what the argument means to them personally. But good reading does not end there. A reader's responsibility is not only to *understand* a writer's point of view but also to *test* it, to see whether the argument holds up under close scrutiny. Put another way, a reader's responsibility is not only to the writer but also to the truth: if every reader simply accepted every writer's claims without question, as if they were the last word on the subject, humankind's quest for understanding would come to an abrupt halt. Only by noticing errors, weaknesses, and limitations in arguments that have already been made by others do we become able to improve on those arguments and get a little closer to the truth. Most writers actually value this kind of critical reading because they see their work not as an end in itself but as a contribution to a larger project, a project of figuring out the answer to a question or the solution to a problem, and this greater goal is one that they share with their readers. In this sense, a critical reader who can see the shortcomings in an argument and correct them is the best reader a writer can hope for. (Note how different this is from merely passing judgment — saying "I liked it" or "I didn't like it." Such blanket judgments don't get us very far.)

But can you, as a first-year college student, raise valid questions against an argument made by an expert? Most of the time, yes. In some situations, you might simply have to take an expert's word for it. But for the most part, if you can make sense of the argument, you can also analyze and assess it. Your knowledge of the subject may be more limited, but you do bring learning and valuable experience to your reading. Your unique perspective may enable you to see something an expert has overlooked. Moreover, you are a reasonable creature, and you can be observant and sensitive, so you are capable of recognizing when something doesn't make sense, when some aspect of the question has been carelessly or superficially argued, or when an important point has been neglected. Questioning whether an argument makes sense is a necessary part of figuring out *how* it makes sense: when an argument doesn't make good sense to you, even after you've considered it carefully, you have as much right as anyone to say so and to explain your misgivings.

The Principle of Charity

But don't be *too* hasty to criticize! Good readers also observe the **principle of charity**. This principle simply states that, as readers, we ought to give the author a chance before we leap in with criticisms and questions. If we find ourselves struggling with a text, we should assume, at least provisionally, that such difficulties stem chiefly from the nature of the ideas being explored, not from the failings of the writer. And we should bring reasonable expectations to the text: a few writers are able to cast their every thought in crystal-clear prose, but we should not expect everyone with good ideas to achieve perfection all the time. So the principle of charity dictates that readers should, within reason, allow for human frailty and accept that even if the writing might be clearer, the text may still be worth reading. (Of course, at the end of the day, you may be forced to conclude that the text was not, in fact, worth the time and effort — but if you make such a judgment before you're sure it's fair, you may be cheating both the writer and yourself.)

The principle of charity has another, more positive aspect. It implies that, to be really good readers, we must temporarily surrender ourselves to the text and let it do its work on us. That is, we must give the writer a chance and, for a time, imagine how the question looks from the writer's point of view. The English romantic poet Samuel Taylor Coleridge wrote in 1817 that poetry requires the "willing suspension of disbelief"; just as poetry or fiction demands that we let our imaginations carry us away from our own worlds and into the world created by the author, so nonfiction also requires a willingness to entertain another person's ideas, and even to immerse ourselves in them. (In "At the Buffalo Bill Museum, June 1988" [p. 413], Jane Tompkins expresses outrage at the killing of animals and implicitly places it on almost the same level as the killing of human beings. Some readers may not accept this moral equation. But they will have to put aside this difference temporarily in order to arrive at a real understanding of Tompkins's point of view.) Eventually, of course, we will need to consider the text in a more detached and critical way, but on a first reading the suspension of disbelief is a useful strategy: the deeper our understanding of the author's position, the more well-founded and persuasive our response will be.

Is it possible to be a sympathetic reader and a critical reader at the same time? Absolutely. Experienced critical readers tend to seesaw as they read, shifting their perspective back and forth, first asking themselves "What does the writer mean?" and then "Does this really make good sense?" The modernist poet and critic T. S. Eliot used the terms "surrender" and "recovery" for this kind of mental circling: readers must first surrender to the text, accepting its way of looking at things, but in good time they must recover their own mind and judge whether this way of looking is acceptable or valid. In this phase, the reader asks questions such as "What is the author failing to see? How else might the question be considered? What are the unstated implications of this argument?"

Clearly, readers who write have many things to do: listen carefully to what the author is saying, taking into account the historical and cultural context; trace the argument and its logical structure; reflect on the argument and start weighing it; begin to think about what they might have to say in response. Readers do not need to do all these things at once, however: that's what rereading is for. And in the next two chapters, we'll offer several strategies for getting all these reading tasks done, effectively and efficiently.

Most students are, in effect, professional readers, and reading plays a central role in the vast majority of college courses. A 2009 national survey of first-year college students showed that 74 percent are assigned at least five books or book-length packs of course readings per year. Thirty-seven percent are assigned more than eleven books, and 13 percent are assigned more than twenty.[5] Your success as a student depends to a great extent on how efficient and capable you are as a reader. And if you think of "success" in education as the attainment of greater wisdom, discernment, and maturity rather than just a matter of grades and credentials, then the way in which you read becomes an even more critical matter. The kind of education you receive — or perhaps "achieve" is the better word — depends not only on what you read but also on how you read. To read attentively, thoughtfully, critically remains an essential skill. In this age of the Internet, information is readily available in vast quantities, but its sheer abundance has made the ability to discriminate between the useful and the not so useful, between the reliable and the dubious, more valuable than ever. "Active reading" means bringing your whole mind to bear on a text, in order to comprehend the text's meaning, to place that meaning in relation to the rest of what you know, and to step back from it to assess its strengths and weaknesses. In the following chapter, we will look at the fundamental strategies for putting this lofty ideal into practice.

✔ Checklist for Reading with a Purpose

Keep the following in mind as you read:

☐ If the reading has been assigned, note its purpose in the context of the course.
  • Ask your instructor for guidance if you are confused.
☐ Clear a space for reading, free from distractions.
  • Find a quiet setting, such as the library.
  • Turn off your cell phone and other devices, close your laptop, and sit upright.

---

[5] National Survey of Student Engagement, Annual Results 2009, 34, http://nsse.iub.edu/NSSE_2009_Results/pdf/NSSE_AR_2009.pdf.

☐ Identify the author and his or her work.

☐ Identify the text's historical and cultural context.
- If necessary and appropriate, research the historical and cultural context.

☐ Identify the text's genre.

☐ Identify the main argument.
- Understand the author's point of view; observe the principle of charity.
- Hold off any criticism until you have a good grasp of what's being said.

☐ Trace the logical structure of the main argument.
- Identify key claims.
- Identify key terms and concepts.

☐ Finally, weigh the argument; note possible weaknesses.

chapter 2

Active Reading

When you have to write about a difficult text, you face a special challenge. Your task is not just to get through the reading, or even to come up with ideas about it, but to meet the author's ideas and develop a response that is *adequate* to them — "adequate" in its root sense: equal, commensurate, or fitting, having been brought up to the same level. A careless reading cannot lead to a response that is equal to the text, one that recognizes and respects the text's meaning. At the same time, the reader who is concerned *only* with the text's meaning and does no more than repeat or summarize the main point will not truly be responding to the text at all and will have nothing to say that another reader might find interesting or useful. The real challenge, then, of **response** is twofold: to comprehend the text's meaning and to respond with fresh and interesting ideas. Active reading strategies help you accomplish both of these tasks. This chapter offers some basic strategies — strategies you should consider using whenever you read a text you will have to write about. The next chapter offers some additional strategies for active reading, ones you can draw on more selectively and which will help you dig deeper into an argument; these are useful when you have to work with an especially difficult or complicated text or when an assignment requires you to explore a text's argument very closely.

> " Curiously enough, one cannot *read* a book: one can only reread it. A good reader, a major reader, an active and creative reader is a rereader. "
>
> **VLADIMIR NABOKOV**

As we noted in the last chapter, in practice understanding a text and responding to it cannot be separated into completely distinct activities — they inevitably overlap — yet first readings tend to focus more on comprehension, and later readings more on responding. You may need to read a difficult text three or more times before you feel comfortable writing about it. This is not unusual, and in fact many students learn that this kind of close, deep work with a writer's ideas — wrestling, pondering, questioning them — can be among the most rewarding kinds of academic experience.

Plan to read a difficult text at least three times if you will be writing in response to it. More than three readings may be necessary, but typically the process has three phases.

- The first reading allows you to get your bearings — to get a general sense of the sort of text you are dealing with and the work that lies ahead.

- The second reading usually provides a better sense of how the pieces fit together into a whole, and now you can begin to map the text's argument or structure so that you arrive at a strong sense of "the lay of the land."

- On the third and subsequent readings, you define, clarify, and strengthen a position of your own.

Although at first the text may feel like a wilderness, if you take the time to explore, survey, and map it, you can soon feel at home in it. With the help of a few strategies, you can approach this kind of work with confidence and even a sense of adventure.

Reading through the Text for the First Time

Read from Beginning to End

The principal aim of a first reading is to develop a general sense of the text as a whole, to "get your bearings," so that when you begin to concentrate on discrete passages, you will be able to use your understanding of the whole to make sense of them. In this first reading, try to push on from the beginning to the end of the essay or chapter with minimal interruptions and without worrying too much about passages whose meaning is not immediately clear. Focus on the main argument, and try to follow the thread that runs through the whole text, connecting paragraph to paragraph and section to section. Glance at footnotes or endnotes, but don't let them distract you from this thread. If for a moment you lose your sense of how the pieces are fitting together, don't get discouraged. Keep reading. Later passages may help to clarify earlier passages, and examples and anecdotes may help to make sense of abstract generalizations. But for now, you need only get a sense of the "shape" of the text, the principal features of the landscape. As you read, keep an eye out for the author's main purpose and argument so that later you can confidently identify it.

Keep a Notebook and Pen Nearby

It's always a good policy to keep a notebook and pen nearby so that you can mark up the reading or write notes if the need arises or inspiration strikes — and if it does, go ahead and write, even if it means interrupting your reading for a few minutes. (Of course, you can also use a computer for your writing.) Capture your thoughts and put them into words while they are fresh. The value of this kind of informal and unstructured writing is immeasurable, and, we contend, "freewriting" at various stages of the reading and drafting process is essential to a good final product. Its purpose is not only to record your thoughts; the very act of writing helps to clarify and develop them and to begin a conversation with the text. Your thoughts may be tentative, random, and sketchy at first, but that should not discourage you. The process of thinking things through on paper is valuable even when the writing itself turns out to be no more than a stepping-stone to more usable writing later on.

Mark Up the Text

A brand-new book, with its crisp pages and clean margins, is an object you may want to keep in mint condition. But textbooks are not coffee-table books. They are the tools of your education, and writing in them does not desecrate them. For centuries, readers have **annotated** — or marked up — books with notes and made their copies into unique records of a thoughtful engagement with the author's ideas. (Notes in the margins of a book are known as **marginalia**.) "Annotation," writes H. J. Jackson in *Marginalia: Readers Writing in Books*, "used to be taught as part of the routine of learning. Marking, copying out, inserting glosses, selecting heads, adding bits from other books, and writing one's own observations are all traditional devices, on a rising scale of readerly activity, for remembering and assimilating text."[1] Owning a book allows you to record your conversation with the author; that conversation begins with the choice of what to underline or what to jot down in the margins. (The marginalia of the poet Samuel Taylor Coleridge, mentioned in the last chapter,

---

[1] H. J. Jackson, *Marginalia: Readers Writing in Books* (New Haven: Yale University Press, 2001), 87.

CHAP. 13.   *That Faith onely justifieth before God.*

No piecing or partial Cauſ (said *Luther*) approacheth thereunto; For Faith is powerful continually without ceaſing; otherwiſe, it is no Faith. Therefore what the works are, or of what value, the ſame they are through the Honor and Power of Faith, which undeniably is the Sun or Sun-beam of this ſhining.

Melanct. ſeventh Replie.

In *Auſtin* (ſaid *Melancthon*) theſe words (*Solâ fide*) excludeth directly the works.

Luther's Anſwer.

Whether it bee ſo or no: Theſe words of *Auſtin* do ſufficiently ſhew, that hee is of our opinion, where hee ſaith, Well may I bee afraid, but I do not therefore deſpair: For I think upon and remember the wounds of the Lord. And further, *in Libro Confeſſionis*, hee ſaith, Wo bee to the life of that humane Creature (bee it never ſo good and worthie of praiſ) that diſ-regardeth God's Mercie.

Hereby (ſaid *Luther*) hee ſheweth plainly, that Faith is Active and powerful in the Beginning, Middle, and End, that is, continually. As alſo the *Pſalm* ſaith, By Thee is forgiveneſs, &c. Alſo, *Enter not into judgment with thy ſervant*, &c.

Melanct. eighth Replie.

Is this ſaying true, The Righteouſneſs of works is neceſſarie to Salvation?

Luther's Anſwer.

No, (ſaid *Luther*) works do not procure nor obtein Salvation, but they are preſent by and with Faith, which obtaineth Righteouſneſs; as I of neceſſitie muſt bee preſent at my ſalvation. The opinion of *Sadoletus* may bee this, that faith is a work required by God's Laws, as Love, Obedience, Chaſtitie, &c. Therefore, hee that believeth hath fulfilled the firſt part of the Law, and ſo hath a beginning to Righteouſneſs, but when this beginning is preſent, then other works are required which are commanded in the Law, which muſt bee don after and beſides Faith.

Hereby wee ſee (ſaid *Luther*) that *Sadoletus* underſtandeth nothing in this Caſe: for if Faith were a commanded work, then his opinion were right, and faith in that ſort would regenerate one in the beginning, as other good works would alſo renew one afterwards.

But wee ſaie, That Faith is a work of God's Promiſs, or a gift of the holie Spirit, which indeed is neceſſarie to the fulfilling of the Law, but it is not obtained by the Law nor by works. But this preſented gift (Faith)...

Figure 2.1 A page from Martin Luther's *Colloquia Mensalia* (1652). Annotations by Samuel Taylor Coleridge.

became celebrated and valued for their insight and wit. See Figure 2.1 for an example.) Your notes in the margins make the book more completely your own.

But on reading a text for the first time, avoid marking it up too heavily. Instead, read through the text completely at a steady pace, knowing that later on you'll come back to it and mark it up thoughtfully.

Underline sparingly — just key phrases or sentences that you know you will want to come back to; and in the margins, jot down a question mark next to puzzling passages, or a brief keyword as a heading, and so on. When you reread and have a stronger sense of the shape of the argument as a whole, you will mark up the text more heavily (see p. 55). For this kind of work, a thick highlighter marker may be better than nothing, but in the long run it reveals its shortcomings. After several rereadings, devotees of the highlighter often end up with a text so heavily highlighted that nothing stands out any longer in the great sea of yellow or pink — and so it defeats its purpose. A pencil or a fine-point pen, on the other hand, offers plenty of flexibility — underlining; circling words or phrases; writing words, symbols, and simple diagrams in the margins; and so on — and allows you to mark up pages and write notes in a notebook without constantly switching between tools.

Here is an example of annotations a student made during a first reading. This is the first paragraph of Adam Gopnik's essay "Bumping into Mr. Ravioli." (The full piece is reprinted on p. 384.)

7½ years old

My daughter, Olivia, who just turned three, has an imaginary friend whose name is Charlie Ravioli. Olivia is growing up in Manhattan, and so Charlie Ravioli has a lot of local traits: he lives in an apartment "on Madison and Lexington," he dines on grilled chicken, fruit, and water, and, having reached the age of seven and a half, he feels, or is thought, "old." But the most peculiarly local thing about Olivia's imaginary playmate is this: he is always too busy to play with her. She holds her toy cell phone up to her ear, and we hear her talk into it: "Ravioli? It's Olivia . . . It's Olivia. Come and play? OK. Call me. Bye." Then she snaps it shut and shakes her head. "I always get his machine," she says. Or she will say, "I spoke to Ravioli today." "Did you have fun?" my wife and I ask. "No. He was busy working. On a television" (leaving it up in the air if he repairs electronic devices or has his own talk show).

Here are the annotations of the same paragraph that the student made during a second reading. Note that he has expanded his use of marginalia.

"imaginary friend"
why weird name?

New York

My daughter, Olivia, who just turned three, has an imaginary friend whose name is Charlie Ravioli. Olivia is growing up in Manhattan, and so Charlie Ravioli has a lot of local traits: he lives in an apartment "on Madison and Lexington," he dines on grilled chicken, fruit, and water,

Charlie - 7½ years old

and, having reached the age of seven and a half, he feels, or is thought, "old." But the most peculiarly local thing about Olivia's imaginary play-mate is this: he is always too busy to play with her. She holds her toy

imitates adults with toy cell phone

cell phone up to her ear, and we hear her talk into it: "Ravioli? It's Olivia... It's Olivia. Come and play? OK. Call me. Bye." Then she snaps

pretend frustration?

it shut and shakes her head. "I always get his machine," she says. Or she will say, "I spoke to Ravioli today." "Did you have fun?" my wife and I

examples of conversation

ask. "No. He was busy working. On a television" (leaving it up in the air if he repairs electronic devices or has his own talk show).

Note the Knowledge Problem, Thesis Statement, and Key Claims

As you read, look for an explanation — even a very compressed one — of the **knowledge problem** that the author is addressing — the question that remains unanswered, the mystery that remains unsolved, or the need that remains unfilled. As we noted in Chapter 1, scholars typically identify the important unknowns in their field and attempt to contribute something large or small toward answering these knowledge problems. Usually, scholars tell the reader quite early in the article the nature of the problem, question, or need they are addressing. However, since they are often writing for other specialists in their field, they may refer to this problem in shorthand, with a brief allusion rather than a full explanation. Still, if you look carefully in the first few paragraphs, you can usually find at least a hint of it. And recognizing the knowledge problem will help you understand the author's main purpose and the general direction of the argument.

Closely linked to the problem is the **thesis statement**: a proposition, in one or two sentences, that stands for the argument of the text as a whole. You might think of the thesis as the author's answer to the knowledge problem — perhaps just a small part of the answer, but something worth contributing to the conversation about this problem. Writers do not always position the thesis statement at the end of the first paragraph, as you may have learned to do, but it usually does appear somewhere near the beginning of the essay or somewhere near the end. Writers will sometimes restate a thesis in different forms as their argument evolves; for example, a short version might appear at the beginning of the essay, and a more detailed one at the end. Many accomplished writers resist following predictable formulas, so they might decide to hold the reader in suspense and disclose the argument a little later than expected, or they may want to begin with a lengthier introduction that makes it necessary to place the thesis statement in the fourth or fifth paragraph rather than in the first or second. A complex argument may even require breaking the thesis statement into several parts that appear throughout the essay. So be on the lookout not only for the thesis statement but for all statements that disclose the author's sense of the purpose and direction of the argument.

As you work your way through an argument, you may notice that it contains interlocking parts: one argument has to be made to support another argument, and each argument or supporting argument works together with others to make the author's overall case for the thesis. Each argument contains one or more **claims** (assertions) and support for those claims. As you read, identify the major arguments and their claims — you will often find them at or near the beginning of paragraphs. Notice also *how* the author supports such claims — perhaps through stories, or with data, or by referring to the work of other researchers.

Not all essays make straightforward arguments in support of a thesis, however; some essays are much more exploratory and questioning (Jane Tompkins's "At the Buffalo Bill Museum, June 1988" is one example). In these cases, notice how the exploration unfolds, developing the theme and considering fresh points of view, leading the reader from one question to another, defining the problem more sharply and drawing the reader more deeply into it. Look for the key questions that indicate where this exploration starts and where it ends. And look for statements that indicate why this exploration matters.

Note Divisions, Turning Points, and Signposts

Whether you're reading an exploratory essay or a thesis-driven argument, note and mark the major divisions in the text; where the author shifts from one topic or theme to another; and how each topic or theme relates to the thesis of the essay as a whole. If necessary, write headings in the margins.

Many writers leave signposts for the reader at key turning points in the text. These signposts may be a single word such as "however" or "nevertheless" that reveals a shift in the direction of the argument, perhaps to introduce some exception or qualification. But sometimes an author very explicitly states where we will be heading or where we have come from, perhaps using a phrase like "I will argue that . . ." or "Having demonstrated that . . ." This kind of writing (sometimes called **metadiscourse**) often helps the reader take a step back from the details of an argument to get a stronger sense of its general direction, or it reminds the reader of the global argument after a long detour. Statements like these often appear at **turning points** in the text. Consider an example from an influential essay by the historian Frederick Jackson Turner, "The Significance of the Frontier in American History" (1893). Because his essay is necessarily full of facts and references that support his argument, he wants the reader to be able to navigate through the wealth of detail and still keep sight of the destination, so he offers an entire paragraph at about the midpoint that functions as a large signpost.

> Having now roughly outlined the various kinds of frontier, and their modes of advance, chiefly from the point of view of the frontier itself, we may next inquire what were the influences on the East and on the Old World. A rapid enumeration of some of the more noteworthy effects is all that I have time for.[2]

This kind of metadiscourse is "programmatic" — it reveals the author's project — and reassures the reader that the vessel is still on course and that the destination is just over the horizon. In any complicated or difficult reading, these signposts are worth looking out for and worth marking or underlining so that you can come back to them whenever you need a reminder.

Note Things That Puzzle You

At this stage, your first reading, don't spend a lot of time trying to figure out everything in the text you find confusing. Simply make a note in the margin of things that you'll want to come back to later on, or copy out a brief phrase from the text and a page number, so that you can identify the passage easily. In one or two sentences, write down your question, as clearly as you can at this stage, or simply put a question mark next to the passages you don't understand.

Gloss Unfamiliar References

As noted earlier, one of the most effective and efficient ways of making better sense of a text is to look up unfamiliar words (and familiar words that seem to be used in unfamiliar ways) in a college-level dictionary. It is also useful to look up unfamiliar allusions and references, either in a traditional encyclopedia or using the Internet. A *gloss* is an explanatory note in the margins of a text or in a separate notebook. Instead

---

[2] Frederick Jackson Turner, *The Significance of the Frontier in American History* (New York: Ungar, 1985), 44.

> **Try This   Mark Up the Text**
>
> Read Cornel West's essay "Malcolm X and Black Rage" (p. 450) steadily from begin-
> ning to end, marking up the text as you go. Follow the guidelines offered above, as
> best you can. Mark or underline West's statement of the problem, his thesis state-
> ment, and some of his key claims. (If on a first reading you cannot identify all those
> elements, simply make a note of those you need to keep looking for as you re-read.)
> Identify divisions, turning points, and signposts in the essay. And note anything that
> puzzles or surprises you—as well as anything you find especially interesting or
> thought-provoking. Finally, in the margins or on a separate page, gloss unfamiliar
> terms and references.

of interrupting your reading every few minutes, however, consider using a code to
mark unfamiliar terms, and look up several at once when you reach a convenient
break in the text. For example, you might underline and put a "d" in the margins next
to words you need to look up in the dictionary, and underline and put an "a" in the
margin next to unfamiliar allusions or references.

Every reader encounters the problem of changing cultural knowledge. Culture
changes constantly, and readers today tend to be much less familiar with, say, the
Bible or Greek myths or even Shakespeare's plays than were readers of just a few
decades ago. Writers once took for granted that readers would understand allusions
to "Niobe's tears," for example, or "the patience of Job." Today, readers may not recognize the source or immediately catch the meaning, but they can easily look such
things up on the Internet. Try Encyclopedia.com or *The Columbia Encyclopedia* (at
bartleby.com/65).

Reading Journal: Thoughts, Claims, and Questions

Keep a reading journal, either in a notebook reserved for this purpose or in a special
folder on your computer. You'll want to be able to review your entries easily, so it's
important to keep them together in one place. In your first entry, include three parts:
your first thoughts, a list of two or three important claims that you noticed in the
text, and a list of two or three good questions about the text.

Don't be too concerned about the quality of your work at this point; you need only lay the groundwork for more productive writing you'll do later on. But this groundwork *is* valuable, as a word or phrase that might seem insignificant now can inspire an important insight later.

Record Your First Thoughts

After reading the whole text once, put it aside and spend at least ten minutes writing freely and unreservedly about what you've just read. First, note the date and time at the top of the page or document. Then write continuously; don't stop to worry about grammar, spelling, word choice, or even whether your thoughts are any good. This freewriting is for your eyes only — a chance simply to record your initial response to the text, however basic or incoherent. Here are some questions you might ask yourself if you're stuck — remember, though, that there are no firm rules for this, and you certainly don't have to cover all (or any) of these questions.

- What is the text about? How would you describe the author's *main* purpose, as you understand it at this point?
- Of everything you just read, what most stands out in your memory?
- What do you think of the author's ideas at this point?
- What was it like to read this text? Hard work? Easy going? Stimulating? Arduous? Describe the experience.
- How do you feel you performed as a reader? (Note your strengths as well as your weaknesses.)

Here's an example of one student's initial response after reading Cornel West's "Malcolm X and Black Rage" (p. 450).

Student Sample Reading Journal, First Entry

March 31, 2011, 8:20pm

I think Malcolm X's idea (or maybe Cornel West's idea of Malcolm X's idea?) of psychic conversion is interesting. It contains a lot of truth about the whole business of achieving equality. Maybe not all the methods that Malcolm X used were correct. But in order for someone to demand equality and rights he or she must see themselves as better than the oppressors, but they must never separate themselves completely because that will lead to their alienation from

→ **Try** **This**   **Record Your Initial Response in a Journal Entry**

If you have not already done so, read Cornel West's essay "Malcolm X and Black Rage" (p. 450) once from beginning to end. Then put it aside and spend ten to fifteen minutes writing in a journal, either on paper or on a computer. First record the date and time at the top of the page, and then write freely and continuously. If you get stuck or feel unsure of your direction, turn to the questions listed in the "Record Your First Thoughts" section (p. 53). At some point in your writing, attempt to express in your own words the nature of the problem that West is addressing. In addition, try to record from memory two or three of the claims he makes. And note two or three questions about the text that occurred to you as you were reading or that occur to you now. (You need not do all these steps in any particular order. Remember: the main thing is simply to record your initial response to the text.)

society, leaving problems and not resolving anything. One must never look at him- or herself through the eyes of others, but instead try to see through their own eyes because those are the only truth tellers. Cornel West uses Michael Jackson as an example to demonstrate how if one does not achieve psychic conversion, then he or she may be in denial of the truth and live in a constant need to be like the majority (whites) because of a pre-existing sense that they are somehow better.

Identify the Problem (If Possible)

If you can, explain in your own words the nature of the problem that the author is concerned with, or as much about it as you can grasp at this point. In some instances, this may be difficult after only one reading; if so, simply write a word or two reminding you to come back to this step after a rereading or two.

Restate Two or Three Claims

Next, identify from memory two or three of the author's claims. If you can confidently identify one of these claims as the author's thesis, then do so. (Perhaps mark a capital "T" next to it in the margin.) But if you're not sure of the thesis yet, don't worry: the claims you identify at this point need not be the most important ones, just ones that you recall. But try to be sure that they are indeed *claims* — arguable propositions — and not simple statements of fact.

Ask Two or Three Questions

Finally, write down two or three good questions about the text. A "good" question is simply a genuine question about some aspect of the text that interests or puzzles you — the sort of question you'd like to raise in a discussion and that might lead to a deeper understanding of the text, or some aspect of it, rather than a merely factual question with a yes/no answer or a "quiz" question that would only be asked to make sure the class had done its homework.

Rereading

Read Slowly

To some, this may not sound like a productive reading strategy; we tend to assume that, as the ads for speed-reading courses tell us, better readers are faster readers. But in fact, good readers vary their pace to suit their purpose and the nature of the material. They might skim quickly through a newspaper article or a Web page, but they will take the time to absorb, weigh, and ponder a densely argued text, especially if they expect to be writing or talking about it. Read at a pace that's comfortable, but don't hurry. Especially for your second and subsequent readings, you'll get much more out of a text if you give it the time it requires.

Develop Your Marginalia

Your most important task is to identify the author's argument and follow it throughout the text. To do so, you will need to mark up the text more heavily. If you don't have a lot of margin space (or are unwilling to mark up your book even with a pencil), consider making a photocopy of the essay so that you can use the larger margins as well as the white space on the reverse. Or you might attach Post-it notes to the book; one advantage of this approach is that, by aligning the edge of the note with the edge of the page, you can easily locate them later, and of course you can detach them if needed.

A Basic Dialectical Notebook

The **dialectical notebook** is a simple and powerful method of taking notes developed by Ann E. Berthoff.[3] Here's how it works. Draw a line down the center of a page in your notebook. You can also use a computer. At the top of the left-hand column, write "What It Says." Here, you'll take notes about *what the author is saying.* These might be quotations of key phrases, whole sentences, or even whole paragraphs. They might be paraphrases or summaries of parts of the text. Or they might outline a section of the text. The form they take is up to you — but the left side of the page belongs to the author's words and ideas. (Be sure to record the page number that corresponds to each quotation or paraphrase so that you can find it and cite it later.) At the top of the right-hand column, write "What I Think." Here, you'll take notes about *what you think* about what the author is saying. These notes might consist of comments, questions, reactions, reflections, or even symbols and punctuation marks (!, ?, *, huh?). They can be as long or as short as you like. At first, your notes on the right side may be quite brief compared to those on the left, but it's important to write something on the "What I Think" side. In particular, write down your questions. The act of formulating your questions in words will help make them clearer and more definite. You can come back to them and rephrase them more precisely later on. You'll be able to try out possible answers to these questions and find patterns that will help you see things that were hidden before.

The word "dialectic" refers to a method of arriving at insights through debate, discussion, or an exchange of ideas. The double-entry format of the dialectical notebook lets you keep one foot in the text, so to speak, and one foot in your own reactions to it. This close and continuous interaction with the text produces a dialectic that, like good talk, leads somewhere. But you've got to keep up your end of the conversation. The notes you take on the right, notes that record and develop what is going on in your head as you reread, may be different from the sort of notes you usually take. Berthoff described this record-keeping as an **audit of meaning**. An audit is a methodical review or examination. Recording your responses, and then reviewing them and recording your responses to your responses, is the key to establishing a real dialogue with the text. This dialogue, as Berthoff argues, is the essence of critical reading and writing: "The reason for the

---

[3] Ann E. Berthoff, with James Stephens, *Forming, Thinking, Writing,* 2nd ed. (Portsmouth, NH: Heinemann–Boynton/Cook, 1988).

double-entry notebook will become apparent to you as you begin to see that you are conducting the continuing audit of meaning that is at the heart of learning to write critically."[4] This method of note-taking may seem time-consuming, but it helps to generate critical reading and ideas for writing so effectively that it is worth giving it a try.

If initially you have very little on the right side of the page, reread with the sole aim of recording your responses, however vague or inarticulate they might be at this early stage. Then work through your notes and write brief responses to the quotations and paraphrases that you noted on the left — as many of them as you can. If you're at a loss, use these questions as prompts.

- Why did this passage seem noteworthy or puzzling to you?
- What can you say about its meaning?
- What questions can you ask about the passage?
- If the passage is confusing, can you identify where the difficulty lies? For example, is there a particular word, phrase, or sentence structure that is unclear?
- How might you connect this passage to something else in the text, or to other texts in the course, or to your own knowledge or experience?

Don't worry at this point about whether your thoughts are impressive or essay-worthy or "right." You can edit later, and you can use as much or as little of these dialectical notes in your final product as you like. For now, they need only be a record of your own thoughts as you read.

Layers: The Dialectical Notebook as Palimpsest

The real power of the dialectical notebook becomes clear when you start working over the notes that you took on a first and second reading. With each subsequent reading, you can build up the notes on each side, and as they become denser and more fully developed, you can begin working solely with your notebook, amplifying and elaborating your thoughts until you have whole sentences and paragraphs, referenced to relevant passages in the text. For example, on a first reading, you

---

[4] Berthoff, *Forming, Thinking, Writing,* 27.

might copy out on the left side a passage you found especially puzzling, and on the right write down nothing more than two question marks next to it. But on a second reading, some ideas about the meaning of the passage may occur to you, and so you jot them down. Returning to this page later, you might realize that your ideas were basically right but that you can now explicate the text with more confidence and more precision, so you edit your notes and add to them.

In this way, your notes develop layers, and your pages become a kind of "palimpsest." This word derives from a Greek root that literally means "scraped again." Before the invention of paper, writing surfaces were expensive and were often reused rather than thrown out. A palimpsest is a manuscript of papyrus or parchment from which the text has been scraped away, but not completely erased, to make room for a new layer, so that the first layer is still legible beneath. By extension, the word is often used to refer to a text that bears more than one layer of writing, one superimposed on another. In our case, the first layer of writing will not be erased to make room for a new layer, but rather serves as a foundation for subsequent layers that fill in the white space around it.

The three examples that follow provide a glimpse of a student actively using this method of note-taking. These cumulative entries on Cornel West's "Malcolm X and Black Rage" (p. 450) show the student's newest notes in blue.

Double-Entry Notebook with a First Layer of Notes

<u>WHAT IT SAYS</u>	<u>WHAT I THINK</u>
"Rather, Malcolm believed that if black people felt the love that motivated that rage the love would produce a psychic conversion in black people; they would affirm themselves as human beings, no longer viewing their bodies, minds, and souls through white lenses, and believing themselves capable of taking control of their own destinies." (p. 451)	love/rage (?) "psychic"?
Dangers of such conversion, danger of pride: "Strange Fruit" on trees in South	Billie Holiday's song. (Who wrote it?)

Double-Entry Notebook with a Second Layer of Notes

WHAT IT SAYS	WHAT I THINK
"Rather, Malcolm believed that if black people felt the love that motivated that rage the love would produce a psychic conversion in black people; they would affirm themselves as human beings, no longer viewing their bodies, minds, and souls through white lenses, and believing themselves capable of taking control of their own destinies." (p. 451)	love/rage (?) people tend to associate Malcolm with rage; West wants them to see the love behind the rage "psychic"? means extrasensory, often. But can also mean "of the mind" or "of the soul" (*Webster's*). Here, perhaps both mind *and* soul?
Dangers of such conversion, danger of pride: "Strange Fruit" on trees in South	Billie Holiday's song. (Who wrote it?) Googled it: Abel Meeropol, a white, Jewish teacher in NYC

➔ Try This   Creating a Dialectical Notebook

You can set up a dialectical notebook on paper or on your computer. Divide the page down the middle and give each column the appropriate headings: "What It Says" on the left and "What I Think" on the right. (If you're using a computer, you can insert two text boxes side by side to create two columns. This takes a few minutes, but you can save the blank dialectical notebook template for future use.) Read or reread your assigned essay with your dialectical notebook open, and take notes in the "What It Says" column as you go. Respond to these notes in the "What I Think" column. Leave some space so that you can develop these notes later. (For further detail, see "A Basic Dialectical Notebook," p. 56.)

After reading and making notes once, read through the text a second time and develop your notes with a second layer. Record new insights and observations, and pay special attention to any notes on the right-hand side that suggest an idea, a question, or a puzzlement that needs to be worked out. Respond to your earlier responses, so that your notebook begins to become an audit of meaning.

Double-Entry Notebook with a Third Layer of Notes

WHAT IT SAYS:	WHAT I THINK:
"Rather, Malcolm believed that if black people felt the love that motivated that rage the love would produce a psychic conversion in black people; they would affirm themselves as human beings, no longer viewing their bodies, minds, and souls through white lenses, and believing themselves capable of taking control of their own destinies." (p. 451)	From rage to love (see Baldwin) love/rage (?) people tend to associate Malcolm with rage; West wants them to see the love behind the rage "psychic"? means extrasensory, often. But can also mean "of the mind" or "of the soul" (*Webster's*). Here, perhaps both mind *and* soul?
Dangers of such conversion, danger of pride: "Strange Fruit" on trees in South	Yes — *almost* a religious conversion but not exactly religious: a profound shift in consciousness. Reminds me of Du Bois and "double consciousness" Billie Holiday's song. (Who wrote it?) Googled it: Abel Meeropol, a white, Jewish teacher in NYC. Sorrow songs? Du Bois again

Reading Journal: Further Thoughts

After you've finished rereading, spend twenty to thirty minutes with your reading journal. The purpose is to give you an opportunity to collect your thoughts while the reading is still fresh in your mind, to develop these thoughts by the act of writing (remember: writing tends to *generate* ideas, not just record them), and to capture some words or phrases that might be useful later. You've already laid the groundwork with your entries in your dialectical notebook: this is an opportunity to begin building on it — in a very rudimentary way, perhaps, but you never know what might happen. The point is to give your mind the opportunity to create thoughts.

Here is an example of what one student, Mariana Gonzalez, wrote in her journal after reading West's essay and working with her dialectical notebook. Notice how she has begun to shape and structure her observations.

Student Sample Reading Journal, Second Entry

West also mentions W. E. B. Du Bois's idea of "double-consciousness," which is when one looks at oneself through the eyes of others — not just on occasion but habitually. Double-consciousness is exactly what Malcolm X believed to be wrong because he states that the person who looks for approval and assimilation will never have true freedom and love for the black people. Psychic conversion can be seen as a sort of exact opposite to double-consciousness, but I'm not sure how anyone decides which one of the two is correct. Cornel West seems to believe that Du Bois's double-consciousness appears to make black people enter into an eternal quest for acceptance by white racists. Psychic conversion instead offers a more effective way by letting black people see that they do not need the approval of whites, but only their own love and appreciation.

Timed Freewriting

First, spend another ten minutes writing continuously in your reading journal. Again, don't be too concerned with the quality of your writing. But focus this time on what you are now able to say about the text, beyond what you could say after the first reading. How has your understanding of the text changed? Did you notice anything different or new this time through? What are your thoughts now about the author's argument?

Two or Three More Claims

Write down from memory two or three more of the author's claims, ones that you overlooked the first time. This will give you a more complete sense of the author's argument.

Respond to Your First Questions

Take a look at the questions you wrote down after your first reading. Can you respond to any of them now? If so, write a paragraph or two.

Write Down Two More Questions

Add two more questions to your entry. Perhaps you'll find this time that your questions are even more penetrating and interesting — that they go deeper into the main concerns of the text.

Of course, you can read the text a third time, or as many times as you wish, and repeat the same process of freewriting, identifying claims, responding to questions, and posing new ones. Beyond providing material you can bring to class discussion, your notebook may well contain good material for your writing too.

✅ Checklist for Active Reading

Here are some guidelines to help you get the most out of reading a text. Remember: difficult texts are difficult for most readers, and good readers expect to reread.

☐ The first time you read a text, read it through from beginning to end.

☐ Mark up the text.
- Underline and make marginal notes — but sparingly.
- Keep a notebook and pen nearby.
- Note key claims, turning points, and signposts.
- Note things that puzzle you.
- Gloss unfamiliar references.

☐ Keep a reading journal.
- Record your first thoughts and questions.
- Identify three or four important claims.
- Write down at least two good questions about the text.

☐ Reread the text.

☐ Read slowly.

☐ Develop your marginalia.

☐ Keep a dialectical notebook.

☐ Add further thoughts to your reading journal.
- Write down two or three more claims.
- Respond to your first questions.
- Write down two more questions.

chapter 3

Further Strategies for Active Reading

In the epigraph on the right, Henry David Thoreau issues a kind of challenge to his readers: to approach reading with real seriousness and dedication — like professional athletes, pushing their limits, striving always to improve. Perhaps he makes reading sound rather grueling, but another way of looking at it is to consider that, like athletes in training, readers do improve with practice and find that the heavy work gets easier over time. Thoreau also reminds us that the art of reading is one that nobody ever *perfects*, that every text is in some way

> " To read well, that is, to read true books in a true spirit, is a noble exercise, and one that will task the reader more than any exercise which the customs of the day esteem. It requires a training such as the athletes underwent, the steady intention almost of the whole life to this object. Books must be read as deliberately and reservedly as they were written. "
>
> **HENRY DAVID THOREAU**

unique and poses fresh challenges. Certainly as a college student, you'll find that attentive critical reading is something you'll be practicing regularly, but you'll also discover that your skills as a reader will be stretched and strengthened as you

63

tackle more challenging texts, especially as you take more advanced courses. You will learn to adapt your reading strategies for different purposes, requirements, and time frames; you'll learn what works best for you and for the kinds of courses you're taking.

This chapter presents specialized techniques to analyze arguments more closely and to learn their strengths and weaknesses. The techniques we discussed in the last chapter — marking up the text, taking dialectical notes, and keeping a reading journal — are basic tools for active reading, and you'll probably use at least one of them whenever you read for your courses. But other strategies can be useful in particular situations. Question-centered notes are useful if you are expected to take a stand on a controversial issue. Quotation-centered notes may be appropriate for an assignment that requires close reading (in a literature course, for example). Responding to a particularly complicated or nuanced argument might require analyzing its rhetorical structure by mapping it, as either an outline or a radial diagram.

You may want to experiment with these techniques immediately, or you may want to store them away for later. But it's important to have the tools to dig into an argument and probe it more deeply, questioning it not in a hostile way, but to find out how it stands up to scrutiny, just as you might walk through a wood-frame structure and test the posts and struts and foundation. Just as you might have come to know pieces of music intimately by repeated listening and could sing almost every part from memory, so too you can become as familiar with a text as its author is (as Thoreau suggests readers should do) through a combination of re-reading and critical analysis. Some of these ideas may seem time-consuming, but that might not be a bad thing — just ranging around in a text, being absorbed in it, often prompts good ideas.

Variations on the Dialectical Notebook

A Question-Centered Triple-Entry Notebook

This is another kind of dialectical notebook, a variation on the double-entry notebook suggested by David Jolliffe in his book *Inquiry and Genre: Writing to Learn in College.*[1] This method works especially well with texts that take a stand on a debat-

---

[1] David Jolliffe, *Inquiry and Genre: Writing to Learn in College* (Boston: Allyn and Bacon, 1999).

| → **Guidelines** | **Taking Double- or Triple-Entry Notes on a Computer** |

If you prefer to work on your laptop rather than with paper and pen, you can still take notes in parallel columns. If you are working in Microsoft Word or Apple's Pages, use the "Text Box" tool (in the "Insert" menu) to draw the columns on a blank page. After filling in a heading at the top of each column, save the page as a blank template that you can use repeatedly. (Avoid using the "Columns" command in the "Format" menu, which is designed to make text flow from one column to the next; it does not let you move back and forth between the columns.)

---

able issue. As in a double-entry notebook, you audit meanings in the text in one column and your responses to the text in another, but in a third column you also keep an audit of *the question or problem that the text addresses*. This "question column" helps you focus your responses on the issues — the fundamental questions — that underlie the argument.

To begin a triple-entry notebook, divide a page into three columns. The first column will contain questions that you formulate by figuring out what question the text is answering, explicitly or implicitly. (Expect to write roughly two or three questions per page of text — or about one question for each substantial paragraph — but there is no rigid rule for this kind of work.) In the middle column, note how the text answers the question that is (often implicitly) being addressed; in the right-hand column, record thoughts about your own answer to the question and how the text's answer fits with your own experience and views. To avoid getting your columns confused, write a heading at the top of each column: for example, write "Question" over the left column, "Text's Answer" over the center column, and "My Response" over the right column. Often, the most difficult aspect of the triple-entry approach is figuring out the question to which the text responds. Some texts make the question explicit or obvious, but other texts require careful thought to identify the unstated, underlying question that the argument is addressing. But taking the time to do so can make it much easier to work out your response and to know where you stand in relation to the text's argument.

Here is an example of one student's notes on Cornel West's "Malcolm X and Black Rage" (p. 450) in a question-centered triple-entry notebook.

Question-Centered Triple-Entry Notebook

QUESTIONS THE TEXT IS ANSWERING	HOW WEST ANSWERS THE QUESTIONS	MY OBSERVATIONS AND RESPONSE
What was good and worth hanging onto in Malcolm X's thought? How did he contribute something positive to the civil rights struggle?	Malcolm X was motivated by *love* for black people: this lay behind his rage. He hoped to inspire a "psychic conversion" in black Americans.	I'm a little confused here because I've always thought Malcolm X was a defender of violent means or "any means necessary." This sounds like a very nonviolent strategy. What is "psychic conversion" anyway?
Why was psychic conversion so important that Malcolm X and others were willing to risk their lives with it?	Malcolm X knew that to be a truly self-loving person he had to *embody* or "crystallize" the confrontation between self-affirmation and early death.	This is a pretty interesting and powerful way of thinking about Malcolm X's death. A martyrdom? But wasn't he killed by one of his own men?

A Quotation-Centered Triple-Entry Notebook

Another kind of dialectical notebook is quotation-centered. To create such a notebook, you copy out important or difficult passages from the text in one column. In the second column, you write an **exegesis** (an interpretation, an explanation, or a paraphrase) of each passage. In the third column, you record your own observations, reflections, questions, or any other kind of response, such as a connection with one of your own experiences, ideas, or beliefs.

This is a very simple but effective method of generating close readings of, and responses to, key passages in a text. The simple act of copying out the words forces your attention to stay on the passage and helps to clarify the meaning. (Be sure to note page numbers so that you can locate these passages in the original text later on.)

Note that an exegesis explores *inside* the text, while commentary works from the text to something *outside* it. Exegesis combined with commentary might be most appropriate for working with difficult texts, as it lets you work out the meaning of complicated or dense passages but also forces you to think about the meaning of these passages *for you*. This approach allows you to move back and forth between the text's meaning and your meaning. Feel free to write a lot about even a short passage, exploring not only what the passage says but also how the passage says it and what thoughts and feelings the passage suggests. You may be surprised at how much you can get out of a passage that may not seem very promising at first.

Here is an example of this technique applied to Cornel West's "Malcolm X and Black Rage" (p. 450).

Quotation-Centered Triple-Entry Notebook

QUOTATION	EXEGESIS	COMMENTARY
"Malcolm X's notion of psychic conversion can be understood and used such that it does not necessarily *entail* black supremacy; it simply rejects black captivity to white supremacist ideology and practice" (p. 454).	It's possible to make use of this notion of "psychic conversion" without having to believe that one race is superior to others. The notion of "psychic conversion" just means that blacks (or other minorities) can escape from the dominant way of thinking and acting that puts whites above blacks.	West is trying here to *detach* a concept he values — "psychic conversion"— from one that he rejects — the notion that any race is by nature superior to another. This seems like a key move in the essay.

Also, this detaching makes it possible for *any* minority to use this concept of psychic conversion: the disabled, gays, racial minorities, etc. |

Adapting the Dialectical Notebook Method

Once you've tried some of the dialectical note-taking methods described above, you might begin to experiment with your own versions of this technique. For example, some writers like to work with smaller notebooks — half the size of the standard 8.5-by-11-inch type. In this kind of notebook, you might write only on a fresh page on the left-hand side while you're reading. These notes might be quotations, paraphrases, or reflections. Later, when you review these notes, you can write on the right-hand side, tying themes together, developing thoughts, sketching out ideas. For some writers, a notebook becomes a kind of scrapbook, a repository for ideas and reflections: they add sticky notes when they run out of space; they incorporate doodles; they tape in short articles or images; they use different colored inks to highlight ideas that seem important.

These notebooks become an archive of your dialogue with a text and thus represent the beginning of the writing process. As Ann E. Berthoff notes,

> In all its phases, composing is conversation you're having with yourself — or selves, since, when you're writing, you consciously play the roles of speaker, audience, and critic all at once. You do the talking; then you do the answering; and you listen to the dialogue between the speaker and the respondent. When you're making meaning in sentences, gathering sentences to compose paragraphs and paragraphs to construct arguments, you're doing the same kind of thing you do when you carry on a conversation.[2]

Ideas come to us at strange moments. Keeping a small notebook with you at all times will let you work on your ideas when they come to you, on the subway or in the waiting room at the dentist's office or wherever ideas happen to find you.

Many writers find it helpful to make a habit of writing every day, even if there's no requirement to do so. A daily reflection journal is a powerful tool for writers, helping them generate and develop ideas without having to worry about anyone judging or criticizing them. Perhaps more important, it allows the writer to set aside that inner critic who is often the great enemy of writing. Set aside thirty minutes a day to freewrite in a journal, without stopping to think and without judging the quality of your thoughts or expression. Don't share the journal with anyone else, and for the

---

[2] Ann E. Berthoff, with James Stephens, *Forming, Thinking, Writing,* 2nd ed. (Portsmouth, NH: Heinemann–Boynton/Cook, 1988), 23.

first month, don't reread what you've written. You'll find that much of what you write may simply be "process": a kind of prolonged throat-clearing. But sooner or later, you'll find gems among the ore.

Combine and mix strategies to come up with a method that works best for you. But bear in mind that notebooks should record not only others' ideas but also your own response to them.

Analyzing the Argument

As we have already said, an argument is a kind of logical structure, combining **claims** and **evidence**. "In the long run, this car costs less to drive because it gets twice as many miles per gallon as its competitor." The claim: "In the long run, this car costs less to drive." The evidence: "it gets twice as many miles per gallon as its competitor." In this case, the argument is only one sentence long, and the evidence is a single piece of data, so we need only figure out whether the evidence is true or false to assess whether the claim has any validity. The logical structure of this argument is as simple as it could be, made up of a premise and a conclusion, a simple "if . . . then" relation. If the car gets twice as many miles per gallon as its competitor (the premise), then perhaps in the long run it would cost less to drive (the conclusion). (Of course, a full calculation would have to take in many factors, such as the price of the car and the price of gas. But the present argument is a simple one.) A more complicated argument — and most arguments are a good deal more complicated — will have a more complicated logical structure, combining multiple premises and multiple conclusions. Evidence is rarely a simple statement of fact; often it is itself another claim, and arguments are often complicated structures of claims built on claims. Some claims are unlikely to be controversial, and some are ones that readers could verify (or negate) for themselves with a little research. Sometimes evidence is a straightforward statement of fact; more often it's a "near fact," one that is likely to win the reader's consent but could be disputed by a skeptical reader. So tracing an argument often demands considerable powers of attention.

Let's look at "To Err Is Human," a brief essay by the late Lewis Thomas, a biologist and medical doctor who wrote a regular column in the *New England Journal of Medicine*, where this essay first appeared in 1976.[3] At that time, computers were still rare and somewhat primitive: computers that filled large rooms were typically less

---

[3] Lewis Thomas, "To Err Is Human," *New England Journal of Medicine* 294, no. 2 (1976): 99–100.

powerful than a modern calculator; the personal computer had only recently been introduced; and the Internet did not exist. Yet Thomas's argument is as relevant today as ever, because it concerns fundamental differences — and similarities — between the way that humans and machines think. His argument has both a whimsical and a serious side to it. Read the essay twice and try to follow Thomas's argument as closely as you can.

Lewis Thomas
To Err Is Human

Everyone must have had at least one personal experience with a 1
computer error by this time. Bank balances are suddenly reported to have jumped from $379 into the millions, appeals for charitable contributions are mailed over and over to people with crazy-sounding names at your address, department stores send the wrong bills, utility companies write that they're turning everything off, that sort of thing. If you manage to get in touch with someone and complain, you then get instantaneously typed, guilty letters from the same computer, saying, "Our computer was in error, and an adjustment is being made in your account."

These are supposed to be the sheerest, blindest accidents. 2
Mistakes are not believed to be part of the normal behavior of a good machine. If things go wrong, it must be a personal, human error, the result of fingering, tampering, a button getting stuck, someone hitting the wrong key. The computer, at its best, is infallible.

I wonder whether this can be true. After all, the whole point 3
of computers is that they represent an extension of the human brain, vastly improved upon but nonetheless human, superhuman maybe. A good computer can think clearly and quickly enough to beat you at chess, and some of them have even been programmed to write obscure verse. They can do anything we can do, and more besides.

It is not yet known whether a computer has its own con- 4
sciousness, and it would be hard to find out about this. When you walk into one of those great halls now built for the huge machines, and stand listening, it is easy to imagine that the faint, distant

noises are the sound of thinking, and the turning of the spools°
gives them the look of wild creatures rolling their eyes in the
effort to concentrate, choking with information. But real thinking, and dreaming, are other matters.

On the other hand, the evidences of something like an uncon-   5
scious, equivalent to ours, are all around, in every mail. As exten-
sions of the human brain, they have been constructed with the
same property of error, spontaneous, uncontrolled, and rich in
possibilities.

Mistakes are at the very base of human thought, embedded   6
there, feeding the structure like root nodules. If we were not provided with the knack of being wrong, we could never get anything
useful done. We think our way along by choosing between right
and wrong alternatives, and the wrong choices have to be made as
frequently as the right ones. We get along in life this way. We are
built to make mistakes, coded for error.

We learn, as we say, by "trial and error." Why do we always   7
say that? Why not "trial and rightness" or "trial and triumph"?
The old phrase puts it that way because that is, in real life, the way
it is done.

A good laboratory, like a good bank or a corporation or govern-   8
ment, has to run like a computer. Almost everything is done flawlessly, by the book, and all the numbers add up to the predicted
sums. The days go by. And then, if it is a lucky day, and a lucky laboratory, somebody gets a mistake: the wrong buffer, something in one
of the blanks, a decimal misplaced in reading counts, the warm
room off by a degree and a half, a mouse out of his box, or just a misreading of the day's protocol. Whatever, when the results come in,
something is obviously screwed up, and then the action can begin.

The misreading is not the important error; it opens the way.   9
The next step is the crucial one. If the investigator can bring himself to say, "But even so, look at that!" then the new finding, whatever it is, is ready for snatching. What is needed, for progress to
be made, is the move based on the error.

---

turning of the spools   Early computer memory was on spools of magnetic
tape. [Editor's note]

Whenever new kinds of thinking are about to be accom- 10
plished, or new varieties of music, there has to be an argument
beforehand. With two sides debating in the same mind, harangu-
ing, there is an amiable understanding that one is right and the
other is wrong. Sooner or later the thing is settled, but there can
be no action at all if there are not the two sides, and the argument.
The hope is in the faculty of wrongness, the tendency toward
error. The capacity to leap across mountains of information to
land lightly on the wrong side represents the highest of human
endowments.

It may be that this is a uniquely human gift, perhaps even 11
stipulated in our genetic instructions. Other creatures do not
seem to have DNA sequences for making mistakes as a routine
part of daily living, certainly not for programmed error as a guide
for action.

We are at our human finest, dancing with our minds, when 12
there are more choices than two. Sometimes there are ten, even
twenty different ways to go, all but one bound to be wrong, and
the richness of selection in such situations can lift us onto totally
new ground. This process is called exploration and is based on
human fallibility. If we had only a single center in our brains,
capable of responding only when a correct decision was to be
made, instead of the jumble of different, credulous, easily conned
clusters of neurons that provide for being flung off into blind
alleys, up trees, down dead ends, out into blue sky, along wrong
turnings, around bends, we could only stay the way we are today,
stuck fast.

The lower animals do not have this splendid freedom. They 13
are limited, most of them, to absolute infallibility. Cats, for all
their good side, never make mistakes. I have never seen a mal-
adroit, clumsy, or blundering cat. Dogs are sometimes fallible,
occasionally able to make charming minor mistakes, but they get
this way from imitating their masters. Fish are flawless in everything they do. Individual cells in a tissue are mindless machines,
perfect in their performance, as absolutely inhuman as bees.

We should have this in mind as we become dependent on 14
more complex computers for the arrangement of our affairs. Give
the computers their heads, I say; let them go their way. If we can

learn to do this, turning our heads to one side and wincing while the work proceeds, the possibilities for the future of mankind, and computerkind, are limitless. Your average good computer can make calculations in an instant which would take a lifetime of slide rules° for any of us. Think of what we could gain from the near infinity of precise, machine-made miscomputation which is now so easily within our grasp. We would then begin the solving of some of our hardest problems. How, for instance, should we go about organizing ourselves for social living on a planetary scale, now that we have become, as a plain fact of life, a single community? We can assume, as a working hypothesis, that all the right ways of doing this are unworkable. What we need, then, for moving ahead, is a set of wrong alternatives much longer and more interesting than the short list of mistaken courses that any of us can think up right now. We need, in fact, an infinite list, and when it is printed out we need the computer to turn on itself and select, at random, the next way to go. If it is a big enough mistake, we could find ourselves on a new level, stunned, out in the clear, ready to move again.

---

slide rule   An instrument resembling a ruler with a sliding strip in the center, used for making rapid calculations before the widespread availability of electronic calculators and computers. [Editor's note]

To begin analyzing the argument as a logical structure, we will first need to ascertain what the author is arguing and then move ahead to look more closely at the relation among the various subordinate claims and at the relation between the claims and the evidence or reasoning that supports those claims.

Notice that the first two paragraphs are introductory; the main argument does not really begin until paragraph 3. The first paragraph introduces the topic of computer errors and establishes common ground with the reader; the second paragraph defines a common assumption about these computer errors — one that Thomas will challenge. But it's only in the third paragraph that Thomas presents an alternative view, suggesting that the computer "at its best" may be fallible. With paragraph 4, the argument really gets under way, so let's trace the argument carefully from the fourth to the ninth paragraphs. Then, if you wish, you can continue the work on your own from paragraph 10 to the end of the essay.

In paragraphs 4 and 5, Thomas compares the "mind" of a computer to that of a human being, dividing the question into two parts: "Does a computer have consciousness?" and "Does a computer have unconsciousness?" He puts aside the first question as unresolvable (perhaps hinting that the answer is "no"), but the second question produces an important result: the computer's capacity of making mistakes is "equivalent" to a human's unconsciousness. Paragraph 6 argues that mistakes are not only central to human thinking, "feeding the structure [of human thought] like root nodules," but also necessary to us: we "get along in life" by choosing between alternatives. Paragraph 7 offers some general evidence for this claim, in the familiar saying that we learn by "trial and error." Paragraphs 8 and 9 give further evidence, but this time from a specific example: a laboratory. Normally, a laboratory operates like a computer, mechanically, performing the same routines exactly. But the occasional error or unexpected result can lead to new discoveries that no one could have foreseen. In paragraph 9, Thomas elaborates: it's not the error itself that produces progress; it's the willingness of the investigator to pay careful attention to the unexpected.

In these paragraphs, then, Thomas argues that the human capacity for error is essential to the process of learning and discovery, and he suggests that the capacity of computers for errors may be potentially beneficial rather than just harmful or a nuisance. This is a thesis: a central claim or proposition, one that can be disputed but which the author defends. To make the argument, Thomas must do more than just state his thesis, of course. He must break it down into subordinate claims and provide evidence or reasoning to support those claims. In paragraphs 4 and 5, he does break the argument down, dismissing one-half of the question in order to bring the other half into focus. While paragraph 6 states a premise that underlies the main argument and supports it with logical or "deductive" reasoning, paragraph 7 provides factual evidence for the premise. Paragraph 8 supports the same premise with an example from life (one that most of the essay's original readers would recognize from experience), and paragraph 9 draws inferences from the example.

A partial outline that identifies claims and the support for these claims (evidence, reasoning, further claims) might look something like the following.

Partial Analytical Outline of "To Err Is Human"

Paragraphs 1, 2, 3

1. Introduces and defines "computer error." Establishes common ground with the reader by describing experiences that are familiar to all.
2. Defines a common assumption about computer errors.

    3. Proposes an alternative view, with the hypothesis that the computer, "at its best," may be fallible.

Paragraphs 4, 5

    4. Main argument begins: compares the computer's "mind" to the human mind by asking whether computers have consciousness. Puts aside the question as unresolvable.

    5. Claims that computers do have unconsciousness. Evidence: they make errors (examples have been given in paragraph 1).

Paragraphs 6, 7

    6. States central premise: mistakes are basic to human thought. Reasons that human brains are built to make mistakes; this is how humans learn.

    7. Familiar saying provides evidence for these claims.

Paragraphs 8, 9

    8. Further evidence, from an example: a laboratory. Errors often produce the most profitable results.

    9. Draws inference: progress requires error.

Complete the outline, if you wish, devoting one or two lines to each paragraph. The real point, however, is that even an argument like this, one that might seem relatively casual and lighthearted, makes it possible to trace a logical structure of claims and evidence. Doing so — whether formally (as above), in the margins of the text, or even mentally — makes it possible to assess the argument's strengths and weaknesses. (For example, Thomas states in paragraph 5 that computers "have been constructed with the same property of error, spontaneous, uncontrolled, and rich in possibilities." Does he provide strong evidence of this? If not, does it make a difference to his main point?)

➡ **Try** **This**   **Summarizing an Argument**

Read and reread the first eight paragraphs in Cornel West's "Malcolm X and Black Rage" (pp. 450–53). Construct a summary and an outline of the argument that West makes in those paragraphs, similar to the one offered above. You may need to sketch it out in draft form and then revise it as your sense of the argument gains in clarity.

Mapping the Text

There is more than one way to map a text, and over time you may find that you develop your own unique way of constructing a map. But the goal is always to enable you to see and to analyze the logical structure of the text's argument or exploration, in skeleton form. The great value of a map is that it requires you to look at the entire argument, rather than focusing exclusively on just selected passages. The two methods described below each have their strengths: the first is linear and hierarchical and perhaps works best with texts that make an argument in support of a thesis; the second is flexible and pictorial and perhaps works best with texts that are exploratory and circuitous.

What It Says/What It Does

By taking a moment to consider what each paragraph says and does, you can construct an outline of the text's rhetorical structure. This method may take some time, but it produces a clear picture of the argument's main claims and the evidence and reasoning that support those claims. (See the partial analytical outline on pp. 74–75.) This can be invaluable not only for comprehending an argument but also for evaluating it. All arguments have a structure. That is, an argument in its simplest form presents a relation between a claim and the evidence for that claim. Here's an example from paragraph 5 of Cornel West's essay "Malcolm X and Black Rage" (p. 452):

> In short, Malcolm X's notion of psychic conversion is an implicit critique of W. E. B. Du Bois's idea of "double-consciousness." Du Bois wrote:
>
>> The Negro is a sort of seventh son, born with a veil, and gifted with second-sight in this American world,—a world which yields him no true self-consciousness, but only lets him see himself through the revelation of the other world. It is a peculiar sensation, this double-consciousness, this sense of always looking at one's self through the eyes of others, of measuring one's soul by the tape of a world that looks on in amused contempt and pity.
>
> For Malcolm X this "double-consciousness" pertains more to those black people who live "betwixt and between" the black and white worlds—traversing the borders between them yet never settled in either. Hence, they crave peer acceptance in both, receive genuine approval from neither, yet persist in viewing themselves through the lenses of the dominant white society. For Malcolm X, this "double-consciousness" is

less a description of a necessary black mode of being in America than a particular kind of colonized mind-set of a special group in black America. Du Bois's "double-consciousness" seems to lock black people into the quest for white approval and disappointment owing mainly to white racist assessment, whereas Malcolm X suggests that this tragic syndrome can be broken through psychic conversion. But how?

The first sentence in this quotation makes a claim, one that West needs to make in order to build a persuasive analysis of Malcolm X's ideas. He claims that Malcolm X's notion of psychic conversion makes an "implicit critique" of W. E. B. Du Bois's idea of double-consciousness. This is not a statement of fact, but rather a statement of West's *belief*: a reasonable reader might doubt or disagree with the claim, so West must provide evidence for it. The quotation from Du Bois does this. It shows the contrast between Malcolm X's position and that of Du Bois and yet also shows how the two concepts — psychic conversion and double-consciousness — are related: both concern the way that an individual's mentality is shaped or misshaped by the experience of oppression, but double-consciousness is more like a diagnosis while psychic conversion is something like a remedy. West's analysis or "exegesis" in the remainder of the paragraph brings this relation into focus, as he explains how Du Bois's ideas would have looked from Malcolm X's point of view.

Of course, this argument is just one small part of a larger argument that West makes about this notion of psychic conversion. Complicated arguments present a number of related claims and various kinds of evidence for these claims, so that one claim supports or qualifies another. Once you have analyzed the structure of the argument — how evidence supports claims, how claims are related to one another, how all the parts fit together — you are in a much stronger position to assess the argument's strengths and weaknesses.

You will need to approach a rhetorical analysis of this kind in two steps. In the first step, you will analyze each paragraph in the essay for "what it says" and for "what it does." In the second step, you will use this analysis to construct an outline that illustrates the argument's structure. (If the text is lengthy, this may be a good activity for a group: divide up the text into sections, with each group taking one or two sections.)

Step 1 Draw a line down the middle of a page in your notebook, creating two columns. At the top of the left column, write "What It Says"; at the top of the right column, write "What It Does." For each paragraph in the essay, write one or two sentences in the left column that summarize what the paragraph says, and one or two in the right column that state the *function* of this paragraph in the argument.

WHAT IT SAYS	WHAT IT DOES
Epigraph 1 (de Tocqueville, 1840). If the US undergoes revolutions, they will be due to black race.	Places civil rights struggle in long historical perspective.
Epigraph 2 (same, 1835). Democracy is an obstacle to civil rights.	Suggests depth of the problem that a minority faces in a democracy.
Paragraph 1. Malcolm X's "commitment to affirm black humanity" made him "the prophet of black rage."	Introduces reader to Malcolm X, giving an overview of his beliefs that puts them in a positive light, as a genuine contribution to the struggle for civil rights.
Paragraph 2. Malcolm's "rage" was caused by a deep love for black people; he wanted this love to inspire "psychic conversion."	Introduces theme of "psychic conversion," presenting it as the positive, constructive motive underlying the well-known "rage." (A step toward rehabilitating Malcolm X?)
Paragraph 3. Psychic conversion was dangerous in 1950s and 1960s. Malcolm himself "sharply crystallized" the relation between self-affirmation and "early black death."	Places Malcolm's ideas in historical context, thus helping to explain his militancy.
Paragraph 4. Psychic conversion means blacks "must no longer view themselves through white lenses." Example of Michael Jackson's "facial revisions": views himself "through white aesthetic lenses." But this is common among black professional class; this explains their "ambivalent" reaction to Malcolm X, who was their "skeleton in the closet."	Defines term. Uses familiar example to explain it. Places Malcolm X in *contemporary* context: generalizes from the specific example to the experience of black professional class today. Describes typical attitude to Malcolm X's ideas.

Figuring out the function of each paragraph can be tricky, but it is the key to any analysis of rhetorical structure. Avoid summary here, and avoid repeating what you've already written in the left column. Instead, work out how the paragraph contributes to the writer's argument, how it moves the argument forward. If the paragraph were absent, what would the argument be missing? What kind of "move" is the writer making? What is the writer doing that serves the larger purpose of the essay? Although this work will take some time and some trial and error, it helps you understand how experienced writers develop an effective argument. In the example based on Cornel West's "Malcolm X and Black Rage" (opposite), the entries in the left-hand column briefly summarize the epigraphs and the first four paragraphs of West's essay, while the entries on the right explain what these paragraphs *do* for the argument, how they contribute to its construction. At times, a paragraph's function might not be immediately clear. If so, leave the right column blank for a moment and fill it in later. But complete the right-hand column before you move on to Step 2.

Step 2 Now construct an outline of the argument's structure, based on the right-hand column of your "What It Says/What It Does" notes. Begin by identifying how paragraphs with a similar function can be grouped together. For example, several paragraphs might all be telling one story or explaining one example, and these might provide support for a claim, and this claim might, in turn, support one aspect of the author's main thesis.

In the case of Cornel West's "Malcolm X and Black Rage," a complete "What It Says/What It Does" analysis shows that West does not *fully* reveal his thesis until the final section of the essay, where he discusses the realities of race in contemporary American society and explains that Malcolm X's notion of psychic conversion, though flawed, remains relevant and useful. Nevertheless, West makes his general purpose clear in the first few paragraphs of the essay: to reconsider Malcolm X's thought, paying special attention to the notion of psychic conversion.

Let's refer to the sample "What It Says/What It Does" notes to begin analyzing how these first few paragraphs can be grouped by function.

Introductory elements
> Epigraphs
> Paragraph 1. Introduces Malcolm X; overview of his beliefs in a positive light.

"Psychic conversion"
> Paragraph 2. *Introduces* "psychic conversion." Presents it as the positive motive underlying the "rage" motivated by love.

Paragraph 3. Historical context helps to explain Malcolm X's militancy.

Paragraphs 4–5. *Defines and explains* "psychic conversion."

Paragraph 4. Uses familiar example (Michael Jackson), contemporary context, generalizes from specific example to the experience of black professional class today and the typical attitude to Malcolm X's ideas.

Paragraph 5. Claim: psychic conversion makes implicit critique of double-consciousness.

Quotes Du Bois, analyzes how Malcolm X would have read this; contrast with psychic conversion.

Leads to conclusion (Malcolm X suggests that "psychic conversion" can break this syndrome) and question: *How?*

Critique

Paragraphs 6–8. Malcolm X does not offer direct answer.

1. Distinction between two mentalities ("house negroes" versus "field negroes") does not match up with professional class versus laboring class, as Malcolm X suggested.

2. Black nationalism does not have a monopoly on black self-love, self-determination.

Example: Marcus Garvey: black armies, navies are not essential to black self-love, self-respect.

Likewise Elijah Muhammad: black self-love, self-respect does not mean accepting black supremacy.

This analysis makes it clear that West devotes one paragraph to a general introduction to Malcolm X's thought and then introduces the specific concept of psychic conversion. He devotes two paragraphs to a general discussion of this concept before moving to an extended *definition* of it, which runs across two paragraphs. This leads to a conclusion (Malcolm X suggests that "psychic conversion" can break the "double-consciousness" syndrome), a question (How?), and West's response (Malcolm X failed to provide a direct answer).

The pattern of indentations helps to represent the logical structure of West's argument. By creating distinct levels, the outline shows how concepts are introduced and defined, how examples support definitions and lead to claims, how further examples support claims, and so on. Every essay will have a different structure.

Often the main thesis appears much earlier in the essay, and each paragraph in the essay makes a claim in support of the thesis, and each paragraph offers evidence and reasoning in support of that claim. In writing up an analysis, you need not include one line for every single paragraph in the essay: the purpose is to produce a framework of the logical structure of the text as a whole.

Some word processors, including Microsoft Word, include an outlining function that enables you to format text as headings with different levels (Heading 1, Heading 2, Heading 3, and so on). The program will indent lower-level headings automatically, and you can hide lower-level headings in order to see only the main headings.

Constructing a Radial Map of the Text

A radial map is a diagram of a text, using boxes and circles to arrange its elements in such a way that the structure of the text becomes visible on a single page, with subheadings radiating out from the main theme at the center or down from the top. The map itself is a useful tool to have on hand as you begin thinking and writing about a text, but you may find that the greatest benefit of this map comes from the process of constructing it. The process requires that you collect all the important elements of an argument or exploration, consider how all these elements fit together, and arrange them under headings that connect to the central theme so that the entire essay can be visualized at once. Radial maps are especially useful when you are working with a text that is full of detail; perhaps they are most helpful for readers who are visually inclined.

If you have access to a drawing program on a computer, you can block out themes and main points first and then move them around and experiment with different arrangements.

Begin constructing your map by writing down the theme of the essay in a box at the center or the top of the page. Next, begin arranging main headings around or below this box. Now begin to elaborate the diagram by arranging subheadings and subtopics in relation to each of these main headings. You should be able to begin this work on a second reading, but you may not be able to complete the map until you've read the text a third or even a fourth time. As the map becomes more complicated and more complete — and as the structure of the argument becomes more clear — you will almost certainly find that you need to rearrange the map and perhaps even start over.

Different texts lend themselves to different arrangements. This diagram for the first half of West's essay has two columns.

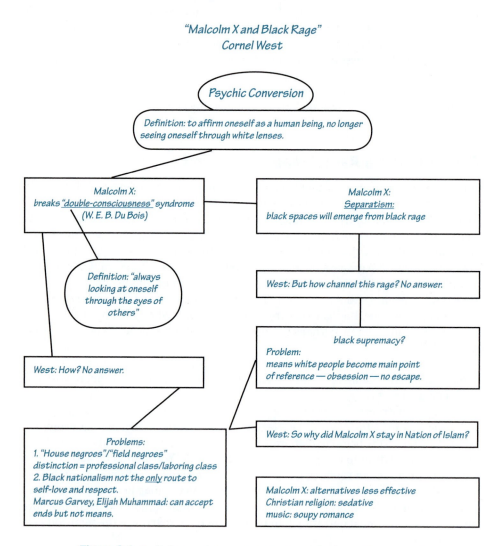

"Malcolm X and Black Rage"
Cornel West

Psychic Conversion

Definition: to affirm oneself as a human being, no longer seeing oneself through white lenses.

Malcolm X:
breaks "double-consciousness" syndrome
(W. E. B. Du Bois)

Malcolm X:
Separatism:
black spaces will emerge from black rage

Definition: "always looking at oneself through the eyes of others"

West: But how channel this rage? No answer.

black supremacy?
Problem:
means white people become main point
of reference — obsession — no escape.

West: How? No answer.

West: So why did Malcolm X stay in Nation of Islam?

Problems:
1. "House negroes"/"field negroes"
distinction = professional class/laboring class
2. Black nationalism not the only route to
self-love and respect.
Marcus Garvey, Elijah Muhammad: can accept
ends but not means.

Malcolm X: alternatives less effective
Christian religion: sedative
music: soupy romance

Figure 3.1 **Radial Map of Cornel West's "Malcolm X and Black Rage"**

In another example below, based on Jane Tompkins's "At the Buffalo Bill Museum, June 1988" (p. 413), the map has two halves. The top half represents the journey round the four museums. The bottom half represents the aftermath of Tompkins's visit: her reading and her reflections on the experience as a whole.

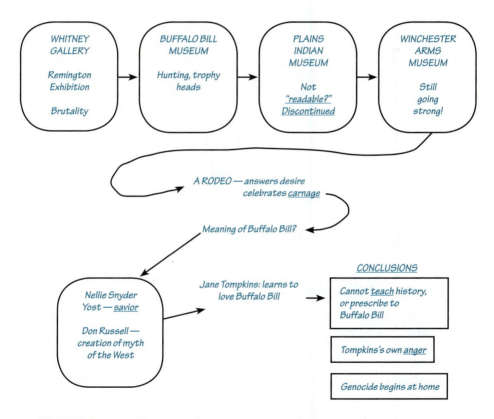

Figure 3.2 Radial Map of Jane Tompkins's "At the Buffalo Bill Museum, June 1988"

Evaluating the Argument

Reading with and against the Grain

Your first one or two readings of the text focus on what the author is saying: you try to look at the question from the author's point of view, and in so doing, you "try on" his or her ideas. The principle of charity, discussed in Chapter 2, states an essential precept for this kind of thinking: you need to be a "friend" to an argument and give it a fair chance, before you can justifiably be its critic. When you read in this way, attempting to look at the world through the writer's eyes, you are reading "with the grain" of the essay: you are turned in the direction that the essay points. But there is also value in reading "against the grain" and bringing a more skeptical mind to bear on the text. (When working with wood, it is easiest to cut with the grain, the direction of the tree's growth; cutting against the grain is harder work because of the wood's resistance.) Reading against the grain doesn't mean demolishing the argument or dismissing it unfairly, forgetting everything you learned from reading with the grain. Rather, you need to *test* the argument, to find out its weaknesses, and to imagine alternatives to it.

This exercise might produce any number of outcomes. You might find fatal flaws in the author's argument and decide that an opposing argument, or **counter-argument**, has much greater merit. You might discover that, although other points of view and other arguments are possible, the author's argument is a very strong one, and you are more convinced by it than ever. Most likely, though, you'll find some weaknesses and some strengths, and you'll have to weigh them carefully to see where you stand. But this process is a necessary part of critical reading and formulating a response.

Believing and Doubting

The "believing and doubting game" is a strategy developed by the scholar and teacher Peter Elbow.[4] The word "game" is used because this strategy requires you to play roles: to step away from what you really believe and to pretend for a moment that you are someone different. The believing game is an extension of the reading-with-the-grain exercises that you've already been practicing. But now, take it a step further.

---

[4] Peter Elbow, *Writing without Teachers,* 2nd ed. (New York: Oxford University Press, 1998), 147–91.

Write out all the reasons that someone might have for believing this argument, and see if you can imagine other arguments for believing it, in addition to those that the writer has given. In other words, be the writer's strongest advocate and ally. Give this the time it needs: twenty to thirty minutes at least for a substantial essay.

Now play the doubting game. Put yourself in the shoes of a person who is deeply skeptical of the writer's views. First, you'll need to work out what the opposing view — the counterargument — would look like. Write it out as a thesis statement. Then imagine the details of the counterargument. Ask yourself, "What possible reasons could such a person have for taking a contrary position?" Make a list of them — as many as you can think of. Include weak reasons as well as strong ones. (Writing out weak reasons may help you think of other, stronger reasons. And sometimes, after some thought, weak reasons turn out to be not so weak after all!) Then select the most persuasive of the arguments you've listed, and write them out as an argument.

An important aspect of the doubting game, indeed of any critical reading, is to identify weaknesses, if any, in the writer's rhetoric. Some kinds of argument are inherently flawed because they involve mistakes of reasoning, called **fallacies**.

Example: All Americans love their country.
Paul McCartney loves his country.
Therefore, Paul McCartney is an American.

Of course, the error here lies in the fact that while it *might* be true that "all Americans love their country," it is not true that *only* Americans love their country. Paul McCartney is English, so it's quite possible for him to love his country and not be an American. The mistake here is quite obvious, but this kind of logical error can often be subtle and easy to miss. Other kinds of fallacies are not logical errors but ethically questionable strategies. For example, an argument might appeal to the baser instincts of the reader — the tendency to go with the crowd, perhaps, rather than examine an argument on its merits, no matter how unpopular.

Representing Another's Ideas Fairly and Accurately

A final observation has to do with both reading attentively and reading critically. Any writer who works with another writer's ideas may be tempted to shape those ideas to suit his or her own purposes, and thereby risks misrepresenting or distorting them. To do so deliberately would be a serious breach of ethics. But a writer can sometimes misrepresent ideas through carelessness or neglect, without intending in any way to be dishonest. For example, a writer might need to summarize another writer's argument as part of the evidence that supports a new argument of her own. But in doing so, she might accidentally omit certain details and qualifications that actually make a considerable difference to the other writer's point. The result may be that she not only misrepresents the other writer's point but also constructs an argument that does not really stand up to scrutiny. There's a difference between using other writers' ideas and abusing their ideas — and sometimes the difference is subtle. Imagine, for example, that a student is writing a philosophy paper about artificial intelligence and is discussing the problem of whether a computer is truly a kind of mind. Suppose that he has decided to argue that there's no fundamental difference between a human mind and a computer and that therefore we should consider a computer to be a kind of mind. Having read "To Err Is Human," the student wants to enlist Lewis Thomas in support of his argument and writes a paragraph such as this:

> In an article that appeared in the *New England Journal of Medicine* in 1976, Dr. Lewis Thomas, a biologist, argues that computers do possess "unconconsciousness" in the form of a capacity for error, and this makes them able not only to think like humans but also to make mistakes like humans. Therefore, they can also make unexpected discoveries in very much the way that human beings do. "Your average good computer can make calculations in an instant which would take a lifetime of slide rules for any of us," he writes. "Think of what we could gain from the near infinity of precise, machine-made miscomputation which is now so easily within our grasp. We would then begin the solving of some of our hardest problems" (73). Thus Thomas argues that computers not only function but also *malfunction* in the same way that a "mind" does.

The difference between what Thomas says and what this paragraph claims he says may be subtle, but it's important. Thomas does not quite say that computers make discoveries; he suggests only that they might play a role in helping human beings make discoveries. And he does not argue that computers function in the same way a mind does (rather, he suggests that they malfunction in the way a mind does). Moreover, Thomas approaches the topic with a certain humor and irony; he does have a serious point to make, but it's not really about the similarity between computers and human brains. So it's misleading to suggest that Thomas's argument directly pertains to the philosophical debate about computers and minds. The student writer

> ⊖ **Try**
> **This**   **Paraphrasing a Passage**
>
> Select a brief passage (10–15 lines) from one of the essays that have been reprinted in Part 5 of this book. Draft a paraphrase of the passage by expressing the writer's ideas in your own words. Now reread the original passage a couple of times (you might also need to reread the paragraphs that precede and follow it, in order to get a clearer sense of the context). Revise your paraphrase so that it represents the writer's thought more accurately, but take care not to use the writer's own words. If you must use one or two phrases from the original, put them in quotation marks to avoid plagiarizing.

should have taken Thomas's argument in the spirit in which it was made and avoided twisting it out of shape to fit his needs.

Academic writers (whether freshmen or professionals) are sometimes tempted to misrepresent or oversimplify (even unconsciously) when faced with deadlines and high expectations. We are often looking for something when we read, perhaps something specific or perhaps just anything we can use, and it's easy to be a little too eager to find it — and to pretend we've found it even if it's not quite there. We must frequently paraphrase and summarize other writers' ideas, and we must do so in a way that shows the relevance and meaning of those ideas to our own argument. It's much more difficult to accurately represent the ideas of others than it is to oversimplify or reconstruct or slant or slightly exaggerate those ideas. (Chapter 10 presents strategies for paraphrasing and summarizing.)

Writing a Letter to the Author

Another way to work out your response to a reading is to write a letter to the author. This technique helps you focus your thoughts, formulate your questions and ideas, and "speak back" to the text. For many writers, the personal letter is a familiar mode of writing, one that allows them to write honestly and openly, whereas note-taking can lead them to write in more formal, detached, and inhibited ways. Writing a letter to the author provides an "enabling fiction": imagining a real person as the audience of your remarks is an effective way to enter into a conversation with a text and to sidestep anxieties about formal, graded academic writing that can restrain your creativity.

Talking Out Your Ideas

Use Class Discussion

In class, your dialectical notebook can do double duty. On one hand, it contains questions and observations that you can put to your classmates, and you can develop your notes on the basis of their comments. On the other hand, discussion can spark ideas to record in your notebook and work out more fully later on. In many college courses, discussion plays a crucial role. Its purpose is to give students the opportunity to think ideas through and to arrive at their own understanding of a text, rather than simply relying on the professor's interpretation and taking it at face value. Students are expected to come to class with comments and questions prepared and to express their views clearly and reasonably for the class to consider. Instructors hope you will work out your own views and come to your own insights; they do not want to see their own views echoed back in a dozen or more identical papers. Class discussion affords an opportunity to figure out where you stand and how your views compare to others so that you can make a strong and interesting argument in your writing. A dialectical notebook can be an essential tool in making such discussions work for you.

Discuss with a Friend, Classmate, Tutor, or Professor

If you read actively, and especially if you use some of the strategies you have learned in Part 1, you will soon reach a point where you have some ideas about the texts you are reading, but these ideas may be vague or confused at first. It might help to get some feedback at this point. Just listening to yourself talk out your ideas can help to clarify them and give you a sense of their strengths and weaknesses. But feedback from a colleague, a friend, or an instructor can be just as helpful. There's nothing wrong with seeking feedback of this sort, and it doesn't make your ideas any less your own.

☑ Checklist of Further Strategies for Active Reading

Although you are unlikely to use all of these methods for one piece of writing, add these to your toolbox of reading strategies, and use the ones that best suit your purpose.

☐ Use a question-centered triple-entry notebook.

☐ Use a quotation-centered triple-entry notebook.

☐ Construct an analytical outline of the text.

☐ Map the text.
  • Construct a "What It Says/What It Does" analysis.
  • Construct a radial map.

☐ Read with and against the grain.
  • Play the "believing and doubting game."

☐ Write a letter to the author.

☐ Talk out your ideas.
  • Use class discussion.
  • Discuss with a friend, a classmate, a tutor, or an instructor.

Checklist of Revision Strategies for Active Reading

part 2

Composing and Revising

chapter 4

Writing to Discover and Develop Ideas

The Value of Exploratory Writing

Writing is in some ways a mysterious business. Some days, we sit down at our desks, and the words just tumble out; ideas delight and surprise us as they parade across the page. It all seems fun and stress-free, hardly like work at all. Yet the next day, for some reason, words refuse to cooperate, and nothing we write seems the least bit interesting or worthwhile. We get distracted, take a coffee break, watch YouTube, return to our work. But it's as if the words we need are bottled up in some hidden recess of the brain, and we just can't seem to get them out. At those times, writing can be brutally hard work, like carving granite with a teaspoon.

It's just as hard to account for the enormous differences in how writers experience the creative process. Some write slowly and with difficulty, others quickly

> *The formulation of a problem is often more essential than its solution, which may be merely a matter of mathematical or experimental skill. To raise new questions, new possibilities, to regard old problems from a new angle, requires creative imagination and marks real advance in science.*
>
> **ALBERT EINSTEIN**

93

and easily; some keep to a strict routine, others change their methods frequently — yet many different working styles can be equally productive in the end. Each writer must learn through experience how to get his or her best work done, and many aspects of the whole complicated business — how the mind finds words, how words give form to ideas, how one idea leads to another — may never be fully understood.

But even though these mysteries lie at the heart of the writing process, most experienced writers agree on certain productivity strategies. First, the writing process is typically **recursive**: it loops back through the phases of the process as many times as necessary. So reading leads to note-taking, note-taking leads back to reading, further note-taking leads to drafting, then some difficulty arises that leads back to additional reading, and so on. (We'll return to this theme in Chapter 5.) Second, experienced writers tend to agree on the importance of separating out two distinct phases of the writing process: **informal writing** to discover and develop ideas, and **revising** and **editing** this writing to make those ideas clear to the reader.

We're all tempted to believe that we can hammer out good writing in one sitting, simply pouring out our brilliance onto a computer screen. Oh, a bit of editing and polishing might be necessary afterward, but (we tell ourselves) it ought to be possible to express ideas directly and clearly (shouldn't it?), as we do routinely when we speak.

In reality, however, that's not how writing works.

Here's the problem: if we approach the first draft as if it were the final version, we require ourselves *to do two conflicting things at the same time*: we must figure out our ideas for ourselves and at the same time we must make sense of these ideas for the reader. To do both at the same time is not exactly *impossible* — we manage it with simple pieces of writing like text messages and short e-mails, and some of us could even cobble together something resembling an essay this way — but it is certainly inadvisable. It's inadvisable because college-level writing must possess qualities that few of us can achieve all at once on the first pass: preciseness, nuance, clarity, complexity, and logical rigor. We will write a better essay, and the work will go more smoothly, if we separate out the informal exploratory writing from the formal essay writing. When the writing process does clog up and break down, it's usually because we are trying to do both the writerly and the readerly at the same time.

The Writerly versus the Readerly

When writing informally to discover and develop ideas, you are working toward meeting *your own need* to develop and clarify your thoughts. When rewriting, revising, and editing, you are working toward meeting *your reader's need* to understand and appreciate your ideas. Writers sometimes refer to the first kind of writing as **writerly** and the second as **readerly**,[1] terms that express the different audiences and, so to speak, the different beneficiaries of each. In the writerly, exploratory phase, you focus your attention on sorting out, clarifying, and developing your ideas; you allow your ideas to change as they take shape, even to contradict what you said just two sentences before. You never know quite where this kind of writing will lead: you are pursuing an insight, you are on a voyage of discovery, an expedition into the unknown, and the more surprising and new the revelations, the better.

In the readerly phase, you focus attention on your reader. You try to see your writing through the reader's eyes, to imagine what those eyes will see as they work their way through your text and how the mind behind those eyes will respond. You arrange your arguments in the most effective order; you delete sentences, paragraphs, even whole pages that do not belong; you add new material where something is missing; you iron out wrinkled sentences and find apt words to replace awkward ones. You carefully craft a text designed to persuade readers to believe, think, feel, or do something.

Even if lots of good ideas have already occurred to you as a result of rereading and taking notes, it would be unwise to skip the exploratory, writerly phase. It truly is the energy center of the writing process, the most creative and, for many, the most enjoyable of writing activities. As novelist and screenwriter Evan Hunter said, "The only true creative aspect of writing is the first draft. That's when it comes straight from your head and your heart. . . . The rest is donkey work. It is, however, donkey work that has to be done."[2] Devoting adequate time to working out and developing your ideas — thinking and rethinking them — will result in a final product that is clearer, richer, and more interesting. Informal writing enables you to correct weaknesses that were previously invisible and to become aware of possibilities that at first you could not have imagined. Moreover, low-stakes experimentation with words and strategies smoothes out the whole writing process, reducing the anxiety that can otherwise be overwhelming. It supplies the raw material, the ingredients, that you need for the readerly phase that comes later.

---

[1] These terms were coined by the twentieth-century French critic Roland Barthes; see Barthes, *S/Z: An Essay,* trans. Richard Miller (New York: Hill and Wang, 1974).
[2] Quoted in Jon Winokur, *Advice to Writers* (New York: Random House/Vintage, 2000), 104.

Exploratory Writing

There are, of course, many kinds of writerly, informal writing — journaling, note-taking, planning, and so on. This chapter focuses on exploratory writing for the purpose of developing ideas, a pleasurable and unpressured kind of writing in which there are few rules and no wrong moves. Exploratory writing can feel more like play than work. It gives you the opportunity to puzzle things out, to delve deeper, in a writing space where no one will judge or criticize you. You can freely exercise your creativity and ingenuity, because at this stage even apparently outlandish ideas are just fine. You can safely write about your personal thoughts and experiences too. You can worry later about whether to keep such material in your final paper; for now, just explore. This is writing for no one's eyes but your own.

The twentieth-century English novelist E. M. Forster famously posed the question, "How can I tell what I think until I see what I say?"[3] At first, this may seem counterintuitive: Doesn't thinking come before writing? But what Forster describes is a familiar experience to writers: somehow the act of putting ideas into a sequence of words and arranging words in a sequence of sentences clarifies and *shows* us what we think. We can begin writing with very little sense of what we might have to say about a subject and can use the writing process as a tool for discovery, figuring things out as we go.

Most of us talk to ourselves — if not out loud, then silently. We speak thoughts in our heads in order to consider and test them; we might even improvise a little debate to weigh the pros and cons of an idea. But usually we don't sustain these interior conversations for very long, and we end up with no record of the conversation except unreliable memory. Recording thoughts in writing makes it possible to *see* these thoughts — quite literally — and to work with them. As the teacher and scholar Peter Elbow writes, "A principal value of language . . . is that it permits you to *distance* yourself from your own perceptions, feelings and thoughts. Try, then, to write words on paper so as to permit an interaction between you and not-you. You are building someone to talk to."[4] Seeing our words makes it possible not only to weigh them but

---

[3] E. M. Forster, *Aspects of the Novel* (Harmondsworth, UK: Penguin/Pelican, 1962), 108. It must be said that Forster does not quite endorse this view, which occurs in a chapter on plot. There he posits it as the words of "an old lady" who refuses to believe in logic and would agree with the French novelist André Gide, whose book *Les Faux Monnayeurs* (1925) tries to do away with plot and replace it with "real life." Forster is doubtful about the wisdom of this approach. Nevertheless, the old lady's question has justifiably been adopted by writing teachers as a succinct expression of the aims of exploratory writing.

[4] Peter Elbow, *Writing without Teachers*, 2nd ed. (New York: Oxford University Press, 1998), 55.

also to respond to them — to improve and extend them — so that writing leads to more writing. Thus writing does not merely express thinking; it *produces* thinking (from the Latin *producere*, "to lead forward").

Many writers enjoy exploratory writing enormously. Their thoughts about scholarly matters and private matters get mixed up together — and this has the effect of enriching and deepening both. Some writers prefer to write longhand, in small notebooks or on blank pages of copier paper; others prefer to type their thoughts on a computer. Many prefer to work somewhere quiet, where there's nothing to distract them — no phone or TV or e-mail. Other writers work best in crowded, noisy environments like cafés or fast-food restaurants, where the music and chatter become a kind of white noise that actually helps them think. Some people need the comfort and privacy of a special writing place — a bedroom or an office. Personalities differ; the important thing is to figure out by experimentation where you do your best work, and then make a habit of going there regularly.

Knots and Questions

With time, writers tend to develop individual methods of exploratory writing to suit their own personalities and situation (such as the particular requirements of an assignment or a project), but the variations typically follow a basic pattern. In all exploratory writing, two types of activity are of particular value: posing questions and playing with "knots." A knot is anything that's puzzling or unclear or even mysterious about the text (or whatever is on your mind) — some difficulty, something that bothers you about it. We're all familiar with crime dramas in which the detective fastens onto some detail that doesn't quite make sense — the butler's shoes weren't muddy — and of course it leads to the solution of the whole mystery: the butler was innocent of murder, after all; it was the baron's estranged half-sister who committed the crime! That little detail is the knot that the detective plays with until it unravels and reveals the truth. A knot might at first look like an awkward inconvenience: a fact that doesn't quite fit with the theory. But knots are frequently doorways to fresh, surprising ways of looking at something. Once you've identified a knot, either from memory or from your notes, toy with it, untangle it, see where it leads you. Be patient: if you just pull on the ends of the string, you might only make the knot tighter. Exploratory writing offers the opportunity to approach it with a light touch, to get the knot to yield by taking time to analyze it, prod it, gently interrogate it. It's possible the knot leads nowhere — but it might lead to a whole new way of seeing things.

Questions are the best tool we have not only for undoing knots but also for find-ing them. Knots can be hard to identify at first, but questions are easy to come by. We can always pose some kind of question to get things started, even if it seems obvious or pointless. The writing process gives us an opportunity to rephrase, correct, or sharpen the question, and a well-crafted question clears a pathway to a good idea. One question leads to another, and a good idea leads to further questions.

We sometimes speak of "entertaining" a question, a turn of phrase that suggests precisely what is needed: invite the question in, offer it a cup of tea, urge it to sit down and chat. Worthwhile questions can't be turned away immediately with a sim-ple yes or no answer. They demand our hospitality before they divulge everything they know. To use a different metaphor, questions function as the engine of the whole process: they keep the exploration moving forward into new territory. If you get to the point where your exploratory writing hits a dead end or seems to peter out, try simply listing questions for a while. Compile a dozen questions and then choose one to work with until it opens up further questions.

Sample Exploratory Writing

First-year student Brita Bero is working on an essay assignment with an open topic. In these exploratory writing sessions, she thinks through the meaning of some themes and quotations from Cornel West's "Malcolm X and Black Rage" (p. 450), paraphrasing some of his ideas, raising questions, and drawing some conclusions.

Session 1, March 29, 2011

The idea of psychic conversion is very important to this essay. Very hard to understand, though. I think it has to do with African Americans viewing themselves with "white lenses," which means they measure themselves and their self-worth against white Americans. Malcolm X felt this was bad, because African Americans shouldn't try to measure their self-worth by what their oppressors thought was right, but what they think is right. Michael Jackson example sort of goes along with this. Basically, why should African Americans want to be like the people that hold them back?

Malcolm X was also afraid, maybe (?), or at least didn't like the idea of black and white culture mixing. It seems like he advocated the idea of whites and blacks in America being totally separate, or would support that if anyone ever mentioned it to him. Ideally, black Americans wouldn't care what their white counterparts were up to, because they'd be living in their own Black America. 2 problems with this. (1) It couldn't happen because white Americans, at that time, were too oppressive. (2) Black and white America were already merging. Malcolm is an example himself, essay mentioned that his grandfather was white (did he ever mention that in public? or acknowledge it?). Also, essay mentions music as hybrid as well.

Malcolm's fear of the whole mixing thing really interesting. Also, the part about black middle class relating to Malcolm X. How they understood his message the most, but supported him publicly the least. Sort of irritating to me that just because he has some radical ideas, he isn't given the same respect as MLK Jr. He seemed/seems to be a very important part of African American history, and American history. Where's Malcolm X's day?

Session 2, March 30, 2011

"That which fundamentally motivates one still dictates the terms of what one thinks and does — so the motivation of a black supremacist doctrine reveals how obsessed one is with white supremacy." (West 454)

Quote illustrates how Malcolm X's ideas are different from other African American leaders, because while others focused on their black identity as a reaction to counter white identity and what white Americans thought African Americans should be, Malcolm X's idea of psychic conversion is based on the fact that African Americans won't/shouldn't care about white Americans. More clearly, others measured their blackness by how *not* white it was, Malcolm advocated measuring blackness by how *black* they were. Subtle, but major difference. So, quote explains a doctrine before Malcolm X's.

Quote continues, "This is understandable in a white racist society — but it is crippling for a despised people struggling for freedom, in that one's eyes should be on the prize, not on the perpetuator of one's oppression." (West 454)

This illustrates an idea more like Malcolm X's. If the goal is to be a strong African American, then why should one take the unnecessary step of defining one's self as *not* white American? Psychic conversion forces African Americans to view themselves as black Americans in a black society, not black Americans in a white society. How black someone is (the metaphorical prize) is measured by how black society sees them, not by how different they are from white society (the "perpetuator of one's oppression").

Therefore, psychic conversion is Malcolm X's unique idea, is based not on measuring one's self against the opposite of what one wants to become, but measuring up to one's own ideals. It's as if there are two yardsticks, one is white and the other is black. To see how black you are, use the black one to measure, not the white one. Or, more clearly, you don't see how red a piece of paper is by holding it next to a green piece, you compare it with other reds.

✔ Checklist for Exploratory Writing

Just as computers and pens are the physical tools for exploratory writing, so knots and questions are the mental tools. But we still need some practical guidelines for this kind of writing. Here, then, is a list. Keep in mind, however, that these are only guidelines. Eventually, you'll develop an exploratory writing practice of your own that might work differently.

☐ Remember that this writing is for your eyes only.
- No one will read it except you, unless you choose to show it to someone.

☐ Write steadily for a set period.
- Try twenty minutes at first. But fifteen minutes or thirty minutes will work too. In any case, decide on your time frame in advance.

☐ To start with, put your notes aside and work from memory.
- What you remember is probably what interests you most: for some reason, it got lodged in your mind.

☐ If nothing occurs to you from memory, begin anywhere.
- You may have nothing to say at first. You may have nothing to say for the full writing period. That's okay. Just write "I can't think of anything to say. I still can't think of anything to say" until something occurs to you, however trivial or superficial it might seem. Thoughts are stirring in the back of your mind. When something about the reading or the problem does strike you, write about it.

☐ Keep moving forward.
- Don't edit. Don't worry about grammar, spelling, punctuation, or formatting. Don't go back and erase or cross out anything you've written, no matter how pointless or silly it seems.

☐ Entertain questions and knots.
- However silly or inappropriate they may seem, use them as the engines of exploration. Dwell on knots. Stay for as long as possible with the knots that you come across — anything that's puzzling or interesting. Do what you can with them. One may lead to another or begin to change its appearance as you dwell on it.

☐ Open a space for reflection.
- Talk things out. Speculate freely. Ponder. Give yourself time to focus at length.

☐ Put away your dictionary and thesaurus for now.
- Use your own words, even if they may not be exactly right. Save perfectionism for the readerly phase.

☐ Expect a lot of garbage in this writing.
- That's exactly as it should be. You need to generate a lot of material in order to produce a few good ideas.

The Benefits of Writing Daily

This book or any book can teach you only so much about writing. Writing is a craft, and crafts are learned by doing. Like learning to play the piano or paint or knit, learning to write means writing regularly, and writers benefit from practice more than anything else. Instruction is helpful, but we learn far more from sitting down regularly to put words on paper, discovering over time our themes and our voices, steadily gaining confidence and fluency, recognizing our strengths and limitations, developing an ear for what works and what's labored or florid or wordy, getting a sense of how to begin, how to keep going, how to finish.

Although this book deals with writing in academic settings, we strongly encourage you to write a daily journal about whatever you like. Use a notebook or, if you prefer, a computer, and save your entries in a special folder. Write two or three pages a day — and write every day, preferably at a regular time. (The best time is probably soon after you get up, before your busy life eats up the rest of the day.) This journal will be for your eyes only, with no restrictions on what you write about. Though journals are often used for recording experiences, feelings, and speculations, they don't have to be. You can write stories or dreams or fantasies, describe what's around you wherever you happen to be, or just write aimlessly about nothing in particular. It's all perfectly fine. Any kind of daily writing will help you become a more proficient writer. (In fact, the word "journal" comes from an Old French word meaning "daily.")

→ Try This   Practicing Exploratory Writing

Option 1. Try your hand at exploratory writing. Go to your college library or another quiet spot where you can work without interruption. Briefly review the notes that you have made on one of the readings included in this book. Then open a new page of a notebook and write for twenty minutes. Search for a good theme for an essay, on any topic related to the reading. If you find one before twenty minutes are up, don't stop: continue to explore the theme, testing its strengths and weaknesses and developing its implications.

Option 2. As a subject for exploratory writing, consider this painting by René Magritte, entitled *The Liberator* (1947). Try to work out an interpretation: What, in your view, is the painting saying? What does it mean? Devote thirty to forty-five minutes of exploratory writing to this activity.

Option 3. Choose an intriguing poem, photograph, painting, or piece of

The Liberator (1947), by René Magritte.
(Source: The Art Archive/Private Collection/Gianni Dagli Orti. © 2011 C. Herscovici, London/Artists Rights Society [ARS], New York)

music as a subject for exploratory writing. (Choose one to which you have access so that you do not have to rely on memory and can examine it repeatedly.) It should be a work that is unfamiliar to you so that your exploration of it has a chance to yield fresh and unexpected insights.

> ## ⊝ Guidelines   Keeping the Censor at Bay
>
> To avoid the negative thinking that blocks writing, keep the following guidelines in mind:
>
> - Recognize that the negative, critical voice in your head is the enemy of creativity and insight.
> - Write daily in a journal for no one's eyes but your own. Write whatever you want.
> - Permit yourself to write badly in your journal.
> - Relax. Go where your mind takes you and enjoy the ride.

Writer and teacher Julia Cameron notes that creative people (and that might be virtually everyone) tend to be highly self-critical.

> We are victims of our own internalized perfectionist, a nasty internal and eternal critic, the Censor, who resides in our (left) brain and keeps up a constant stream of subversive remarks that are often disguised as the truth. The Censor says wonderful things like: 'You call that writing? What a joke. You can't even punctuate. If you haven't done it by now you never will. You can't even spell. What makes you think you can be creative?' And so on and on.[5]

Daily journal writing helps us learn to ignore the Censor's negative and disabling voice. We can let that voice carp away, while we just keep on writing whatever we feel like writing. In time, we learn that the Censor is merely a "blocking device"[6] that serves no useful function, and it slowly loses its power over us.

Making Meanings

As a college student, you are likely to find journaling particularly valuable because you are being bombarded throughout the day with so many new ideas, experiences, and people. You need not only a place to record your impressions but also a way to

---

[5] Julia Cameron, *The Artist's Way* (New York: G. P. Putnam's Sons, 1992), 11.
[6] Ibid., 12.

sort it all out. Ideas and questions occur to you constantly, but you need to take the time to reflect, develop these thoughts, and dwell with them.

Ideas become meaningful to us when we find a way to integrate them into our entire body of knowledge. As long as they float around in a space where they are cut off from the rest of our concerns and experiences, they will never be very meaningful. Notebooks, journals, "morning pages," freewriting — all these are forms of "heuristic" writing, or writing to discover. But done in a sincere and committed way, they become the means of discovering not just ideas but meanings, not just thesis statements and arguments that serve to finish an assignment but also connections and relationships between the readings and your own interests. Too often, schoolwork, assigned by different instructors in courses that may have little in common, exists in isolation, detached from students' actual experiences and questions. One of the most effective ways of making readings and assignments meaningful is to begin by writing for yourself, rather than writing for a grade. Ultimately, the two things can merge so that the writing you do for yourself evolves into the writing you submit for a grade. Exploratory writing can function as the bridge between the two, the means by which schoolwork can become more personally meaningful and satisfying.

The process is frequently surprising. You might start out in one direction and find yourself suddenly veering off in a different one altogether, and this new direction takes you places you never imagined going. You might write something on Monday that seems unremarkable and insignificant, but when it comes to mind on Wednesday, it opens up all kinds of unforeseen possibilities, becoming the beginning of a whole new line of inquiry. In her essay "On Keeping a Notebook," essayist and novelist Joan Didion explores the purpose of the notes that she has been taking — regularly but unsystematically — for many years. Their value, it turns out, is less in what she actually records on paper than in the memories that these notes can conjure up.

> At no point have I ever been able successfully to keep a diary; . . . and on those few occasions when I have tried dutifully to record a day's events, boredom has so overcome me that the results are mysterious at best. What is this business about "shopping, typing piece, dinner with E, depressed"? . . .
>
> In fact I have abandoned altogether that kind of pointless entry; instead I tell what some would call lies. "That's simply not true," the members of my family frequently tell me when they come up against my memory of a shared event. "The party was not for you, the spider was not a black widow, it wasn't that way at all." Very likely they are right, for not only have I always had trouble distinguishing between

what happened and what merely might have happened, but I remain unconvinced that the distinction, for my purposes, matters. . . .

How it felt to me: that is getting closer to the truth about a notebook. I sometimes delude myself about why I keep a notebook, imagine that some thrifty virtue derives from preserving everything observed. . . . Remember what it was to be me: that is always the point.[7]

Likewise, the point of exploratory writing is always to find out what something means to you. Don't expect any sort of heuristic writing to pay off quickly: most of the time, you won't arrive at the insight or thesis statement that you need for your essay with your very first writing session — or even your second. The process is meant to be recursive. The result of the first session becomes the starting point for the next one. You may be surprised how many sessions you have time for. If you have five days between reading/note-taking and revising/polishing, and if you devote just ninety minutes a day to exploratory writing, broken into three sessions, you will complete fifteen half-hour sessions. At three pages per session, that's forty-five pages of exploratory writing. More to the point, it's a journey that may lead you far from your point of departure and, in all likelihood, toward ideas of real value.

Recursive exploratory writing is sometimes called looping; this rhythm of writing and resting, of tension and relaxation, helps ideas to form. Here's how it works:

- Write for ten, twenty, or thirty minutes. Take a break, roughly equal to the amount of time you've spent writing. Pick up a promising thread from the writing you just completed, and write for another ten, twenty, or thirty minutes. Then take another break. Keep this going for several loops.

- Enjoy yourself. Don't hesitate to explore thoughts that you don't expect to include in the finished version of your paper. You never know what may spark an idea, so trust your thoughts and let them lead you forward.

You Can Always Write More

One of the most valuable outcomes of exploratory writing is the effect it will have on your attitude toward revision. When writing feels difficult and demands enormous effort, writers tend to become too attached to their words. They become reluctant to

---

[7] Joan Didion, "On Keeping a Notebook," in *Slouching Towards Bethlehem* (New York: Farrar, Straus and Giroux, 1968), 133–36.

cut or revise passages that, no matter how much perspiration they cost or how delightful they may be in themselves, really must go, for the greater good of the whole. By contrast, writers who know from experience that they can readily generate more writing whenever it's needed can revise with confidence and can revise more effectively, because they are willing to abandon material. To revise well, we need to know that our words are not so very precious: we can always write more. As the late British comic Spike Milligan used to say: "Ingle jingle jangle jom / There's more, my friend, where that came from."[8] And as, more soberly, Annie Dillard writes: "the path is not the work."[9] The writing that we abandon was useful for getting us where we need to be, but once it has served its purpose, we must be willing to part with it. Perhaps every writer finds this process of deleting words and ideas a little difficult to do, but the habit of exploratory writing and unpressured drafting does make it easier. We no longer feel that words are precious, hard-to-find things but instead feel that they are plentiful and easy to come by. We can afford to be generous with them.

Focused Exploratory Writing

As we've seen, exploratory writing can serve many purposes and be about anything at all. But there will be times when you'll want to use exploratory writing to make progress toward completing an academic essay. For the purpose of academic writing, first focus on figuring out exactly what the question or problem or issue is. Once you've got a clear sense of that, you can begin to work on finding a solution to it.

Focused exploratory writing is useful whether you are writing in response to a specific assignment — perhaps one that presents you with a specific question or problem to address — or writing on a topic of your own. Even if the assignment is phrased as a question or problem rather than a topic or a directive, first you'll need to understand the question *for yourself*, in your own terms and in relation to your own thinking. Patiently thinking the question through — figuring out what it's *really* asking, what it's getting at — is the first and most necessary step toward arriving at an answer.

If the assignment asks you to respond to a particular reading, begin by focusing on the problem that the author is addressing. The author may explicitly mention the

---

[8] Spike Milligan, *Muses with Milligan,* recorded 1965, Decca LK 4701, vinyl LP.
[9] Annie Dillard, *The Writing Life* (New York: Harper and Row, 1989), 4.

problem (usually in the opening paragraphs), or you may have to infer it from the text by asking, "What sort of question, problem, or issue does the author's argument shed light on or take a stand on?"

Then, work out your take on the problem. Explain, in as much detail as possible, where you stand and where the author stands. Do you agree or disagree with the author? Your sense of this may be vague at first, and it may shift or even reverse itself as you write, but that's fine: you're just exploring, not laying out a consistent argument.

Pose questions whenever they occur to you. Questions help you see more clearly where you need to direct attention; they will move you forward.

Next, begin working out your reasons for your position. If you get stuck, work on key passages (a few sentences) in the text. Perhaps copy out the most relevant ones, or ones that feel like knots, and focus on answering these questions:

- What is the author saying in this passage?
- What might it have to do with the problem?
- How does it relate to my position?

Keep it loose: you are not yet writing for anyone's eyes but your own. The trick to exploratory writing is to keep moving toward your objective even though you don't know what it looks like. Move toward the articulation of an idea, or the framing of a question, or the formulation of an argument. Eventually, perhaps repeatedly, you will find that the elements of your puzzle resolve themselves in a little "aha" experience as something obscure emerges into clarity. Then you've got something. This something may not be the final thing — ideas can always be polished, developed, elaborated, refined — but it's a beginning.

➤ Try This   Practicing Exploratory Freewriting

The following activities will give you the opportunity to try your hand at exploratory freewriting, to get the feel of it, and to experience how it works. For now, follow the guidelines that have been offered in this chapter. To get more practice with exploratory freewriting, choose one or more of these activities. Before you begin, decide how much time you will devote to the activity you've chosen, and divide it into segments of ten, fifteen, or twenty minutes so that you can practice looping.

(continued)

Option 1: Focused Exploratory Writing for an Essay Assignment. If you have been assigned a topic for a paper, use it as a springboard. Read over the assignment instructions carefully. Consider the following questions as you write.

- What is the assignment asking you to do? What central problem does it set for you? Paraphrase the problem as you see it (put it into your own words).
- What can you say in response to this problem as a result of your reading, note-taking, and thinking so far? Work first from memory, but if you get stuck, turn to your notes.
- What passage in the text speaks most directly to the problem given in the assignment? What does this passage say (paraphrase it)? Explain the connection to the problem, as you see it. What conclusions can you draw from this passage? What ideas does it suggest to you?
- What other passages relate to the problem? What do they say? Repeat the step above for each relevant passage: paraphrase it, explain how it relates to the problem, develop the ideas it suggests to you.
- What seems to be the purpose of the assignment? Why might this problem be important? How does it relate to the course and its objectives?
- Does the assignment offer any clues as to the direction your essay should take? Many assignments include both a directive — a statement of what you must do — and suggestions or hints for things you might do, or might want to think about, as you develop your ideas.

Option 2: Exegesis and Commentary. As we said earlier, exegesis is an explanation or interpretation of a text. For this activity, choose a short passage from the text—between two sentences and one paragraph in length. (You might work with one of the essays included in this book or use a text that you've been assigned in your coursework.) It should be a passage that seems important to the meaning of the text as a whole but also contains difficulties or puzzles of some kind—in other words, a passage that seems likely to reward close attention, one that's worth dwelling on for a while.

Begin by stating in your own words what you think the passage means. Try to clarify any parts that seem obscure. (You may need a dictionary; if so, quote useful definitions in your writing.) Work over the passage in detail, so that your writing unfolds its meaning as exhaustively as possible. Consider how its parts work together, how words, phrases, and sentences relate to one another to form a meaningful whole. Stay alert for meanings that might not have been obvious at first, especially ones that differ from—or even contradict—your first impression.

Once you have done all you can with the passage itself and have completed your exegesis, shift your focus to making connections between the passage and something else—other texts, ideas, experiences, and facts. (In the exegesis phase of this activity, you work inside the passage; in the commentary phase, you work between the passage and something else.) Almost any kind of connection could produce a useful insight. How does your chosen passage relate to the major themes of the text as a whole? How does it relate to particular passages in the text that seem memorable or important? What connections do you find between this passage and other things in the world, such as your experiences or other texts you've read or social issues or political events?

After writing about one or two connections of this kind, go back to the text and consider it in isolation once more. What more do you see in it now?

Option 3: Exploratory Writing on a Knot of Your Own Choosing. Use some problem or puzzle in your own work or life as a subject for exploratory writing. You may or may not solve the problem, but write continuously and explore different ways of looking at it. Try to bring greater clarity to the problem, and perhaps some kind of solution will emerge—if not immediately, then later on.

Option 4: Freewriting. Try freewriting without any subject or starting point at all. See what emerges as you follow where the writing takes you. As you proceed, try to identify a topic, a question, or a problem. Articulate and refine it to the best of your ability, and try to develop some kind of insight into it. Use the looping technique to get some distance and perspective on your topic between bouts of writing.

✓ Checklist for Focused Exploratory Writing

Keep the following points in mind as you write to discover and develop ideas.

☐ Identify the problem, issue, or question that the assignment or text addresses.

☐ Establish your own position and seek a solution or an answer. Make a contribution to the conversation.

☐ List your reasons or justification for this stand.

☐ Pose questions.

☐ Seek knots.

chapter 5

Developing an Argument

Argument as Structure

If you were to build a house, a barn, or a cathedral — any structure meant to last — you would need not only good materials but also an understanding of structural and architectural principles. You would need to

> 66 The aim of argument, or of discussion, should not be victory, but progress. 99
>
> **JOSEPH JOUBERT**

know how to arrange spaces that serve people's needs, how to place doors and windows, how to make the walls and roof strong enough to withstand ice and rain and wind. Developing an argument is similar. Of course, you need materials, like ideas and quotations and notes, but you also need an understanding of the principles that make it possible to bring the various parts together to form a structure that holds up, that invites readers in and leads them through its points, and that can withstand careful scrutiny. Like the best buildings, the best arguments are sturdy, well proportioned, and pleasing. Achieving these goals requires an understanding of some basic principles of logic and rhetoric.

This chapter focuses on planning, designing, and assembling an argument. To construct a strong argument, writers must understand argument's component parts and how these parts relate to one another. In the fourth century B.C.E., the Greek philosopher Aristotle distinguished between two aspects of argumentation: **logic** (systematic reasoning) and **rhetoric** (the art of persuasion). You might think of logic as the invisible interior principles that hold an argument together — like the structural principles that keep a building standing — and rhetoric as the external features that make it attractive. This chapter is concerned primarily with logic — with making the argument fundamentally sound. (Rhetoric, the art of making an argument appealing, is discussed in the next chapter.)

The Components of Argument: Motive, Claim, and Support

As you will recall from Chapter 3 (p. 69), we use the word "argument" here not in the sense of a two-sided dispute in which one opponent tries to defeat the other, but in the sense of a single logical structure in which one individual *makes* an argument. Like any structure, arguments have several component parts — namely, motive, claim, and support.

Motive

We noted in the Introduction that academic essays usually offer a solution or partial solution to a problem, a question, or an issue of some kind. Usually, this problem (or question or issue) also concerns other scholars in the field; the writer will usually mention or explain it in the first paragraph or two. This reference to a problem reveals the writer's purpose and also why readers might want to pay attention to the essay. In other words, they explain the argument's "motive": its basic purpose and reason for existing. (As we noted in Chapter 4, sometimes the problem, question, or issue is *implied* rather than stated outright. But if so, the reader can usually figure it out.)

Academic writing is often concerned with problems of an intellectual nature — we might call them "knowledge problems" — rather than practical problems. In many academic disciplines, the job of researchers is to expand our understanding of the world, so their work seeks to answer questions and solve problems at the cutting edge of knowledge. Some practical usefulness might appear somewhere down the road, but often the main reason for solving the problem is simply to satisfy human curiosity. In the academic world, this is motive enough. Arguments published in magazines and newspapers, typically intended for general readers rather than professional research-ers, are more usually concerned with practical problems.

While a concern with knowledge problems is a distinctive feature of academic work, academic writing can also focus on practical problems. College writing assign-ments in particular often ask students to address practical problems: for example, political problems ("Should the electoral college be abolished?"), social problems ("How can American cities best deal with homelessness?"), or technological and engineering problems ("How can a smarter robot be built?"). Whether you are deal-ing with an intellectual problem or a practical one, you will need to provide a strong sense of the problem, question, or issue you are addressing so that the reader can understand why your argument matters and is worth reading.

Claim

Every argument, including academic arguments, proposes some idea to readers — the solution to a problem, the answer to a question, the correct approach to an issue. In other words, it makes a claim — an assertion that something is true or valid.

A claim differs from a fact in that a claim *awaits* proof or strong evidence, while a fact has already been well established. For example, the following is a claim:

> Information comes to seem like an environment.
>
> (Sven Birkerts, "Reading in a Digital Age")

This is a novel idea, one that readers might not accept without some sort of support-ing evidence. However, the sentence that comes next in Birkerts's article can be called a fact because it describes a familiar experience that readers are likely to accept without further argument or support: "If anything 'important' happens any-where, we will be informed."

On its own, a claim leaves the reader wondering, "Why should I believe that?" or "Why is that true?" A claim is yet to be proven, just as a claim that you stake on some-thing, such as a piece of land, has not yet been fulfilled: it is a demand that you're *expecting* to be fulfilled at some later time. A claim hangs in the balance, waiting to be proven or disproven.

A claim is also different from an opinion, though the difference can be subtle. When you express an opinion — for example, "I think it is wrong to conduct experi-ments on animals," or "In my opinion, it was a terrible performance," or "I believe that most people are basically good" — you just state a belief, and it may or may not be possible or necessary to make a rational argument for it. It could be an expression of taste, bias, or faith, perhaps a feeling or a hunch — that brussels sprouts are delicious, that Cameron Diaz is the greatest actor ever, that capital punishment is murder — and you are not asserting that your belief is objectively "true." But when you make a claim, you do state it *as true*. You're prepared, at least in theory, to back it up. Here are several actual claims.

> There is no fundamental difference between man and the higher animals in their mental faculties. (Charles Darwin, *The Descent of Man*)

> To the frontier the American intellect owes its striking characteristics.
> (Frederick Jackson Turner, "The Significance of the Frontier in American History")

> The current design revolution recognizes that sensory experience is as valid a part of our nature as our capacity to speak or to reason.
> (Virginia Postrel, "The Design of Your Life")

> It's an overwrought Gothic melodrama that has a nice first act before it descends into shameless absurdity. (Roger Ebert, review of the film *Asylum*)

These claims come from very different sources, but each one *requires* a supporting argument to persuade the reader that it is valid or true. On their own, they aren't either valid or invalid, true or false. (You can probably imagine directly contrary claims that might be made.)

> **➡ Try**This **Working with Claims**
>
> 1. Make up supporting statements for each of the claims listed above. Use your imagination, or search for facts that provide strong support.
> 2. Make up three or four claims of your own. Discuss them in class: What sort of support does each require? (Some possible topics: the effect on children of two working parents; the right to text while driving; the dangers of mixed martial arts or "ultimate fighting"; the need for print journalism in the Internet age.)

Support

Without **support** (evidence and reasoning), claims are no more than a series of assertions, backed by nothing (such claims are called "empty claims"). If readers have no reason to believe them, claims lack all force and impact. So support is essential. But what counts as support? Support includes both evidence, such as data and facts, and **reasoning**, a sequence of logically connected statements. There are only two requirements for support: first, it must be *valid* in itself; second, it must be *relevant* to the claim. Consider the following one-sentence arguments:

> Animals should be treated humanely because they are just like you and me.

> Animals should be treated humanely because at least 60 percent of American households include a pet.

In the first example, the claim that "animals should be treated humanely" is supported by a statement that is not necessarily valid in itself. (*Are* all animals "just like" you and me? Are any?) In the second example, the claim is supported by a statistic that may well be accurate but is irrelevant: Why should this fact mean that all animals should be treated humanely?

A stronger argument might go something like this:

> Animals should be treated humanely because they feel pain as acutely as humans do; moreover, scientists have shown that animals also experience similar emotional distress, including feelings of shame, loss, and depression.

(Of course, this argument holds up only if scientists have in fact shown all this. The relevant studies would need to be cited.)

Support gives us a reason (or reasons) for believing a claim to be true, but it is not the same thing as absolute **proof**. (In fact, proofs are rarely, if ever, 100 percent airtight, except perhaps in mathematics.) We can rarely *prove* arguments; all we can do is support them as strongly as possible. There will always be *some* room for doubt.

Still, in the strongest arguments, the relation between claims and their support is a tight fit, so tight as to be virtually irrefutable. In a weak argument, there are holes in the reasoning, gaps between the claims and the support and between different claims. Objections can easily be raised. The whole structure comes tumbling down under the least pressure.

The Modes of Persuasion:
Ethos, Pathos, and *Logos*

The philosopher Aristotle identified three "modes" or methods by which writers (or speakers) can persuade readers (or an audience): *ethos* (credibility), *pathos* (emotion), and *logos* (logic or reasoning). That is, a writer might persuade readers by convincing them that he or she is a credible source — sincere, fair, caring, amiable, and so on. Or a writer might persuade by appealing to readers' emotions, by bringing them to tears, arousing their anger, or stirring their pride. Finally, a writer can persuade readers by appealing to reason, by explaining how the evidence forces them to reach a particular verdict, for example, or by showing that certain conclusions necessarily follow from principles on which they all agree.

In academic writing, *logos* is the most important of the three modes of persuasion. Yes, an academic essay should show that you are credible (matters like correct spelling, formatting, and grammar suggest that you are a careful writer), but readers are unlikely to be persuaded by *ethos* alone. And yes, appealing to readers' emotions might help to bring home a point or convince them that your argument really does matter (a poignant anecdote to clinch your argument in the last couple of paragraphs can be effective), but an academic essay will rarely persuade by *pathos* alone. Instead, academic arguments persuade primarily by means of *logos*, because the purpose of academic writing is not to win over the reader by any means, but to seek and offer truth. (The only test for *ethos* and *pathos* is whether they have the desired effect. But *logos*, as Aristotle recognized, obeys its own set of rules — which gave birth to the science of logic and ultimately to the scientific method.) By comparison, *ethos* and *pathos* are merely ornamental — not unwelcome, but not the stuff that forms the substance of the argument. It's worth taking a moment, then, to consider how reasoning and logic — *logos* — function in academic writing.

Types of Reasoning

As we noted earlier, an argument is different from a proof. The purpose of academic writing is rarely to *prove* something, but rather to make an argument that is as convincing as possible, given the available evidence. A good academic essay need not make an argument that is unassailably "right," but the reader should feel, by the conclusion, that there's a good chance the argument is right, that its claims are insightful and supported by strong evidence and careful reasoning.

Sound reasoning is essential to academic writing. In developing your argument, you will need to guard against errors of reasoning known as "logical fallacies." In addition, you must explain your reasoning adequately, so that the steps that lead from one claim to another will be clear to the reader. To create a persuasive argument, make sure that your evidence is valid and supports your claims and that your claims support your thesis.

The science of formal logic, concerned with the precise conditions that produce absolutely valid conclusions from premises, need not concern us in detail. (In fact, real-world arguments rarely meet the strict standards of formal logic.) But it may be helpful to distinguish between two kinds of reasoning — inductive and deductive — and to distinguish between two types of deductive reasoning — the syllogism and the enthymeme.

Deduction

Deduction is the term used for deriving a conclusion from other statements, known as **premises**. Thus, a proof can be formed by building a chain of statements, in which each statement rigorously follows from prior statements.

Syllogism   The basic tool of deductive reasoning is the syllogism. Aristotle introduced the syllogism in his *Prior Analytics* as a means of testing the validity of deductive reasoning. He defined the **syllogism** as "discourse in which, certain things being stated, something other than what is stated follows of necessity from their being so."[1] The words "of necessity" are the key here: The deduced statement does not follow because Aristotle wanted it to, or because the ancient Greeks believed in syllogisms, or because the writer finds some advantage in it. The deduced statement *must* be true if the other statements are true.

In simple terms, a syllogism contains two related premises and a conclusion. For example:

> All humans are mortal. **(MAJOR PREMISE)**
> All Greeks are humans. **(MINOR PREMISE)**
> Therefore, all Greeks are mortal. **(CONCLUSION)**

The subject ("Greeks") and predicate ("mortal") in the conclusion occur in the premises, and both premises also contain a third term ("humans") known as the "middle term," which does *not* occur in the conclusion. The syllogism functions like a machine for producing truths. If you have two related truths, the syllogism makes it possible to deduce a third, new truth. The next two examples are perhaps a bit more practical.

---

[1] Aristotle, "Prior Analytics," trans. A. J. Jenkinson, in Jonathan Barnes, ed., *The Complete Works of Aristotle: The Revised Oxford Translation,* Bollingen Series 71, Vol. 1 (Princeton, NJ: Princeton University Press, 1984), 39.

All drinks containing caffeine affect Michela's sleep.

Cola contains caffeine.

Therefore, cola will affect Michela's sleep.

All the apples in the basket have green spots.

Some of the apples in the basket have red spots.

Therefore, some of the apples in the basket have both green spots and red spots.

In real life, no one argues by means of strict syllogisms, but they show how the validity of an argument can be subjected to strict and precise analysis.

Moreover, in reality we rarely find ourselves working with universally true premises, so it is necessary to argue what is probably true, based on probable premises, rather than what's necessarily true. The point is that you should carefully examine the logic of your deductive reasoning to make sure that your conclusions follow from the premises. Your conclusions don't need to be absolutely, necessarily valid proofs, but they do need to have a high degree of probability.

Enthymeme In formal logic, one conclusion follows strictly from another, and in the process of deducing conclusions from premises, no steps may be omitted. In real-life arguments, however, we can and do omit steps, expecting readers to supply them. An **enthymeme** is an informal syllogism, in which one of the premises is missing. In practice, we're much more likely to say "Caffeinated drinks affect Michela's sleep, so cola will affect her sleep too" or "Cola contains caffeine, so it will affect Michela's sleep" than to spell out the entire syllogism. And this works perfectly well, as long as the reader will understand the missing step. So omit only those steps that you can expect the reader to understand.

Induction

Induction is the method of reasoning from a part to a whole or from particulars to a generalization. When a scientist gathers data from laboratory experiments and draws a conclusion based on that data, he or she is reasoning inductively — reasoning from particulars to a generalization. Of course, some generalizations have greater validity than others; usually, it all depends on the size of the sample on which the generalization is based. Take this statement, for example: "American cars are more reliable than European cars." Although this is a broad generalization, a study of the overall reliability of millions of American and European cars might show that it is valid (or invalid). A smaller study would only be able to *suggest* that it might be valid or invalid.

Types of Evidence

Evidence includes textual evidence, anecdotes from personal experience, statistics, expert authority, graphs and other visuals, facts, and comparisons or other analogies. Each type has its hazards as well as its strengths (see Table 5.1), and each may be more or less appropriate depending on the assignment and the context.

Table 5.1 **Types of Evidence**

Type of Evidence	Example	Strengths	Hazards
Textual evidence, such as quotations, paraphrases, and summaries	West writes, "This is understandable in a white racist society — but it is crippling for a despised people struggling for freedom, in that one's eyes should be on the prize, not on the perpetuator of one's oppression." (p. 454).	Expected if the assignment asks you to analyze or do a close reading of a text. Introduces evidence directly into your essay, showing the reader exactly how you drew your conclusions.	If used excessively, direct quotations can obscure the argument you are making. They must be fully integrated into your argument with analysis and commentary, as they rarely speak for themselves.
Stories or anecdotes, including personal anecdotes	De Waal tells the story of visiting the *omphalos* near Delphi, Greece.	Usually engaging, they can be moving, dramatic, powerful.	They often appeal to the emotions (*pathos*) rather than reason (*logos*). May be logically weak, as they describe particular instances rather than general truths.
Statistics	The phrase "banking concept of education" occurs sixteen times in the first two pages of Paulo Freire's essay.	An economical way to summarize a wealth of evidence.	Often abused. They often look compelling, but may be incomplete (see Darrell Huff, *How to Lie with Statistics*).

Table 5.1 Types of Evidence (*continued*)

Type of Evidence	Example	Strengths	Hazards
Expert authority	As Frans de Waal argues, the principle of avoiding anthropomorphism can sometimes cause scientists to fail to understand animal behavior.	Reliable sources, especially leading scholars in a particular field, writing in peer-reviewed journals, provide strong evidence.	Is the source reliable? No one is beyond question. Some sources, especially Web sites, may seem more authoritative than they really are.
Visuals, including graphics that display statistical data	See Tompkins's use of a painting by Frederic Remington.	Economical yet often rich.	Use only if they truly strengthen the argument, never for decorative purposes.
Facts	Snowboarding debuted at the Olympics in the Winter Games of 1994, in Nagano, Japan.	Can be difficult to dispute. At best, they are unambiguous, intelligible, clear.	Facts are often more complex than they appear. Cite the source of facts that are not general knowledge.
Analogies, including comparisons, metaphors, and similes	Since fraternities have been able to give up hazing traditions, it is likely that the football team will be able to do likewise.	Analogies use facts or conditions that the reader acknowledges to elicit assent to a new idea.	Must be a very close fit, or they will be confusing and ineffectual.

As noted earlier, evidence must be both valid (quotations need to be accurate, facts need to be correct, and so on) and relevant to the claim it supports. Sometimes weaker evidence can be combined with other types of evidence to produce reasonably strong support for a claim.

In college writing, the best kind of evidence is often determined by the nature of the assignment. For an assignment that asks for a close reading of one or more texts, the strongest evidence is typically the words on the page. For a research assignment that asks for a study of a local subculture, the strongest evidence might be your direct observations or the testimony of interviewees. Usually, your assignment will either clearly state or strongly hint at the kind of evidence that you are expected to use. If you are unsure, ask your instructor.

Drafting a Thesis Statement

Arguments can be short and simple — a single claim and some support for the claim.

> Come with me to the hockey game. Our star defenseman has finally recovered from injuries and will be in the starting lineup.

> **THE CLAIM:** You should come with me to the hockey game.
>
> **THE SUPPORT:** Our star defenseman will be in the starting lineup.

But academic arguments are more lengthy and complicated than this example, so they need a "master claim" to keep them focused and organized. We call this master claim the **thesis statement**. The body of the essay typically provides support for this master claim, support that will include many other claims — supporting claims — along the way. The thesis statement is often presented in one or two sentences somewhere near the beginning, usually toward the end of the first or second paragraph. It represents the argument boiled down to its essence — a single claim that shows what the essay contributes toward the solution of a problem or that reveals the author's stand on an issue.

The purpose of all the thinking you do while rereading, taking notes, and doing exploratory writing is to produce an idea that you'd like to present in an essay — a thesis. If you feel that you still don't have anything to say, return to the strategies discussed in Chapters 2, 3, and 4. (Sometimes the creative process can be a struggle. There's no fail-safe formula for generating ideas, but the strategies and activities that we've discussed in these chapters should move the process forward.)

If you do have a sense of what you want to say, even a vague one, it's time to draft a working thesis statement. Think of your working thesis statement as a building tool: it will help you develop your argument even if it has to be substantially revised several times during the writing process. You need not feel committed to your words at this point, but your working thesis statement will give you a sense of direction as you begin developing an argument.

The Role of the Thesis Statement

As you begin thinking about a working thesis statement, it will be helpful to remember what a thesis statement is and isn't.

The word "thesis" is an ancient Greek term that originally referred to the stressed syllables in a line of poetry or stressed notes in a musical phrase, and to the beating of a hand or foot in time to a rhythm. Eventually, it came to be used for statements that were "put forth" or "put down" in a related way, often in a debate or conversation. This sense is still implied in its modern usage. Just as we sometimes use the expressions "Let me float this idea" or "Let me put this thought out there," the word "thesis" suggests an idea that a writer wants to test or try out. (Similarly, the word "essay" comes from the French verb *essayer*, meaning "to try or test.")

This nuanced meaning of "thesis" is useful to keep in mind as you sketch out a working thesis. Student writers are sometimes tempted to play it safe, feeling that they ought to have the "right answer" to a problem, even if their idea is self-evident or one that anyone else in the class might have come up with. But to construct a lengthy argument to support an obvious point is a waste of your time as well as your reader's. And an essay assignment is not like an exam: instructors rarely expect a "right answer." When they read exams, instructors usually expect to find a certain sameness; but when they read essays, instructors look forward to reading as many different arguments as there are students in the class.

A thesis statement is much more than a **topic** or general subject. It suggests what the essay seeks to accomplish rather than merely what it talks about. A topic is static and lifeless — it makes no particular assertion and needs no proof. But a thesis statement — as a type of claim — requires a supporting argument. And it relates to a recognized problem, question, or issue — it has a motive. Thus a thesis has an energy and a direction that will keep the essay moving forward.

For example, "the problem of greenhouse gas emissions" is a possible topic. Here's a thesis statement from a student essay:

> Congress can take several effective measures to diminish the emission of dangerous greenhouse gases, without limiting either the freedom or the prosperity of American citizens.   (Student writer Amy Britten)

In her opening paragraph, this writer had explained the problem: greenhouse gases contribute to global warming, which scientists agree is changing the climate more quickly than living things can adapt to such changes. She then proposed that part of the solution may be action on the part of the federal government, as action can be taken without great cost to America's freedom or prosperity. So the essay's motive is clear. But the thesis calls out for a supporting argument: the reader needs to know not only what specific measures she is proposing but also how these measures can be implemented without diminishing the freedom or prosperity of American citizens.

Here are some further examples of thesis statements from actual academic essays and articles, some by students and some by professional scholars. Note how each of these makes an original claim, related to a problem, a question, or an issue. Each leaves support for later, provoking the reader to ask, "Really? Now, why should you think that, and why should I agree with you?"

> Given these discoveries, we must be very careful not to exaggerate the uniqueness of our species. The ancients apparently never gave much thought to this practice, the opposite of anthropomorphism, and so we lack a word for it. I will call it anthropodenial: a blindness to the humanlike characteristics of other animals, or the animal-like characteristics of ourselves.
>
> (Frans de Waal, "Are We in Anthropodenial?")

> Why is it that so many of us are obese? . . . Although answers are beginning to emerge, there can be no meaningful discussion of the subject until we resist the impulse to assign blame. Nor can we hold to the simple belief that with willpower alone, one can consciously resist the allure of food and precisely control one's weight. Instead, we must look at the facts dispassionately and uninfluenced by the numerous competing interests that drive debate on this subject.
>
> (Jeffrey M. Friedman, "A War on Obesity, Not the Obese")

> The athletics scholarship must be abandoned in favor of institutional need-based aid. The athletics scholarship at its foundation is the biggest barrier to athletes' getting a genuine educational opportunity. When you are paid to play, regardless of the form of "payment," everything takes a back seat to athletic performance.
>
> (John R. Gerdy, "For True Reform, Athletics Scholarships Must Go")

> Although a supporter of states' rights and the Missouri Compromise, President Franklin Pierce signed the Kansas-Nebraska Bill into law because he believed that the advantages of a transcontinental railroad were worth the political price: the potential benefits to the country outweighed the anger that the repeal of the Compromise would surely provoke.   (Student writer Zach Peikon)

Jane Tompkins's main argument is that reflecting seriously about history is a personal moral responsibility. But instead of just stating this argument, Tompkins *shows* the reader what this means and demonstrates how to do it. In the end, the essay's meaning is to be found more in what Tompkins *does* than in what she says. It presents its "moral" more in the indirect way that films or plays or even paintings do, than in the direct way that most scholarly essays do.

(Student writer Diana Taylor)

We wish to put forward a radically different structure for the salt of deoxyribose nucleic acid. This structure has two helical chains each coiled round the same axis.

(James Watson and Francis Crick, "A Structure for Deoxyribose Nucleic Acid")

Credentialing, not educating, has become the primary business of North American universities.   (Jane Jacobs, "Credentialing versus Educating")

To sum up, a thesis statement helps readers recognize an essay's purpose and point, but it also serves the needs of writers during the writing process, in that it gives them a clear sense of their argument's direction and helps them stay in control of their purpose. As you draft your working thesis for the first time, bear in mind that a good thesis has two qualities, which work in tandem:

1. It is fresh, insightful, and interesting.
2. It can be supported with evidence and strong reasoning.

These two criteria are equally necessary: a thesis should not be so "interesting" or far-fetched as to be insupportable, nor should it be supportable but obvious or trivial. Just as an argument that states only the obvious is a waste of time, so are arguments that are merely frivolous or facetious.

Drafting the Argument

An Argument Matrix

Your notes and informal writing have supplied you with a good deal of raw material to work with. But it *is* raw. You could simply work through all this material and mark or copy out the ideas you plan to use. But the process of working out arguments to support your thesis — including identifying claims and the evidence to support

> **→ Guidelines**   **Making a Three-Column Document**
>
> To make a three-column document in Microsoft Word, follow these steps.
>
> - Open a new document and choose "Insert" under the "Table" menu. A dialog box will pop up.
> - In the "Number of columns" text box, type "3."
> - In the "Number of rows" text box, type "2." Click "Okay" and a table will appear in the document.
> - In the top row, type "Claims" in the left-hand column, type "Evidence" in the middle column, and type "Discussion" in the right-hand column. If you wish, select each of these words and click on the icon for centered text and the icon for boldface. Your first entry will begin in the second row.
> - You can add rows as needed: under the "Table" menu, choose "Insert" and then choose "Rows Below" on the submenu that appears.

those claims, and working out possible counterarguments — can be made more efficient by using a simple device called an **argument matrix**: a document with three columns, headed "Claims," "Evidence," and "Discussion."

The value of an argument matrix is that you can start in any of the three columns, but at some point you will need to enter notes in all three columns to complete the supporting argument. It reminds you to provide evidence, wherever possible, for your claims and to explain that evidence with discussion (evidence doesn't speak for itself). For example, in the "Evidence" column, you might list a quotation that you feel supports your argument well. Next, in the "Discussion" column, you might add some sentences that explain why this quotation supports your argument. Finally, after this work has clarified how the quotation works in relation to your argument, you can formulate a claim in the "Claims" column. Or you might begin with a claim that you believe to be true and then locate the evidence (a quotation or a fact) that supports the claim.

This method also helps to prevent inadvertent plagiarism, since quotations (other people's words) are clearly distinguished from discussion (your words). Be sure to identify quotations in the "Evidence" column with page numbers. Although your "Evidence" column might include many useful quotations, you don't need to include them all, word-for-word, in your final essay. You can write paraphrases and summaries or simply insert page numbers. (See Ch. 9's "Integrate sources effectively," p. 322.)

Gather material from your notes as well as from the text. Reread the text and your notes with your argument in mind, building support for your thesis.

The following example of an argument matrix is taken from an essay in progress on Jane Tompkins's "At the Buffalo Bill Museum, June 1988" (p. 413).

CLAIMS	EVIDENCE	DISCUSSION
The word "genocide" is significant. Although it refers to the murder of Native Americans and perhaps also to the slaughter of buffalo, it also brings to mind other genocides.	Since she can't resolve the main problem, she offers instead a conclusion that "for a while will have to serve." The last line of the essay states, "Genocide matters, and it starts at home." (p. 430)	Tompkins suggests that we must not fail to judge those who committed atrocities in America's past, just as we wouldn't fail to pass judgment on Hitler and anyone who participated in genocide.
The outrage Tompkins felt at the historical center is not actually contradicted by what she says in the essay's last paragraph.	As she exits the historical center, her indignation stems from her *horror* of violence and destructiveness. At the end of the essay, she's still horrified by it: see reference to "genocide" in last paragraph.	Her indignation was never really violent or destructive; she still feels indignation.

(continued)

CLAIMS	EVIDENCE	DISCUSSION
Tompkins does not really reject the "anger" she had felt. Nor should she.	"I cannot resolve the contradiction between my experience at the Buffalo Bill Historical Center with its celebration of violent conquest and my response to the shining figure of Buffalo Bill as it emerged from the pages of books. . . ." (p. 430)	Her feelings about Buffalo Bill are still uncertain. She has not simply given herself up to "love" for him. This suggests that she has not completely renounced her moral indignation.
Analyzing the paintings in the Whitney Gallery of Western Art, Tompkins arrives at a key insight about the contradictions between the tension-filled paintings and the bland placards next to them. Such "contradictions" emerge throughout her visit.	"The uneasiness of the commentary, and my uneasiness with it, were nothing compared to the blatant contradictions in the paintings themselves. A pastel palette, a sunlit stop-action haze, murderous movement arrested under a lazy sky, flattened onto canvas and fixed in azure and ochre — two opposed impulses nestle here momentarily. The tension that keeps them from splitting apart is what holds the viewer's gaze." (p. 414)	She notices a contradiction between the curator's placards and the subject matter of the paintings — which presented scenes of violence and suffering in settings of striking beauty. She concludes that art cannot be separated from history, that the neutral, purely informational, and nonjudgmental placards miss the essential truth about these paintings.

Anticipating and Incorporating Counterarguments

The "Claims" column is also the place to list counterarguments and your rebuttals to them. A counterargument is an argument that opposes your own argument. For example, if a writer is arguing in favor of legalizing marijuana, the counterarguments would be the arguments *against* legalizing marijuana. Why should you bring up arguments that oppose your own position? For two reasons: First, an intelligent reader may well be thinking of these counterarguments already, and by preempting these objections and responding to them, you can put them to rest. Second, by addressing counterarguments, you show yourself to be someone who thinks an argument through carefully and thoroughly, someone who has considered every aspect of the argument and is neither neglecting nor hiding any part of it. By anticipating and rebutting counterarguments, you make your own argument stronger.

Frequently, counterarguments are addressed toward the end of an essay, after the main argument has been presented, but they may be included almost anywhere in the essay. They may be introduced with phrases such as "although some might argue . . ." or "some readers might object to this argument, saying. . . ." No argument should ignore the possible counterarguments. At the very least, take some time during this phase of the writing process to play the role of a skeptical reader and imagine how such a reader might challenge the argument you are making. Experienced academic writers learn to play this role constantly as they work, continually seeking out the weaknesses and limitations of their arguments and figuring out a reasonable reply as they put together their claims and support.

You might discover a counterargument that you cannot rebut. This is not a disaster. It might indicate that your thesis needs to be rethought — and at this early stage in the process, it can be. If you've drafted a working thesis with the expectation that you will revise it, you will be less reluctant to shift your direction. At times, however, a counterargument is not so strong as to require a total revision of the thesis; it simply indicates that unanswered questions remain. In such a case, don't suppress the question; instead, acknowledge it, and show how it might suggest a possible direction for further research.

In your argument matrix, identify counter-claims clearly as such in the left-hand column. For counter-claims, your discussion notes should be a refutation of the claim.

⊖ Try This   Developing Arguments

This activity provides an opportunity for practice in refining arguments.

Step 1. Choose one of the propositions from the list below and work out an argument for it, based on your own experience, beliefs, and general knowledge. (If time allows, conduct research in the library or on the Internet, but research is not required.) As you develop the argument, write out your claims in full sentences, and spell out the support for each claim as fully as you can.

Step 2. Trade your work with a classmate. Examine your classmate's argument carefully. Look for places where, in your estimation, your classmate has presented the arguments fully and persuasively, as well as places where the argument needs more development.

Step 3. Look over your classmate's comments on your own work. How might you strengthen your argument by explicating the ideas more fully? With your classmate's help, develop and strengthen your original argument.

Step 4. Work out counterarguments and then address them. Identify two or three unanswered questions or problems that remain.

- Video games do [or do not] have real educational value.
- Americans are [or are not] becoming too materialistic.
- Smoking tobacco should [or should not] be illegal.
- Taxpayer dollars, through government grants, should [or should not] be used to support the arts.
- Physical education classes, three times a week, should [or should not] be a required element in the curriculum throughout grade school, middle school, and high school.
- The United States should [or should not] dismantle all its nuclear weapons, unilaterally.
- Gay men and women should [or should not] have the right to legal marriage in all fifty states.
- Owners of SUVs should [or should not] have to pay a special "gas guzzler" tax.

Drafting Paragraphs

Now that you have some claims, evidence, and discussion, you are ready to begin drafting paragraphs. Think of each major paragraph in the body of your essay as making a little argument of its own, beginning with a claim and developing the evidence and discussion that support the claim. The introductory paragraph (or paragraphs) works a little differently, though, as it normally serves to present the purpose of your essay and your thesis statement. The final shape, number, and arrangement of these paragraphs will change as your work progresses, but it's helpful to put together at least three or four paragraphs as soon as you can so that you have a skeletal structure to build on.

Drafting an Introduction

In an argument essay, the introductory paragraph (or paragraphs) serves chiefly to introduce the reader to the essay's purpose. In general, the purpose of an argument essay should be clear by the second or third paragraph. Few readers have the patience to read much further without a sense of where the essay is going.

The introductory paragraph needs to do more than just present the thesis. As we noted, a good thesis offers the solution to a problem, the answer to a question, or a stand on an issue. Moreover, the writer must demonstrate that the problem is real and, if it's not obvious, that it matters because it produces some sort of error or cost. This is the argument's motive. Explaining the motive could require several paragraphs, so your solution — your thesis statement — might not appear until the second, third, or even fourth paragraph. However, in an argument essay, it is usually wise to present the thesis promptly once the motive is clear; delaying it may lead the reader to wonder whether you have anything to contribute.

Consider the following example of how an argument's motive might be presented. The bare thesis statement in this case is "the federal government must develop a more complex method of calculating wealth, one that accounts for local differences in the cost of living." In itself, this doesn't mean much. But an introductory phrase (shown underlined) can be added that positions it as the solution to a problem.

> In order to obtain an accurate count of the number of Americans who live in poverty, the federal government must develop a more complex method of calculating wealth, one that accounts for local differences in the cost of living.

The problem is that government researchers lack an accurate count of the number of Americans who live in poverty. Adding the introductory phrase is an improvement over the bare thesis, of course, because the phrase explains *why* the government should develop better methods of calculating wealth. But it still doesn't explain why solving this particular problem is important. An additional sentence (shown underlined) following the thesis can help.

> In order to obtain an accurate count of the number of Americans who live in poverty, the federal government must develop a more complex method of calculating wealth, one that accounts for local differences in the cost of living. Only when more precise estimates of the number of Americans in need of federal help become available will it become possible to spend taxpayers' money wisely and effectively.

This more complete account of the problem shows that it also entails a *cost* and that the solution confers a benefit. In this case, providing this information can be done simply by indicating that without an accurate count of the number of Americans living in poverty, it's impossible to spend taxpayers' money wisely and effectively. For some arguments, though, you'll need to write more than one or two sentences: if the problem, its costs, and the solution's benefits are not obvious, and if they require a paragraph or more of explanation, be prepared to supply it.

In certain situations, you might need to go even further and relate the narrower problem explicitly to the broader work of the discipline as a whole. Again, the example is underlined.

> In order to obtain an accurate count of the number of Americans who live in poverty, the federal government must develop a more complex method of calculating wealth, one that accounts for local differences in the cost of living. Only when more precise estimates of the number of Americans in need of federal help become available will it become possible to spend taxpayers' money wisely and effectively. Economists have suggested several alternatives to the method currently in use, but so far none have been considered politically acceptable.

Whether such additional detail is needed depends on the audience and the assignment. In an essay for an economics course, for example, such a statement might not be necessary because any professional economist could be expected to know this; thus you can leave some aspects of the motive unstated and implied. If you are confident that the reader shares your concern with the problem under discussion, you might not need to provide an explicit link between the problem and the aims of the discipline as a whole.

➔ **Try**This   **Examining the Problem and Solution**

Examine Frans de Waal's essay "Are We in Anthropodenial?" (p. 432) carefully, looking for statements that discuss the problem he is addressing. Is it a practical problem or a knowledge problem? What does he suggest, explicitly or implicitly, about the cost of the problem? What does he suggest about the value of the solution he proposes?

Argument essays sometimes begin with a story or description of a representative case that paints a vivid picture of the problem. A paragraph or two of this kind of narrative can be especially effective because readers will almost always read to the end of a story, simply to find out how it ends.

Drafting Body Paragraphs

In exploratory writing, writers often leave the claim until late in the paragraph, perhaps even the last sentence, because they develop clarity about what they want to say only gradually, through the process of writing it out. They'll begin with some detail that stands out for them, make connections to other details, work out a sense of how it all adds up, and finally state what it means for their argument at the end of the paragraph. Such a process is quite normal in the early writerly stages. But a paragraph organized in this way makes heavy demands on readers, because it reveals the actual *point* so very late. Readers must hold a mass of perplexing details in their heads for several sentences — until finally at the end of the paragraph the point becomes clear. Some readers may get annoyed; some may lose patience and stop reading altogether.

As you draft the body paragraphs of your essay, bear in mind that the first sentence sets the direction. If the reader gets a clear sense of a paragraph's theme from the first sentence, and if the rest of the paragraph keeps to the theme, even as it develops and elaborates it, then your reader will feel that the paragraph has **unity**.

Readers need to find a **topic sentence** — a sentence that declares the paragraph's main concern, theme, or point — at the beginning of the paragraph so that they understand its purpose from the outset and do not have to puzzle through information that lacks any clear purpose. In fact, this need to find the paragraph's main point is so powerful that the first sentence tends to function as the paragraph's topic sentence *whether it is meant to or not.* So, since your reader will assume that your first sentence signals the topic of the whole paragraph, your task is to make sure that it does so as clearly and precisely as possible.

However, an argument essay is not composed of a series of topics. As we've seen, an argument is made up of claims and support for those claims. So in an argument essay, the purpose of most paragraphs will be to present a claim and to support it. The claim really governs the paragraph, as everything else in the paragraph should support it. At least initially, placing your claim in the first sentence is a safe strategy: your point will be clear from the outset.

You can then develop the support for this claim in the rest of the paragraph. Present it fully, laying out the evidence and explaining in detail how the evidence supports the claim. As writers, we tend to assume that readers will understand how a piece of evidence supports a claim — for us, it's perfectly obvious — but to any reader who is new to your ideas or has a different point of view, the relation may not be obvious at all. Spell it out. Evidence — whether it's data, a quotation, or an observation — rarely speaks for itself; it almost always needs to be explained. The "Discussion" column in your argument matrix should give you some words and phrases to begin developing this explanation.

If the point you want to make is complicated and the paragraph must be long, you can strengthen the paragraph's unity by incorporating words or phrases into later sentences that link back to the main topic or theme, thereby showing how these sentences relate to it. Repeating the exact same word frequently will create a sense of tedium, but words and phrases that are related but not identical, that work as variations on a theme, can forge connections and develop your point at the same time.

Here is one of the longer paragraphs from Cornel West's "Malcolm X and Black Rage" (p. 450). Note that the verb in the first sentence is "misdirected": for Malcolm, religion and music had misdirected black rage into dreamy sentimental romance. This notion quickly emerges as the theme of the paragraph, a theme that West sustains and emphasizes by repeating the idea of "romance" in the first half of the paragraph and incorporating the notion of "channeling" black rage (related to "misdirected") in the second half.

> Yet, for Malcolm, much of black religion and black music had <u>misdirected</u> black rage away from white racism and toward another world of <u>heaven and sentimental</u> <u>romance</u>. Needless to say, Malcolm's conception of black Christianity as a white man's religion of <u>pie-in-the-sky</u> and black music as soupy "I Love You B-a-b-y"

romance is wrong. While it may be true that most — but not all — of the black music of Malcolm's day shunned black rage, the case of the church-based civil rights movement would seem to counter his charge that black Christianity serves as a sedative to put people to sleep rather than to ignite them to action. Like Elijah Muhammad (and unlike Malcolm X), Martin Luther King, Jr., concluded that black rage was so destructive and self-destructive that without a broad moral vision and political organization, black rage would wreak havoc on black America. His project of nonviolent resistance to white racism was an attempt to channel black rage in political directions that preserved black dignity and changed American society. And his despair at the sight of Watts in 1965 or Detroit and Newark in 1967 left him more and more pessimistic about the moral channeling of black rage in America. To King it looked as if cycles of chaos and destruction loomed on the horizon if these moral channels were ineffective or unappealing to the coming generation. For Malcolm, however, the civil rights movement was not militant enough. It failed to speak clearly and directly to and about black rage. (p. 455)

Drafting a Concluding Paragraph

At this stage, a concluding paragraph is not really necessary; you can leave it for the revision stage, when your argument is already solid enough that you can step back and reflect on it. At this point, it's enough to say that a conclusion should not repeat points that you have already made clear. Rather than closing off the essay, the conclusion should really open it up, giving the reader a sense of its importance and its broader implications or suggesting directions for further research or questions that remain unanswered. The conclusion should give the reader something to think about, a send-off rather than a wrap-up.

Revising: A Recursive Process

Perhaps owing to the pressure of deadlines, some student writers revise their writing only slightly before submitting it. But failing to revise — or failing to allow enough time to revise — is to miss the opportunity for thinking and learning that writing assignments offer, and almost certainly it means submitting work that misrepresents your real abilities.

Revising is not the same as editing or proofreading. The word "revise" — from the Latin *revisere,* "to look at again" — means to *see* your work *again*. When you revise, you don't just clean up your writing or correct it; you step back from it, identify its strengths and weaknesses, and then do whatever's necessary to improve it — cut, add, rewrite, rearrange, rethink, even start again.

In a sense, writing *is* revision. You began your work with notes in the margins of a text as you read and reread; you developed some of these impressions into phrases and sentences in a notebook; you further developed some of these ideas in your informal, writerly explorations. Finally, as an argument emerged, you began to focus on a thesis, and you developed some paragraphs for a first draft of your essay. At every stage, you *revised* — reconsidered, selected, expanded, developed — some sort of writing that already existed. (You could even call your first reading of a text a kind of revision — a "re-seeing" of the author's point of view by bringing your own point of view to bear on it.) Selecting, rethinking, and rewriting have been essential to the process.

Susan Sontag, one of America's most highly regarded essayists, remarked:

> I don't write easily or rapidly. My first draft usually has only a few elements worth keeping. I have to find out what those are and build from them and throw out what doesn't work, or what is simply not alive. So there is a process of rewriting, of accumulation.[2]

Although her published essays seem spontaneous and confident, Sontag suggests that a great part of her work involves discerning what's worth keeping and what must be cut. We naturally become attached to passages that took a lot of time and effort, and it takes backbone to cut such passages. But cut we must. A careful reader (perhaps a fellow student, a tutor, or a professor) can help identify what should be kept and what needs to go. (Most writers rely on such readers at some stage in the writing process.) But an awareness of what to keep and what to cut also comes from a growing sense of the whole argument that emerges during the revision process.

Revising Your Thesis

The process of developing an argument is recursive: it moves forward by looping back to activities already performed. This is necessary because an argument evolves as its elements become clearer — as claims and support become articulated in full sentences, as the relation between claims and support and between the various

---

[2] Charles Ruas, *Conversations with American Writers* (New York: Knopf, 1985), 186.

claims themselves begins to emerge distinctly on the page. And as the argument emerges, it becomes possible to shape the thesis statement into a more perfect expression of the argument's central idea. Perfecting the thesis statement, in turn, makes it possible to refine the argument with greater clarity and confidence. A strong argument emerges only by cycling through the process several times. In essence, you must constantly move between the argument in progress and the evidence, in order to check, refine, and strengthen your argument.

Inexperienced writers, especially when under the pressure of a deadline, sometimes write out a thesis statement in a first draft and never bother to go back and revise or sharpen it. The result is usually disappointing: either the actual argument doesn't fit the thesis statement very well, in which case the reader can only be confused about the essay's purpose, or the argument gets molded to fit the thesis, no matter what the facts actually show, in which case the reader can only be left feeling unconvinced. But ideas evolve as the writing happens, and both the thesis and the argument must evolve together, with each continually adapting to the changing shape of the other, a process that may be described as "dialectical."

A **dialectic**, as we said in Chapter 2, is a thinking method that moves forward by means of two or more elements that test and correct each other. Often this involves a process of exposing and correcting errors or flaws. This dialectical process of refining a working thesis as an argument evolves resembles the method of empirical science known as the "data-model loop" (see Figure 5.1). Laboratory scientists start with a model or prediction of an experiment's outcome. Next, they devise an experiment that will test this theory as conclusively as possible. Typically, the results of the experiment — the data — reveal how the initial model needs to be corrected or revised, and this new model will then be tested by further experimentation. By this recursive process of theorizing and testing, science gets steadily closer to the truth, and advances are made. Thus the loop is really a spiral that steadily advances upward, since the cycle doesn't return to the same point; each refinement in the model represents an advance in knowledge.

Writers rarely formulate a perfect thesis statement before the argument is fully formed because they seldom have a crystal-clear sense of the entire argument when they first sit down to write. Clarity emerges through the activity of writing and rewriting. A working thesis and an evolving argument have a dialectical relation: as the argument emerges more clearly, it requires corrections in the working thesis, but a clearer and more precise thesis also makes a stronger argument possible. As you develop your argument, expect to revise your thesis several times as your ideas become clearer through the writing process.

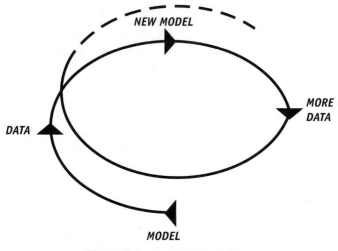

Figure 5.1 The Data-Model Loop

Limiting Your Thesis

Earlier in this chapter (p. 123), we identified two criteria for a good thesis: it is fresh, insightful, and interesting; and it can be supported with evidence and strong reasoning. The second of these criteria means that the **scope** of the thesis must be appropriate for the assignment. That is, if the thesis is making a claim that's too broad to argue within the assignment's page limit, you don't have much hope of persuading your reader. For professional researchers, it makes sense to limit the scope of the problem they are working on; the more limited the scope, the better the chances of solving the problem and making a genuine contribution. Likewise, you should narrow your thesis to make it more manageable. Student essays are usually between five and twenty pages. If your thesis is too broad or too ambitious, you won't be able to support it in such a confined space. So it usually helps to limit your thesis, narrowing it down to a specific proposition that you can adequately treat in the pages you have available.

One of the chief functions of a thesis statement is to fence off the territory of your argument, so it needs to *define*, or draw limits around, your main idea. A thesis statement needs to give both a complete and precise synopsis of your argument. As you revise your working thesis statement, look for words and phrases that will sharpen it and indicate its limits. Consider the following examples:

Too broad: There are ideas in Rousseau's *The Social Contract* that can be applied to today's world.

Appropriate: Rousseau's analysis of democracy, with its four essential components (a "small state," "simplicity of manners," "large measure of equality," "little or no luxury" [bk. III, ch. 4, p. 113] can help resolve the political crisis of our time as more Americans lose faith in the workings of a democratically elected government.
                                                            (Student writer Ben Dauksewicz)

Too broad: President Franklin Pierce signed the Kansas-Nebraska Act because he thought it was the best thing for the country.

Appropriate: Although a supporter of states' rights and the Missouri Compromise, President Franklin Pierce signed the Kansas-Nebraska Act into law because he believed that the advantages of a transcontinental railroad were worth the political price: the potential benefits to the country outweighed the anger that the repeal of the Compromise would surely provoke.   (Student writer Zach Peikon)

Too broad: The minimum wage should be increased.

Appropriate: The minimum wage should be raised to a level at which workers can cope with the rising cost of living in each state as determined by the Consumer Price Index (CPI), which "is a measure of the overall cost of the goods and ser-vices bought by a typical consumer." Each of the fifty states should be required by a federal mandate to have their own minimum wage based on the average cost of living in each respective state.   (Student writer Tao Lin Pao)

Hedging

Some argument essays are polemic (from the Greek word *polemos*, meaning "war"): their purpose is to defeat a real or imagined opponent, so they state their claims as strongly as possible. But defeating an opponent is rarely the purpose of academic writing; rather, the goal is to get as close to the truth as possible. As a result, academic writers are typically cautious, and they often qualify their claims with words or phrases such as "probably," "perhaps," "possibly," "may," "might," "in most cases," or "could be considered." These are called *hedge words.* Their purpose is not to weaken the argument or to make it wishy-washy. Rather, such words enable writers to convey their degree of certainty. If you present an idea as a possibility rather than a certainty, readers will take you no less seriously; indeed, when you refuse to overstate your claims, you are more likely to be received as a careful and responsible thinker.

But "hedging" is not merely a matter of using qualifiers. It is also a matter of providing an accurate assessment of the strength of the evidence, not only in the thesis statement but throughout the essay. In the following passage, the animal scientist Temple Grandin argues that certain dog breeds are more aggressive than others. Notice how she carefully hedges her claim — not just with hedge words and phrases, but with a frank account of the evidence that makes it impossible to offer more than an educated guess about this matter.

The genetics of aggression is an especially thorny issue with dogs. Most people don't want to believe that there are some breeds, like pit bulls and Rottweilers, that are more aggressive by nature. (Pit bulls aren't an established AKC [American Kennel Club] breed.) Usually these folks have known or owned individual Rotties or pits who were sweet and good-natured, so they conclude that when a Rottweiler or a pit bull shows aggression the problem is the owner not the dog. But the statistics don't support this interpretation, although it's true that statistics on dog bites aren't hard and fast.

There are lots of problems with dog bite reports. For one thing, there are a few different kinds of dogs that are called pit bulls, including some purebreds like the American Staffordshire terrier and some mixed-breed dogs. Another problem: large dogs do more damage when they bite people, so they're probably overrepresented in the statistics. Also, lots of purebred owners fail to register their dogs with the AKC, so it's impossible to know exactly how many purebred Rottweilers there are in the country and compare that figure to the number of reported dog bites committed by Rottweilers.

Because dog population data is imprecise, no one can nail down *exactly* what each breed's "aggression quotient" is compared to other breeds. Still, you can get an overall picture of which breeds are most dangerous by looking at medical reports of dog bites. *On average*, Rottweilers and pit bulls are so much more aggressive than other breeds that it's extremely unlikely bad owners alone could account for the higher rate of biting. And if you're looking only at anecdotal evidence, there are plenty of cases of nice, competent owners with vicious Rottweilers or pit bulls. Aggression isn't always the owner's fault. Writing about pit bulls, Nick Dodman says, "Originally bred for aggression and tenacity, pit bulls, if provoked, will bite hard and hang on, making them as potentially dangerous as a handgun without a safety lock." . . . [T]hey can become quite civilized, developing into loyal and entertaining companions. But the *potential* for trouble is always lurking somewhere, as a result of their genes and breeding.[3]

Grandin is speculating here, but speculation is perfectly valid as long as it is presented *as* speculation, and not as near certainty. The purpose of the hedging in this passage is to establish a just relation between the nature of the evidence and the strength of the claim. This hedging is an important part of what it means to be a responsible writer: to overstate or understate, whether deliberately or carelessly, is to engage in a kind of deception, and in academic writing especially, such deception is to be scrupulously avoided.

Revising Paragraphs

Revision gives writers an opportunity to reshape paragraphs so that readers can absorb the ideas in a more effortless and satisfying way. Often, this means identifying the topic and purpose of the paragraph and stating it clearly at the beginning of the paragraph rather than further down. In an argument essay, where the purpose of a paragraph is often to establish a claim that supports the main thesis, the writer must locate the paragraph's claim — whether it is clearly stated or not — and move it to the beginning of the paragraph.

The first requirement of revision is to shift perspective and think like a reader. There are two ways of looking at a paragraph: the map view and the globe-trotter's view. The map view is a bird's-eye view that sees the whole paragraph at a glance. When thinking about how sentences are arranged in a paragraph, we often take this view, looking at the whole thing from above — topic sentence at the top, supporting material beneath, perhaps a closing sentence at the bottom. Readers do not experience paragraphs this way, however. Rather, they experience them more like a hiker moving through a landscape or a sailor navigating a sea dotted with islands. That is, readers encounter one sentence at a time and work to make sense of each one in relation to previous sentences and paragraphs. The horizon constantly changes as readers move through the text. They don't know what's coming later; the argument or the story unfolds one piece at a time. Revising draft paragraphs requires taking both the map view and the globe-trotter's view.

---

[3] Temple Grandin and Catherine Johnson, *Animals in Translation: Using the Mysteries of Autism to Decode Animal Behavior* (New York: Harcourt/Harvest, 2006), 148–49.

Beginning the Paragraph: Transition, Topic, and Claim

When we discussed drafting body paragraphs, we said that the first sentence sets the paragraph's direction and that normally body paragraphs should open with a claim, followed by the supporting evidence and reasoning. But not *every* paragraph has to be structured in exactly the same way; in fact, some variety helps prevent monotony and lets you accommodate exceptional situations (for example, paragraphs that tell a story or raise a question rather than make an argument).

Now that you have drafted a few paragraphs, we can complicate things a bit and distinguish three separate functions that the opening of a paragraph should fulfill: transition, topic, and claim. Recognizing these three functions makes it possible to try different ways of structuring paragraphs while still keeping the argument clear and strong.

Transition

A transition guides the reader from the previous topic to the topic of the new paragraph. Transitions can be a word ("moreover," "however," "furthermore," "nevertheless"), a phrase ("in contrast," "in addition," "for example"), or a whole sentence ("Now that we have considered the historical record, let's look at the situation in America today"). Of course, transitions can be used between sentences and clauses as well, but they are often especially helpful when the reader moves from one unit of the argument to a new one — which typically involves moving from one paragraph to another. Transitions give the reader a sense of the relation between this new paragraph and the previous one, whether it be one of contrast, addition, or something else. Avoid using transition words and phrases mechanically or thoughtlessly. A transition is not *always* necessary, but it is often helpful. Think like a reader and use your best judgment. As a rule, make your transitions no longer than necessary; you want to keep the argument moving.

Topic

As we suggested earlier, a topic and a claim are not the same thing. The topic is the general subject of a paragraph, while the claim is the *point* you want to make, the paragraph's real purpose. The first sentence of the paragraph *must* give readers a clear sense of the *topic*; this opening sentence is the chief means by which a paragraph coheres. But as long as the topic is clear, the claim can be moved elsewhere in the paragraph.

Claim

While placing the claim in the first sentence generally works well, it is not absolutely necessary. As long as the paragraph's first sentence clearly states the topic, the claim *can* appear later in the paragraph. It can appear in the second sentence or at the end of the paragraph — both prominent positions. Occasionally, the claim might appear elsewhere. Moreover, the claim can be split between two sentences. For example, it might be stated in general terms at the beginning of the paragraph (to make the main point clear) and in more precise terms later on. Or it can be stated in part early in the paragraph and in part later on.

The main thing to avoid is burying the claim in other material, where it might be overlooked.

In a longer essay, variations in paragraph structure help prevent monotony and predictability. But if there's any possibility of confusion, remember that the point of the paragraph is usually clearest if the claim appears early. To sum up:

- The topic *must* occur in the first sentence.
- The claim may occur in the first, the second, or even the last sentence.
- The claim may be split between two sentences.

It is useful to recall these structural principles as you *revise* a thesis-driven essay because when you draft ideas, there is a natural tendency to begin a paragraph with evidence and end it with a claim. This occurs because we gain clarity as we write: usually we need to work through the evidence before we can be sure what our claim *is* — that is, what claim is truly justified by the evidence and what words best express our claim. Therefore, to work well as readerly arguments, writerly drafts often need to be reorganized: the thesis has to be moved from the last paragraph to the first, perhaps, and claims need to be repositioned at the beginning of paragraphs instead of the end.

Varying Paragraph Length

Paragraphs are sometimes described as the building blocks of the essay. The word "block" does suggest unity and cohesion, qualities that paragraphs do need to have. But building blocks are usually alike in shape and size, and the analogy suggests a sameness that could lead to a plodding, repetitive structure. The architectural metaphor we introduced in the opening of this chapter, that of rooms in a well-planned home, might be more useful. Each room is distinct — kitchen, living room, dining room, bedrooms — and each serves a particular purpose. And ideally each room has been designed and furnished to be both functional and pleasing.

Imagine walking into such a home and taking a tour. There are transitions — doors and hallways that connect one room to another. Each room is unique, but each is complete and fulfills its function. As you walk from room to room, you begin to get a sense of the house as a whole, of how the various spaces fit together to make a complete home, one with its own particular character and style. Getting to know the layout is a gradual process, but if the house has been well designed, it's an easy and pleasant process.

Paragraphs work rather like rooms: each paragraph should have its own character and purpose, but each should contribute to the whole. As a writer, you must bear in mind that readers cannot initially see the essay as a complete whole. They make their way through the essay one paragraph at a time. Gradually the shape of the whole argument begins to emerge.

A paragraph break marks a pause and a turn from one unit of thought to another. Paragraphs give readers a sense of where one unit ends and another begins, a sense of how the argument develops by moving from one topic to the next. Since readers usually see the length of the paragraph (perhaps unconsciously, out of the corner of their eyes) before they read the actual words, they know whether to brace themselves for a long trek or whether to relax a little. Paragraphs let the reader digest one idea at a time without becoming overwhelmed.

While paragraphs should cohere, they can be almost any length (though probably not much more than a page). You can experiment with paragraph breaks, creating shorter or longer paragraphs to suit your argument's needs.

In modern academic writing, paragraphs are usually less than a page in length. But it's rare to find many short paragraphs (of, say, less than four lines) in a row. A typical paragraph is roughly ten to twenty lines in length. But there will be variety. Short paragraphs are sometimes needed for other purposes besides laying out a component of the argument. For example, a transitional paragraph might be needed at a certain point in order to sum up all that's been established so far and to hint at where the argument will go from here.

And sometimes short paragraphs can simply underscore a point.

Concluding Paragraphs

In the body of the essay, you've been taking your reader through a forest of details. But by the conclusion, it may have become difficult, as the saying goes, to see the forest for the trees. Here, you may need to speak to the reader about the forest, the big picture: why all this matters and what it means. As we said earlier, a concluding paragraph should never be redundant and should never merely restate an argument that should already have been made clear. Instead, it should offer *summation,* not summary — a more distant perspective, not repetition. A good conclusion answers the question "So what?" or "What now?" or "Where do we go from here?" or "What else must we consider in connection with this problem?"

So while the concluding paragraph brings the essay to a close, the closure need not be airtight. The most effective closings resonate, leaving the reader with something to think about. The concluding paragraph is often the place to point out questions that remain unanswered or to suggest directions for further research. (You might choose to end the essay with a question.) In this sense, the conclusion is less an ending than a send-off: you are passing the baton to the reader now, to go out and act or reflect or investigate further, as the case may be.

If the rest of the essay has done its job and made a strong case for your thesis, then you might choose to close with a gentle tug at the reader's heartstrings, especially if you feel that action or assent is urgently needed. Earlier in this chapter, we discussed Aristotle's concepts of *logos, ethos,* and *pathos* and noted that in an academic essay *pathos* — an appeal to the emotions — typically takes a backseat to *logos* — an appeal to reason. But the concluding paragraph can be the right place for a little *pathos.* For example, if your opening paragraph describes a problem and its costs, your concluding paragraph might return to the subject of these costs, reminding the reader of the reasons that it is important to address the problem as soon as possible.

In the great scheme of things, a thesis is not an end point but a starting point for rethinking bigger questions that exceed the scope of the paper you're writing. What, then, is the significance, the importance, of the thesis you've argued? If you think of your essay as a contribution to a conversation, your concluding paragraph needs to invite some response, some reflection on the part of the reader. The word "conclusion," then, is somewhat misleading, because it implies closure, shutting the door on the topic, wrapping it up so that it can be put away. But this is just what a closing paragraph should *not* do; instead, it should open doors. In a word, it needs to put the ball back in the reader's court.

A Case Study of Paragraph Structure

To understand better how paragraph structure works in practice, let's look at the first four paragraphs of an essay by economist James Surowiecki that appeared in his column "The Financial Page" in *The New Yorker*.[4] Here, Surowiecki is arguing that the federal government, through the Food and Drug Administration, should shift its focus to the benefits and risks of drugs that are already on the market and should stop devoting all its energy to testing drugs *before* they go on the market. He does not explicitly state his thesis until the sixth and final paragraph, but his purpose does become clear by the middle of the second paragraph.

The essay begins with an anecdote, so that the structure of the first paragraph is narrative. The sentences are arranged chronologically: the first sentence tells what happened first, and the last sentence tells what happened last.

James Surowiecki
A Drug on the Market

Last month, a fierce and costly battle erupted over the diabetes drug Avandia after an article in *The New England Journal of Medicine* suggested that the drug raised the risk of a heart attack by 43 percent. In the publicity storm that ensued, the number of new Avandia prescriptions shrank by 21 percent, and investors lopped more than $12 billion off the market capitalization of the drug's maker, GlaxoSmithKline. Then came a furious backlash. The article's lead author, Steven Nissen, was accused of being a publicity-seeking crusader with a conflict of interest (Nissen had previously received research support from the maker of one of Avandia's competitors). GlaxoSmithKline dismissed Nissen's work, which was a meta-analysis of forty-two other studies, and published interim results from its own long-term study of Avandia's safety, which it claimed proved to be no more dangerous than its competitors. There were complaints about the "tabloid" hype that journals attached to their stories, and the British medical journal *The Lancet* said that "alarmist headlines and confident declarations help nobody."

1

---

[4] James Surowiecki, "A Drug on the Market," *The New Yorker,* June 25, 2007, 40.

Having worked our way through this story, we are probably asking ourselves, "Okay, but what's the point?" The purpose of the second paragraph is to give the answer.

> This kind of brouhaha, with volleys of personal attacks and ² fights for the biggest headline, doesn't look much like science. But it's all too typical of the way we measure the safety and efficacy of drugs. The United States has no rational system for "post-market surveillance" — the evaluation of drugs after they've been approved. Instead, oversight is left to a motley collection of altruists, academics, lawyers, self-publicists, and drug-companies, who make their own arbitrary decisions about which drugs to study, how to evaluate them, and what risks to look for. Somehow, the truth is expected to rise to the surface from among all these competing interests and random decisions.

The focus here is more on the problem than on the solution, so at this point the essay's thesis is partly implied rather than stated, but the implication is nevertheless clear: the United States lacks a system for "post-market surveillance" — and it needs one. This claim appears in the second and third sentences of the paragraph, and the fourth and fifth sentences continue to detail the problem.

Now let's look at the structure of the third paragraph.

> One might expect the Food and Drug Administration to ³ bring order and rationality to the system. But the way the F.D.A. is configured and run prevents it from doing so. Before a drug has been approved, the F.D.A. has tremendous leverage over pharmaceutical companies, and can require them to do the studies that it deems necessary. As soon as the agency actually approves a drug for sale, though, its authority is markedly diminished. The agency can recommend that the manufacturer of a drug already on the market conduct studies, but it can't, with a few exceptions, force the company to do so. Furthermore, it can't limit their advertising or sanction them in any real way. As a result, most post-market studies promised by drug companies have never been started, and, of those which have, nearly three-quarters remain incomplete.

Here, Surowiecki splits the topic and the claim between the two first sentences. The first sentence makes a claim of sorts, but it isn't the claim that he argues in the rest of the paragraph. It's really just an announcement of a topic: the Food and Drug Administration, which he has not mentioned previously but which will be central to his argument. So his claim is in the second sentence. The sentences that follow provide explanation and support.

The fourth paragraph is organized in a similar way. The first sentence merely brings up a topic or an issue: the FDA's own capacities. The claim appears in the second sentence. The details that follow support the claim: that the FDA has neither the money nor the "infrastructure" to run drug trials of its own.

> Instead of relying on drug-makers to test their own products, 4
> the agency could, in principle, run or commission its own trials.
> But it lacks both the money and the infrastructure to do so. While
> there is an office devoted to "surveillance and epidemiology,"
> which is theoretically responsible for post-market monitoring,
> its budget is startlingly small, it does not function as an indepen-
> dent agency, and its recommendations are often overruled. The
> F.D.A. as a whole is far more focussed on what happens to drugs
> before they enter the market: for every seven employees who
> work on drug approval, only one works on post-market safety.

Why does Surowiecki structure his essay this way? It's not hard to see why he begins with a story: he's writing for the general reader, not for economists or political scientists, so he has to arouse our interest immediately in a problem that might otherwise seem obscure and, in the scheme of things, not especially urgent. But once we start reading a story (and this one concerns "a fierce and costly battle"!), we usually want to know how it ends, so we'll stick with Surowiecki for the span of that paragraph at least. And by its end, we're committed: he's shown us that there's something fishy going on — and that concerns all of us.

But why, in the paragraphs that follow, does Surowiecki split the topic and the claim into two or even three sentences? There may be several reasons, but here's one possibility: The problem he describes is fairly complex, and it involves terms, structures, and systems that are unfamiliar to most of us. So he needs to keep his sentences short: "Here's a topic. Here's my claim about the topic." That's easier for readers to handle than longer sentences that introduce a new topic and a new claim at once.

Notice that paragraphs 2 through 4 each have a second sentence that begins with the word "But." And in all three paragraphs, the first sentence offers a sort of naive, commonsense point of view, the point of view of the layman, while the second offers the more informed point of view of the expert. "Here's what you might think at first. But here's what I can tell you that will make you see the situation more clearly." In this way, Surowiecki plays the role of a guide: he can understand how things look from the ordinary person's perspective, but he can also claim some expertise in the subject. He is thinking like a reader. It's an effective strategy for a writer on complicated economic issues to use in a weekly magazine for general readers like *The New Yorker.*

➔ Try This   Analyzing Paragraph Structure

Choose a passage of several paragraphs from one of the readings in this book. Conduct an analysis of the way each paragraph is structured. The above analysis of Surowiecki's article and the following analysis of paragraphs 10 and 11 from Cornel West's "Malcolm X and Black Rage" (p. 450) may be taken as general models.

> The project of black separatism—to which Malcolm X was beholden for most of his life after his first psychic conversion to the Nation of Islam—suffered from deep intellectual and organizational problems. Unlike Malcolm X's notion of psychic conversion, Elijah Muhammad's idea of religious conversion was predicated on an obsession with white supremacy. The basic aim of black Muslim theology—with its distinct black supremacist account of the origins of white people—was to counter white supremacy. Yet this preoccupation with white supremacy still allowed white people to serve as the principal point of reference. That which fundamentally motivates one still dictates the terms of what one thinks and does—so the motivation of a black supremacist doctrine reveals how obsessed one is with white supremacy. This is understandable in a white racist society—but it is crippling for a despised people struggling for freedom, in that one's eyes should be on the prize, not on the perpetuator of one's oppression. In short, Elijah Muhammad's project remained captive to the supremacy game—a game mastered by the white racists he opposed and imitated with his black supremacy doctrine.

The first sentence states both the topic ("the project of black separatism") and West's claim (it "suffered from deep intellectual and organizational problems"). What these problems were, exactly, he does not say in this topic sentence. Instead, he specifies one of them (the intellectual rather than the organizational) in the second sentence, and this problem becomes the theme of the paragraph: the obsession

(continued)

with white supremacy. The remainder of the paragraph chiefly explains why this was a problem, with a focus more on logic than on historical facts, but West seems to be implying that events reflected this logic. The final sentence of the paragraph sums up his point and restates it in more precise language than he has done earlier. West has divided his claim between the beginning of the paragraph and the end—a common strategy.

> Malcolm X's notion of psychic conversion can be understood and used such that it does not necessarily *entail* black supremacy; it simply rejects black captivity to white supremacist ideology and practice. Hence, as the major black Muslim spokesperson, he had many sympathizers but many fewer Muslim members. Why did Malcolm X permit his notion of psychic conversion to result in black supremacist claims of the Nation of Islam—claims that undermine much of the best of his call for psychic conversion? Malcolm X remained a devoted follower of Elijah Muhammad until 1964 partly because he believed the other major constructive channels of black rage in America—the black church and black music—were less effective in producing and sustaining psychic conversion than the Nation of Islam. He knew that the electoral political system could never address the existential dimension of black rage—hence he, like Elijah, shunned it. Malcolm X also recognized, as do too few black leaders today, that the black encounter with the absurd in racist American society yields a profound spiritual need for human affirmation and recognition. Hence, the centrality of religion and music—those most spiritual of human activities—in black life.

The paragraph concerns Malcolm X's reasons for remaining faithful to the Nation of Islam despite the problems with it and even though the notion of psychic conversion can be separated from them. But this topic is not introduced until the third sentence, with a question. The first sentence states the *general topic*, but not the specific topic, of the paragraph. The claim does not appear until the sentences that follow.

Checklist for Developing an Argument

Keep the following in mind as you develop your argument.

- ☐ The argument
  - The argument needs to have a motive. It should respond to a need, such as a problem, a question, or an issue.
  - The argument must make a claim. It needs to offer a solution, suggest an answer, or take a stand.

- The argument has to support its claim(s) with evidence and reasoning that are both valid and relevant. The type of evidence should be appropriate for the particular assignment.

☐ The thesis statement
  - The thesis statement functions as the "master claim" of the essay.
  - It should be fresh, insightful, and interesting.
  - It can be supported with evidence and reasoning.
  - It may be revised as your argument develops. You can limit and "hedge" the thesis statement as necessary.

☐ Paragraphs
  - The introductory paragraph(s) should present the essay's motive and thesis.
  - Body paragraphs should usually begin with a claim; support for the claim should fill out the rest of the paragraph. However, if the first sentence makes the topic of the paragraph clear, you can position the claim elsewhere in the paragraph. But avoid burying the claim in a place where it might be overlooked.
  - Where necessary, begin paragraphs with transition words, phrases, or sentences. Think like a reader!
  - Address counterarguments in one or more paragraphs.
  - Vary the length of paragraphs.
  - The concluding paragraph should offer a "send-off."

chapter 6

Organizing the Essay

Thinking Like a Reader

In Chapter 4, we introduced the distinction between the "writerly" and the "readerly." Up to this point, your concerns for the most part have been writerly: you've been concerned chiefly with figuring out what you want to say — with developing ideas and building an argument. Now it's time to shift your focus to the reader's needs. Your reader hopes to be enlightened, informed, stimulated, inspired, perhaps even charmed and entertained. Rather than putting your energy into generating ideas, you now need to think like a reader — to take a step back from your words and adopt the point of view of someone who has no notion of what you want to say or the thinking process that led to it. How will you arrange your thoughts so that you guide the reader along a clear path through your argument, all the while anticipating the reader's questions and providing satisfying replies, and at last bringing the essay to an effective close?

> " It's part of my feeling that what a writer does is to try to make sense of life. I think that's what writing is. . . . It's seeking that thread of order and logic in the disorder, and the incredible waste and marvelous profligate character of life. What all artists are trying to do is to make sense of life. "
>
> **NADINE GORDIMER**

Organization is most apparent to a reader when it is lacking; good organization is transparent. The reader of a well-organized essay simply proceeds steadily through the argument, admiring how one thought flows smoothly and logically into another and how every question seems to be answered as soon as it arises. The sequence of ideas seems natural, inevitable, even obvious. On occasion, writers achieve this sense of easy flow without effort: the order in which the ideas spilled out onto the page turns out to be the right and best order. But most of the time, writers must give careful thought to the best way to arrange ideas and organize paragraphs. They must work hard to make the organization seem natural and inevitable.

No two essays are organized exactly alike, and no simple formula exists for organizing an essay, because if the writer has anything new to say, the essay will be unique. Organization should be organic in the sense that it should suit the particular subject matter, serve the writer's purpose, and meet the needs of the occasion. (The word "organize," from the Greek word *organon*, meaning "a tool of thought," suggests not just an orderly structure but one that suits its purpose.) So organizing an essay requires some craftsmanship; arguments cannot simply be squeezed into a one-size-fits-all mold, such as the five-paragraph essay format you may have learned in high school or middle school. This format may function well as training wheels — for learning basic principles of argument and paragraph structure — but it lacks the necessary flexibility for the more complicated arguments that college instructors expect. Professional scholars and writers do not employ the five-paragraph format because their ideas can almost never be distilled into just three body paragraphs. Every argument must take its own particular shape, filling as many paragraphs as it requires. The number depends on the nature of the argument.

But even though every argument differs, writers can organize essays most effectively when they bear in mind certain principles and keep a few strategies at hand.

Organizing an Argument Essay

A well-crafted essay follows certain basic principles of organization. These are *principles* rather than rules because variations are certainly permissible (and sometimes advisable, as we shall see later). But even when straying from them, be sure to keep these principles in mind.

Keep Your Own Argument in the Foreground

The first principle of essay organization is to keep the argument in the foreground; that is, make the argument clear at the outset and keep it prominent throughout the essay. Here are some techniques (again, these are not rigid rules).

Place a Well-Crafted Thesis Statement Near the Beginning of the Essay — Usually toward the End of the Introduction. This is where readers expect to find the thesis statement, because the purpose of an introductory paragraph (or paragraphs) is usually to explain the essay's purpose and set the stage for the argument that follows. You may state your thesis again, in different words and perhaps in greater detail, at the end of the essay; however, postponing it entirely could be disastrous if it forces your reader to struggle through the entire essay without grasping your purpose.

Place the Topic and the Claim at the Beginning of the Paragraph. (See Chapter 5, pp. 112–13, for a discussion of the placement of topics and claims.) The first one or two sentences tend to govern the paragraph as a whole because readers expect sentences to indicate the paragraph's topic and to contain the claim. If the paragraph ends up being about something unrelated to the first couple of sentences, readers may become confused. Since complex arguments often require complex supporting evidence — data, reasoning, quotations, claims that support other claims, and so on — readers can easily lose sight of the main point while working through all the details. Placing the claim at the beginning of the paragraph (in the first or second sentence) establishes its importance and shows that the matter that follows is its support.

Create Links between Claims and the Thesis. Use key words and phrases that link back to your thesis statement to show how new arguments connect to the essay's main purpose. Do this thoughtfully and creatively, however, to avoid a tiresome repetition of the same words and phrases throughout. To give yourself a variety of terms and phrases to choose from, take a few minutes to list five or six different ways of expressing your main point. These need not be full sentences; you need just a small storehouse of words and phrases for you to draw from as you revise.

For example, a student writer of an essay arguing that human rights should not be extended to the great apes listed the following connected terms and phrases:

- rights, privileges, entitlements, protections
- recognize, enshrine, preserve, respect
- human being, person, animal, nonhuman animal, primate, ape, great ape
- difference, distinction, contrast

In the end, the writer did not use all these words, but having them on hand made it easier to forge varied and appropriate links between claim sentences and the main argument.

Separate Out Claims and Develop Each Argument Fully

An expository essay (one that explains an idea or [...] [...] line of thinking in a systematic and reasonably c[...] the reader to weigh the ideas fairly. It *exposes* t[...] view. A common weakness in such essays is a fail[...] oughly, to spell out the component parts and s[...] problem, of course, is that the writer is already so[...] or she forgets to explain crucial elements in it.) A good argument essay does not merely state the thesis and the main claims; it also provides evidence for the claims, reasons out the argument, and considers its implications. It addresses as many sides of the issue as possible.

Avoid clumping arguments together or passing over key elements so swiftly that one argument hides behind another. When we first begin to organize an argument in our minds, we need to cluster ideas, chiefly to give us a sense of how the pieces fit together into a whole. But after getting a sense of the argument's main parts, we usually need to shift focus to how each of these component parts will become a fully developed **stage** or "chunk" of the essay — a paragraph or a group of paragraphs on closely related topics (sometimes called a **stadium**; the plural is "stadia"). In other words, after ideas have been brought together into clusters, they need to be separated out into individual paragraphs, and each idea needs to be *fully* developed and articulated.

A good argument answers all the relevant questions that a reader may have and doesn't leave the reader thinking, "Well, if claims x and y are true, then I suppose the argument would be valid. But I'm not sure that claims x and y *are* true." Or, to give a more concrete example: "If it's true that frequent testing helps students remember material better, and if remembering material is the point of a good education, then I suppose the author is correct: teachers should give more tests. But I'm not sure that those assumptions are true." It's the writer's job to produce the strongest possible reasons for believing that claims x, y, and all the others are true. This often means analyzing each argument or component of an argument for implied but unstated claims, or for stated but unsupported claims, and working out support for them. For each of the claims we make, we must ask ourselves, "Why do I believe this to be true? What reasons do I have for making this claim?" Often the reason is another claim, which will need to be supported in a whole new paragraph.

Now, some claims are so well established already, so unlikely to be at all contro-versial, that elaborate support and explanation are unnecessary. Other claims may be more controversial, but, having been persuasively argued by another writer, they can be covered by a citation or a footnote without being exhaustively re-argued. But every claim that is essential to the argument needs to be treated fully, in one or more paragraphs.

For example, the sample essay "Human Rights for Apes: A Well-Intentioned Mistake" (p. 171) could conceivably be reduced to this: "Human rights should not be extended to apes and the distinction between apes and humans should be preserved, both in law and in ethics, because although apes may be in many ways similar to

→ Try This   Developing a Claim

Work through the notes, informal writing, argument matrix, and other material that you produced for earlier chapters. Identify one interesting claim of your own, and copy it out at the top of a blank page or word processing document.

Now look through your notes for support for the claim — perhaps a quotation from the text, or evidence of another kind, or your own ideas. List this support under the claim.

Next, generate as much additional support for the claim as you can. You might find other quotations that support it, other evidence, other reasons. Don't be afraid to go a little overboard as you brainstorm; you can always cut out the weaker sup-ports once you have plenty of material. Ultimately, however, the *number* of supports doesn't matter so much as the fact that you have thoroughly considered all the possibilities.

Now develop your material into an argument paragraph. Begin the paragraph with your claim, and explain the support for the claim in the body of the paragraph. Don't simply list the evidence, however; explain as fully as you can how and why each piece of evidence relates to and supports the main claim.

You may find that your paragraph becomes too long and needs to be split in two or even three paragraphs. That's fine. Figure out the best places for a break, and incorporate transitional words or phrases to make it clear that the new paragraphs are still focusing on the claim of the first paragraph.

humans, they lack the cultures and belief systems that make the concept of 'rights' necessary." Such an argument would have the merit of being shorter, but what reason would the reader have for believing the writer's claims? The claims that are being made in this one-sentence version need to be teased out and treated separately, and each must be developed into a sound argument by providing evidence that supports it.

Address the Counterarguments

As we said in Chapter 5 (p. 127), a counterargument is an argument for the *opposing* side or point of view. You should address counterarguments because they will occur to many readers anyway, and so it is prudent to deal with them. The usual readers of student essays are instructors, who are trained to think critically and are in the habit of scrutinizing arguments for their strengths and weaknesses. Often, in fact, they are already deeply familiar with the debate or conversation that you have entered. You are more likely to persuade your readers if you can refute all of the strongest counterarguments or, if not refute them, can at least show that you have considered them and then explain why you believe your own position is stronger.

➔ **Try This** **Addressing Counterarguments**

If you completed an argument paragraph or paragraphs for the previous "Try This" activity, trade your work with a classmate. Read your classmate's argument carefully and list as many questions and counterarguments as you can, even if you find the argument convincing. (Keep in mind that the ultimate purpose of this exercise is to help make the argument stronger, so you are not really attacking the argument.) Explain your counterarguments as fully as possible. Then exchange papers with your classmate. Using your classmate's counterarguments, as well as any others that occur to you, write one or two paragraphs that address and refute two or three of the strongest counterarguments. (You might begin these paragraphs with a phrase such as "Some might argue that . . .")

Some essays devote more space to addressing counterarguments than to presenting the positive side of the argument. This is appropriate when the proposal itself is quite simple and straightforward but when many objections have been voiced against it. For example, an argument in favor of government-funded day care might focus chiefly on the supposed obstacles to it, as there may be general agreement that, if feasible, free day care would be a good thing.

Establish Common Ground with the Reader

In presenting your argument, you don't want to alienate your reader by seeming too aggressive. You are not trying to score points against an adversary; you're trying to win over readers to your way of thinking. Remind your readers of the points on which they probably already agree with you. In this way, you get your readers to consent before you introduce more controversial ideas later on.

In the sample essay "Human Rights for Apes: A Well-Intentioned Mistake" (p. 171), the writer disagrees with those who argue that human rights should be extended to apes but concedes that apes should be considered as having certain rights — animal rights. He makes this concession in the second paragraph, immediately following the thesis statement, in order to put to rest any supposition that he may want to deny any kind of right to apes. In this way, he narrows the scope of his own argument at the outset to the specific question of whether human rights should be extended to apes. And he shows that he is approaching the problem in a fair-minded and reasonable way.

Drafting an Organizational Plan

Clustering and Diagramming

Although at this point you should already have a good sense of your main ideas, you've probably amassed a profusion of notes and informal writing that might seem a little overwhelming. How do you bring order and shape to all these ideas and present them in a way that's clear, economical, and persuasive?

Often, the difficulty is that you've spent so much time arriving at your position that the validity of your argument now seems almost self-evident. You can lose sight of the long road that led to this point. You got here by taking a meandering route through data, questions, arguments, and counterarguments, but your reader has not taken this journey. To the reader, your argument is not at all obvious; in fact, the reader might hold a view of the matter that shares nothing with your own. How, then, can you conceive of your argument as a series of logical steps, a direct path from problem to solution? How will you know where to start and end and how to show the steps that lead to your main argument?

The most practical way to break an argument into steps is to group ideas into clusters. You can then arrange these clusters in a diagram and thereby visualize your whole argument's shape and get a sense of the big picture. As you work, you should be able to see how related ideas can be gathered into groups. The important thing is to begin to see relations among ideas — ways of bringing elements together or separating them.

Diagramming your ideas makes it possible to develop a clear and strong organizational scheme, to keep your main argument in focus throughout your draft, and to concentrate on one element of your argument at a time as you write. It also helps you identify what to keep and what to cut.

If you produced a radial diagram as a reading strategy (see Chapter 3, pp. 81–83), you are already familiar with this technique. You can produce a cluster diagram on your computer or with pencil and paper. Each has advantages and disadvantages, though the computer usually gives a tidier final product. (Nothing is simpler than clustering ideas and drawing diagrams with a pencil, but moving clusters around and making revisions means erasing and rewriting, which can get messy and tedious.) Most word processing programs will let you create a cluster diagram. While it might take some time to learn all the program's tools and commands, you will be able to rearrange and revise to your heart's content. (See p. 158 for guidelines for creating cluster diagrams on a computer.) If you're working on a long essay involving a complex argument, consider using a pencil initially and moving to the computer later.

There are no firm rules for this kind of work; in fact, playing with your ideas and experimenting with different arrangements and clusterings is part of the point. But a good way to get started is to write out your thesis statement in the center of the page. Arrange main topics at some distance from the center so that you have plenty of room for other notes. Use a brief phrase to note each main point below each topic heading. (You may find that some headings end up with very few notes. That's fine. It doesn't necessarily mean the topic is weak or unimportant.)

> **→ Guidelines**   **Creating Cluster Diagrams on a Computer**
>
> **Using Microsoft Word to Create a Cluster Diagram** Different versions of Word
> have slightly different icons, but the method of drawing diagrams is similar. With a
> little trial and error, you will become proficient.
>
> - Use the "Insert" tab and click on "Text Box." Clicking on the icons allows you to
>   draw rectangles and other shapes and to join them with lines or arrows.
> - Resize a text box or shape by dragging one of its "handles."
> - Double-click on a shape to change the "fill" color (for example, from blue to
>   white).
> - Click on the text-box icon and position the cursor within a shape in order to type
>   words inside it.
>
> **Using Apple's Pages to Create a Cluster Diagram**
>
> - Click on the "Shapes" icon to draw rectangles, circles, arrows, and other
>   shapes.
> - Click on the "Text Box" icon to create a space for typing text. You can move the
>   text anywhere on the page by dragging it.
> - Resize a text box or shape by dragging one of its "handles."
> - You can group items, such as a text box and a shape, so that they can easily be
>   moved together. Use shift-click to select multiple items. Then use the "Group"
>   command in the "Arrange" menu.
> - You can place an item behind or in front of another item by selecting it and
>   choosing the appropriate command from the "Arrange" menu.
> - You can fix items onto a specific location on the page by choosing the "Lock"
>   command.

At first, simply focus on clustering, on gathering up the main points that each topic, or component of your argument, requires. Your cluster diagram might look something like Figure 6.1.

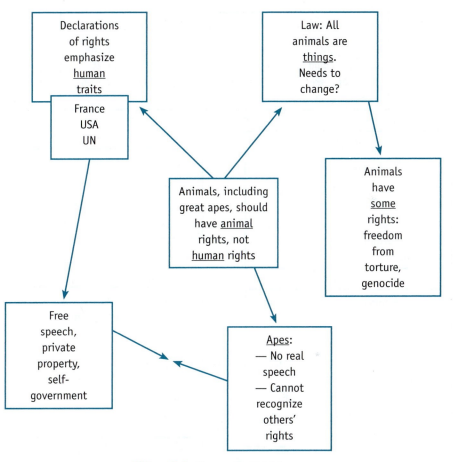

Figure 6.1 **Cluster Radial Diagram**

Once you've got most of the main components on the page, you can begin arranging the clusters. Now you can move the thesis statement to the top of the page and can refine and arrange the arguments in a logical order below it, as in Figure 6.2 (see p. 160).

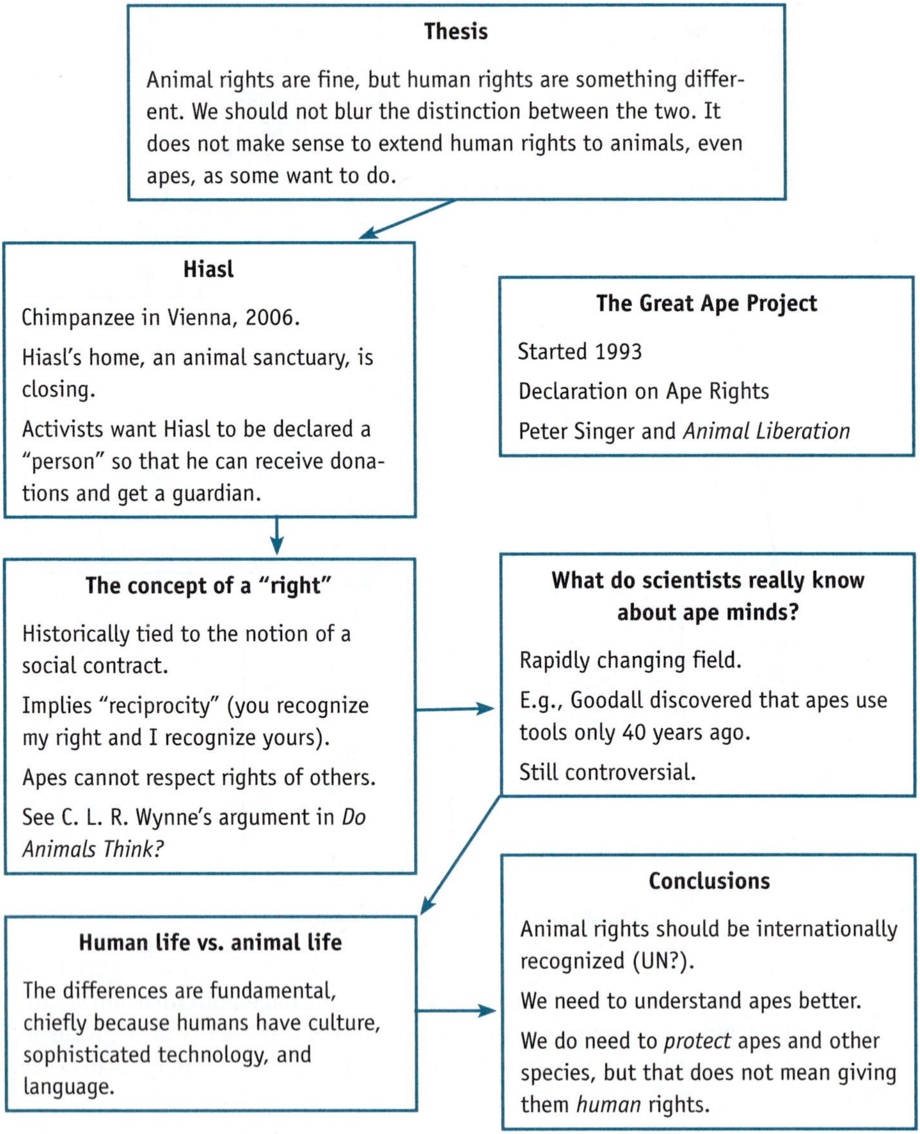

Thesis

Animal rights are fine, but human rights are something different. We should not blur the distinction between the two. It does not make sense to extend human rights to animals, even apes, as some want to do.

Hiasl

Chimpanzee in Vienna, 2006.

Hiasl's home, an animal sanctuary, is closing.

Activists want Hiasl to be declared a "person" so that he can receive donations and get a guardian.

The Great Ape Project

Started 1993

Declaration on Ape Rights

Peter Singer and *Animal Liberation*

The concept of a "right"

Historically tied to the notion of a social contract.

Implies "reciprocity" (you recognize my right and I recognize yours).

Apes cannot respect rights of others.

See C. L. R. Wynne's argument in *Do Animals Think?*

What do scientists really know about ape minds?

Rapidly changing field.

E.g., Goodall discovered that apes use tools only 40 years ago.

Still controversial.

Human life vs. animal life

The differences are fundamental, chiefly because humans have culture, sophisticated technology, and language.

Conclusions

Animal rights should be internationally recognized (UN?).

We need to understand apes better.

We do need to *protect* apes and other species, but that does not mean giving them *human* rights.

Figure 6.2 Cluster Diagram Revised into Logical Order

Revising Organization: Constructing a Sentence Outline

Now that you have diagrammed the components of your argument, you are in a position to develop an outline. We have deliberately left a discussion of outlining until after you have developed an argument, even if only a rudimentary one. An outline is a revision tool, one that helps you arrange or rearrange ideas that already exist. If you use an outline too soon, it easily becomes a straitjacket: it inhibits your thinking and shuts out good ideas that haven't yet occurred to you. You need to have material for your argument before you can begin to arrange that material.

You can begin organizing your argument with a very simple outline — little more than your thesis, your motive, one or two claims, and perhaps a note about the evidence that supports these claims. At first, forget about the sequence of ideas as you already have them in your notes and informal writing. Start fresh, and think about the clearest and simplest way to arrange your ideas for others to get their gist. For this purpose, it helps to put into words the **nucleus** or essence of your argument in the form of two or three propositions that explain its basic reasoning (for example, "I think [my thesis] is valid because . . ."). This will help you begin a basic outline. The important thing is to use *full sentences* in the outline, and not merely words or brief phrases that represent topics. An argument is composed not of a string of topics but of ideas that have a logical relationship to one another. Only full sentences can represent your ideas and their relationships.

In your draft, lines in the outline can be fleshed out as paragraphs; paragraphs you have already drafted can be summarized in the outline as one sentence (often one claim). Paragraphs are the building blocks of the essay, and organizing is largely a matter of arranging paragraphs in an order that makes good sense.

A sentence outline can clarify your sense of the overall shape of the argument and of what each paragraph in the essay needs to do. Even after your outline becomes more complete, however, expect to revise it as your essay evolves. Paragraphs may cease to correspond neatly to the outline. One paragraph might grow to the point where it needs to become two, or unexpectedly a certain paragraph might work better if placed earlier in the essay. This is just as it should be, part of the adventure of the writing process: the organization of an essay changes as it develops. Your outline and your draft will complement each other and take on a reciprocal relationship, each changing to reflect changes in the other. But as the complete essay takes shape as paragraphs rather than outline notes, your gauge for making judgments about organization will begin to shift away from the outline and toward an imagined reader — "the reader over your shoulder." In the end, you must focus your attention on the experience a reader will have in reading the essay through from beginning to end without the benefit of an outline.

Work Out the Nucleus of Your Argument

To begin, you need to have a reasonably clear sense of your argument's general shape — not yet paragraph by paragraph, but in larger chunks or stages. You can clarify your sense of the main stages by writing out a two- or three-sentence summary of the argument you want to make in support of your thesis. (This summary is not the same thing as the thesis statement itself: rather than being the main point your essay will make, the summary lists the *reasons* that your point is valid.) This nucleus will help you see the logical structure of your argument more clearly. Every argument will differ, of course, but to speak in the most general terms, the nucleus will probably take a form something like this: "If you understand this, then you'll see this next thing. And if you understand that, then surely you'll agree that my thesis is valid." Or "Here's a true story. Here's the lesson I take from the story. If this lesson is valid, it suggests that x [a commonly held belief] may not always be true after all." Or "Because x seems to be true, it follows that y is probably true too. And there's good evidence for z as well. If both y and z are true, then, as you see, my thesis is probably valid. Now, some may say y and z are false, but their arguments are flawed because a, b, and c."

A summary statement includes several stages, and if we separate them out, we have the beginnings of an outline. Each stage might require several paragraphs in the finished essay. (The number of paragraphs assigned to each stage here is just for the purpose of illustration; the actual number would depend on the nature of the particular argument.) Figure 6.3 shows one possible arrangement and paragraph count for the body of an essay.

The model in Figure 6.3 tells us that the body of this essay might require seven paragraphs. (With an introductory paragraph and a concluding paragraph, the complete essay might have nine paragraphs.) But as your writing moves along, you may realize that your summary statement has too few or too many paragraphs. No problem: the outline is not meant to imprison you; its purpose is to help you think like a reader and transform writerly drafting into a readerly finished product.

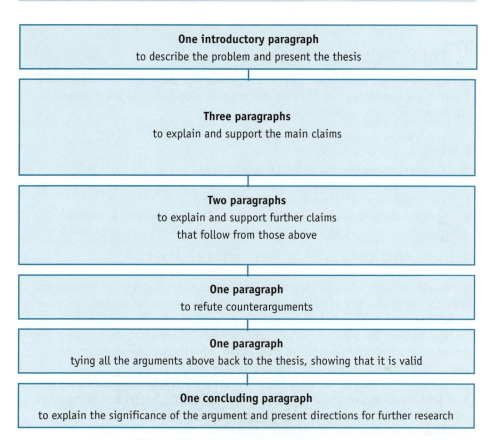

Figure 6.3 Model of a Summary Statement

If you can write out the logic of your argument in two or three sentences, you can usually see its general shape and get a rough sense of how it will need to be organized. You can see what the stages of the argument are and begin to work out what points must be made in order to establish each stage. These points are the claims that make up the skeleton of your argument. Typically, each claim that needs to be argued will require a separate paragraph. Some claims, however, need very little argument, either because they are common knowledge or because a reliable authority has already demonstrated their validity; in such cases, all you need to do is to cite

➡️ **Try** **This** **Sketching an Argument**

You can easily try sketching an argument's logical structure by experimenting with an issue that is already familiar. For example, you may already have a point of view regarding one of the following issues:

- Should capital punishment be banned?
- Should marijuana be legalized?
- Should soft drinks be banned from public schools? ˙
- Should sex education be taught in grade schools?
- Should cigarettes be banned?
- Should the drinking age throughout the United States be lowered to eighteen?
- Should the United States adopt a four-day workweek to reduce unemployment?

Or you can select another issue on which you have a clear opinion.

First write out your position (for example, "I believe that capital punishment should not be banned"). Then add the word "because" and list the two or three main reasons why you believe in this stand. Consider what a reader would need to understand in order to be persuaded. This will be the nucleus of your argument.

Now consider the arguments that might be made in opposition to your views and the questions that might be raised. Write some notes on how you would answer or refute these questions and counterarguments.

Now create an outline similar to the model in Figure 6.3, but incorporate your content: your thesis and your main arguments, as well as your response to counterarguments. The outline should not contain all the details or all the supporting evidence, but it should illustrate the logical structure of the argument you envision.

the source. Claims that need little or no argument can usually be folded into other paragraphs.

Get Started with a Basic Sentence Outline

At this point, you are ready to construct a simple outline composed of complete sentences. You should have a clear sense of your motive (the problem or question you are working on), your thesis, and two or three of the main reasons that your thesis is valid.

You can construct this outline on paper, especially if you begin by leaving lots of space between each of the lines. But it's easier to do it on a computer, where you can move lines of text around without having to erase or cross out. Here's how to create a basic sentence outline, along with a few software tips.

- Begin by stating the *problem* that your argument addresses in one or two sentences at the top of the outline. (The wording need not be perfect; get the idea down.)

- Underneath it, write out your working thesis statement. If you're working on a computer, give both the problem and the thesis statement a "heading 1" format.

- Refer to your nucleus to identify the main stages or sections of your argument. Write these out as complete sentences. Indent them one-half inch from the thesis and motive statements. (Or format them as "heading 2.")

- Try to identify two or three of the claims that each stage requires. If you're not there yet, work with the claims that you believe are important for your argument. Indent them one-half inch from the statements of stages. (Or format them as "heading 3.")

- Where possible, briefly explain the evidence or reasoning that supports each of these claims. In each case, use one or two complete sentences. Indent these sentences one-half inch from the statements of claims. (Or format them as "heading 4.")

Be sure to use complete sentences throughout, not words or short phrases that merely represent topics or stand for complex ideas. The purpose of this outline is to represent and clarify the logical structure of your argument — the relationships between ideas — not merely to list a series of subjects to discuss. A mere series of topics — one thing after another, with no logical or meaningful development — is really no organization at all.

Here is an example of the initial, basic sentence outline Marc Dumas created for the paper that he eventually titled "Human Rights for Apes: A Well-Intentioned Mistake" (p. 171).

Sample Basic Sentence Outline

Problem: The problem is the controversy over the rights of great apes. Scientists and others in the Great Ape Project argue that the great apes are biologically, intellectually, and socially so much like humans that they should have human rights — and that they need them.

Working Thesis: Chimps and other great apes should not be given the same rights as humans.

   I. The concept of "human rights" is linked to *human* qualities and to *human* society.
      A. For example, free speech and private property are rights that apes cannot exercise.
      B. See Declaration of the Rights of Man and of the Citizen (France) and American Bill of Rights (USA).
      C. See Universal Declaration of Human Rights (UN).
  II. Apes cannot recognize human rights — or even ape rights — so recognizing rights is a one-way street.
      A. Apes can't sit on juries or recognize others' rights or even understand what it means to have a "right" for themselves.
      B. See Clive Wynne, page 226: rights must be "reciprocal."
 III. If we lumped together ape rights and human rights, we would have to limit human rights severely.
  IV. So we should be *protecting* apes rather than creating controversies based on things we can't know about their minds and their feelings.
      A. We don't know much about what apes want, because we cannot really communicate with them.
      B. Maybe the Great Ape Project is a publicity stunt?

Revise the Outline

At this point, you can begin arranging, or rearranging, paragraphs in your draft, or you can continue to flesh out the outline, adding further claims and support for the claims.

Continue working through your diagram, notes, and informal writing to gather up your material, distinguishing claims from supporting evidence and arranging the

> **→ Guidelines**   ## Constructing an Outline
>
> ### Using Word's Numbering Feature to Construct an Outline
> In Microsoft Word, go to the "Format" menu and choose "Bullets and Numbering." Then click the "Outline Numbered" tab. Each line you type will appear with a number or letter to identify its position. To move an item up or down a level, click the icons on the toolbar or formatting palette that decrease or increase the indent.
>
> ### Using Apple's Pages to Construct a Sentence Outline
> To begin a sentence outline in Apple's Pages, choose "New from Template Chooser" in the "File" menu. Then, in the chooser window, click "Outlines" under the "Word Processing" heading in the menu on the left. For a sentence outline, select either the "Harvard outline" or the "Research outline." (The others can be adapted but are less suitable for outlining an argument.) You can then fill in the template's language with your own content.

material within stages in your outline. Move toward an outline that lays out the argument claim by claim.

While you are doing this, you may find that your list of claims changes as you find material that doesn't quite belong with any of the claims you've already listed. This is normal — and part of the recursive or looping nature of the writing process. Each new step tends to require revisions to earlier work, but with each revision the work becomes stronger. The important thing at this stage, as you group supporting material under claims, is to keep claims in the foreground as headings.

Look for Relationships That Suggest an Organizational Plan

Many arguments can be organized in only one way, because certain ideas cannot be introduced until others have been well established. In such cases, the organization of ideas is at least partly dictated by logic and must move from a premise to a conclusion — that is, from an idea that has to be established first (a premise) to an idea that follows from it (a conclusion).

For example, imagine an argument that same-sex couples in America should have the right to marry. First, the writer might argue that there is strong evidence that homosexuality is not typically a choice but is biologically determined or in some other way "hardwired." If this is true, then America includes citizens who are by nature homosexual, citizens who pay taxes and fulfill the other obligations of citizenship. Now (the argument might run) if same-sex marriage does no harm to others, then homosexuals should enjoy the same right to marry as heterosexuals, since to deny this right would be an arbitrary injustice against a subset of the state's own citizens. Arguments like this proceed according to a logical order: if x is true, then y is true, and if y is true, then z must follow.

But you may find that not every element in the argument falls into place according to a strict and necessary logic. Here are some alternative arrangements.

- *Weaker-to-stronger order.* Sometimes, an effective strategy is to proceed from weaker arguments to stronger ones, so that readers feel increasingly persuaded as they read (rather than increasingly doubtful). The weaker-to-stronger arrangement works when you can support a thesis with several distinct arguments, each of which is independent of the others, so that you can sequence them in order of strength.

- *Chronological or narrative order.* When you are discussing events, historical or fictional, it often works best to discuss them in the order of occurrence.

- *Arrangement by theme or type.* Arguments may be grouped by type. For example, arguments that rely on surveys or statistical evidence might be grouped together, and arguments that rely on deductive reasoning might be grouped together. Similarly, arguments that have in common a theme or scholarly discipline may be grouped together. For example, in an essay arguing that the electoral college should be abolished, it might make sense to keep all the arguments from history together and then move on to arguments based on political philosophy.

Organizing a Long Essay

In a long essay (more than about eight pages) involving a complicated argument, you may identify stages within stages, and each substage might involve several points. To keep it all under control, you might want to divide the essay into sections. You might even write a separate nucleus and a separate outline for each section. Each section can be numbered or given a subtitle, or both. You may choose not to keep the section breaks in the final essay, but working with sections of a manageable length at this stage will make it easier to organize them.

> **→ Guidelines**   ## Outlining with a Computer
>
> If you're writing a long essay in Microsoft Word, you can use the "Document Map" feature in the Navigation Pane as an additional outlining tool. This works only if you have used headings in your document and styled them as headings. To do this:
>
> - First make the formatting toolbar visible. (Choose "Formatting" from the "Toolbars" submenu under the "View" menu.)
> - Then click in a heading and choose a heading style for it from the drop-down menu on the left of the formatting toolbar.

Marc Dumas worked on his basic outline, enlarging it and adding further claims and support for them. Here is his revised outline.

Revised Sample Sentence Outline

Thesis: The distinction between the rights of animals and those of humans ought to be preserved, both in ethics and in law.

    I. But legislative bodies should recognize certain *animal* rights.

      A. Under Austrian law Hiasl is considered a "thing."

      B. No third category exists for animals.

      C. But it does not follow that he should be made legally a human. Instead, the law should recognize a distinct category for animals.

    II. The concept of "human rights" is linked to distinctly human qualities and to uniquely human society.

    III. Declaration of the Rights of Man and of the Citizen (France, 1789) emphasizes right to *free speech* and *private property*.

      A. So does American Bill of Rights (USA, 1791).

      B. Universal Declaration of Human Rights (1948)?

      C. These rights are not relevant to apes.

    IV. Only an understanding of differences between cultures and histories makes it possible or necessary to recognize "universal" human rights.

      A. Apes lack this understanding.

V. Recognizing ape rights can go in only one direction — apes cannot recognize human rights, or even ape rights.
    A. See Clive Wynne, page 226 quotation: rights must be reciprocal.
    B. Apes can't sit on juries or recognize others' rights or even understand what it means to have a "right" for themselves.
    C. Extending rights to apes might mean we would have to dilute or restrict human rights.

VI. We should be protecting apes rather than creating controversies based on things we can't know about their minds and their feelings.
    A. We don't know much about what apes want because we cannot really communicate with them.
    B. Acquisition of language is still controversial.
       See Donald Griffin, *Animal Minds*.

VII. **Counterargument:** Great Ape Project says apes' inability to defend their own rights is not a real problem: children and disabled humans need guardians too (p. 5).
    A. But apes don't have human family members to speak for them.
    B. And children and some disabled do not have the same rights (e.g., voting) as others.

VIII. **Closing paragraph:** We need a Universal Declaration of Animal Rights.

Organizing an Argument Essay: A Basic Model

The following student essay by Marc Dumas, "Human Rights for Apes: A Well-Intentioned Mistake," is based on the outline above. It offers a basic model of essay organization. As you might expect, it begins with a one-paragraph introduction that includes a thesis statement. Seven body paragraphs follow, each presenting a distinct argument in support of the thesis. The second paragraph establishes common ground by conceding a point, and the sixth paragraph rebuts a counterargument. The essay ends with a concluding paragraph that suggests some directions for further research and reaffirms the writer's position. As we will see, this structure may be too simple to serve all purposes, but it does provide a starting point for further discussion and exemplifies several principles of good organization. (This essay is in MLA format. See Chapter 10 for details about formatting conventions.)

Marc Dumas

Professor Taylor

Composition 101

9 November 2012

Human Rights for Apes:

A Well-Intentioned Mistake

Uses recent news item to show problem vividly and poses a question.

Recently, animal rights advocates in Vienna, Austria, went to court to ask a judge to declare that a chimpanzee named Hiasl (pronounced "heezle") is a "person" ("How to Protect"). To some, their case might sound frivolous, but for at least two decades a group of influential scientists and philosophers has been waging an international campaign to extend human rights to the great apes (chimpanzees, orangutans, and gorillas). The great apes certainly do face dire threats, and recent genetic research has shown just how closely related they are to human beings. But does it therefore follow that *human* rights ought to be extended to a species of nonhuman animal or that this step can be taken without fundamentally changing the very meaning of human rights? I

Thesis statement declares writer's response to the question.

would argue that, while it makes good sense to recognize that higher animals should have "rights" of some kind, we should preserve a clear distinction, in law and in ethics, between the rights of animals and those of humans.

First sentence states claim, concedes that some animal rights should be recognized. Reference to Hiasl establishes link to previous paragraph. Rest of paragraph provides support (facts, reasoning, expert opinion).

The case of Hiasl does demonstrate the need for legislative bodies to recognize certain *animal* rights. The chimpanzee's caretakers went to court because the animal sanctuary where he lived for twenty-five years was bankrupt, and Hiasl would soon be homeless. Caring for a chimpanzee is expensive (food, medical bills, and housing cost about US$6,800 a month), and Hiasl's supporters argue that the

Dumas 2

chimp's best hope is to be allowed to receive donations from the public and to be awarded a legal guardian ("How to Protect"). The problem is that Austrian law permits only "persons" to receive personal donations or be adopted. In law, a chimp is merely a "thing"; no third category exists for animals. Hiasl's supporters argue that seeking the status of "person" for Hiasl is their only option ("How to Protect"). However, if Austrian law were not so restrictive, this recourse would not be necessary. It does not follow that Hiasl and every other great ape should be placed in the legal category of human persons. As Rutgers University law professor Gary Francione argues, it would make better sense to recognize animal rights, in particular the right *not* to be treated as a thing, as a distinct category (24).

New claim introduces new argument. Reference to differences between apes and humans establishes link to previous argument. Claim supported by reasoning.

True, animal behaviorists have shown that apes have rich and complex social and emotional lives. Nevertheless, fundamental differences between apes and humans make it inappropriate to grant both species the same rights. Humans live out their lives within cultures and societies characterized by particular belief systems. The differences among these belief systems are what makes a concept of universal "human rights" — a kind of minimum entitlement for every human being — necessary. Similarly, it is only an understanding of a world beyond immediate experience, and a sense of history — both of which are unique to humans — that make it possible to recognize and respect the rights of others.

New claim introduces new argument. Reference to human rights establishes link to previous argument. Claim supported by historical fact, reasoning, expert opinion.

Historically, the notion of human rights has been closely linked to distinctly human qualities and to uniquely human society. It was first worked out during the eighteenth century in Europe. Chief among the rights mentioned by the Declaration of the Rights of Man (1789), issued during the French

Dumas 3

Revolution, and the U.S. Bill of Rights (1791) are the rights to free speech and property — neither of which is relevant to apes. More recently, the Universal Declaration of Human Rights, adopted by the United Nations in 1948, was never intended for nonhuman animals, and Article 1 specifically notes that human beings are "endowed with reason and conscience" — qualities that, as Charles Habib Malik, one of the drafters of the Declaration, commented, "distinguish them from animals" (qtd. in Morsink 298).

New claim introduces new argument. Reference to intellectual capacity of apes establishes link to previous argument. Claim supported by expert opinion (in citations).

In order to apply human rights to animals, we would have to pick and choose the few that are relevant to them. This is what the Great Ape Project has done, identifying specifically the right to life, freedom from slavery, and freedom from torture (4). But even these selected rights can apply in only one direction: we could never expect apes to recognize the rights of humans or even of other apes. Animal behaviorist Clive D. L. Wynne argues that rights, to be meaningful, must be reciprocal:

> As my right to swing my arm stops at my neighbor's nose, so rights in general imply responsibilities. And responsibilities demand comprehension: a defendant must be able to understand what they have been charged with. To express one's rights and accept one's responsibilities one needs a comprehension of others' motivations. . . . (226)

No expert has claimed that any of the great apes except *homo sapiens* is capable of such comprehension.

Background introduces new claim (third sentence) and counterargument (fourth sentence). Rest of paragraph rebuts it (facts, reasoning, expert opinion) to support claim.

We do not really know what any animal, including apes, wants and needs. In the decades since Jane Goodall studied the chimpanzees of Tanzania, our understanding of apes has been improving rapidly, yet primatologists still

Dumas 4

disagree about whether apes are capable of reason, whether they have a true sense of self, and to what degree their emotional and social lives resemble humans'. The root of the problem is that we cannot communicate with apes to understand their way of understanding of the world, except in the most limited ways. Apes can be trained to use words as symbols for things; perhaps some apes have even learned to use a simple form of grammar by combining three or four signs in American Sign Language — but this too remains controversial. As Donald Griffin notes, many scientists who have been studying the evidence carefully for years remain unconvinced that apes are using language at all: "Terrace and others have concluded that signing apes are not using anything that deserves to be called a language, because of the almost total lack of rule-governed combinations of signs" (223). And of course, only apes trained in captivity acquire signing skills. No ape uses language as humans do, to communicate with others of their species about any number of topics. Only a handful of apes have ever learned to use even a hundred signs (Griffin 232).

New claim, supported by reasoning. Reference to legal rights establishes link to thesis.

Our aim should be to protect apes, not to assume more than we really know about their needs and desires or to blur the profound differences between apes and humans. So by extending human rights to apes, we risk diluting and weakening the meaning of those rights. No animal can participate in the rule of law, or participate in the protection of the rights of others, or even understand what it means to have a legal right themselves. Does this mean, then, that those who cannot or will not respect the rights of others can expect to have their own rights respected?

Dumas 5

Introduces another counterargument. Reference to legal person status establishes link to previous paragraph and thesis. Rest of paragraph rebuts counterargument (facts, expert opinion, reasoning).

The argument that a chimpanzee ought to be given the same basic rights as humans and deserves to be considered a legal "person" has been developed in detail by the Great Ape Project, the brainchild of philosophers Paola Cavalieri and Peter Singer. The project is supported by a number of respected biologists, psychologists, and ethologists. According to the organization's "Declaration on the Great Apes," the fact that apes cannot defend their own interests is not a serious problem. The Great Ape Project argues that "human guardians should safeguard [apes'] interests and rights, in the same way as the interests of the young or intellectually disabled members of our own species are safeguarded" (5). But the young and intellectually disabled have parents or other family members who can speak for them and typically make decisions about their interests. And in fact, we *do* limit the rights of the young and the intellectually disabled, as appropriate to their particular capacities. Small children have very few rights as individuals, as do nonverbal mentally handicapped adults (Singer 55).

Conclusion restates thesis, adds detail, identifies directions for further research.

Hiasl was denied a legal guardian and ended up at the Vienna Animal Protection Center (Stafford). Whatever Hiasl's ultimate fate, however, his case illustrates the problem that societies face when human rights are enshrined in law but no provisions are made for animal rights. This is the case in the United States today. We need to do more to protect ape habitats and defend them from attack, but I believe that the United Nations should compose a Universal Declaration of Animal Rights. Such a declaration might encourage all countries to spare not only the great apes from suffering and indignity but all species of animals.

Dumas 6

Works Cited

Francione, Gary L. "One Right for All." *New Scientist* 8 Oct. 2005:
    24. Print.

Great Ape Project. "A Declaration on Great Apes." *The Great Ape
    Project: Equality beyond Humanity.* Ed. Paola Cavalieri and
    Peter Singer. New York: Griffin-St. Martin's, 1993. 4-8. Print.

Griffin, Donald. *Animal Minds.* Chicago: U of Chicago P, 1992.
    Print.

"How to Protect Ape's Rights? Make Him a Person." *MSNBC.com.*
    MSNBC Digital Network, 5 Apr. 2007. Web. 17 Oct. 2012.

Morsink, Johannes. *The Universal Declaration of Human Rights:
    Origins, Drafting, and Intent.* Philadelphia: U of
    Pennsylvania P, 1999. Print.

Singer, Peter. *Animal Liberation.* 3rd ed. New York: Ecco-
    Harper, 2002. Print.

Stafford, Ned. "Chimp Denied a Legal Guardian." *Nature.com.*
    Nature Publishing Group, 26 Apr. 2007. Web. 15 Oct. 2012.

United Nations. Gen. Assembly. Universal Declaration of Human
    Rights. *UN.org.* United Nations, 2011. Web. 15 Oct. 2012.

Wynne, Clive D. L. *Do Animals Think?* Princeton: Princeton UP,
    2004. Print.

Organizing an Argument Essay: A Second Example

As we noted earlier, there are many ways to organize an argument essay, and no single method can work for every argument. To follow one model every time you wrote an essay would quickly become limiting. In order to understand better the general principles that underlie the organization of argument essays, even sophisticated ones, we can see how they work in a second student paper. This paper, by

Wendy Sung, includes paragraphs with greater structural variety than those we saw in the paper by Marc Dumas. (This essay is in MLA format.)

Wendy Sung

Professor Scott

Composition 101

2 April 2012

A Campaign for the Dignity of the Great Apes

Introduction is two paragraphs.

René Descartes (1596-1650), often called the father of modern philosophy, believed that animals are "natural automota" — thoughtless and soulless machines (285). In many ways, modern science held to this view even after Charles Darwin showed that *homo sapiens* evolved from primates and after the close similarity of ape and human brain structures and DNA became known. More recently, scientists have learned, both through observation and through direct communication in sign language, that the great apes (chimpanzees, bonobos, gorillas, and orangutans) have rich emotional and even intellectual lives and that they not only sense pain but can suffer in more profound ways as well, experiencing complex emotions such as grief, loneliness, and disappointment. In 1993, two philosophers, Paola Cavalieri and Peter Singer, inaugurated the Great Ape Project, a campaign to secure for great apes fundamental rights that have traditionally belonged only to humans. These rights include the right to life, the protection of individual liberty, and the prohibition of torture, rights that reflect the basic sameness of human and ape needs (Great Ape Project 4).

Sung 2

All the great apes are endangered. Although exact numbers are hard to estimate, great ape populations have declined rapidly in the last two decades, because of hunting, loss of habitat, and diseases such as SIV[1] and Ebola; most experts predict that the great apes will be extinct in fifty to a hundred years (Bowman; "Species Fact Sheet" 1). Yet despite this risk, and all that we now know about their impressive mental and emotional capacities, apes continue to be used in traumatizing laboratory experiments and to be hunted for meat. America's Animal Welfare Act provides little protection for apes used in research, and none for apes in their natural habitats overseas. Nonprofit organizations such as the World Wildlife Fund, the Jane Goodall Institute, and Save the Chimps are doing what they can with limited funds and powers. But laws are needed that recognize the dignity of the great apes, guarantee their fundamental rights, and prohibit their use in experimental research. Legislation can also provide the means to preserve ape habitats and to help end the hunting of apes for meat, and perhaps can turn the tide in the battle to save apes from extinction.

Thesis: laws are needed to protect apes.

Fifty years ago, chimpanzees in Africa numbered in the millions. Today only about 200,000 remain ("Chimp Facts"). Their habitats are disappearing as the expanding human population turns forest into farmland, and chimpanzees (and their close relatives, bonobos) continue to be hunted both for meat and so that infants can be taken for the live animal trade

---

[1] Simian immunodeficiency virus: Although strains of this virus do not usually cause AIDS in the natural host, they may do so when they cross to another species.

Sung 3

Table 1 Population, Status, and Habitat of Great Apes

Species	Chimpanzees	Bonobos	Gorillas	Orangutans
Estimated population	172,700 to 299,700	5,000 to 60,000	Western gorilla: 100,000 Eastern gorilla: 700	Borneo: 55,000 Sumatra: 7,500
International Union for Conservation of Nature (IUCN) status	Endangered	Endangered	Endangered	Endangered to critically endangered
Location	Central and western Africa	Central Africa	Central Africa	Borneo and Sumatra (Asia)

Source: Data from "Species Fact Sheet: African Great Apes"; photos from Getty Images.

(Goodall 207). Much of the slaughter would be unnecessary were it not for local economic factors: hunters are driven to killing apes because other sources of income have disappeared. Social scientist Kerry Bowman's interviews with bushmeat hunters reveal that most of them would accept other employment if it were made available. "All stated they are looking for economic alternatives," he reports.

Statement of fact leading to claim.

Of the roughly 2,400 chimpanzees in the United States, the vast majority — about 1,700 — are being used for

Sung 4

biomedical testing. Only about 500 live in sanctuaries. About 700 are held captive in zoos or used by the entertainment industry ("Chimp Facts"). Although the Animal Welfare Act was intended to protect captive animals from abuse, researchers are exempt from its regulations. Animals used in laboratory experiments often suffer horribly after being infected with diseases or poisoned with toxins ("Animal Testing"). This situation persists because we assume that human suffering is more real than ape suffering, and science still treats apes as objects to be used rather than intelligent fellow creatures.

Paragraph begins with a claim.

The cosmetic industry has found alternatives to the use of animals for research, and medical research can do the same. Most — perhaps all — lab research involving apes is unnecessary or even counterproductive, since therapies that work in one species often do not work in another (Singer 89). According to People for the Ethical Treatment of Animals (PETA), 92% of drugs that pass animal tests fail when tested on human beings ("Animal Testing"). The genetic differences between apes and humans mean that clinical trials involving chimpanzees are often of little value. As Peter Singer shows in *Animal Liberation,* experiments that cause animals to suffer are frequently performed but rarely produce new knowledge. Most aim only to confirm the results of earlier research or to repeat an experiment with some minor variation (52-60).

Counterargument is addressed.

Some argue that animals do not have enough understanding of their circumstances to *suffer* in the sense that humans do. But apes almost certainly can suffer. They recall what has been done to them in the past, and they

Sung 5

can fear what may happen in the future (Byrne 115). Over the last three decades, scientists have come to understand a good deal about the minds of apes, in particular by communicating with apes that have learned to use human sign languages such as American Sign Language, or ASL. Apes can be taught to communicate not only with humans but also with each other; they have even attempted to teach one another signs in some instances. While many of their signs focus on immediate needs, apes also converse about social interactions, emotions, private thoughts, and memories (Fouts and Fouts 32). While chimpanzees and bonobos are known to be the most intelligent of the great apes and the ones most closely related to human beings, other great apes are nearer humans in intellectual capacity than we used to think. Psychologist Francine Patterson has tested the IQ of the gorilla Koko repeatedly, using five different tests over the space of five years, and found that his IQ score averaged 80.3 (Patterson and Gordon 61), roughly equivalent to that of a typical four-year-old human. Not only do apes demonstrate self-awareness and have long memories, but they can also anticipate future events. As Richard Byrne writes: "In almost every case, the evidence — though not always conclusive — has pointed to one group of primates, the great apes, as having some ability to imagine future possible states of affairs" (122).

Claim is implied: if humans of low intelligence cannot be killed, neither should apes.

Most people would consider it immoral to deny basic rights to human beings with low intelligence or limited language skills. Modern societies do not consider it acceptable to murder them or use them in medical experiments or use them in any way as the means to an end, no matter how great

Sung 6

the rewards of that end might be. Neither intelligence nor the ability to speak is considered necessary for being included in the "human race" and enjoying human rights. If any faculty is considered necessary, it is the ability to feel and to suffer. Only when a person becomes "brain dead" — permanently incapable of thought or feeling — do we take away life support. But researchers no longer doubt that chimpanzees and other apes are clearly able to think, feel, and experience a range and depth of emotion not very different from that of *homo sapiens*.

This paragraph has an exploratory structure. It includes questions at the start and near the end.

Granted, human beings are different from other animal beings — we build cities, create works of art, send vehicles to Mars, and worry about our fashion sense — but does it make sense any longer to draw one rigid line dividing the human animal from all others? We humans are biologically even closer to chimpanzees than chimpanzees are to orangutans. We share with chimpanzees more than 98% of our DNA. We also share a common ancestor who lived about six million years ago. Richard Dawkins has shown how relatively short a time this is, in evolutionary terms: if parents and children were to hold hands and form a chain representing all the generations between us today and this common ancestor, the chain would stretch less than 300 miles (84). Humans can accept blood transfusions and even organ transplants from chimpanzees (Teleki 298). How can we treat them and other great apes as "just animals" — with the same moral status as the chicken we eat for dinner? I suspect that more of us would understand our special kinship with apes if we could observe them in the wild. Biologist Geza Teleki writes movingly about such an experience in the forests of Gombe, Tanzania:

> As I sat alone on the crest of a grassy ridge watching
> a spectacular yet common sunset over the silvery

waters of Lake Tanganyika in wonderful solitude and silence, I suddenly noticed two adult male chimpanzees climbing toward me on opposite slopes. They saw one another only as they topped the crest, just yards from my seat beneath a tree, whereupon both suddenly stood upright and swiftly advanced as bipeds through waist-high grass to stand close together, face to face, each extending his right hand to clasp and vigorously shake the other's while softly panting, heads bobbing. Moments later they sat down nearby and we three watched the sunset enfold the park. When dusk fell my two companions went off to build platform nests high in the trees of the valley. Nevermore, I realized as I hastened homeward to my own bed (a lower platform) at the field station before darkness fell, would I regard chimpanzees as "mere animals." (297)

Paragraph begins with a claim.

It is not necessary to make extravagant claims for the intelligence or language skills of great apes in order to believe in their rights. Controversy continues to surround the question of whether apes can really acquire "language" skills in the full sense, as they appear to be unable to form grammatical sentences, but only able to use signs individually or in combinations of two or three. Thus Columbia University ethologist Herbert Terrace and other researchers argue that signing apes "are not using anything that deserves to be called a language" because their signing is ungrammatical and repetitious (Griffin 242). But Donald Griffin counters that, while Terrace's findings have caused many "to dismiss the whole effort to teach language-like communication to apes as unimpressive and insignificant, this dismissal is based on the absence or near

Sung 8

absence of combinatorial productivity [that is, grammatical phrases], and it does not seriously detract from the significance of signing as evidence of what apes are thinking" (223).

Conclusion

Some scientists remain skeptical of the notion that apes and other animals might have emotional lives that resemble our own. But, as primatologist Frans de Waal argues, biologists and animal behaviorists have been so thoroughly trained to avoid anthropomorphizing animals that they may put up excessive resistance to the suggestion that apes are in some ways like us. And consequently, when faced with arguments that apes think and feel much as humans do, they may demand a level of proof that is unattainable in practice. After a critical review of various claims for animal consciousness, animal psychologist Clive D. L. Wynne concludes: "Animals don't need legal rights to be accepted as valuable and worthy of our protection. They are valuable to us because of who we are, not who they are. Things don't have to be like us to be important to us. They don't have to be able to feel pain to deserve our concern" (242). But we are not just failing to value and protect the animals that are most like us; we are actively destroying them, to the point of extinction. Wynne, I believe, is wrong: animals do sometimes need legal rights. When it was recently announced that an animal sanctuary in Vienna, Austria, would be closing, animal rights advocates went to court to ask that one of its residents, a chimpanzee named Hiasl, be granted the legal status of a "person" so that he could be awarded a guardian and become the recipient of donations that would cover the cost of food and shelter ("How to Protect"). Now that we have failed so thoroughly to do what Wynne suggests and to value the great apes "because of who we are," perhaps it is time for stronger measures.

Sung 9

Works Cited

"Animal Testing Is Bad Science: Point/Counterpoint." *PETA.* People for the Ethical Treatment of Animals, n.d. Web. 8 Feb. 2012.

Bowman, Kerry. "The Demise of the Great Apes in Africa." *Canadian Ape Alliance.* The Canadian Ape Alliance, 20 Apr. 2010. Web. 27 Jan. 2012.

Byrne, Richard W. "Primate Cognition: Evidence for the Ethical Treatment of Primates." *Attitudes to Animals: Views in Animal Welfare.* Ed. Francine L. Dolins. Cambridge: Cambridge UP, 1999. 114-25. Print.

Cavalieri, Paola, and Peter Singer, eds. *The Great Ape Project: Equality beyond Humanity.* New York: Griffin-St. Martin's, 1993. Print.

"Chimp Facts." *Save the Chimps: Speaking Out for Them.* Save the Chimps, Inc., n.d. Web. 8 Feb. 2012.

Dawkins, Richard. "Gaps in the Mind." Cavalieri and Singer 80-87.

Descartes, René. "Animals Are Machines." *Environmental Ethics: Divergence and Convergence.* Ed. Susan J. Armstrong and Richard G. Botzler. New York: McGraw, 1993. 281-85. Print.

de Waal, Frans. "Are We in Anthropodenial?" *Discover* July 1997: 50-53. Print.

Fouts, Roger S., and Deborah H. Fouts. "Chimpanzees' Use of Sign Language." Cavalieri and Singer 28-41.

Goodall, Jane. *Reason for Hope: A Spiritual Journey.* New York: Warner, 1999. Print.

Great Ape Project. "A Declaration on Great Apes." Cavalieri and Singer 4-8.

Sung 10

Griffin, Donald R. *Animal Minds: Beyond Cognition to Consciousness.* Chicago: U of Chicago P, 2001. Print.

"How to Protect Ape's Rights? Make Him a Person." *MSNBC. com.* MSNBC Digital Network, 5 Apr. 2007. Web. 7 Mar. 2012.

Patterson, Francine, and Wendy Gordon. "The Case for the Personhood of Gorillas." Cavalieri and Singer 58-78.

Singer, Peter. *Animal Liberation.* 3rd ed. New York: Ecco-Harper, 2002. Print.

"Species Fact Sheet: African Great Apes." *WWF (panda.org).* World Wildlife Fund, May 2007. Web. 15 Feb. 2012.

Teleki, Geza. "They Are Us." Cavalieri and Singer 296-302.

Wynne, Clive D. L. *Do Animals Think?* Princeton: Princeton UP, 2004. Print.

Wendy Sung's essay takes a different position from that of Marc Dumas's essay. But it also takes a different approach. Rather than seeing rights for apes as a knowledge problem, Wendy sees the issue chiefly as a practical problem, one that requires action on the part of the reader. She argues that the rights of the great apes should be legally protected.

Wendy's essay also differs from Marc's in structure. Her introduction is more elaborate: it comprises two paragraphs rather than the typical one paragraph; a thesis statement does not appear until the end of the second paragraph. The first paragraph consists of background information that sets up the issue at stake, so a second paragraph is needed in order to present Wendy's position on that issue.

From that point forward, her position remains clear throughout the essay, so clear that there is little danger of it becoming buried. Consequently, she can take some further liberties with paragraph structure; she doesn't need to begin every single paragraph with a claim. Of course, some paragraphs do begin with a claim, such as paragraphs 5 and 9. But others, such as paragraph 4, begin with a statement of fact and lead up to a claim that appears later in the paragraph. In paragraph 7, the claim is never stated outright, yet it is sufficiently clear: if we would never condone the killing of human beings with low intelligence and limited verbal skills and would not condone their use in medical experiments, then we shouldn't do such things to apes, either.

Wendy includes a visual element in the form of a table, to present data in a format that the reader can easily grasp and to avoid tediously listing numbers and facts in a paragraph of background information.

Toward the end of the essay, she includes a paragraph (para. 8) with an exploratory structure: it begins and ends with questions. These are partly rhetorical questions — questions with a clearly implied answer. But the purpose of the paragraph is not simply to argue; it is also to speculate and pose the real question, "Why do we hold onto a rigid distinction between our species and others?" Wendy's concluding paragraph is a little more open-ended than Marc's: she introduces views held by two leading scholars that complicate her argument a little and broaden the perspective, though they do not change the argument fundamentally. The effect of these departures from standard paragraph structure is a degree of variety and unpredictability that is missing from a more basic essay structure.

Clarification Strategies

No matter what kind of essay you are writing, you can employ strategies to clarify your ideas and their organization for the reader. The best time to use these strategies is when your essay is fairly close to its final form, when you have already organized your ideas around a structure and can read a complete draft as if through the eyes of a reader. At this stage, you can ask an actual reader to help identify places where clarification is needed.

Metadiscourse and Programmatic Statements

As we said in Chapter 2, the term "metadiscourse" means writing that refers to the text in which it appears. For example, if I were to write, "You are reading Chapter 6 of *Writing in Response*; this chapter concerns ways to organize a college essay," my words would be making reference to this text itself, rather than to something outside the text. In other words, they would be *discourse about this discourse*. Writers often use metadiscourse to explain their intent or purpose or to bring the reader back to the main argument or to remind the reader of their purpose after a long detour. For example:

"I am arguing that..."

"We have now reviewed the various types of . . . ; next, we must look at how these types..."

"This essay has argued that..."

"Looking back over this exploration, I see that..."

In a complicated argument, metadiscourse is a useful strategy for clarification. But many essays — perhaps most — require no metadiscourse at all: the argument unfolds without the need for announcements and explanations of purpose and intent. Bear in mind that excessive metadiscourse can be tedious for a reader and can feel like a pointless delay if it's not necessary. Reserve it for moments when clarity truly demands it.

Here is a fairly elaborate example from a book by historian Hayden White, in which he pauses at the end of a lengthy theoretical discussion in order to provide the reader with a road map for the rest of the chapter. In this context, most readers probably find the metadiscourse helpful and welcome.

All this is highly abstract, of course, and in order to be made convincing requires both theoretical amplification and exemplification. In what follows, therefore, I will try to characterize the historical discourse in somewhat more formal terms and then analyze a passage of "proper" historical prose in order to explicate the relationship that obtains between its manifest and latent (figurative) meanings. After that, I will return to the problem of the relation between "proper" historiography and its historicist counterpart, on the one side, and to some general remarks on the possible types or modes of historical representation suggested by figurative analysis, on the other.[1]

Transitional Expressions

While whole sentences of metadiscourse can clarify the overall direction and purpose of an essay, brief transitional expressions provide a way to express the relationship between ideas. Some examples include "however," "but," "nevertheless," "moreover," "at the same time," "still," and "on the one hand . . . on the other hand."

---

[1] Hayden White, *Tropics of Discourse* (Baltimore, MD: Johns Hopkins University Press, 1978), 106.

You may use words like these even in your readerly drafts, but you might omit them when the relationship between two ideas seems obvious to you. To the reader, however, such words greatly help to clarify your thinking.

Definitions

Definitions are of two kinds: stipulative definitions and dictionary definitions. A stipulative definition is a special definition for a particular purpose, a meaning that a writer stipulates in the essay. Thus, in an essay on science fiction, a writer might explain, "For the purpose of this essay, the word 'fancy' refers to a particular kind of creative imagination, the faculty of imagining beings and places that do not exist in reality." Writers often need to invest ordinary terms with a special meaning, and these may well need definition since the reader cannot simply go to a dictionary to find the meaning. If the writer does not explain the term, it will remain unclear.

In high school, you sometimes might have included a dictionary definition of a key word in your essay as a clarification strategy, but in a college paper you should assume that readers will use the dictionary themselves, if necessary, to find the general meaning of terms. Include a dictionary definition only if a word has a technical or specialized sense that would not be familiar to an educated reader.

Composing Titles

Titles are an important element in any college essay. The title is a clarification strategy because an effective title gives the reader a sense of the scope of the essay, its purpose and argument. Craft a title that points to what is unique about your essay. Titles in the humanities tend to be structured differently from those in the natural sciences. In the humanities, writers often give their essays a

> **→ Try This   Working with Transitional Expressions**
>
> Working with a classmate, choose two different passages from one of the essays included in this book. Rewrite one of the passages, omitting all the transitional expressions. Your classmate will rewrite the other passage. Exchange your notebooks and write out the passage once more, this time putting transitional expressions back into the passage by considering where they are most needed and which expressions would work best. Compare your rewritten passages to the original. Which is clearer? (You may have made some improvements!)

two-part title separated by a colon. The first part of the title is more imaginative, and the second part is more descriptive. In the natural sciences, titles tend to be strictly descriptive. Consider the following examples, taken from a variety of professional journals:

Ethos and Error: How Businesspeople React to Errors

The Monster in the Rainbow: Keats and the Science of Life

Deep Play: Notes on the Balinese Cockfight

Incorporating Nonverbal Behaviors into Affect Control Theory

Sustained Photobiological Hydrogen Gas Production upon Reversible Inactivation of Oxygen Evolution in the Green Alga Chlamydomonas reinhardtii

The second-to-last title, for a sociology article, resembles the last title, for a plant physiology article, in that it is strictly descriptive. But the first, second, and third titles — for articles in composition, English, and anthropology — each have two parts, a more poetic and intriguing first half and a more descriptive second half. This reflects the fact that these disciplines do not insist on detachment, impersonality, and objectivity to the same extent as do the natural sciences. But all these titles strive to signal the essential purpose of the article and help to clarify this purpose for the reader.

✔ Checklist for Organizing an Argument Essay

Be sure to include the following kinds of paragraphs in your argument essay.

☐ Introductory paragraph(s) (usually one, but no more than two)
- Describe a problem of some kind (a knowledge problem or a practical problem).
- Offer a solution in a thesis statement, usually in the first paragraph, usually of one or two sentences.

☐ Body paragraphs (usually at least three)
- Begin with a claim, followed by support for the claim.
- Develop a new component of the argument. (Complex components may need more than one paragraph.)
- Address counterarguments, typically toward the end of the essay.

☐ Concluding paragraph(s) (usually one, but no more than two)
- Bring closure to the essay.
- Mention questions that remain unanswered and/or directions for further research or thinking.
- Offer a send-off, not merely a reiteration of the main argument (which should already be clear).

Organizing an Exploratory Essay

Normally a thesis is the solution to a problem — either a practical problem or a knowledge problem. But many problems, while interesting and important, are too difficult or complex to be neatly solved, even with a good deal of research. The exploratory essay lets writers explore a difficult problem without necessarily having to offer a complete solution. Such an essay *seeks* a solution, but it may or may not arrive at one — or it may arrive at a partial or provisional or tentative solution. Its chief purpose is to shed light on the problem by thinking it through carefully and to arrive at a deeper understanding of the issues.

Many essays are exploratory in form and purpose — from the essays of Michel de Montaigne, the sixteenth-century French writer generally considered to be the inventor of the essay form, to those we now find in magazines and blogs. Exploratory essays are not the norm in academic writing, where writers typically present the results of scholarly research and make a case for their solution to a problem. However, in some disciplines, especially in the humanities, exploratory essays are becoming more common. As a college student, you may be required to write an exploratory essay in a composition course or perhaps a philosophy or women's studies course, or you may encounter an assignment that, in your view, lends itself to an exploratory approach (but be sure to ask your instructor whether such an approach will be acceptable).

In some respects, an exploratory essay looks like the informal writing that you do when seeking a thesis for an argument essay (see Chapter 4, p. 98): exploratory essays often trace a more circuitous path around a problem and adopt a more informal style than does the typical thesis-driven essay. However, exploratory essays, though they may appear to be more freely organized, are nevertheless highly polished and carefully structured — and therefore more readerly than informal writing usually is. They often tell a story, with less emphasis on overt claim and evidence.

Exploratory essays may emphasize suggestion and implication over argumentation, at least until the conclusion. They often move from topic to topic by association rather than strict logic.

The essay "At the Buffalo Bill Museum, June 1988" by Jane Tompkins (p. 413) is a good example of an exploratory essay. While the first four sections describe the author's responses to the exhibits in each of the four museums that make up the Buffalo Bill Historical Center, the final section (pp. 424–30) raises questions about the myth and reality of Buffalo Bill himself. At the conclusion of the essay, Tompkins poses some tough questions that reach, at least implicitly, beyond the particular case of Buffalo Bill to ask how it is possible to pass judgment on history: "I cannot resolve the contradiction between my experience at the Buffalo Bill Historical Center . . . and my response to the shining figure of Buffalo Bill. . . . But I have reached one conclusion . . ." (p. 430). She leaves the reader with a great deal to think about, but no simple, tidy answers. (You might see the meaning of her questions differently, and that's fine: they are big questions.) Exploratory essays typically offer not solutions but food for thought.

While the form of the exploratory essay is freer than that of the argument essay, several general principles can guide us. First, instead of being centered on a thesis that governs or drives the argument throughout, an exploratory essay is driven by a central question or problem. So whereas we can describe the argument essay as thesis-driven, we can describe the exploratory essay as question-driven. The sense of the question or problem may evolve as the essay proceeds, but the essay does not meander aimlessly. The search for insight keeps it moving forward. One reason that college instructors assign this kind of essay is that sustaining

⊙ **Try This**   **Analyzing an Exploratory Essay**

Analyze Jane Tompkins's exploratory essay "At the Buffalo Bill Museum, June 1988" (p. 413) as a story of a quest. Identify the beginning, the middle, and the end. Identify the stories within the story. Distinguish passages of reflection from passages of narrative. How does Tompkins sustain the quest by introducing new questions when a solution emerges? How does she offer an ending without offering a fully formed thesis?

such a quest over several pages requires students to think deeply about the problem at hand.

The notion of "story" provides the framework for structuring exploratory essays. A story always has a structure: a beginning, a middle, and an end. In the case of the exploratory essay, the beginning and the ending are clear enough: the beginning defines a problem or question, and the end is some epiphany, clarification, or moment of understanding. So what happens in the middle? There are many possibilities, but here is a common way of structuring the middle of an exploratory essay: For a start, you can propose some way of solving the problem, a path or strategy, and then pursue this path. Then you must assess your progress. You can either move forward or perhaps circle back, redefine the problem, imagine alternative ways of solving the problem, and (in sum) describe what happened on the way to the insight. The exploration is sustained by bringing new questions to bear even when a possible solution emerges, so that the essay does not rest with some premature answer to the puzzle but instead insists on digging deeper, exploring further, examining more closely. That is why such an essay will be question-driven rather than thesis-driven: instead of being organized around a thesis, and the needs of an argument in support of that thesis, it is organized around a central question as it tells its story. The exploratory essay presents the story of a quest, an intellectual quest. Still, exploratory essays need not consist exclusively of storytelling. They frequently combine several different modes of writing, including autobiography, narrative, analysis, reflection, and argumentation, because different modes of thinking make up the quest and become part of the story.

Comparing the Argument Essay and the Exploratory Essay

Table 6.1 (see p. 194) provides a quick overview comparing the two essay forms.

One way to see the difference between the organization of an exploratory (or question-driven) essay and an argument (or thesis-driven) essay is to look at two sample essays on similar topics, one in argument form and the other in exploratory form. In a course on "The Frontier and American Identity," the instructor assigned a three-to-five-page midterm essay on this topic: "Why did President Franklin Pierce sign the Kansas-Nebraska bill (1854) into law?" One student,

Table 6.1 Comparison of Argument and Exploratory Essays

	Argument Essay	Exploratory Essay
Purpose	To persuade the reader that an idea is valid	To explore and deepen the reader's understanding of a problem
Impetus	Thesis-driven	Question-driven
Structure	Logical structure	Mostly narrative structure
Modes of discourse	Keeps primarily to argument mode	Often combines several modes of discourse

Kelly Rivera, conducted extensive research in her college library and was ultimately able to draw some conclusions. Even though the historical situation was complicated, she decided that the question posed could be answered, and she felt strongly about the position she had adopted. So she wrote an argument essay in thesis-driven form.[2]

Sample Essay in Argument Form

This essay in argument form presents a thesis at the end of two introductory paragraphs. Body paragraphs present claims that support the thesis. The writer integrates sources to provide support for her claims.

---

[2] Although this paper and the one by Greg Fernandez (p. 205) were written for a dual-credit English and history course and so use MLA documentation, papers for history classes often employ the documentation system outlined in the *Chicago Manual of Style* (see Chapter 10 for more information). Be sure to check with your instructor about the system you should use.

Rivera 1

Kelly Rivera

Professor Lyman

RHET/HIS 201: The Frontier and American Identity

31 October 2012

A Fatal Compromise: President Franklin Pierce

and the Kansas-Nebraska Bill of 1854

Why did Franklin Pierce sign the Kansas-Nebraska bill of
1854 into law? This bill established two new territories in land
that had been acquired as part of the Louisiana Purchase and
later set aside as Indian Territory. In order to establish these
new territories, Congress had to address the delicate question
of whether slavery would be allowed in them; it was this
aspect of the bill that made it a turning point in American
history. Southerners were determined to see that slavery
would be permitted, but many in the North feared the political
power of the southern slave states and were equally
determined that slavery would be prohibited. Earlier
agreements on the slavery question left an ambiguous
precedent. The Missouri Compromise of 1820 had restricted
slavery to territories that fell below 36°30′ latitude. But the
Compromise of 1850 that established the territories of New
Mexico and Utah left the decision in the hands of local
residents rather than Congress: in other words, these new
territories would decide the slavery question for themselves.
The Kansas-Nebraska bill applied this principle of "popular
sovereignty" to Kansas and Nebraska and explicitly repealed
the Missouri Compromise, which was incompatible with this
principle. It was the repeal of this compromise that provoked
anger in the North and ultimately led to the creation of the

*Introduction begins
with historical
context.*

Republican Party and a political stand-off that would drag the country into civil war.

President Franklin Pierce, elected in 1852, had always supported the principle that the federal government should avoid interfering in matters that concerned individual states, so he was a strong supporter of the Compromise of 1850 and the principle of popular sovereignty. But he was reluctant, at least initially, to repeal the Missouri Compromise, anger northerners, and reopen the slavery question once more. Though a northerner, he agreed with many of his fellow Democrats, especially those from the South, that slavery was a question of "states' rights." And he believed, or hoped, that the whole question had been settled once and for all by the agreements of 1820 and 1850. However, he became convinced that only a bill that explicitly repealed the Missouri Compromise had any chance of passing in the House of Representatives. And he felt that the advantages of opening the new territories to a railroad through the center of the continental United States were worth the political price: the potential benefits to the country overshadowed the anger the bill would surely provoke. For these reasons, Pierce signed the bill.

Pierce, like many northerners, was never morally opposed to slavery. He believed that slavery was a states' rights issue, and his cabinet included several southern Democrats who believed deeply that slavery, the South's "peculiar institution," was morally defensible and protected by the Constitution. In the words of one biographer, Pierce saw the United States as "the creation of sovereign states with each state retaining the right to allow slavery within its border"

End of introduction presents thesis.

Claim: Pierce was not morally opposed to slavery but saw it as a states' rights issue.

Rivera 3

(Gara, *Presidency* 79). However, he was opposed to repealing the Missouri Compromise of 1820; he knew that this would reawaken a bitter controversy. But he probably overestimated the strength of the Democratic Party in the North and underestimated the depth of the anger that the repeal would arouse (Wolff 128).

For many northerners, slavery was more objectionable for the threat that it posed to the balance of power than for the way it abused human beings. The Constitution declared that slaves were to be counted as three-fifths of a white person; they could not vote, of course, but this method of calculating population meant that southern slave states held a larger number of seats in Congress relative to the actual voting population than free states. Most northerners opposed "slave power" rather than slavery itself, so they were more concerned about preventing the spread of slavery than about abolishing it altogether. Few northerners were strict abolitionists; even the Free Soil Party was more concerned with containing the power of the slave states than it was with the conditions or rights of the slaves themselves (Gara, "Slavery" 5-6). Those who did oppose slavery in principle generally saw it as the business of the southern states to abolish it. If northern states were to interfere with southern affairs, after all, what was to stop the South from interfering in northern affairs? As Larry Gara explains, southerners "feared that free territory to the west would make their own slave property insecure. They insisted, through [Senator] Atchison, that legislation creating a new western territory include a provision repealing the 1820 compromise. That was the spark that set a major Free Soil fire

Claim: fear of "slave power" was greater than opposition to slavery.

Rivera 4

in the North. It was clear evidence to the northerners of the influence of the slave power" (*Presidency* 89).

The chief reason for organizing Kansas and Nebraska into territories had less to do with new settlements than with a transcontinental railroad. The Kansas-Nebraska Act came about as a result of a "railroad mania" that was sweeping the country from 1847 to 1857 (Hodder 4). Since the acquisition of California, following the war with Mexico, a transcontinental railroad was considered essential. Pierce, like most of his

Claim: Pierce felt a railroad would unite the nation.

countrymen, believed strongly in the need for a railroad that would stretch across the country and help unite the nation. He foresaw the "emergence of the United States as a potential two-ocean power requiring transcontinental railroad and telegraph lines to link its various sections" (Gara, *Presidency* 74). A route across the South, from New Orleans to San Diego, had been made possible by the Gadsden Purchase, but such a route would be unacceptable to northerners, who would gain no advantage

Claim: a central route was key.

from it. Uniting the country meant finding a central route, and this meant abolishing what Patricia Nelson Limerick calls the "lingering fiction" of a permanent Indian Territory. Stephen A. Douglas expressed the problem succinctly:

> The idea of arresting our progress in that direction . . . has become so ludicrous that we are amazed, that wise and patriotic statesmen ever cherished the thought. . . . How are we to develop, cherish and protect our immense interests and possessions on the Pacific, with a vast wilderness fifteen hundred miles in breadth, filled with hostile savages, and cutting off all direct communication. The Indian barrier must be removed. (qtd. in Limerick 92-93)

Rivera 5

For most white Americans, Indian interests were now of little concern. And in fact, even some Indians, the Wyandot tribe, supported the organization of Nebraska into a territory so that they could receive federal protection (Gara, *Presidency* 89).

The "key to the whole matter," argues Roy F. Nichols, is "the process of becoming" (197). Nichols argues that we can only understand why the Kansas-Nebraska Act came into being when we stop looking for its cause in the will, ambition, or hope of particular individuals, such as Senator Stephen A. Douglas or Representative Alexander H. Stephens, and instead look at the way that the bill in its final form came into being: it was the product of a long process of bartering and deal-making with congressmen from all over the country who held a wide variety of interests and convictions. The Whig Party was disintegrating, and the Democratic Party was undergoing a transformation. The "real history" of the bill, says Nichols, "is the analysis of how a bill ostensibly to organize a territory had been made an instrument of the fundamental political reorganization that that disintegration of the old parties had made inevitable" (211). This struggle within the parties determined the bill's final form, so that in the end it bore little resemblance to the first bill that Douglas had introduced in 1853. The struggle to win support had resulted in a bill that no single individual really authored. It does not follow that Pierce's support was inevitable, but this does suggest that Pierce too was swept up in a tide of change that he could not control.

Pierce became persuaded that repealing the Missouri Compromise was inescapable during a meeting with Douglas, Jefferson Davis, and other leading senators (Gara, *Presidency* 90). Missouri senator David R. Atchison, president of the

Claim: repeal had become necessary.

Rivera 6

Senate (and in effect vice president since the death of Vice President William King shortly after the inauguration), was particularly insistent that the Missouri Compromise must be repealed. Missouri's slave owners worried that if land to the west of their state was free, their own slaves would run away (Gara, *Presidency* 89). Therefore, even though many southerners did not demand the repeal of the 1820 compromise, the insistence of a powerful few made it seem unavoidable. Without the repeal, no territories, and without the territories, no central railroad. Once Pierce became convinced of this, he worked hard to get support for the bill in the House. Historian Gerald Wolff writes that although Pierce is often described as "an inept and weak President," he proved to be "on the whole, both competent and effective" in winning support for the Nebraska bill among northern Democrats in the House (80).

The election that brought Pierce to the White House had been a triumph for the Democratic Party; in fact, it represented the death of the Whig Party. Pierce could not have foreseen that the Kansas-Nebraska Act would galvanize its opponents, uniting them in opposition to the expansion of slavery, and lead to the establishment of the Republican Party. Nor could he have foreseen the bloodshed in Kansas and the Civil War.

Claim: consequences were unforeseeable.

Perhaps a president of stronger and more determined character would have been able to resist Senator Douglas and the others who insisted on the repeal of the Missouri Compromise. It is tempting perhaps, but ultimately unfair, to pass judgment with the benefit of hindsight. President Pierce

Rivera 7

was in a difficult position and perhaps no one could have prevented the return of a conflict between North and South that had been intensifying throughout the first half of the century. And perhaps, if the Kansas-Nebraska Act did hasten the country toward the complete abolition of slavery at last, it was not an entirely bad thing.

Conclusion: we can't judge fairly from the present.

Rivera 8

Works Cited

Gara, Larry. *The Presidency of Franklin Pierce.* Lawrence: UP of Kansas, 1991. Print.

---. "Slavery and Slave Power: A Crucial Distinction." *Civil War History* 15 (1969): 5-18. Print.

Hodder, Frank Heywood. "The Railroad Background of the Kansas-Nebraska Act." *Mississippi Valley Historical Review* 12.1 (1925): 3-22. Print.

Limerick, Patricia Nelson. *The Legacy of Conquest: The Unbroken Past of the American West.* New York: Norton, 1987. Print.

Nichols, Roy F. "The Kansas-Nebraska Act: A Century of Historiography." *Mississippi Valley Historical Review* 43.2 (1956): 187-212. Print.

Wolff, Gerald W. *The Kansas-Nebraska Bill: Party, Section, and the Coming of the Civil War.* Brooklyn: Revisionist, 1977. Print.

Analysis

The essay's argument is governed by a clear thesis: "Though reluctant at first to repeal the Missouri Compromise, Pierce signed the Kansas-Nebraska bill because he believed the bill was worth the price." As you would expect, the purpose of the essay is to demonstrate by means of evidence and reasoning that this thesis is valid. So the thesis statement is the essay's main claim, and the other claims play a supporting role. The organization becomes clearer when we look at the essay in outline form, as a sequence of claims that support the thesis. Each claim represents the focus of a different paragraph.

Introduction: historical context of the question.

Thesis: Despite his reluctance, Pierce signed the Kansas-Nebraska bill because he believed the bill was worth the political cost of repealing the Missouri Compromise.

    I. Pierce could accept repeal of the Missouri Compromise because:

        A. He was never morally opposed to slavery as such.

        B. He saw it as a "states' rights" issue.

        C. To the extent that he did oppose slavery, it was due to fear of southern power or "slave power."

    II. Pierce believed that the need for a transcontinental railroad made the repeal of the Missouri Compromise worthwhile.

        A. He believed a railroad would unite the nation.

        B. This meant finding a central route, through Indian Territory, in preference to a southern route.

    III. Repeal of the Missouri Compromise became necessary, even though many southerners had not really wanted it, because of the demands of certain senators whose votes were necessary.

    IV. Pierce could not have foreseen the consequences of repealing the Missouri Compromise.

Concluding reflections/send-off: Is it fair to pass judgment with the benefit of hindsight?

Note that the thesis statement makes a master claim, and each of the sentences below it makes a supporting claim. The sentences that stand as major headings (I, II,

⊘ **Try This**   **Writing an Exploratory Essay**

Write an exploratory essay on the subject of rights for great apes, using the two sample essays (p. 171 and p. 177) as starting points. If you wish, develop your ideas by conducting research in the library or on the Internet, using the bibliographies that follow each of the sample essays as a starting point.

III, and IV) each represent key claims that must be made in order to make an argument for the thesis. In other words, Kelly can make a strong case for her thesis by making a case for each of these claims, or subtheses. Each claim is a kind of miniature thesis, and the sentences that stand as minor headings (A, B, C) also make claims that support the claims that stand above them in the hierarchy.

An essay structured in this way makes it easy for the reader to follow the argument because the structure guides the reader along point by point or claim by claim. The main thesis appears at the end of the introduction, just where the reader expects to find it, and the components of the argument, the claims, have been placed in prominent positions, at the beginning of paragraphs. Thus the argument is firmly in the foreground, and the supporting evidence does what it should do: supporting the claims, not burying them.

Sample Essay in Exploratory Form

Let's now look at an exploratory (or question-driven) essay on the same topic as Kelly Rivera's argument (or thesis-driven) essay. Greg Fernandez did similar research but ultimately felt that the topic left more questions in his mind than answers. He could see that certain kinds of answers might suffice from certain points of view, but for him the question of why President Pierce signed the Kansas-Nebraska bill opened up perspectives that only led to further questions. After discussing his ideas with his professor, Greg asked if he could write an essay that explored his questions rather than one that made an argument for a definite thesis. Greg's professor encouraged him to give it a try.

Fernandez 1

Greg Fernandez

Professor Delgado

RHET/HIS 201: The Frontier and American Identity

31 October 2012

Exploring the "Whys" of History:

Franklin Pierce and the Kansas-Nebraska Bill of 1854

Why did President Franklin Pierce sign the Kansas-
Nebraska bill into law in 1854 and thereby repeal the Missouri
Compromise of 1820 and reopen the slavery question? At the
start of my research, I found myself focusing almost
obsessively on the word "why." It puzzled me because it
seemed to point directly toward the question of Pierce's
motivation, and motivation can be considered from any
number of perspectives. A person might approach it from the
point of view of biography: How did the events in Pierce's life
story lead him to this crucial decision? Or from the point of
view of culture: How did the culture of his time make it
possible to allow slavery to expand? Or from the point of view
of politics: How did political forces make it necessary for
Pierce to sign a bill he may have personally disliked? Or from
the point of view of psychology: How did his own inner
conflicts make him follow Congress rather than lead it?

And these were, I suspected, just a few of the
possibilities.

At this point, it seemed that to provide anything like a
sufficient answer to the question "Why?" would be impossible —
not only because I faced the usual limitations of time and space
but also because it would be impossible to "get inside the head"
of a man who lived a century and a half ago. As far as I could

Introduction: this is the question that drives the essay.

Fernandez 2

tell from the biographies, Pierce never left a complete explanation of why he signed the bill, and even if he had, it would be difficult to know how much of it to believe (Gara, *Presidency* 119). But after further reading and research, I began to feel that my initial doubts might be a kind of trap and that, in a way, I was already answering my question. That is, it may well be impossible to give any *complete* answer, but the fact that I had already been able to carve up the question into different approaches suggested that I might be able to find *some* kind of answer. As I read historians' accounts of the journey of the bill from its beginning as one man's idea to its destination as the law of the land, I realized that historians do know enough about the events of that time to make it possible to draw some conclusions and make some educated guesses.[1] I decided to start with the approach that seemed most practical and feasible: the political perspective. So I looked at the question in this way: President Pierce and the Democrats hoped and believed that the slavery question had been settled by the Compromises of 1820 and 1850, so how did *political* forces influence Pierce to sign this bill that repealed the Missouri Compromise of 1820 and reopened the whole question?

In Larry Gara's biography of Franklin Pierce and in Gerald Wolff's *The Kansas-Nebraska Bill: Party, Section, and the Coming of the Civil War,* I found some clues. Many, perhaps most, southerners were not especially eager to see the

A way forward: answer doesn't have to be complete; multiple approaches are possible.

---

[1] For a striking example of a historian's educated guesswork, about Stephen Douglas's motivation for promoting the bill with such energy, see Limerick 111.

Fernandez 3

Missouri Compromise repealed. After all, it did seem to
prevent further interference by northerners in the southern
way of life. But some southern politicians, and in particular
some from Missouri, were worried that the new territory to
their west, Missouri's next-door neighbor, would pose a danger
to their own "property" (i.e., their slaves) if it was free. Their
only hope for the creation of a slave state on the western
border of Missouri was to get the Missouri Compromise
repealed; thereafter they might see to it that the referendum
in Kansas went in favor of slavery (Gara, *Presidency* 89-90;
Wolff 160). Senator Atchison of Missouri was particularly
powerful: he was the president of the Senate and, since the
death of William King in 1852, vice president of the United
States. Without his support, and the support of his cronies
(the so-called "F Street Mess"), the bill was dead, and there
would be no new territories and no railroad across the country
(Nichols 204; Hodder 11-14). So Pierce saw that the repeal of
the Missouri Compromise was necessary, and he gave his
support to the bill. From that point on, it was inevitable that
he would sign it into law once it passed through Congress.

Political approach.

This gave me one kind of answer: a political answer — a
partial answer looking at the question from one point of view.
What about the other points of view — the personal, the
cultural, the psychological, and so on? These angles might call
for more speculation, but even here it seems possible to say
something.

Transition to other approaches.

The cultural or moral aspect of the question had already
become fairly clear: How could Pierce allow himself to sign the
bill, repeal the Missouri Compromise, and open the new

Fernandez 4

territories to slavery? Pierce was not opposed to slavery in
principle, it appears, and though he was a New England lawyer
and not a southern slave owner, he appointed a number of
southern slave owners and defenders of slavery to his cabinet

*Cultural approach:
racism.*

(Gara, *Presidency* 44-47). Racism in the mid-1800s was not
confined to the South; it seems to have been a widespread
attitude. Most whites seemed to have thought that whites were
superior, a point of view supported, they believed, by scripture
and by nature. Racist views were deeply ingrained in the
American mind and openly expressed by leading politicians of
the North as well as the South. For example, in 1839 Lewis Cass
wrote in the *North American Review,* "There can be no doubt . . .
that the Creator intended the earth should be reclaimed from a
state of nature and cultivated" (qtd. in Gara, *Presidency* 75).
Senator Thomas Hart Benton asserted that whites had the best
claim to the land because they "used it according to the
intentions of the CREATOR" (qtd. in Gara, *Presidency* 75). There
was even talk of transforming Indians into Christian farmers
who would gradually become part of white society, but this
suggestion met resistance (Limerick 40). Caleb Cushing, a
Massachusetts politician, would not admit as his equals "either
the red man, of America, or the yellow man of Asia, nor the
black man of Africa" (qtd. in Gara, *Presidency* 75), and Stephen
A. Douglas referred to the trans-Mississippi West as "filled with
hostile savages" (qtd. in Limerick 93).

   It is difficult for a student today to comprehend these
attitudes, to understand how intelligent, religious, and
apparently moral men and women could be so indifferent to
the rights of individuals of a different race or culture. Perhaps

Fernandez 5

Cultural approach: religion.

one clue can be found in the religious language used by politicians quoted here: perhaps they genuinely believed that God had made Europeans superior to other races, and men superior to women. Perhaps they believed that the Bible, the Word of God, declared this. They thought of the United States as white and Protestant (Gara, "Slavery" 16). Yet not *all* Americans believed this. Christians like Gerrit Smith believed that slavery was evil and must be abolished, and the former slave Frederick Douglass was revealing the dark truth about slavery; northerners could not really plead ignorance (Rawley 165-66). Did the majority truly believe in white superiority, or did they just persuade themselves of what they wanted to believe, what was convenient to believe?

Why could not Pierce, who, if not a great statesman, was not an evil man, see the evil that slavery represented? Why couldn't most Americans? The Constitution stated that all men were created equal, but evidently Americans did not take this literally or did not apply it to African American slaves. And still today, we cannot say that we have achieved full equality among the citizens of this country: women, blacks, gays, and lesbians remain in certain respects unequal.

Personal approach.

It may be more difficult to draw firm conclusions about the way Pierce's personal life and character influenced his decision, yet I found myself more fascinated with this aspect of the question than with any other. After all, Pierce's personal qualities must have entered into the equation somehow, though it might be hard to say exactly how. I was struck by historians' low estimation of Pierce's abilities and achievements. The reader cannot help pitying him a little: he was a kind of accidental

Fernandez 6

president who never sought the office. His party nominated him because he seemed to provide a way out of a stalemate, and he won the election only by being less objectionable than the Whig candidate, Winfield Scott. He was relatively young, just forty-seven at the start of his presidency, and a heavy drinker, perhaps even an alcoholic. And from the beginning, his presidency was beset by tragedy. After having lost three children in infancy, Pierce and his wife lost their only surviving child shortly before the inauguration. In front of their eyes, he was crushed in a train accident ("Franklin Pierce"). Not long after, Pierce lost his vice president, William King, and a close friend and ally, Charles Atherton (Gara, *Presidency* 76). Perhaps this left the new vice president, Senator Atchison of Missouri, in a position of even greater influence over Pierce.

At the end of my research and after all my reflections and speculations, I felt satisfied that I had learned something about why Pierce signed the Kansas-Nebraska bill. But I also arrived at a further conclusion. In history, answers are always going to be fragmentary and partial — just educated guesses, really. Our knowledge of history is full of holes, like a moth-eaten quilt, and it will always remain so. That, I suppose, is why historians are always debating one another and always coming up with new angles from which to look at old issues. Why did President Pierce sign the Kansas-Nebraska bill? Perhaps we can never know fully *why* historical events occur: the causes are too many, and the record is too thin. But we can discover plausible possibilities. The record teaches us, at least, how one ordinary, flawed human being shaped the country's destiny, without the benefit of foresight.

His conclusion is somewhat tentative.

Fernandez 7

Works Cited

"Franklin Pierce." *Encyclopaedia Britannica Online.*
Encyclopaedia Britannica, 2011. Web. 28 Oct. 2012.

Gara, Larry. *The Presidency of Franklin Pierce.* Lawrence: UP of
Kansas, 1991. Print.

---. "Slavery and Slave Power: A Crucial Distinction." *Civil War
History* 15 (1969): 5-18. Print.

Hodder, Frank Heywood. "The Railroad Background of the
Kansas-Nebraska Act." *Mississippi Valley Historical Review*
12.1 (1925): 3-22. Print.

Limerick, Patricia Nelson. *The Legacy of Conquest: The
Unbroken Past of the American West.* New York: Norton,
1987. Print.

Nichols, Roy F. "The Kansas-Nebraska Act: A Century of
Historiography." *Mississippi Valley Historical Review* 43.2
(1956): 187-212. Print.

Rawley, James A. *Race and Politics: "Bleeding Kansas" and the
Coming of the Civil War.* Philadelphia: Lippincott, 1969.
Print.

Wolff, Gerald W. *The Kansas-Nebraska Bill: Party, Section, and
the Coming of the Civil War.* Brooklyn: Revisionist, 1977.
Print.

Analysis

This essay is governed by its opening question: "Why did President Franklin Pierce sign the Kansas-Nebraska bill into law in 1854 and thereby repeal the Missouri Compromise of 1820 and reopen the slavery question?" The paper explores this question, coming at it from several different angles. While there is no clear thesis, or master claim, that drives the paper and supplies a method of organization, the possible answers to this question (which make up the body paragraphs) serve that purpose. The paper's organization will become clear as we examine its structure. The introduction proposes the question. It is followed by "a way forward," laying out the terms of the writer's intention; Greg writes that his answers may be incomplete but that there is merit in the exploration. This is followed by an explanation of several approaches — political, cultural, and personal — that offer insights into the question. The final paragraph offers a tentative conclusion. Here is the essay in outline form.

I. Definition of the problem: the difficulty of answering the question "why," especially because it seems to ask about motivation and we can't get inside his head.
II. A way forward:
    A. My answer doesn't have to be complete to be worthwhile.
    B. I can choose from among the different angles as a way to get started.
III. First approach: the political angle.
IV. Further lines of investigation:
    A. The cultural approach (attitudes toward race and religion).
    B. The personal approach: his tragedies — death of his son and vice president.
V. Tentative conclusion or upshot: History doesn't offer certain answers — it's a quilt full of holes.

As we mentioned above, an exploratory essay is structured as a narrative, or story. Any question-driven, exploratory essay will contain three elements — a begin-

> ➔ **Try This** **Writing the Story of Your Quest**
>
> Begin with a problem from a textbook or a writing assignment. Write first to work toward a better understanding of the problem or question. Then figure out ways to find answers: What work does it entail — rereading? research? interviews? a museum visit? archival work? Keep a careful moment-to-moment journal of your work. At some point, you should come to a conclusion of some kind — perhaps not an answer, but at least a point of view, or a theory, or even just a deeper understanding of the question. Then write this up as a quest narrative: identify the key moments in the quest, the missteps as well as the steps forward, and shape your freewriting into a readerly essay.

ning, a middle, and an end. And since the story is your story, it will typically talk about you. Therefore, you will need to use the word "I" to tell your story, as Greg does.

Now, the story may contain several stories, as well as passages that reflect on the meaning or significance of those stories. For example, in order to define the central problem or question of the essay, you may need to tell the story of how you came to recognize its importance or urgency. Notice how Greg discusses his obsession and puzzlement in his introduction. A vivid account of the context or occasion of the problem is often essential to the reader's understanding of why the question matters and is interesting. And your account of the things you did in order to solve the problem or answer the question may include stories: for example, you might have gone to the library and read a book about some episode in history or someone's life, and such a story might become part of your larger narrative. Or you might have conducted an interview with someone, and this interview becomes a story (itself perhaps containing the interviewee's stories) within your narrative. The skills of storytelling are thus essential to the exploratory essay. The best exploratory essays tell good stories, ones that hold readers' interest and keep them reading even though they do not know what the story's outcome will be. As you revise, bear in mind that the exploratory essay is not the quest itself, but rather a crafted narrative of the quest. You will need to select, shape, and organize your story so that it effectively takes readers down the path of ideas that you have traced.

✅ Checklist for Organizing an Exploratory Essay

If you are writing an exploratory essay, keep the following narrative structure in mind.

- ☐ Beginning
  - Begin with a truly difficult problem or question.
  - Explain the problem in the opening paragraphs.
- ☐ Middle
  - Describe the journey of your quest for insight into the problem.
  - Dig deeper.
  - Explain shifts in direction (for example, if the nature of the problem changes).
  - Highlight moments of insight or turning points.
- ☐ End
  - Leave the reader with something to think about, such as an insight, a deeper appreciation of the question or problem, or a partial solution.

part 3

Attending
to Style

chapter 7

Crafting Sentences

Sentence Grammar

This chapter offers strategies for crafting effective sentences — ones that are not only clear but also pleasing. Reading poorly constructed sentences is irritating and tedious, but reading well-made sentences, in which the words express thoughts clearly and the sentence structure reflects the movement of thought (its ebb and flow, rise and fall), can be a real pleasure.

In order to revise rough, first-draft prose into effective and elegant writing, it helps to grasp the basics of English grammar. Grammar is often a subject of controversy and confusion. To some people, "correct grammar" is a sign of clear thinking — even of scrupulous or ethical thinking. It is often thought to reflect personal virtues, so for these people a lot is at stake in upholding the traditional rules of grammar. But to others, correct grammar varies across regions, classes, and cultures, so the idea that any one person's — or any social group's — grammar is more "correct" and

> 66 To get the right word in the right place is a rare achievement. To condense the diffused light of a page of thought into the luminous flash of a single sentence, is worthy to rank as a prize composition just by itself.... Anybody can have ideas — the difficulty is to express them without squandering a quire of paper on an idea that ought to be reduced to one glittering paragraph. 99
>
> **MARK TWAIN**

therefore better than another's, as long as communication is taking place, indicates elitism and snobbery.

To clarify this situation, we can distinguish between two different senses of grammar: first, the word "grammar" can refer to the basic structure of language as it is actually used in speech and writing, and second, it can refer to the rules about how sentences work, the conventions of punctuation, and the mechanics of writing. To the extent that this book deals with grammar, we are more concerned with the second sense than with the first, because to succeed as a college writer means becoming familiar with these rules — even if you choose to break them occasionally. In America, the rules of Standard Written English were developed and fixed in the nineteenth and early twentieth centuries, and although they continue to change with the times, the rules for formal writing change more slowly than the conventions of spoken English do. So "formal grammar," in the sense of the rules of Standard Written English, tends to be conservative, even old-fashioned. We need little formal grammar in order to express ourselves orally and little in order to write a draft. But there are practical reasons to care about formal grammar at the revision stage, especially once you begin to focus on polishing sentences for good style and correct punctuation and sentence structure. Every writer must consider his or her audience. Rhetorically, correct grammar is one way to persuade readers of your attentiveness and seriousness (appealing through *ethos*; see Chapter 5, p. 114). In the academic context, Standard Written English is expected, and a certain degree of formality is conventional. The same is true in most business contexts. In order to understand grammar as a whole, let's turn to an examination of the elements of sentences.

Clauses

In order to revise well, a writer must be able to analyze sentences and paragraphs in order to see where they go wrong and how they can be improved. This kind of analysis requires some understanding of grammar and style.

Since grade school, you've known how to recognize a sentence: it begins with a capital letter and ends with a period.

But a sentence. Needs more than. Just a capital letter and a period to be complete. These three phrases are not complete sentences, of course, but *sentence fragments*. A grammatical sentence must contain at least a subject and a predicate. A **subject** is the part of the sentence that performs or is associated with an action. It may be a noun, a pronoun, or a noun phrase. A **predicate** is a statement made about the subject. The predicate must include at least a main verb, but often it includes at least one *object* (or complement) as well:

SUBJECT   PREDICATE

This cheese smells.

SUBJECT   PREDICATE = VERB + OBJECT

Erin likes bats.

The following sentence contains a longer predicate: a main verb ("is") and a series of predicate adjectives.

SUBJECT   PREDICATE = VERB + PREDICATE ADJECTIVES

The air is full of birds, and sweet with the breath of the pine, the

balm-of-Gilead, and the new hay.   (Ralph Waldo Emerson)

The main verb is the key word in the predicate. Thus a distinction is sometimes made between a **simple predicate**, meaning only the verb (or the verb and auxiliary verb, as in "is typing," where "is" is the auxiliary verb), and a **complete predicate**, meaning the verb plus any complements, objects, and modifiers. (Note that some words that are formed from verbs — called verbals — are not *operational* verbs but rather function as adjectives, nouns, or adverbs. For example, in the sentence "Thinking can be hard work," "thinking" is a noun and "can be" is the verb.)

Sentences may contain more than one main verb; we call the predicate of such a sentence a **compound predicate**:

SUBJECT   COMPOUND PREDICATE WITH THREE MAIN VERBS

The judge paused, looked round the courtroom, and proceeded to

deliver his sentence.

Many sentences are even more elaborate: they might contain (like the sentence you are reading now) several subject-predicate combinations, not just one. Each group of words that contains both a subject and a predicate is called a **clause**. A complete sentence must contain at least one clause.

Here are some more examples of one-clause sentences.

Andy Warhol became famous for his paintings of Campbell's Soup cans and Coca-Cola bottles.

His 1963 film *Eat* shows Robert Indiana eating a mushroom, or something like a mushroom, for its entire forty-five-minute duration.

In 1966, Warhol produced the Velvet Underground's album *The Velvet Underground and Nico.*

Warhol was sometimes called "the Pope of Pop."

However, many art historians consider other artists, such as Roy Lichtenstein and Jasper Johns, to be no less significant.

Sentences can also contain two, three, or more clauses. Here are some examples.

Many people are under the impression that all black tea is fermented; actually, almost all black tea is oxidized, a process that, unlike fermentation, requires exposure to the air. Pu-erh tea, made from ancient trees in the Yunnan district of China, is an exception: it is fermented and aged for up to ten years. The fermentation process demands that the tea be deprived of oxygen so that the bacteria on the leaves can flourish. The flavor of Pu-erh tea is unusual and does not appeal to all tea-drinkers: it is strong, earthy, and even musty. Though Pu-erh tea is often sold in the form of loose leaves, it is also available in the form of a cake or bar made of compressed leaves. These are often stamped with attractive designs; indeed, many are intended to decorate a table or a wall rather than to be broken up and brewed.

➔ **Try This**   **Identifying Subjects and Predicates**

We can distinguish between the **complete subject**, or "subject phrase," and the **simple subject**, which is usually just one word. For example, in the second sentence listed above, "His 1963 film *Eat*" is the complete subject. The word "film" is the simple subject. In each of the above sentences, identify the simple subject, the complete subject, the operational verb, and the predicate.

At this point, we can complicate matters slightly. Clauses come in two types: independent (or main) and subordinate (or dependent). An independent clause can stand on its own as a complete sentence, but a subordinate clause cannot.

SUBORDINATE CLAUSE   INDEPENDENT CLAUSE

However, though we continued to be friendly, our relationship was forever changed.

(Glenn Loury)

Here, the word "however" is an introductory word, and the first clause is "though we continued to be friendly." The second clause is "our relationship was forever changed." Note the difference: whereas the second clause could stand alone as a sentence, the first ("though we continued to be friendly") could not. The culprit is the word "though": take it away and suddenly that first clause could stand alone perfectly well. We call "though" a subordinating word: it makes the first clause in this sentence subordinate. So a subordinate clause is one that cannot stand alone as a sentence; it usually begins with a subordinating conjunction (such as "though") or a relative pronoun (such as "who"). Note that a subordinate clause differs from an ordinary phrase. Although a subordinate clause cannot stand on its own as a complete sentence, it is still a clause: it contains a subject and a predicate.

> **Try This   Identifying Clauses**

Identify each separate clause in the paragraph about tea on page 220. For each clause, underline the subject phrase and double-underline the predicate.

Then identify the subordinate clause in the following sentence:

Grand Theft Auto is set in Liberty City, which resembles New York City in many ways.

Phrases

Any group of words that makes sense as a unit but lacks a predicate is called a **phrase**. There are five different kinds of phrases (noun, verb, prepositional, absolute, and verbal), categorized according to the part that they play in the sentence. You will find it useful to be able to distinguish phrases from clauses, so it's worth becoming familiar with them.

Type of Phrase	Definition	Examples[1]
Noun phrase	A noun and its modifiers	*three perfectly happy people*
Noun phrase — appositive	A noun phrase that renames the noun or pronoun that precedes it	I walked up to a tree, *an Osage orange.*
Verb phrase	A main verb and its auxiliaries	as if the leaves of the Osage orange *had been freed*
Prepositional phrase	A preposition, a noun (or a pronoun), and modifiers, if any	*from a spell* *in the form* *of red-winged blackbirds*
Absolute phrase	Usually a noun (or a pronoun) and a participle. It modifies a whole sentence.	Late I lay open-mouthed in bed, *my arms flung wide.*
Verbal phrase — participial	A present or past participle and its modifiers, objects, or complements. It functions as an adjective.	We rock, *cradled in the swaddling band of darkness.*
Verbal phrase — gerund	A gerund (an -*ing* word derived from a verb that functions as a noun) and its modifiers, objects, or complements	The hollow *rushing of wind* raises hair on my neck and face.
Verbal phrase — infinitive	An infinitive (*to* plus the base form of a verb) and its modifiers, objects, or complements. It functions as a noun, an adjective, or an adverb.	The secret of seeing is *to sail on solar wind.*

[1] From Annie Dillard, "Seeing," *Pilgrim at Tinker Creek* (New York: Harper Perennial, 1974, 1998). Longer extracts from Dillard's book appear on pp. 243 and 247–48.

Grammatical Sentence Types

Once you can confidently identify independent and subordinate clauses, you can classify sentences into different grammatical types according to the way these clauses are combined. There are four types of sentences:

- Simple
- Compound
- Complex
- Compound-complex

> → **Guidelines** **Using Grammar Checkers**
>
> Computer grammar checkers are notoriously unreliable. The problem is that a computer does not understand the meaning of a sentence; it can only recognize certain word patterns and make suggestions. Grammar checkers can be helpful if you understand that they offer only basic suggestions and reminders: you must be able to decide for yourself whether these suggestions are appropriate or not.
>
> Nor do grammar checkers distinguish clearly between style advice and grammar advice. Consider the following sentence:
>
> > This sentence contains two independent clauses, but they are separated only by a comma.
>
> The grammar checker suggests changing the second clause to "only a comma separates them"—presumably to avoid the passive voice. That *could* be an improvement. But the original phrasing might be preferable because it puts the word "comma" at the end of the sentence, where it receives some emphasis.

Sentences that contain just one independent clause and no subordinate clauses — no matter how long and densely packed with modifiers and phrases — are known as **simple sentences**: "This sentence is a simple sentence." Sentences that include one independent clause and at least one subordinate clause are known as **complex sentences**. These terms describe the grammatical structure of the sentence, not its length. Complex sentences can be short.

SUBORDINATE CLAUSE   INDEPENDENT CLAUSE

Where there's life, there's hope.

Compound sentences contain more than one independent clause, as in this example.

FIRST INDEPENDENT CLAUSE   SECOND INDEPENDENT CLAUSE

The answers will not be read passively from nature; they do not, and cannot, arise

from the data of science.   (Stephen Jay Gould)

➔ **Try This**   Identifying Independent Clauses

Identify the independent clauses in this sentence.

> The strategies were as varied as the practitioners; they shared only the theme of special pleading for an a priori doctrine—they knew that God's benevolence was lurking some-where behind all these tales of apparent horror.   (Stephen Jay Gould)

Sentences that contain more than one independent clause and one or more subordinate clauses are called **compound-complex**.

> [Intentionality's] presence is about as hard to prove as its absence; hence, caution in relation to animals would be entirely acceptable if human behavior were held to the same standard.   (Frans de Waal)

To use punctuation correctly and confidently, you need to be able to identify grammatical sentence types, to distinguish between independent and subordinate clauses, and to distinguish clauses from other word groups.

There are two ways to join two independent clauses.

- With a comma and a coordinating conjunction (*and, or, nor, for, yet, but, so*), as in this example:

> People say that life is the thing, but I prefer reading.   (Logan Pearsall Smith)

- With a semicolon or, more rarely, a colon, as in these examples:

> They spell it Vinci and pronounce it Vinchy; foreigners always spell better than they pronounce.   (Mark Twain)

> The best of men cannot suspect their fate: The good die early, and the bad die late.   (Daniel Defoe)

If you join a subordinate clause to an independent clause, use a comma if the subordinate clause comes first. Usually the comma is unnecessary if the subordinate clause comes after the independent clause. Compare the following two sentences:

> When your work speaks for itself, don't interrupt.   (Henry J. Kaiser)

> Jill cleaned up whenever Toby made a mess.

Properly punctuated, clauses can be linked together to form compound-complex sentences.

Rhetorical Sentence Types

Now that you can recognize the two types of clauses (independent and subordinate) and four sentence structures (simple, complex, compound, and compound-complex), we can move on to consider sentence structures from another angle, the rhetorical rather than the grammatical. Traditional rhetoric divides sentences into three categories, depending on whether the independent clause appears first, last, or both first and last:

- Loose
- Periodic
- Balanced

If the independent clause appears first, the sentence is called **loose**. Here's an example from Cornel West's "Malcolm X and Black Rage":

> In fact, these tragic facts drove Malcolm X to look elsewhere for the promotion and protection of black people's rights — to institutions such as the United Nations or the Organization of African Unity.

After a brief transitional phrase ("In fact"), the independent clause follows immediately, with the main verb ("drove") appearing immediately after the subject ("these tragic facts"). The sentence continues after the dash with a prepositional phrase (note the absence of a verb — which is why it is a phrase and not a clause). In a loose sentence, most of the detail in the sentence comes *after* the independent clause.

By contrast, a **periodic sentence** places the independent clause, or most of it, at the end of the sentence. This creates a sense of anticipation — but it also requires readers to hold information in their heads as they wait for the subject and main verb that will make sense of it all. Here's a short example from the same essay:

> For Malcolm X, in a racist society, this was a form of social death.

And here's another periodic sentence, by Richard Rodriguez:

> When armies are victorious, when armies are trodden in the dust, when crops fail, when volcanoes erupt, when seas drink multitudes, it must mean God intends it so.

Lengthy periodic sentences are unusual in modern English prose, though before about 1900 writers frequently used them. Here's an example from the great eighteenth-century statesman Edmund Burke:

> To complain of the age we live in, to murmur at the present possessors of power, to lament the past, to conceive extravagant hopes of the future, are the common dispositions of the greatest part of mankind.

In the third sentence type, the **balanced sentence**, two independent clauses stand side by side, often parallel in structure. We often encounter them in political speeches and treatises, as their effect is rather grand and resonant.

> Ask not what your country can do for you; ask what you can do for your country.
>
> (John F. Kennedy)

> Kings are not born: they are made by universal hallucination.
>
> (George Bernard Shaw)

> Put not your trust in money, but put your money in trust.
>
> (Oliver Wendell Holmes)

However, as elegant and impressive as balanced and periodic sentences may be, in modern writing and especially in expository or descriptive writing, the loose sentence is the most common and natural-sounding. The word "loose" should not be taken as pejorative: it simply implies that this sentence structure has great flexibility. When the independent clause appears first, we can freely add phrases and clauses to it and produce a sentence of considerable length that remains perfectly clear. Thus the loose sentence is often **cumulative**; that is, it contains modifiers that develop or qualify the main idea in the independent clause.

> And much about my family life was easy then, comfortable, happy in the rhythm of our living together: hearing my father getting ready for work; eating the breakfast my mother had made me; looking up from a novel to hear my brother or one of my sisters playing with friends in the backyard; in winter, coming into the house all lighted up after dark.   (Richard Rodriguez)

> They regarded me silently, Brother Jack with a smile that went no deeper than his lips, his head cocked to one side, studying me with penetrating eyes; the other blank-faced, looking out of eyes that were meant to reveal nothing and to stir profound uncertainty.   (Ralph Ellison)

Buffalo Bill comes to the child in us, understood not as that part of ourselves that we have outgrown but as the part that got left behind, of necessity, a long time ago, having been starved, bound, punished, disciplined out of existence.

(Jane Tompkins)

➔ Try This   Composing Sentences

1. Compose a single loose cumulative sentence out of the elements listed. Edit them as necessary, and use them in any order, but begin your sentence with an independent clause. Attach phrases and subordinate clauses to the independent clause to include all the remaining elements.

   J. M. W. Turner's 1844 painting *Rain, Steam and Speed — The Great Western Railway* depicts a train.

   The train is crossing a bridge over the River Thames.

   The river flows slowly through the dawn light.

   A tiny rowboat idles in the water.

   The sky is golden, white, and blue.

   The train's black funnel stands out sharply against the sky.

   The train hurtles toward the viewer across the black bridge.

2. Choose a topic of your own, and list five or six attributes or qualities of it. Then combine them into a loose cumulative sentence. Be sure to begin with an independent clause, adding phrases and subordinate clauses as needed to produce an effective sentence.

Writing Longer Sentences by Using Coordination and Subordination

Many writers hesitate to write longer sentences, fearing that a sentence that contains two or more clauses might become a "run-on." However, a run-on sentence is not an excessively long sentence, but one that lacks either the correct punctuation between clauses or a joining word. A short sentence might, in fact, be a run-on. For example:

> Avoid smoking cigarettes, they can kill you.

The sentence contains two independent clauses, but they are separated only by a comma. To avoid the run-on, you can use a semicolon between the clauses or place a coordinating conjunction (such as "for") after the comma.

Writers may feel uncertain about how to recognize clauses, distinguish independent from subordinate clauses, and punctuate them correctly. Usually the result of this avoidance is monotonous, choppy prose. By learning how to write longer sentences, you can escape this pitfall.

Writers need to construct longer sentences chiefly for two reasons. First, expressing complicated or nuanced ideas involves expressing the relationship between ideas. Incorporating more than one thought into a single sentence allows you to express the close relationship between them. In the compound-complex sentence that we considered earlier (p. 224), Frans de Waal expresses a logical relationship by linking two independent clauses together and introducing the second clause with the word "hence": since one can't prove intentionality in the case of humans or animals, why the double standard?

> [Intentionality's] presence is about as hard to prove as its absence; hence, caution in relation to animals would be entirely acceptable if human behavior were held to the same standard.

Second, writing that employs only short sentences will seem choppy and monotonous to readers; a pleasing style varies the lengths of sentences, imparting an almost musical sense of movement and rhythm as it carries the reader along on the swell and ebb of longer and shorter sentences.

Early drafts of an essay tend to rely heavily on simple sentence structures and fairly short sentences. As you revise, you can attend to the rhythm of your sentences. By combining short sentences into longer ones, you can make choppy writing more expressive, elegant, and economical.

Here's a choppy passage from a student's draft.

> Tompkins is plagued by the question of whether to adore or abhor Buffalo Bill. To Tompkins, Buffalo Bill is the antihero. He is the man who roamed the frontier with an itchy trigger finger. Tompkins thinks he also had a knack for spilling blood. Upon further study, he becomes a humanitarian. He tried to save the

buffalo from extinction. He becomes a man of culture. He brought civilization to the West. He is also the man who brings a picture of the Wild West back to the civilized East. Bill Cody's final portrait is that of an American hero. He is the "poster boy" of the new era of expansion.

Not only does the prose sound awkward because of the repetition of short, simple sentence structures, but it also feels wordy because of the repetition of empty phrases like "he is." Moreover, the relationship of ideas is less than clear because each clause stands alone, bearing the same relation to the preceding clause as to the following one. However, when the writer, Brendan Barrett, combined closely related sentences into longer ones, the passage improved greatly.

Tompkins is plagued by the tearing question of whether to adore or abhor Buffalo Bill. To Tompkins, he is primarily the antihero, the man who roamed the frontier with an itchy trigger finger and a knack for spilling blood. Upon further study, he becomes a humanitarian who tries to save the buffalo from extinction; he becomes a man of culture who brings civilization to the West as well as a picture of the Wild West back to the civilized East. Indeed, Bill Cody's final portrait is that of an American hero, the "poster boy" of the new era of expansion.

Brendan took the sentences "He is the man who roamed the frontier with an itchy trigger finger. Tompkins thinks he also had a knack for spilling blood" and turned them into a single **appositive phrase** — that is, a phrase that expands on the term that immediately precedes it (in this case, "antihero"). However, he chose to keep the repetition of "he becomes a" in the next sentence because this repetition helps keep the point clear as the reader enters the more complicated phrases about the Wild West and civilized East that follow. So Brendan joined the second of these sentences to the first with a semicolon, producing a balanced sentence made of parallel clauses. Finally, he turned the last sentence into another appositive phrase, this time expanding on the word "hero."

Combining sentences in this way is called **coordination** and **subordination**. When we combine two sentences and keep them equal to each other (as Brendan has done with the two clauses that begin "he becomes a"), the process is called "coordinating." Coordination is accomplished by joining together clauses, either with a semicolon or with a coordinating conjunction (*and, or, nor, so, yet, but, for*). Some rewording may be necessary.

Turning a sentence into a phrase or a subordinate clause is called "subordinating." Subordination is accomplished in several ways.

Using Subordinating Words Use a subordinating word to turn one of the clauses into a subordinate clause. Subordinating words include subordinating conjunctions (such as *after, because, so that, when, though, in order that*) and relative pronouns (*who, whom, whose, which, that*).

Consider this sentence:

> When propagandists are not demonizing the enemy, they are remaking themselves
> in its image.   (Daniel Harris)

In this example, the clause "propagandists are not demonizing the enemy" has been subordinated to the independent clause ("they are remaking themselves in its image") by placing the subordinating conjunction "when" in front of it.

Here is another example:

> Because there is a generally poetic element in all historical writing, an element that
> appears in prose discourse as rhetoric, great historical works, whether by historians
> or historicists, retain their vividness and authority longer after they have ceased to
> count as contributions to "science."   (Hayden White)

In this case, the first clause ("there is a generally poetic element in all historical writing") has been subordinated by placing the subordinating conjunction "because" in front of it.

And here is another example of a sentence that uses subordination:

> One of the grand myths of the American Religion is the restoration of the Primitive
> Church, which probably never existed.   (Harold Bloom)

In this example, the second clause ("which probably never existed") has been subordinated by using the relative pronoun "which" as the subject.

A final example:

> The concept of irony was rediscovered by I. A. Richards, who defines irony . . . as "the
> bringing in of the opposite, of the complementary impulses," in order to achieve a
> "balanced poise."   (D. C. Muecke)

Here, the second clause has been subordinated by using the relative pronoun "who" as the subject.

Cutting Words You can also subordinate by cutting unnecessary words and turning a clause into a phrase, as in the following example.

> Land in Holland being so scarce and expensive, Dutch gardens were miniatures, measured in square feet rather than acres and frequently augmented with mirrors.
>
> (Michael Pollan)

This sentence combines one independent clause and three verbal phrases, of which each could have been an independent clause. In the draft stage, it might have been four separate sentences:

> Land in Holland was scarce and expensive. Therefore, Dutch gardens were miniatures. They were measured in square feet rather than acres. They were frequently augmented with mirrors.

But the repetition of the empty pronoun "they" and the verb "were," the cumbersome "therefore," and the staccato effect of four short sentences in a row all make this version inferior.

Using Appositives   The appositive phrase — a phrase that expands on the term it follows — is an especially useful and effective subordination device. Consider the differences between these versions:

> **Original**   Gioacchino Rossini (1792–1868) is the composer of *The Barber of Seville, William Tell,* and other masterpieces of opera. At age thirty-seven, he suddenly stopped composing, though he would live for another forty years.

> **Revised**   Gioacchino Rossini (1792–1868), the composer of *The Barber of Seville, William Tell,* and other masterpieces of opera, suddenly stopped composing at age thirty-seven, though he would live for another forty years.

The appositive in the revised version is "the composer of *The Barber of Seville, William Tell,* and other masterpieces of opera." It simply expands on "Gioacchino Rossini." But the revision is preferable to the original not only because it contains fewer words but also because the first sentence of the original version is dull: it merely explains who Rossini is. Sentences formed around "is" or another form of the verb "to be" are often good candidates for this kind of subordination.

Expanding on Key Words   You can also subordinate by picking up a key word, repeating it, and developing it:

→ Try
This   Combining Sentences

Combine the following pairs of simple sentences into one compound sentence using coordination. You can delete and add words, but don't alter the meaning of the sentence.

1. The *Washington Post*'s Style Invitational is a weekly contest. In Week 278, readers were asked to take any word from the dictionary.
2. The word may be altered by adding, subtracting, or changing one letter. Readers must supply a new definition of the word.
3. For example, one reader made up the word "sarchasm." The reader defined it as "the gulf between the author of sarcastic wit and the person who doesn't get it."
4. Another reader offered the word "inoculatte." It means "to take coffee intravenously when you are running late."

Combine the following pairs of simple sentences into one complex sentence using subordination.

5. The winning entry defined the word "intaxication" as "euphoria at getting a tax refund." It lasts until you realize it was your money to start with.
6. The word "cashtration" refers to the act of buying a house. It renders the subject financially impotent for an indefinite period.

Combine the following sentences into a complex-compound sentence, using both coordination and subordination. Change the order of the sentences if you wish.

7. Some submissions made reference to local landmarks. One of these was awarded "first runner-up." It was sent in by a reader from Arlington, Virginia. He offered the word "giraffiti." He defined it as "vandalism spray-painted very, very high, such as the famous 'Surrender Dorothy' on the Beltway overpass."

Combine the following sentences into a complex sentence, using subordination to subordinate two of the sentences.

8. The word "bozone" was defined as "the substance surrounding stupid people." It stops bright ideas from penetrating. However, the bozone layer unfortunately is showing no signs of erosion.

> Rather it is a reconstruction of the field from new fundamentals, a reconstruction
> that changes some of the field's most elementary theoretical generalizations as well
> as many of its paradigm methods and applications.   (Thomas Kuhn)

When you combine sentences using coordination and subordination, bear in mind that the aim is to use these techniques judiciously so that the relations between ideas are more clearly and elegantly expressed. Don't simply string clauses together. There's no single correct way to do this. Practice and use your best judgment.

Telling a Story with Active Sentences

When writing seems lively and vivid, precise and varied, verbs typically play a prominent role in many of the sentences. Verbs, especially active verbs, do more than simply link nouns together; they give a sentence energy and movement.

Think of a sentence as a very, very short story. A story comes from the combination of a character (the subject of your sentence) and some sort of action (the verb). Often, the character does something to someone else (the object of the sentence). Consider the following sentence:

> In Sophocles' play *Oedipus Rex*, the murdering of his father and the marrying of his
> mother are actions taken by King Oedipus of Thebes.

The meaning of the sentence is clear enough, but something's wrong: it seems wordy and convoluted. The sentence fails to tell the story of the play in a forceful, logical way. The operational verb, "are," is a dull one, and the subjects of the verb are "murdering" and "marrying" — nouns formed from the verbs "murder" and "marry" (that is, gerunds).

The problem with the sentence is that murdering and marrying are really the *actions* in the story, not the *actors*. When the actor is the grammatical subject of the sentence and the action is the grammatical verb, the writing becomes clearer. If we rearrange the sentence so that the true actor becomes the subject and the actions become verbs, we get this:

> In Sophocles' play *Oedipus Rex*, King Oedipus of Thebes murders his father and
> marries his mother.

Let's consider some more examples. Compare the original and revised versions in these three pairs.

Original   The publication of Sigmund Freud's *Die Traumdeutung* occurred in 1899, a translation of which later appeared in English as *The Interpretation of Dreams.*

Revised   In 1899, Sigmund Freud published *Die Traumdeutung,* later translated into English as *The Interpretation of Dreams.*

Original   It was in this book that the introduction by Freud of the theory of the Oedipus Complex took place.

Revised   In this book, Freud introduced the theory of the Oedipus Complex.

Original   The claim of this theory is that the experience of young children is to have a feeling of desire for the parent of the opposite sex and a feeling of hatred for the parent of the same sex.

Revised   This theory claims that young children feel desire for the parent of the opposite sex and hatred for the parent of the same sex.

As we can see, sentences that tell a story are stronger, shorter, and more direct — not only when they concern actual plots (literal people and actions) but also when they concern abstract matters. In the last sentence above, the actor is the word "theory," and the action is "claims." Since theories *do* make claims, we can think of this abstract statement as a kind of story, with an actor and an action.

The more wordy and indirect phrasing that we find in the original sentences is often described as **periphrastic**. Typically, such sentences use a form of the verb "to be" (*is, are, was, were*) as the operational verb, and they frequently use noun forms, adjective forms, or adverb forms of verbs rather than operational verbs.

The way to untangle such sentences is to look for the verbs hiding in the nouns, adjectives, and adverbs. Then revise the sentence so that the actors in the sentence are subjects and objects and the actions are verbs. Table 7.1 (opposite page) shows a small sample of nouns and their verb, adjective, and adverb forms. Though most nouns can be turned into other parts of speech, not all words take all forms.

Table 7.1 Some Nouns and Their Forms

Noun Form	Verb Form	Adjective Form	Adverb Form
creation	create	creative	creatively
declaration	declare	declarative	declaratively
discovery	discover	discovered	
finding	find	found	
imagination, imagining	imagine	imaginative	imaginatively
initiation, initiative	initiate	initial	initially
opening	open	open	openly
speech	speak	spoken	
verbalization	verbalize	verbal	verbally
writing	write	written	

→ **Try This** **Working with Word Forms**

Fill in the missing words in the list below.

Noun Form	Verb Form	Adjective Form	Adverb Form
origin, original	originate	_____	_____
_____	emote	emotional	_____
_____	complete	_____	completely
_____	_____	_____	apologetically
_____	reason	rational	_____
compression	_____	_____	
_____	_____	representative	

→ Try This   Revising Sentences

Revise the following sentences so that the operational verb is no longer a form of the verb "to be." Aim to keep the meaning as close to the sense of the original as possible.

1. Dr. Frank Drake is the inventor of a formula to estimate the number of extraterrestrial civilizations in our galaxy.
2. In 1960, at a meeting of scientists in Green Bank, West Virginia, Drake's formula was an important subject of discussion.
3. A number of variables, including the number of planets that are capable of supporting life and the length of time that a civilization that is in possession of the technology of mass destruction is likely to survive, are components of the formula.

Revise these noun-form or adjective-form sentences to make them active.

4. Primitive life forms such as bacteria may once have had an existence on Earth's neighboring planet, Mars.
5. Life on Earth, biologists now believe, may have had its origin in extreme conditions, around "thermal vents" or "black smokers" on the ocean floor.
6. Similar conditions may be present on other planets and moons that in other respects do not have much resemblance to Earth.
7. This fact, some argue, makes for a great increase in the number of planets that are able to support life.

For the following sentences, revise expletive constructions to eliminate unnecessary words.

8. So far, there are only 150 planets that have been found outside our own solar system, but there are many astronomers who believe that a great many more must exist.
9. There are many planets that have an orbit that is too close to their suns, or too far away, to permit temperatures that would support life.
10. There are some planets, called "extrasolar" planets, that do not orbit a star. There are quite a few climate researchers who believe that some of these, perhaps as many as half a million, may be capable of supporting life.

Expletive Constructions

Another common type of periphrasis, or indirect construction, is the **expletive**. Expletive constructions use phrases such as "it is . . . that," "it was . . . that," or "there is . . . who," words that can often be omitted without significant loss of meaning. (The word "expletive" derives from the Latin verb *explere*, meaning "to fill out.") Here are a couple of examples.

It was in this book that Sigmund Freud introduced the theory of the Oedipus Complex.

There are some psychologists who dispute Freud's theory of the unconscious.

Still, it is this theory that remains the basis of much modern psychoanalytic practice.

At times, however, expletive constructions are useful. They can throw the emphasis on a particular word in a sentence. Use your ear, and avoid using expletive constructions unnecessarily.

As we shall see in the next chapter, almost every kind of sentence construction has its role to play: passive-verb constructions; active-verb constructions; long sentences and short sentences; loose, periodic, and balanced sentences. The important thing is to keep sentences under control, to be able to construct any type of sentence you need with confidence, analyze sentences for problems, and revise them so that they do what you need them to do.

> ➔ **Try This**   **Examining Sentences**
>
> Choose a passage of several paragraphs (about a page) from one of the essays included in this book. Examine how the writer varies the lengths of the sentences, the grammatical sentence types, and the rhetorical sentence types.

✅ Checklist for Crafting Sentences

As you write and revise sentences, keep the following in mind.

☐ Recognize clauses.
- Distinguish subjects from predicates.
- Distinguish independent clauses from subordinate clauses.

☐ Recognize phrases.

☐ Recognize grammatical sentence types:
- Simple (has only one independent clause)
- Complex (has one independent clause and at least one subordinate clause)
- Compound (has more than one independent clause)
- Compound-complex (has more than one independent clause and one or more subordinate clauses)

☐ Recognize rhetorical sentence types:
- Loose (the independent clause appears first)
- Periodic (the independent clause comes at the end)
- Balanced (two independent clauses appear side by side)

☐ Combine short sentences for clarity and economy using subordination and coordination.

☐ Tell a story with active sentences.

☐ Avoid unnecessary expletive constructions.

chapter 8

Writing with Style

Most of us admire those who exhibit that elusive thing we call "style." Certain celebrities (Lady Gaga, George Clooney, Björk — perhaps) are renowned for their sense of style; you may have friends whose fine sense of style makes them stand out; maybe you yourself are so fortunate. Style is one of those things that we instantly recognize but find difficult

> " Style is not something applied. It is something that permeates. It is of the nature of that in which it is found, whether the poem, the manner of a god, the bearing of a man. It is not a dress. "
>
> **WALLACE STEVENS**

to define — in part, perhaps, because uniqueness would seem to be one of its chief characteristics. But uniqueness isn't the whole story; there are at least a few common qualities that help us pin down what we mean by "style": a certain harmony of manners, dress, and speech, perhaps; a certain daring, and the poise and confidence to go with it. As the poet Wallace Stevens argues in the epigraph to this chapter, style is something more than a suit of clothes, something more than an outer layer that is just added on at the last moment. In the craft of writing, too, style is not just a surface quality. You can say *roughly* the same thing in poor prose as in stylish prose — but not *exactly* the same thing. And the difference is often crucial.

When we consider style in writing, the matter is complicated by the fact that the word gets used in two different senses: in a **normative** sense, which refers to a set of norms or rules that all writers should follow, and in a **descriptive** sense, which refers to the characteristic qualities of a particular piece of writing or a writer's whole body of work. Textbooks typically discuss style in the normative sense because they want to offer guidelines and models for writers. Literary criticism, by contrast, frequently uses the word in the descriptive sense, especially when it aims to identify the distinguishing qualities of a great writer — Ernest Hemingway or Laurence Sterne or Virginia Woolf. This ambiguity in the way that we use the word "style" is more than just a matter of semantic hair-splitting: it affects how we write, and perhaps not always for the better. Writers often feel pulled in two directions at once. On the one hand, they want their writing to express not just their ideas but a personality and a voice. On the other hand, they feel that their writing must observe a set of impersonal rules in order to be acceptable or even intelligible — rules of diction, sentence construction, paragraphing, and so on. In other words, writers may feel torn between style as a set of compulsory standards and style as an aspect of self-expression. This sense of being torn in two directions can sometimes make the writing process difficult and frustrating.

Some Famous Styles

Here are five representative examples of style.

John Lyly

This young gallant, of more wit than wealth, and yet of more wealth than wisdom, seeing himself inferior to none in pleasant conceits, thought himself superior to all in honest conditions, insomuch that he deemed himself so apt to all things, that he gave himself almost to nothing, but practicing of those things commonly which are incident to these sharp wits, fine phrases, smooth quipping, merry taunting, using jesting without mean, and abusing mirth without measure. As therefore the sweetest rose hath his prickle, the finest velvet his brack, the fairest flower his bran, so the sharpest wit hath his wanton will, and the holiest head his wicked way. And true it is that some men write and most men believe, that in all perfect shapes, a blemish bringeth rather a liking every way to the eyes, than a loathing any way to the mind.

(From *Euphues: The Anatomy of a Wit*, 1578)

Walter Pater

One of the most beautiful passages in the writings of Rousseau is that in the sixth book of the Confessions, where he describes the awakening in him of the literary sense. An undefinable taint of death had always clung about him, and now in early manhood he believed himself smitten by mortal disease. He asked himself how he might make as much as possible of the interval that remained; and he was not biased by anything in his previous life when he decided that it must be by intellectual excitement, which he found just then in the clear, fresh writings of Voltaire. Well! we are all *condamnés*, as Victor Hugo says: we are all under sentence of death but with a sort of indefinite reprieve — *les hommes sont tous condamnés à mort avec des sursis indéfinis*: we have an interval, and then our place knows us no more. Some spend this interval in listlessness, some in high passions, the wisest, at least among "the children of this world," in art and song. For our one chance lies in expanding that interval, in getting as many pulsations as possible into the given time. Great passions may give us this quickened sense of life, ecstasy and sorrow of love, the various forms of enthusiastic activity, disinterested or otherwise, which come naturally to many of us. Only be sure it is passion — that it does yield you this fruit of a quickened, multiplied consciousness. Of this wisdom, the poetic passion, the desire of beauty, the love of art for art's sake, has most; for art comes to you professing frankly to give nothing but the highest quality to your moments as they pass, and simply for those moments' sake.

(From *The Renaissance: Studies in Art and Poetry*, 1868)

Virginia Woolf

Here then was I (call me Mary Beton, Mary Seton, Mary Carmichael or by any name you please — it is not a matter of any importance) sitting on the banks of a river a week or two ago in fine October weather, lost in thought. That collar I have spoken of, women and fiction, the need of coming to some conclusion on a subject that raises all sorts of prejudices and passions, bowed my head to the ground. To the right and left bushes of some sort, golden and crimson, glowed with the colour, even it seemed burnt with the heat, of fire. On the further bank the willows wept in perpetual lamentation, their hair about their shoulders. The river reflected whatever it chose of sky and bridge and burning tree, and when the undergraduate had oared his boat through the reflections they closed again, completely, as if he had never been. There one might have sat the clock round lost in thought. Thought — to call it by a prouder name than it deserved — had let its line down into the stream. It swayed, minute after minute, hither and thither among the reflections and the weeds, letting the water lift it and sink it until — you know the little tug — the sudden conglomeration of an idea at the end of one's line: and then the cautious hauling of it in, and the careful laying of it out? Alas, laid on the grass how small, how insignificant this thought of mine looked; the sort of fish that a good fisherman puts back into the water so that it may grow fatter and be one day worth cooking and eating. I will not trouble you with that thought now, though if you look carefully you may find it for yourselves in the course of what I am going to say.

(From *A Room of One's Own,* 1929)

Martin Luther King Jr.

One of the basic points in your statement is that the action that I and my associates have taken in Birmingham is untimely. Some have asked: "Why didn't you give the new city administration time to act?" . . .

We know through painful experience that freedom is never voluntarily given by the oppressor; it must be demanded by the oppressed. Frankly, I have yet to engage in a direct action campaign that was "well timed" in the view of those who have not suffered unduly from the disease of segregation. For years now I have heard the word "Wait!" It rings in the ear of every Negro with piercing familiarity. This "Wait" has almost always meant "Never." We must come to see, with one of our distinguished jurists, that "justice too long delayed is justice denied."

We have waited for more than 340 years for our constitutional and God given rights. The nations of Asia and Africa are moving with jetlike speed toward gaining political independence, but we still creep at horse and buggy pace toward gaining a cup of coffee at a lunch counter. Perhaps it is easy for those who have never felt the stinging darts of segregation to say, "Wait." But when you have seen vicious mobs lynch your mothers and fathers at will and drown your sisters and brothers at whim; when you have seen hate filled policemen curse, kick and even kill your black brothers and sisters; when you see the vast majority of your twenty million Negro brothers smothering in an airtight cage of poverty in the midst of an affluent society; when you suddenly find your tongue twisted and your speech stammering as you seek to explain to your six year old daughter why she can't go to the public amusement park that has just been advertised on television, and see tears welling up in her eyes when she is told that Funtown is closed to colored children, and see ominous clouds of inferiority beginning to form in her little mental sky, and see her beginning to distort her personality by developing an unconscious bitterness toward white people; when you have to concoct an answer for a five year old son who is asking: "Daddy, why do white people treat colored people so mean?"; when you take a cross-country drive and find it necessary to sleep night after night in the uncomfortable corners of your automobile because no motel will accept you; when you are humiliated day in and day out by nagging signs reading "white" and "colored"; when your first name becomes "nigger," your middle name becomes "boy" (however old you are) and your last name becomes "John," and your wife and mother are never given the respected title "Mrs."; when you are harried by day and haunted by night by the fact that you are a Negro, living constantly at tiptoe stance, never quite knowing what to expect next, and are plagued with inner fears and outer resentments; when you are forever fighting a degenerating sense of "nobodiness" — then you will understand why we find it difficult to wait. There comes a time when the cup of endurance runs over, and men are no longer willing to be plunged into the abyss of despair. I hope, sirs, you can understand our legitimate and unavoidable impatience.

(From "Letter from Birmingham Jail," 1963)

Annie Dillard

Unfortunately, nature is very much a now-you-see-it, now-you-don't affair. A fish flashes, then dissolves in the water before my eyes like so much salt. Deer apparently ascend bodily into heaven; the brightest oriole fades into leaves. These disappearances stun me into stillness and concentration; they say of nature that it conceals with a grand nonchalance, and they say of vision that it is a deliberate gift, the revelation of a dancer who for my eyes only flings away her seven veils. For nature does reveal as well as conceal: now-you-don't-see-it, now-you-do. For a week last September migrating red-winged blackbirds were feeding heavily down by the creek at the back of the house. One day I went out to investigate the racket; I walked up to a tree, an Osage orange, and a hundred birds flew away. They simply materialized out of the tree. I saw a tree, then a whisk of color, then a tree again. I walked closer and another hundred blackbirds took flight. Not a branch, not a twig budged: the birds were apparently weightless as well as invisible. Or, it was as if the leaves of the Osage orange had been freed from a spell in the form of red-winged blackbirds; they flew from the tree, caught my eye in the sky, and vanished. When I looked again at the tree the leaves had reassembled as if nothing had happened. Finally I walked directly to the trunk of the tree and a final hundred, the real diehards, appeared, spread, and vanished. How could so many hide in the tree without my seeing them? The Osage orange, unruffled, looked just as it had looked from the house, when three hundred red-winged blackbirds cried from its crown. I looked downstream where they flew and they were gone. Searching, I couldn't spot one. I wandered downstream to force them to play their hand, but they'd crossed the creek and scattered. One show to a customer. These appearances catch at my throat; they are the free gifts, the bright coppers at the roots of trees.

(From *Pilgrim at Tinker Creek,* 1974)

Plain Style

Ideas about style in writing, as in fashion, change with the times. A hundred years ago — or two hundred or four hundred — readers brought different expectations to their reading and admired different qualities in writers.

Since the mid-twentieth century, however, a consensus has emerged concerning the desirability of clarity and directness in prose. In "Politics and the English Language" (1946), the English novelist and social critic George Orwell argued that pretentious, obscure, or clichéd language poses a real danger to citizens of a democracy because it allows reprehensible or misleading ideas to pass for truth and reason. Not coincidentally, his essay appeared just after the end of a world war against fascism.

In America in the 1950s, a textbook by William Strunk Jr. called *The Elements of Style* (first published in 1918 but revised by the *New Yorker* essayist E. B. White) became a best seller — and has remained one for half a century. Like Orwell, Strunk and White offered writers a limited set of powerful rules for improving the clarity and freshness of their prose; and like Orwell, Strunk and White assailed the laziness that produces obscure and nonsensical writing: "The beginner should approach style warily . . . and he should begin by turning resolutely away from all devices that are popularly believed to indicate style — all mannerisms, tricks, adornments. The approach to style is by way of plainness, simplicity, orderliness, sincerity."[1] Memorable rules such as "Omit needless words" and "Use definite, specific, concrete language" form the foundation of this approach to "plainness." Like Orwell, and Strunk and White, most other authorities on style over the last century have similarly championed **plain style**.

For good reason. Ornate writing might seem impressive, but obscure diction and perplexing phrasing come between the reader and the subject matter, making it difficult to see what the writer really wants to say. And as Orwell argues, wordiness, stale metaphors, and excessive abstraction may serve as a cover for false, contradictory, or meaningless ideas. "What is above all needed," Orwell writes, "is to let the meaning choose the word, and not the other way about. In prose, the worst thing one can do with words is to surrender to them."[2] The term "plain style," then, does not

---

[1] William Strunk Jr. and E. B. White, *The Elements of Style*, 3rd ed. (New York: Macmillan, 1979), 69.
[2] George Orwell, "Politics and the English Language," in *Essays*, ed. John Carey (New York: Knopf [Everyman's Library], 2002), 965.

mean a dull or flat style; it means a direct, vivid, economical, and readable style, a style that communicates the thought as clearly and precisely as possible.

Any writer who hopes to communicate clearly and effectively would do well to consider the advice of these plain stylists, and we will recapitulate their guidelines in the following sections. But we will also consider two caveats or qualifications to this standard (and mostly very good) advice. First, we can draw some valuable lessons from some of the older ideas about style — ideas that, though they might at first seem to contradict the principles of plain style, are really complementary to them. Second, academic writing has certain stylistic conventions and requirements of its own, so we will discuss these in the final section of this chapter.

Principles of Plain Style

Cut Excess Verbiage

All the principles of plain style can be reduced to this: "If it is possible to cut a word out, always cut it out," as Orwell wrote. Or as Strunk and White famously put it: "omit needless words." In theory, this advice seems easy enough to carry out: just cut any words you can eliminate without changing the meaning. But in practice, it takes judgment and experience to recognize which words are really needed and which ones can be dropped without weakening the sense. How much paring is too much?

When speaking, we tend to use many more words than we need — not just verbal tics such as "you know?" and "like," but whole phrases and sentences that we subsequently retract or reformulate as we work out our ideas. ("This is terrific coffee. Well, not quite terrific, maybe, but very good. . . . Or at least, better than average. Maybe.") Similarly, many of the words in a first draft will prove unnecessary. Some of these you can quickly learn to identify as excess verbiage (see "Cut Empty Phrases" below); others you might find and revise only by experimenting with alternative phrasing. Read the sentence with the word or phrase, then try reading it without, and see whether the result is greater economy or a real loss of meaning.

Cut Empty Phrases   In early drafts, almost all writers use some empty phrases such as those that follow. But experienced writers learn to look out for them as they revise. Cutting them makes the writing more economical, vigorous, and clear. Some phrases can be eliminated entirely.

Phrases That Can Be Eliminated

on the whole

I think that; in my view (in places where it is obvious that the opinion being expressed is your own)

type of; kind of; sort of (when not used literally, as in "Clover is a kind of herbaceous plant")

who is/was (e.g., say "the man in charge" rather than "the man who is in charge")

In other cases, you can substitute a more economical word or phrase for a wordier phrase.

Instead of	Use
come to the conclusion	conclude
the fact that	that
due to the fact that	because
for the reason that	because
each and every	each; every
of a [profound] nature	[profound]
in a [harsh] manner	[harshly]
In [John Updike's story "A & P," he] writes …	In ["A & P," John Updike] writes …
in terms of	with (e.g., say "I am making progress with my essay" rather than "I am making progress in terms of my essay")

In General, Prefer the Active Voice

Compare the following sentences:

In 1971, the FBI recovered El Greco's sketch *The Immaculate Conception*.

In 1971, El Greco's sketch *The Immaculate Conception* was recovered by the FBI.

In the first sentence, the verb "recovered" is in the active voice. That is, the subject of the verb ("the FBI") is the *actor* in relation to the verb: the FBI did the recovering. In the second sentence, the verb "was recovered" is in the passive voice. The subject of the verb ("sketch") is the *receiver* of the action, not the actor. Note that the form of **passive verbs** differs from the form of **active verbs**. Passive verbs comprise two (and sometimes three) words — here, the auxiliary verb "was" and the main verb "recovered." So active-verb constructions are always more economical and direct than passive-verb constructions; although both example sentences express the same idea, the second uses two extra words, because the preposition "by" is also needed to identify the actor.

Passive constructions consign specific mention of the actor to a prepositional phrase ("by the FBI") or omit any mention of the actor. Passive constructions that do not mention the actor sometimes express a writer's wish, conscious or unconscious, to hide the actor's identity. "An increase in your interest rate was deemed unavoidable." Deemed unavoidable by whom? By the lender, of course, but the lender appears to be reluctant to reveal that it is acting in this situation. As a rule, active constructions are more forthright and honest: they tell the reader who is doing what to whom. Passive constructions are often indirect and even evasive: they tell the reader only what is being done to someone or something, and not necessarily who or what is responsible.

Although active-verb constructions (such as "Charlie bit the dog") are usually clearer and more direct than passive-verb constructions, we need to consider some exceptions to the rule, situations in which a passive verb is clearer or less awkward than an active verb. Passive-verb constructions allow you to put the thing that is acted upon in the position of the subject: "The dog was bitten by Charlie."

In the following two situations, you might want to use passive verbs:

1. When you want to emphasize the actor by placing it at the end of the sentence. If the identity of the actor is new information, it might make sense to reveal it at the end of the sentence: "Who bit this dog?" "The dog was bitten by Charlie."

2. When the identity of the actor is unimportant and needs no mention. In the sentence "On June 16, 1903, the Ford Motor Company was incorporated," it may not matter who did the incorporating; the writer only wants to tell us the date on which the event occurred.

Consider this passage from Annie Dillard's "Seeing," in which most of the verbs are active.

> I chanced on a wonderful book by Marius von Senden, called *Space and Sight*. When Western surgeons discovered how to perform safe cataract operations, they ranged across Europe and America operating on dozens of men and women of all ages who had been blinded by cataracts since birth. Von Senden collected accounts of such

cases; the histories are fascinating. Many doctors had tested their patients' sense perceptions and ideas of space both before and after the operations. The vast majority of patients, of both sexes and all ages had, in von Senden's opinion, no idea of space whatsoever.

There's only one passive verb in the passage above. Can you identify it?

If we simply change as many active-verb constructions into passive-verb constructions as we can, we produce a very awkward paragraph.

A wonderful book called *Space and Sight* by Marius von Senden was chanced on by me. When a way to perform safe cataract operations was discovered by Western surgeons, Europe and America were ranged across by them so that dozens of men and women of all ages who had been blinded by cataracts since birth could be operated on. Accounts of such cases were collected by von Senden; the histories are fascinating. Their patients' sense perceptions and ideas of space had been tested by many doctors both before and after the operations. In von Senden's opinion, no idea of space whatsoever was had by the vast majority of patients, of both sexes and all ages.

Conversely, we can sometimes make an awkward passage more elegant by changing passive verbs to active ones, or occasionally vice versa. See what you can do with the following paragraph to improve it.

In 1893, Gandhi and his family moved from Bombay to Natal, South Africa, to practice law for an Indian law firm. Discrimination was suffered by Gandhi, as an Indian in South Africa, and the indignities that were experienced by him there proved to be a turning point in his life. In 1894, the Natal Indian Congress, an organization that was dedicated to working for Indian rights, was founded by Gandhi. Yet at this point in his life, the prevailing racist ideology of South Africa was often reflected in Gandhi's own views. When war was declared by the British against the Zulus, the Indian population of South Africa was encouraged by Gandhi to serve in the British army, and the British regime was urged by Gandhi to accept them. Yet it was during this time that a philosophy of passive resistance was developed by Gandhi, which came to be called "Satyagraha" or "truth-force" by him. In 1915, Gandhi and his family moved back to India.

Sometimes, trying to revise a passive verb creates absurdity.

Mohandas Gandhi was born in 1869.

Would anyone revise this as "Mohandas Gandhi's mother birthed Mohandas Gandhi in 1869"? In such instances, it is better to use the passive voice.

As a Rule, Cast Sentences in Positive Form

Generally, it takes fewer words to express an idea in positive form than to express it in negative form.

Negative   Louise did not cease to smoke cigars.
Positive   Louise continued to smoke cigars.

Negative   Throughout the 1960s, the FBI did not stop searching for El Greco's sketch *The Immaculate Conception.*
Positive   Throughout the 1960s, the FBI kept searching for El Greco's sketch *The Immaculate Conception.*

Negative   Arthur does not hate anyone.
Positive   Arthur likes everyone.

Note, however, that the negative form usually carries a slightly different sense: in the first two examples above, the negative statements are a little more emphatic; in the third, the negative statement could mean that Arthur is indifferent to everyone, not that he positively likes everyone.

Avoid Unnecessary Qualifiers

A **qualifier** is a word or phrase (usually an adjective or an adverb) that modifies, limits, or attributes a quality to another word or phrase (usually a noun or a verb). In the phrase "a tall tree," the word "tall" is a qualifier. Distinguish between necessary and unnecessary qualifiers, and cut the unnecessary ones.

- Some vague qualifiers (such as *rather, very, great, somewhat*) are rarely necessary and should almost always be cut. The sentence will be stronger and more direct without them.

- Similarly, colloquial qualifiers (such as *awesome, terribly, literally, really, awfully, definitely*) are often used carelessly and have become meaningless. These can easily be eliminated.

Check whether the qualifier truly adds something to the sentence, or whether the sentence is stronger, clearer, and more direct without it. In academic style, though, some qualifiers are necessary because they narrow a claim and thereby make it more precise and valid. Without qualifiers, a claim may be too general and therefore inaccurate. (See p. 263 for more on "hedging" your claims.)

➔ Try This   Practicing Concision

Cut excess verbiage from the following paragraphs.

The Great Cost of Information Overload

A company called Basex, which is a business research firm, recently estimated that "information overload" costs American companies $650 billion a year in lost productivity and innovation. Workers are distracted by a steady barrage of e-mails and instant messages throughout the day. "We send too many things out, and we send them to too many people," says Basex's Jonathan Spira. On the whole, the cost to industry is thought to come not only from the frequent distractions but also from the amount of time it takes a worker to refocus on a task following an interruption of this kind.

Another aspect of information overload is the fact that an almost limitless quantity of information is instantly available to workers through the Internet. In 1997, the aforementioned problem was analyzed by David Shenk in his book that is entitled *Data Smog: Surviving the Information Glut*. "Data smog" was the name invented by Shenk to describe the phenomenon of an "overabundance of low quality information." Looking back on his earlier predictions a decade later, Shenk came to the conclusion that the greater the *quantity* of information we must manage, the harder it is to find information that is *quality*. To offer just one example, while search engines have become tools that are more or less essential, one might say, for finding needed information on the Internet, even a search that has been narrowly defined can result in hundreds of thousands of hits, perhaps even more. Sometimes, one might say, more is less.

In fact, the term "information overload" actually predates the personal computer and the Internet. It was introduced, according to Infogineering.net, by futurologist Alvin Toffler in the 1970s, in the course of predicting that the ever-burgeoning availability of large amounts of information would eventually create problems of a severe kind.

In terms of solutions, Infogineering.net offers workers several useful remedies to the problem. First, workers should spend less time on information that is (or may be) "nice to know" and focus instead on what they "need to know now." Second, they should try as far as possible to focus less on quantity of information and more on quality of information. Third, in e-mail, they should make a point of asking questions in terms that are simple and direct, so that the respondent can respond in answers that are short and precise. Fourth, workers should never try to focus on more than one issue at a time, if possible. Fifth and lastly, workers should never forget to spend part of their day disconnected from e-mail, telephone, and all other kinds of interruptions.

Using Clear and Direct Vocabulary

Use Specific Words

In a sense, as the poet T. S. Eliot put it, "words are general, experiences are particular," and so words can perhaps never express ideas with perfect precision. But although the number of words in the dictionary may be finite, the number of ways in which they can be combined is unlimited. Thus language can express ideas with a great deal of preciseness, especially when words are used in fresh and striking ways.

When the exact word doesn't come to mind right away, many writers reach for the thesaurus. Now that computer dictionaries typically incorporate a thesaurus, we needn't even reach for it — a couple of mouse clicks will do. A thesaurus can be helpful, but it can also tempt us to use a word that sounds impressive or fancy but isn't quite right. Before taking a word from the thesaurus, look it up in the dictionary, even if you think you know the meaning. The dictionary will give you a more exact sense of its meaning, and sometimes even its history, and will help you choose the best word. In the end, you may find that the dictionary is more valuable than the thesaurus. Use the thesaurus cautiously; use the dictionary eagerly and confidently.

The seventeenth-century Irish satirist Jonathan Swift defined good style as "proper words in proper places." Your aim should always be to find the exact word, the fitting or felicitous phrase, or what might be called the "happy" expression, in the sense of *fortuitous* — fortunately happened upon.

The dictionary will help you avoid a **malapropism** — using a wrong word that sounds similar to the right one. For example, in 2000, presidential candidate George

> → **Try This** **Get Happy**
>
> Look up the words "cheerful," "happy," "euphoric," and "jolly." How do the meanings of these words differ? Do they carry different connotations? If so, how might you describe these differences?

W. Bush said, "We cannot let terrorists and rogue nations hold this nation hostile or hold our allies hostile." He meant "hostage," of course. But good writing requires something more than just avoiding the obviously wrong word. With so many words in the language (about 250,000), English has many words that convey similar ideas but carry slightly different shades of meaning. By paying careful attention to the best writers' use of language, you will develop sensitivity to these shades and will learn not only a word's **denotation** — the dictionary definition — but also its **connotations** — what it suggests or the feelings and ideas it conjures.

Use Concrete Words

The term **abstract** comes from the Latin word for "drawn away." When a word or concept is distant or remote from lived experience, from things that we can actually see, hear, and touch, we may call it "abstract." The contrasting term is **concrete**, something that is solid and real and exists in material or physical form. Abstractions are necessary and useful, of course. We couldn't possibly limit ourselves to physical objects, especially in academic writing. But words that suggest concrete realities tend to be much more evocative and sensual — and clearer — than abstract words.

Words derived from Latin, such as "operational," "vehicle," and "minimize," often seem more abstract than their near equivalents deriving from Anglo-Saxon: "working," "car," and "lessen." Prefer the shorter, simpler word unless the longer one carries a specific meaning or connotation that you need. Some words are abstract because they refer to concepts that mean different things in different situations and to different people: "democracy," "justice," "progress," "nature," "society," and the like. Such words become devalued over time by overuse or by misuse and should be used with caution.

Abstract words are not bad words — on occasion, they may be exactly the right word in the right place — but most readers object to writing that is *excessively* or *needlessly* abstract, writing that forces them to slog through a thicket of complicated constructions only to arrive at a meaning that could have been expressed more simply.

Compare the following sentences:

The institution of higher education represents an asylum from the obligation to render pronouncements prematurely.

College is a refuge from hasty judgment.   (Robert Frost)

Most readers prefer the second sentence.

Use "Fancy" Words, Jargon, and Neologisms with Caution

Abstract words cannot be avoided entirely, especially in academic writing. But some kinds of words — jargon, neologisms, and pretentious language — should be used with great caution as they risk obscuring your meaning completely.

Jargon is specialized or technical language that a particular group or profession understands but that the average person does not. Computer engineers, for example, necessarily use a good deal of jargon. In an essay on developments in computer technology, some jargon may be necessary, but it should be kept to a minimum if the reader of the essay is not a computer professional. Use technical terms sparingly and define each one when you first introduce it.

Neologisms are words of recent origin that do not yet appear in dictionaries and that readers should not be expected to recognize. Some neologisms do catch on and become acceptable, familiar words; most fade into obscurity. For example, the word "digerati" appeared in the 1990s, formed by combining the words "digital" and "literati," referring to people with expertise in information technology; by 2003, it had entered the *Oxford English Dictionary*, and it is now widely used. The word "multidude" (to describe a group of surfers), by contrast, never caught on and is now a defunct neologism. The term "mouse potato," meaning someone who idles away too much time at a computer, may yet catch on, but for now it remains a neologism.

The Roots of English: Simple Words

English dictionaries usually supply information about the roots, or *etymology*, of words as well as their definitions. You will often see abbreviations such as "OE" (meaning Old English) or "Lat." (meaning Latin) in etymological notes. It helps to know a bit about the history of the English language in order to understand how words made their way from one language to another.

English is a Germanic language; the name comes from the Angles, a Germanic people who migrated from northern Germany to England in the fifth century CE. *Old English,* or Anglo-Saxon, was the language of England until the Norman Conquest of 1066 CE. Within a century (about 1150 CE), French, the language of the conquerors, began to blend with Old English to produce *Middle English.* French being descended from Latin, this process introduced into English not only many French words but also many Latin-based words. From about 1500, the language began to stabilize in the form it takes today, largely because of the spread of printed writing; this form is known as *Modern English.* William Shakespeare's English is Modern English; although many spellings and usages have changed — and will continue to change — our grammar and vocabulary are fundamentally the same as his.

Although the English language includes about 250,000 words (not counting strictly technical and scientific terms), many accomplished writers still favor the simple, earthy Anglo-Saxon words (of which there were fewer than 60,000). Typically, these are one- or two-syllable words that native English speakers know from childhood but that resonate with centuries of usage — words like the following:

> sorrow (*sorge*)
> fear (*fær*)
> heart (*heorte*)
> thought (*thoht*)
> fair (*fæger*)
> write (*writan*)

Latinate words with similar meanings are often polysyllabic:

> misery (*miseria*)
> trepidation (*trepidatio*)
> myocardium (*myocardium*)
> intellect (*intellectus*)
> equitable (*æquitas*)
> inscribe (*inscribere*)

Any good dictionary will provide some information about a word's origins. An etymological dictionary, such as the *Oxford English Dictionary*, also provides quotations that illustrate how each word has been used by writers throughout its history. This can give you insight into the connotations that gather around a word, and thus a much more precise sense of its meaning (or meanings) than any definition can provide.[3]

Here are some examples of how English has changed over the years.

Old English

Mæg ic be me selfum soþ-giedd wrecan, siðas secgan, hu ic geswinc-dagum earfoþ-hwile oft þrowode, bitre breost-ceare gebiden habbe, gecunnod on ceole cear-selda fela, atol yða gewealc, þær mec oft begeat nearu niht-wacu æt nacan stefnan, þonne he be clifum cnossaþ.

("The Seafarer," lines 1–8, from the Exeter Book, copied about 940 CE)

A word-for-word translation: "I can about myself a true poem recite, experiences relate, how I laborious-days and hard times often suffered, bitter breast-cares experienced, explored in [my] boat many care-abodes, terrible tossing waves, where anxious night-watch at the boat's prow often occupied me, when by the cliffs it tosses."

Middle English

Whan that Aprill with his shoures soote
The droghte of March hath perced to the roote,
And bathed every veyne in swich licour
Of which vertu engendred is the flour;
When Zephirus eek with his sweete breeth
Inspired hath in every hold and heeth
The tendre croppes, and the yonge sonne
Hath in the Ram his half cours yronne,
And smal foweles maken melodye,
The slepen al the nyght with open ye
(So priketh hem nature in hir corages),
Thanne longen folk to goon on pilgrimages....

(Geoffrey Chaucer, "General Prologue," *The Canterbury Tales,* about 1390)

---

[3] For more information, see Robert McCrum, Robert McNeil, and William Cran, *The Story of English*, 3rd rev. ed. (New York: Penguin, 2002).

Modern English

. . . Come, poor babe.

I have heard, but not believ'd, the spirits o' th' dead

May walk again. If such a thing be, thy mother

Appear'd to me last night, for ne'er was dream

So like a waking. To me comes a creature,

Sometimes her head on one side, some another;

I never saw a vessel of like sorrow,

So fill'd and so becoming. In pure white robes,

Like very sanctity, she did approach

My cabin where I lay; thrice bow'd before me,

And, gasping to begin some speech, her eyes

Became two spouts. . . .

(William Shakespeare, *The Winter's Tale*, act 3, scene 3, about 1610)

Using Verbs to Bring Life and Action to Sentences

In Chapter 7, we considered how tangled sentences can benefit from being recon-structed so that they tell a story, in which the actor is the grammatical subject and the action is a verb. Strong, fresh verbs inject energy into sentences. As action words, they signify not merely abstract relationships but also movement and force. Con-sciously or unconsciously, the reader sees your ideas in motion when strong verbs show how one concept, thing, or person acts upon another, and your thought becomes a kind of theater, where characters interact and a plot unfolds. The verb "to be" is probably the least vivid and least concrete and yet also the most frequently used verb in the English language. Of course, no writer can (or should) avoid it entirely, but experienced writers know to avoid it when they can; almost any other verb will serve the writer's purpose better than a mere "is" or "was." Many writers find that, in their early draft, the verb "to be" appears too often. But such sentences often hide a verb that can be revealed to express the thought more vividly.

Look for nominalizations that you can revise into verbs or verb phrases. A **nom-inalization** is a noun that has been formed from a verb. (The word "noun" comes from the Latin word *nomen*, meaning "name." "Nominalization" comes from the same root.) For example, the noun "defense" is a nominalization of the verb "to defend"; "pressure" is a nominalization of the verb "to press"; and, as you may have noticed, the word "nominalization" is itself a nominalization of the verb "nominal-ize." So a nominalization hides a verb within it: in the previous sentence, each of the clauses features "is" as the verb. But once we recognize that the word "nominaliza-tion" is itself a nominalization, we have a way to revise: we might write instead, "The noun 'defense' nominalizes the verb 'defend,'" and so on.

➔ Try This   Picking the Better Sentence

Compare these sentence pairs. Note the different wording, and choose which of the versions you prefer, A or B. Explain your choices.

A: At the international physics laboratory known as CERN (the European Organization for Nuclear Research), scientists are replicating conditions that existed in the universe when it was only a trillionth of a trillionth of a second old, the instant when matter, energy, space, and even time itself had just come into being.

B: At the international physics laboratory known as CERN (the European Organization for Nuclear Research), scientists are building a model of conditions that were in existence when the universe was only a trillionth of a trillionth of a second old, when matter, energy, space, and even time itself had just been created.

A: Three hundred feet underground, in a tunnel that spans the border between France and Switzerland, subatomic particles race around a 16.2-mile-long accelerator ring called the Large Hadron Collider (LHC).

B: Three hundred feet underground, in a tunnel that lies across the border between France and Switzerland, subatomic particles move in circles through a 16.2-mile-long accelerator ring known as the Large Hadron Collider (LHC).

A: Driven by 9,300 magnets, two particle beams, each containing trillions of protons and ions (hadrons), move through the collider in opposite directions, reaching a speed equal to 99.9999991 percent of the speed of light (almost 300 miles per second).

B: Propelled by 9,300 magnets, two beams of particles, each containing trillions of protons and ions (which are hadrons), hurtle through the collider in opposite directions, reaching a speed equivalent to 99.9999991 percent of the speed of light (almost 300 miles per second).

(continued)

A: The beams make eleven circuits per second through a vacuum as empty as outer space and then collide with so much force that the energy equals the energy that was released in the first moments following the Big Bang.
B: The beams complete eleven circuits per second through a vacuum as empty as outer space and then crash head-on with such extreme force that it reproduces the energy released a fraction of a second after the Big Bang.

A: The LHC, the world's largest refrigerator, is chilled to a frosty –456.34°F.
B: The LHC, the world's largest refrigerator, is kept to a temperature of –456.34°F.

A: But when particle beams collide, they generate temperatures 100,000 times hotter than the heart of the sun.
B: But when particle collisions occur, there is a production of temperatures that are 100,000 times hotter than the heart of the sun.

Using Figures of Speech and Metaphors

In academic writing, you will not need to concoct elaborate or extended metaphors frequently. But your writing can benefit from an awareness of the metaphors that many English words already contain. Seek out these underlying metaphors in your key terms, and use fitting images and metaphors with care. For example, a writer noticed that she mentioned the "influence" of one thinker upon another: "Walter Benjamin influenced the thinking of John Berger." The word "influence" conceals a metaphor: it comes from a Latin word meaning "flow in." When we speak of how one person influenced another, we are suggesting that something — ideas, probably — flowed from one person into another. So in remarking on how her reading of John Berger changed her understanding of Benjamin, this writer wrote: "The influence flowed against the current of time, however, when I came to read Benjamin's essay in the light of Berger's."

A vivid and fitting metaphor can lodge a memorable image in the reader's mind. (But too many different images can muddy ideas that might otherwise be clear.) In the introduction to his *Complete Poems*, Robert Frost describes the way a poem can take a suprising shape once the writing begins. The poem "has an outcome that though unforeseen was predestined from the very first image of the original mood — and indeed from the very mood." Later in the essay, summing up his thought, Frost writes: "The figure is the same as for love. Like a piece of ice on a hot stove the poem must ride on its own melting."[4]

Avoiding Monotonous Sentence Patterns

In Chapter 7, we identified four grammatical sentence types (simple, complex, compound, and compound-complex) and three rhetorical sentence types (loose, periodic, and balanced). Sentences differ in other ways too — in function (there are questions, declarations, commands, and exclamations), in length, in the number of qualifiers, and so on. As in other matters of style, your goal should not be to vary your sentence patterns merely for the sake of doing so — as decoration only — but rather to suit the meaning. A pleasing variety of sentence patterns will help to keep your reader interested.

One way to create variety in your sentence patterns is to place important words at the end of the sentence for emphasis. The natural order of words in English is subject-verb-object. In English, word order conveys meaning: "man bites dog" means something different from "dog bites man," even though the same words appear in both sentences. In the first example, "man" is the subject of the verb "bites," and "dog" is the object of the verb. In the second, "dog" is the subject, and "man" is the object. Because word order conveys meaning in English, readers unconsciously examine sentence patterns to find meaning, and the subject-verb-object pattern is the simplest and clearest way to express ideas in English.

But we can easily violate this rule, as in the famous saying "To the victor go the spoils." Here, the subject of the verb "go" is "the spoils" (the loot or plunder). By reversing the normal order of words and writing "To the victor go the spoils" rather than "The spoils go to the victor," the writer throws special emphasis on "spoils."

Here are some additional examples:

There but for the grace of God go I.

Behind this information lie years of research.   (John Berger)

---

[4] Robert Frost, "The Figure a Poem Makes," *The Complete Poems of Robert Frost* (New York: Henry Holt and Company, 1949), vi, viii.

As we have seen, word order can be altered by changing an active-verb construction into a passive-verb construction, or vice versa (see p. 247).

My brand-new Mini was wrecked by a moose.

A moose wrecked my brand-new Mini.

The first sentence emphasizes what wrecked the car: a moose. The second emphasizes what was wrecked: the car.

"Copious" Style: Developing Key Ideas

In 1514, the great Renaissance scholar Desiderius Erasmus of Rotterdam published *De Copia* (Of Abundance), a handbook for young writers and speakers that offered models for saying the same thing in a variety of ways. In part, these models were meant for orators who often needed to repeat a thought several times in different words, both for emphasis and while they figured out what to say next. But Erasmus also wanted to give writers ways of amplifying or developing an important thought so that the prose would possess richness and fullness. At first glance, Erasmus's advice might seem to contradict the advice of the "plain stylists" and belong to a bygone era when readers had the leisure to linger over ornamental figures of speech that added little to the sense. (John Lyly, a sample of whose writing appears on p. 240, was celebrated for his richly ornamented style.) But in fact, the ideal of *copia*, or abundance, complements the ideals of plain style. The goal of the **copious style** is never mere redundancy or ornament for the sake of ornament, but rather to describe or express a thing *fully*, doing the thought justice by getting it onto the page in all its dimensions. While the principles of plain style put the writer at risk of paring away so much that the result is meager or impoverished, the principles of copious style entail the risk of verbosity and redundancy. The true goal is to achieve the right balance of richness and plainness. More precisely, the goal should be to express thoughts fully but to make every word count. Some adjectives and adverbs *do* make an idea more meaningful, vivid, or complete; others are merely excess verbiage, and the prose is stronger without them. The trick is to distinguish between the two. Understanding the difference is perhaps the work of a lifetime, but it is never too soon to begin developing this skill.

➲ **Try** **This** **Expanding and Contracting**

Describe an object in front of you or amplify an abstract thought. For fifteen minutes, focus your attention on the object or idea. Write continuously about it, setting down everything that occurs to you. Let your thoughts flow; do not censor or edit them as they arise, but do try to stay focused on the object or idea you are working with. Without using a thesaurus or a dictionary, use as many different words or phrases to describe it as you can think of.

- Think of associations. (What does the object or idea remind you of?)
- Think of similes (comparisons using "like" or "as"). (What is it like? What might it be compared to?)
- Consider the object's or idea's opposite. (What is it *not*?)
- Analyze its components. (What are its parts? Its qualities?)
- Imagine you are explaining the object or idea to a child or to someone who is completely unfamiliar with it. (What are the assumptions that you need to uncover?)

Take a minute to relax, and then come back to the piece you have written. Underline only the words and phrases that seem useful and help to explain the thought. Work these underlined words and phrases into just three or four sentences.

Achieving a Balance of Rich and Plain

All of these rules can and should be broken if doing so clarifies your meaning. Style is a spectrum. Plain style embodies certain values (clarity, simplicity, directness) as well as offering certain techniques and principles, and rich style embodies certain values (variety, abundance, completeness). If the danger at one end of the spectrum is verbosity and redundancy, the danger at the other is of "gutting" your writing, paring away all the nuance, complexity, qualification, and subtlety. Once you have a sense of these values and these dangers, the two keys to developing good style are reading and revising. When you are reading, especially reading writers you admire, notice how their writing works to express their thoughts in effective and pleasing ways. And as a writer yourself, allow time in your writing process to work specifically on style. Experiment with different ways of expressing your thought, and see what works best. As with any guidelines concerning style, the principles of rich and plain style must be applied intelligently, not mechanically. You must rely on your own ear. The aim is to achieve the right balance of rich and plain, cutting wordiness and empty phrases, but not the valuable content, so that every word contributes to the meaning of the whole. Where you find this balance between rich and plain is where you find your own personal style.

Writing in Academic Style

The principles of plain style will serve you well in most kinds of writing — journalism, business correspondence, essays, and so on. Many kinds of writing have their own particular conventions and needs, however, and academic writing is one of them. While its peculiarities do not contradict the principles of plain style, academic writing often displays stylistic qualities that suggest some differences of emphasis. Academic writing is typically formal: it avoids colloquialisms and slang (phrases used in speaking but inappropriate in formal writing, such as "chill out, dude" and "that kind of BS is just plain out of bounds"), "chatspeak" (for example, "ROFL" and "OMG"), and contractions (for example, "isn't," "can't," "I'm"). It prefers precise diction, meaning that it often employs technical vocabulary or specialized terms. And it uses qualifiers to indicate the writer's degree of certainty. Academic style reflects scholarly values and habits of mind.

Some Principles of Academic Style

Maintain a Scholarly Tone. Keep a reasonable and critical tone, the tone of a person who is thoughtful and interested, committed to finding out the truth, willing to look at a question from more than one point of view, and able to rise above a merely personal or local perspective.

Aim to Be Clear but Not Simplistic. Aim for clarity, but do not reduce complex, interesting ideas to simple, banal ones. Readers expect academic writing to make reasonable demands on their attention span, patience, and intelligence. Whereas journalists, writing for the general public, must take pains to enable readers to absorb information quickly and easily, academic writers can expect that readers will take more time to dwell on the nuances and complexities of their ideas.

Follow Disciplinary Conventions in Preferring the Active or the Passive Voice.

In most college writing, the active voice is generally preferred, as it tends to be clearer and more direct. However, certain disciplines, notably in the natural sciences and some social sciences, conventionally use the passive voice. You might be expected to use the passive voice consistently when writing science papers and reports. If you're unsure, check with your instructor.

Use Qualifiers to "Hedge" Claims.

Qualifiers can narrow a claim and thereby make it more precise and valid. Similarly, they can convey the writer's degree of certainty. Academic writers avoid overstating their claims, as they know that new evidence or further argument can always reveal some unforeseen aspect of the question. (For more on hedging, see Chapter 5, p. 137.)

Convey Impartiality.

Be cautious when using words that carry emotional or attitudinal connotations. Wherever possible, express a claim as a conclusion that follows from evidence, not as your "opinion." (Opinion is subjective, tied to the personality and experience of the particular individual who holds it; by definition, opinion rests on "grounds insufficient for complete demonstration.") When a claim is only your opinion, you must express it as such, but as we have seen, a strong argument requires something more: claims must follow from strong evidence.

The word "objective" is sometimes taken to mean "factual," as though academic writing deals only with facts or information. But as we have seen, academics typically write in order to make an argument for conclusions they have drawn through research: evidence (including facts) plays an indispensable role, but a supporting, not a starring role. Academic writing is "objective" in the sense that scholars adopt an attitude of detachment and impartiality. Their ultimate loyalty cannot be to any particular position; it must be to the "truth." (We put the word "truth" in quotation marks, as scholars conventionally do, not because we do not believe in truth but because we can never be entirely sure what it is. Truth is always what remains to be discovered — what, as yet, we only partially know.) Scholars must fix their eyes on the truth; they are not out to win any victories at the truth's expense. Academic style should reflect this attitude.

☑ Checklist for Writing with Style

Understand the principles of plain style.

☐ Cut excess verbiage.
- Cut empty phrases.
- In general, prefer the active voice.
- As a rule, cast sentences in positive form.
- Avoid unnecessary qualifiers.

☐ Choose clear and direct vocabulary.
- Use specific, concrete words.
- Use fancy words, jargon, and neologisms with caution.
- Use verbs to bring life and action to sentences.

☐ Avoid monotonous sentence structures.
- Place important words at the end of the sentence for emphasis.

Understand "copious" style.

☐ Strive to express a thought fully while making every word count.

☐ Achieve a balance of rich and plain.

Observe the conventions of academic style.

☐ Maintain a scholarly tone.

☐ Aim to be clear but not simplistic.

☐ Follow disciplinary conventions in preferring the active or the passive voice.

☐ Use qualifiers to hedge claims.

☐ Convey impartiality.

part 4

Research and Documentation

chapter 9

Conducting Research

"Research" can mean many things: carrying out experiments to test a hypothesis, conducting an e-mail survey, interviewing witnesses to an important event, studying old letters in archives, hunting down scholarly articles in the library — or

virtually any other means of investigating some question or problem. The novelist Zora Neale Hurston memorably described it as "formalized curiosity."[1] It would be impossible to discuss or even anticipate every type of research that college courses might require, but your instructors almost certainly will ask you to conduct research in your college's library and on the Internet — probably frequently. In many upper-level courses, the research paper is the most common type of writing assignment, and these papers often count for a large portion of the grade. Instructors place considerable weight on such assignments because they give students the opportunity to immerse themselves in a scholarly discussion of a problem in a chosen field of study, to think deeply about it, and to propose ideas of their own. In other words, research papers let students do the work that scholars do. They demonstrate a student's ability to exercise the full range of skills — research, interpretation, analysis, critical thinking, and communication — that are needed to work on almost any problem in

[1] Zora Neale Hurston, *Dust Tracks on a Road: An Autobiography* (1942; repr., New York: Harper Perennial, 1991), 127.

the discipline. (These skills are necessary for a great many nonacademic tasks as well.) Research papers allow students to move beyond the more passive and mechanical business of memorizing information and enter into the debates and struggles that represent the leading edge of discovery.

The two most common types of research assignment are the research paper and the research report, which are quite different types of writing. A **research report** usually involves finding reliable information and expert thinking on a topic and presenting your findings in a clear, organized, and objective way. In other words, you present the work of experts. A **research paper** involves not only gathering up information and expert thinking but also developing your own argument, one that is *informed* and *supported* by research but that contributes some new insight or point of view of your own. In this chapter, our focus will be on the research paper, but we will also address most of the information-gathering skills involved in writing research reports.

Whether your campus has one library or a dozen, its collection is likely to be larger and more complicated than your high school's. The library is one of the college's most important resources, and the time you spend becoming familiar with it will be amply rewarded: knowing how to locate material in a large library gives you access to huge reserves of information and ideas. Computers play an essential role in library systems, not only as tools for searching the catalog but also as tools for searching through bibliographic databases and for storing and retrieving complete documents. And the Internet, despite the absence of filters for reliability or quality or value, has nevertheless become an indispensable research tool, providing access to material of all types from sources around the globe. These innovations have made the business of doing research easier and faster — but also more complicated.

Ink and paper, however, are far from being obsolete: the digital revolution is still under way, and libraries are in a state of transition. The computer world and the print world are increasingly linked together, so to do good research, you must know how to work in, and move between, both worlds. This chapter explains how to use some essential tools to find the material you need and offers some strategies for working with that material to help you get the most out of the enormous riches of a modern library system.

The Purpose of Research

The purpose of a research paper is to offer an answer to a question or a solution to a problem. Some questions or problems can be solved, or at least addressed with insight, by consulting just one or two sources — and much of our discussion of college writing up to this point has focused on this sort of essay. But other problems require more extensive research. Research can take many forms:

- Fieldwork: Gathering raw data through observation, experiments, surveys, and interviews.
- Library research: Finding books and print articles in scholarly journals, magazines, and newspapers.
- Internet research: Finding Web sites, discussion boards, and electronic editions of books and articles from scholarly journals, newspapers, and magazines.

The materials of a research project can be grouped into primary research and secondary research. Although the meaning of these terms differs somewhat from one discipline to another, in general **secondary research** is at least one degree removed from the object of study. In **primary research**, you directly investigate the object of study yourself and even create the data yourself — perhaps by conducting an experiment or a survey or by studying original materials, such as the letters of a key player in a historical event. In secondary research, you work with the findings or ideas of other researchers or thinkers, perhaps by reading an article or a Web page or by interviewing a scholar. (The same text could function as either primary or secondary evidence depending on what you are writing about. If you were writing a paper on the work of Jane Tompkins, her essay "At the Buffalo Bill Museum, June 1988" would function as primary evidence. But if you were writing a paper on Buffalo Bill, her essay would function as secondary evidence.) Solving a problem might involve one or both kinds of research. Usually, your assignment will make clear what sort of research is appropriate.

Managing the Research Process

Research is always something of an adventure, like detective work. One day, you might come across a source that cracks the case wide open and gives you a whole new understanding of the subject. Suddenly, your project is moving ahead swiftly. But the next day, you discover there's an important article or book out there that you really can't ignore — but another user has borrowed it, and you won't be able to get your hands on it until after the assignment's due date. Just as suddenly, your project seems to have stalled. What to do?

It may be small consolation to say it, but frustrations and dilemmas like these are all part of the adventure. Wise researchers expect the unexpected and plan for it. If you think about it, unpredictability is in the nature of research, precisely because you don't know in advance where the research will take you; if you did, the research would be unnecessary. So you cannot know in advance what the sources are, which ones are readily available, which ones are essential, and which can safely be ignored. Sometimes the adventure takes less time than you expect, but usually it takes more!

Still, a lot of problems can be prevented by knowing some guidelines for conducting research before you get started. These techniques won't entirely make straight the crooked paths of research, but they will make the journey a little smoother and more enjoyable.

Good research takes both know-how and time management. "Know-how" means possessing the skills to locate the best sources on your topic. Much of this chapter concerns skills of this kind. But time management is equally important: if you allow too little time for hunting down sources or for reading and thinking about them, the writing phase can get so compressed that your best thinking will never make it to the page. So it's important to start a research project early and to gauge, as realistically as possible, just how much time each phase of the project will take and then to schedule these phases around your other commitments. Allow plenty of time for finding sources and developing your argument, as these are the phases in which unforeseeable, time-consuming problems are most likely to occur.

Developing a Research Strategy

Research is a complex and unpredictable process. But inevitably, it involves a number of different phases:

- developing a research focus
- reading background material
- identifying and locating sources
- reading sources and taking notes
- developing an argument
- outlining
- drafting
- revising, formatting, and polishing

Develop a research strategy that's appropriate for your assignment. What kind of sources will give you the best information and the best understanding of your topic? Where will you find these sources? How much time will it take to gather and digest these materials? You may not be able to answer these questions in detail at the outset, but if you create a strategy and start early, you can more easily make adjustments as the road ahead becomes clearer.

Most academic projects will involve some library or Internet research, or both. Although some assignments may call for, or benefit from, field research, such as interviews, surveys, or observations, most undergraduate research at least *starts* with texts (whether in print or electronic form).

A typical research project might proceed in this fashion.

- The project begins with the search for a topic area — by reviewing course readings, browsing the Internet, and brainstorming with classmates.

- Once a topic area has been selected, reading in reference sources (encyclopedias, dictionaries, and almanacs) on the Internet or in print reveals the big picture. This includes historical background (key figures, dates, and terms) and also what is currently being discussed — the hot areas of disagreement and interesting issues.

- A list of search terms makes it possible to locate and select an initial cluster of sources. The library's catalog points to relevant books. Electronic databases and Google Scholar list scholarly journal articles on the topic.

- Skimming and reading in this initial group of sources make it possible to narrow the research focus to a specific problem or question, evaluate each source for relevance and reliability, and choose two or three to serve as a starting point.

- Careful reading (and rereading, as necessary) provides a sense of the scholarly conversation about the problem or issue. The sources' notes and bibliographies reveal other important books, articles, and Internet sources. Your own notes and questions suggest additional directions for research.

- Further reading and thinking lead to a position on the issues and an argument to support that position. Your understanding of the problem deepens as reading proceeds, notes are compiled, and thoughts and hypotheses are generated.

- Informal writing pulls together thoughts, hypotheses, and notes and helps to identify connections and develop ideas, bringing key themes into focus.

- A working thesis emerges, and you begin to draft an argument with claims and evidence, based on what you have learned from your sources.

- Outlining, revision, and development fill out the draft. The thesis becomes revised and refined.

- Further revision, through editing and polishing, brings the paper to completion.

This list makes the research process sound complicated — and it often is! However, the process can be boiled down to two phases: (1) *scouting* and (2) *digging deep*. That is, first get the big picture and select a few good, relevant sources. Then use these sources to narrow your focus and build your bibliography as you become more informed.

Too often, inexperienced researchers simply use the first sources that they stumble upon and let these shape the research paper, no matter whether the sources really speak to a specific question or are even pertinent. The result is inevitably a superficial and poorly informed paper.

Two Sample Schedules for Writing a Paper

Here are two sample schedules, one for writing a short paper (roughly five pages, using five to seven sources) to be completed in three weeks, and another for writing a longer paper (roughly ten pages, using ten or more sources) to be completed in seven weeks. Note that about equal time is allotted for research, reading, and writing. But *thinking* — determining the focus and developing ideas — will be happening continuously throughout the process.

Of course, these are only examples, and you will want to adapt these schedules to the particular circumstances of your assignment and your work habits. You might need to complete the activities in a different order (for example, in some cases a working bibliography might be appropriate earlier than week four, and starting a journal to develop ideas might be the very first thing you do). Also, many of the reading and writing activities are recursive: writers move from reading and note-taking to writing and editing and back to reading and note-taking, and so on. Still, the purpose of a schedule is to allot adequate time to every major phase of the research and writing process, so don't allow yourself to get pulled too far off-track.

A Three-Week Schedule

Week One

a. Brainstorm topics with course readings and classmates.

b. Do preliminary research in encyclopedias and reference sources. Scan their bibliographies and notes to see what has been published on the topic. Gather search terms and concepts.

c. Find some sources on the Internet and in the library. Consult a reference librarian. Narrow the topic to a focused research question.

Week Two

a. Skim sources and select the most useful.

b. Read sources and take notes. Develop a bibliography and locate the additional sources.

c. Keep a journal to develop ideas and formulate an argument. Fill in knowledge gaps with additional research.

Week Three

a. Write the first draft of the paper.

b. Revise and edit.

A Seven-Week Schedule

Week One

a. Brainstorm topics with course readings, classmates, and Google search.

b. Do "big picture" research online. Make a list of key terms and figures. Note frequently cited sources. Make a list of possible research questions.

c. Go to the library and do research in reference sources. Consult a reference librarian.

d. Gather a preliminary group of sources. Skim to select two or three to work with closely.

Week Two

a. Read selected sources carefully and take notes. Begin developing a working bibliography. Place interlibrary loan requests if needed.

Week Three

a. Identify additional sources from reading.

b. Read and take notes. Identify knowledge gaps.

Week Four
    a. Read and take notes.
    b. Brainstorm an argument with informal writing.
Week Five
    a. Read, take notes, and begin drafting.
Week Six
    a. Revise and develop the draft.
    b. Visit the Writing Center.
Week Seven
    a. Revise, correct, and polish the essay. Double-check notes and bibliography.

Getting Started: Scouting for a Topic

We mentioned "scouting" as one of the two main phases of the research process, the phase that precedes "digging deep." Scouting means searching for an appropriate and interesting topic by using available resources, such as course readings, the Internet, your classmates, and your instructor. What it involves will vary considerably from one assignment to another, but typically it means either

1. choosing an aspect of a course's subject matter that strikes you as interesting and important enough to merit a few weeks of concentrated study, or

2. choosing from among a list of suggested topics included in the assignment.

Reviewing course readings and your notes, brainstorming with classmates, and discussing ideas with your instructor can help you select a topic area. But choosing one also means learning something about potential topic areas, such as historical background and current controversies or questions. Here the Internet is a valuable tool for quickly getting a sense of the big picture. Scouting around on the Internet will be merely preliminary research: the information you find at this point may not be wholly reliable or impartial, and you should not place too much weight on it until your research has progressed further. But perusing the Web will usually help clarify whether a potential topic is appropriate and interesting before you narrow your focus and settle on a specific problem, question, or issue.

Understanding the Big Picture

Using an Encyclopedia

After beginning the scouting process with Internet searches (using Google or another search engine), use an encyclopedia (online or in print) to develop your sense of the big picture. (For a discussion of Wikipedia, see the next section.) To conduct a search, you will need to know key terms associated with your topic and their correct spellings.

As you read the relevant articles, note key themes, figures, and dates, as these will help you conduct further research. Most encyclopedias include a brief bibliography with each entry, and some include citation notes. These can guide you to some of the most important books and articles on your topic.

Keep in mind that encyclopedias are an excellent starting point for research, but *not an end point*: they sketch out basic facts, but they take you no further. As you probe more deeply into a subject, you will often be surprised how much more complicated and more interesting the full story is than the mere facts given in an encyclopedia.

A Note on Wikipedia

Wikipedia, founded by Jimmy Wales and Larry Sanger in 2000, differs from other encyclopedias in several important respects. Most notably, it is a free, nonprofit project that allows anyone — not only experts and scholars — to contribute content or edit existing content.[2]

However, Wikipedia does adhere to strict standards and policies. A worldwide community of about 75,000 volunteer editors checks new contributions to make sure these standards are met, and they edit articles as needed. These standards can be summed up as follows.

- Content must adhere to a "neutral point of view."

- Content must be verifiable and must incorporate references to reliable external sources.

---

[2] This includes you, of course. If you wish to be a contributor, see "Starting an article" at en.wikipedia.org/wiki/Wikipedia:Starting_an_article.

- Topics must be "notable" — or covered in at least one reliable and independent source.
- Contributors may not submit articles about their own original research.

Compared to traditional encyclopedias, Wikipedia has some important strengths. Most obvious, perhaps, is its availability on the Web as a free resource. Also, its scope is large and growing: it includes more than 3.5 million entries in the English version alone. And Wikipedia can be more up-to-date than print encyclopedias that publish new editions or supplements only once a year or less frequently. (Mention of the latest news or developments sometimes gets entered into a relevant Wikipedia article within minutes of being reported.) Finally, Wikipedia allows readers to link directly to external sources in citations and bibliographies, making it a convenient starting point for further research.

Any encyclopedia can contain errors (and Wikipedia does not seem to contain more errors on average than other respected encyclopedias do). Over time, Wikipedia seems to be getting more complete and more reliable. In some areas of natural science, Wikipedia may be the best reference available for the general reader.

But Wikipedia has several clear weaknesses too. It is written by amateurs, and articles — especially newer contributions — may be poorly written. As a work-in-progress, many of its articles are incomplete. In addition, articles can easily be sabotaged; though obvious cases are quickly corrected, articles on obscure topics may retain errors or distortions for some time. And because Wikipedia is a collaborative project that relies on consensus among its many users, articles on controversial topics may represent a middle-of-the-road compromise rather than the hard truth.

Wikipedia, like any encyclopedia, should be used only as a starting point for research, not an end point. That is, you should not cite Wikipedia or any other encyclopedia in a paper. Instead, go directly to the sources that the encyclopedia references, assess them for yourself, and draw your own conclusions.[3]

Selecting Sources and Narrowing Your Focus

Once you have chosen your topic, your next step is to pull together an initial collection of sources on your topic — perhaps five to twelve items. Usually these will be scholarly books and articles, but they might also include magazine and newspaper

---

[3] For more detail, see "Wikipedia: About Wikipedia" at en.wikipedia.org/wiki/Wikipedia:About.

articles or other types of sources. From this group, you will select two or three sources for closer study as a starting point for "digging deep."

Using College Research Libraries

College libraries differ from most public and high school libraries both in size — they are typically much larger — and in function. Their purpose reflects the mission of the institution: a large university research library, for example, will usually carry thousands of scholarly journals, but relatively few popular novels. Increasingly, scholarly journals are being published in digital form, and in many cases, even older journals are being stored electronically rather than in paper form. Thus you can do a good deal of your research at your computer, without actually being in the library. But paper is far from obsolete, and thorough research still almost always requires spending time in the library. In addition, the library provides professional problem-solvers in the form of reference librarians.

You may want to begin your research process by finding books on your problem or topic, or you may want to start with journal articles. As a general rule, if your question or problem is a new or very current one, you may find that articles are more up-to-date than books. Otherwise, begin with books, as they are more likely to offer context and a broader frame of reference.

Using Your Library's Electronic Catalog

Some libraries still maintain a card catalog made up of index cards, but today most have made the transition to an online catalog, at least for their main holdings. (Special collections or archives may still rely on a card catalog.) Most library catalogs allow users to search by author, title, **keyword**, or subject (see Figure 9.1). A keyword search typically searches through an entire record (see Figure 9.3, p. 281) for matching terms. Since common words (such as "science," "America," or "war") will usually yield an unmanageable number of hits, keyword searches work best when the terms are fairly specific to a topic or when at least two keywords are combined.

Some library catalogs let users search by subject. Usually this means "Library of Congress subject headings," a limited and systematic set of subject headings published by the Library of Congress to facilitate cataloging and searching. These subject terms are not always the ones you might expect, but you can explore the Library of Congress subject headings in a set of five large red volumes (many libraries display these

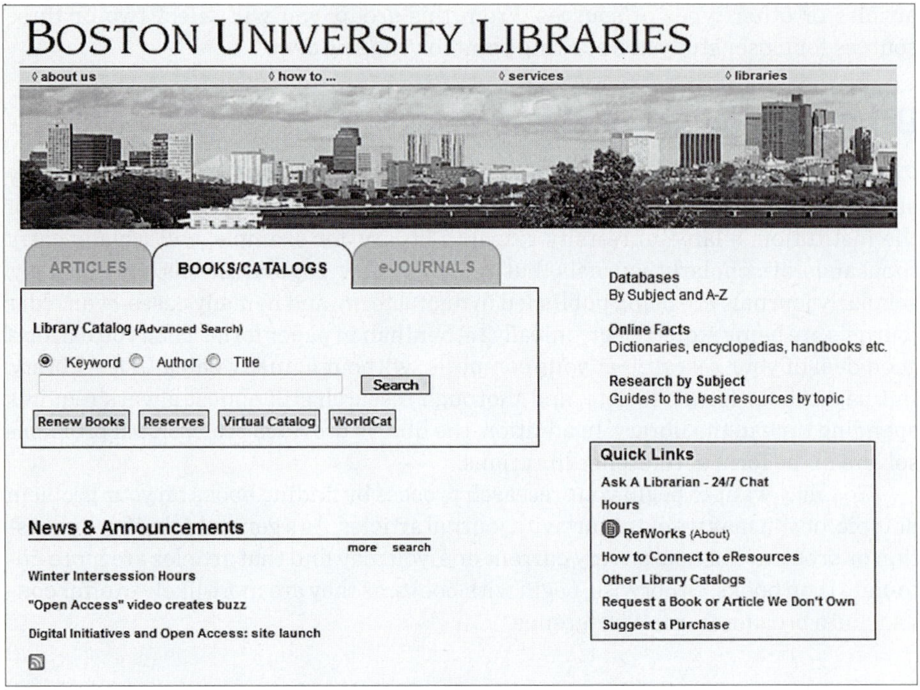

Figure 9.1 Main Search Screen of a College Library's Catalog

volumes prominently in the reference area) or search online at authorities.loc.gov. Alternatively, you can begin with a keyword search, browse the results until you find an item on your topic, and then look at the terms listed under "subject" in the item's record. Many libraries hyperlink subject terms, allowing you to get a complete list of all items on that subject with just one click.

Advanced Searching

Advanced searching allows users to refine a search by including certain criteria and excluding others (see Figure 9.2). The options will differ from one library catalog to another, but the procedure is the same. For example, if you wanted to find a copy of the soundtrack to the 1967 Joseph Strick film of James Joyce's novel *Ulysses*, you

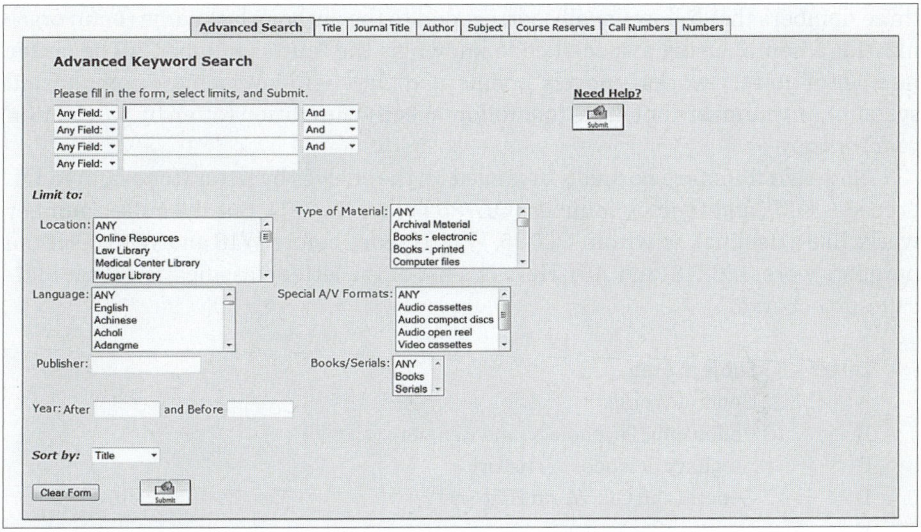

Figure 9.2 "Advanced Search" Screen

could enter "Ulysses" as a title and select "Recordings — music" as "Type of Material." This would eliminate copies of the novel and books about the novel from the search.

Reading a Catalog Record

Catalog records typically contain a good deal of data: in addition to basic information such as author, title, publisher, and edition, they provide a call number and, if your college has more than one library, the location of the item.

The **call number** (for example, QL785 .W126 2001) makes it possible to find the item on the library's shelves (or "stacks"). The Library of Congress classification system, used by most large libraries, begins with one, two, or occasionally three letters that designate subject areas. The first letter corresponds to a broad subject area (see the list on p. 280), and the second and third (if any) letters correspond to a narrower division within that subject area. (Details can be found online at the Library of Congress Classification Outline at loc.gov/catdir/cpso/lcco.) The first set of numbers corresponds to a narrower division of the subject. The letter and the two or three numbers that follow usually correspond to the author's last name (or an organization's name), using a special code known as the "cutter number." (The cutter number of literary works — novels, poems, and plays — follows a more complicated system.) Any numbers or letters that follow specify the edition (often by publication year) or copy.

Note that items are normally arranged on the shelves by letter (for example, QL precedes QM) and then by number (QL785 before QL791). But the cutter number works like a decimal, so within QL785, W126 comes before W18 and W45 (as if the numbers were .126, .18, and .45). Here is a list of the letter classifications that indicate subject area.

Letter	Subject Area
A	General Works
B	Philosophy, Psychology, and Religion
C	Auxiliary Sciences of History
D	General and Old World History
E	History of America
F	History of the United States and British, Dutch, French, and Latin American History
G	Geography, Anthropology, and Recreation
H	Social Sciences
J	Political Science
K	Law
L	Education
M	Music
N	Fine Arts
P	Language and Literature
Q	Science
R	Medicine
S	Agriculture
T	Technology
U	Military Science
V	Naval Science
Z	Bibliography, Library Science, and General Information Resources

A catalog record also includes a bibliographic description of the item, including such information as the number of pages in a preface or prefatory material (in small

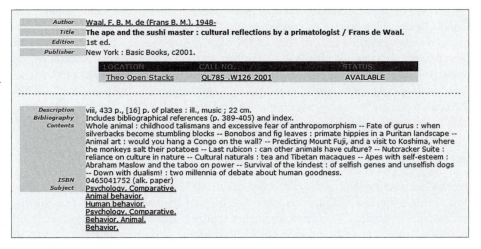

Author	Waal, F. B. M. de (Frans B. M.), 1948-
Title	The ape and the sushi master : cultural reflections by a primatologist / Frans de Waal.
Edition	1st ed.
Publisher	New York : Basic Books, c2001.

LOCATION	CALL NO.	STATUS
Theo Open Stacks	QL785 .W126 2001	AVAILABLE

Description	viii, 433 p., [16] p. of plates : ill., music ; 22 cm.
Bibliography	Includes bibliographical references (p. 389-405) and index.
Contents	Whole animal : childhood talismans and excessive fear of anthropomorphism -- Fate of gurus : when silverbacks become stumbling blocks -- Bonobos and fig leaves : primate hippies in a Puritan landscape -- Animal art : would you hang a Congo on the wall? -- Predicting Mount Fuji, and a visit to Koshima, where the monkeys salt their potatoes -- Last rubicon : can other animals have culture? -- Nutcracker Suite : reliance on culture in nature -- Cultural naturals : tea and Tibetan macaques -- Apes with self-esteem : Abraham Maslow and the taboo on power -- Survival of the kindest : of selfish genes and unselfish dogs -- Down with dualism! : two millennia of debate about human goodness.
ISBN	0465041752 (alk. paper)
Subject	Psychology, Comparative. Animal behavior. Human behavior. Psychology, Comparative. Behavior, Animal. Behavior.

Figure 9.3 Record in a Library Catalog

roman numerals) and in the text proper (in arabic numerals), the number of pages of plates and illustrations, the number of pages in the bibliography, and the size of the item in centimeters (see Figure 9.3). In many cases, the record also provides a list of the contents, the ISBN (International Standard Book Number), and a list of subject terms. Some libraries also include book reviews in catalog records, where available.

Finding Books Online with Google Books and Open Library

Google Books (books.google.com) is a searchable database of more than 15 million books in over 400 languages. It grows continuously as more books are scanned into it. Some of the world's largest libraries have partnered with Google on the project, including Oxford University's Bodleian Library, the Harvard University Library, and the New York Public Library. If you have a Google account (free from Google.com), you can view pages of books that are no longer in copyright and those for which the copyright owner has given permission. For most books in print, you can view only a limited number of pages, if any.

Open Library (openlibrary.org) is a nonprofit wiki project to catalog books and to offer the full text of books in the public domain (that is, books out of copyright). It contains the full text of more than a million books.

Either of these databases can be searched by author, title, and subject. (In Google Books, click on the "Advanced Search" link beneath the "Search Books" button to search by author, title, or subject.) You can also search the full text of books in the database. In practice, this is useful only if you can search for uncommon words or a string of words (frequently occurring words will return too many hits to be helpful). You may not be permitted to read the full book — or even a full page — online, but the search can at least give you some titles, and you can then try to find them in your library or through interlibrary loan.

WorldCat and Interlibrary Loan

WorldCat combines the catalogs of more than 72,000 libraries into one huge catalog containing over 194 million records — not only of books but also of periodicals, audiovisual materials, Web sites, and other media (Figure 9.4 shows a record from WorldCat). Most large libraries in the United States and elsewhere participate in WorldCat. Many college libraries subscribe to WorldCat and make it freely available to students. A free public version is available at WorldCat.org.

Figure 9.4 Detailed Record from WorldCat

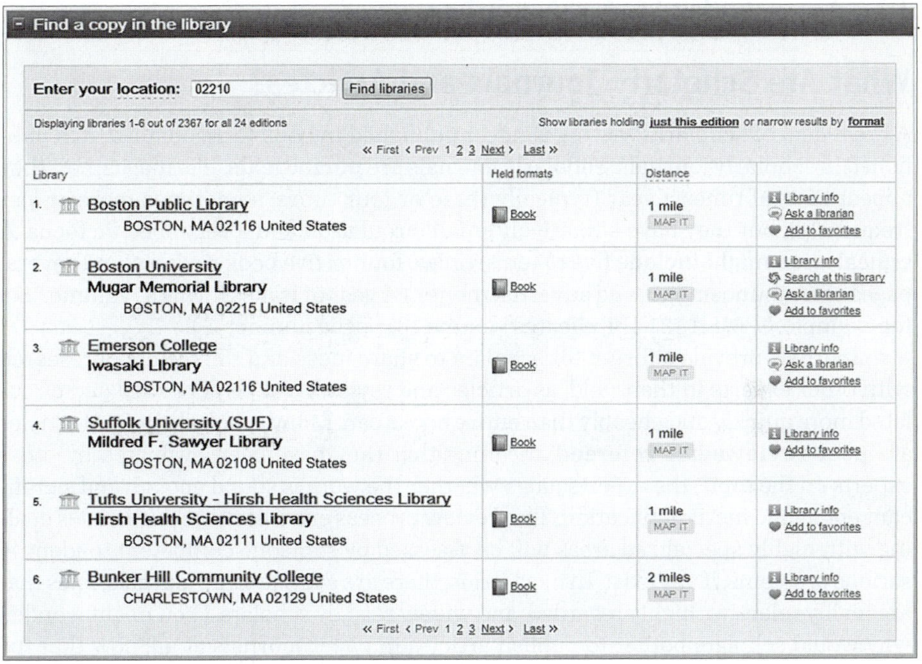

Figure 9.5   **Partial List of Libraries That Own Item, from WorldCat**

WorldCat is "location aware," meaning that the detailed record for each item includes a link to a list of libraries worldwide that own a particular item. (If you are accessing WorldCat through your college's network and if your college owns the item, you will see your college's name next to this link.) This list is organized by state, with your own state listed first (if any libraries in your state hold the item), nearby states listed next, and so on. See Figure 9.5 for a sample listing.

This location-listing feature allows you to expand your reach when researching. If your own library does not hold an item you need, you can use WorldCat to find out if any other libraries in your area (including most public libraries) do hold it. If none does, you might be able to request an interlibrary loan — by which one library lends a requested item to another library for a short period. Ask at the reference desk if your library allows such loans.

Finding Scholarly Articles

What Are Scholarly Journals and Articles?

A great deal of scholarly writing is never published in book form; instead, it is published in scholarly journals. Scholarly journals are **periodicals**: like magazines, they appear several times a year (typically three or four times; sometimes more or less frequently), but they have a relatively small circulation and a very specific focus. A typical issue might include five to ten articles, four or five book reviews, and several pages of announcements and advertisements. (A year of issues forms a "volume." So, for example, "*PMLA* 131.4" indicates volume 131, issue number 4.)

Journals provide a forum for scholars to share ideas and the results of research with other experts in their field, as articles and reviews can be published and circulated more quickly and cheaply than entire books can. Many scholarly journal articles are **peer-reviewed** or **refereed**, meaning that they have been evaluated by other experts on the topic; the experts judge whether the work is sound enough and significant enough to merit publication. This review process ensures that even articles dealing with highly specialized areas will be assessed by someone competent to identify serious problems, if any exist. In most fields, there are a few leading journals, ones that are highly selective, highly regarded, and widely read by scholars. (You might wonder, why would scholars bother to publish articles in paper journals at all, now that the Internet exists? In fact, many journals are moving to the Internet, to make the publishing of research even faster and cheaper, but such a process takes time, and many readers still prefer the clarity, stability, and convenience of paper.)

Using an Interdisciplinary Full-Text Database as a Starting Point

Many college libraries subscribe to one or more interdisciplinary full-text databases, such as JSTOR (short for "Journal Storage") and Project MUSE. Both of these databases give users access to complete articles from journals in a wide range of academic disciplines (Project MUSE focuses chiefly on the humanities and social sciences). Users can read these articles online, print them, or download them as PDF (portable document format) files. JSTOR offers the full text of more than a thousand journals, but the actual number of journals available to you will depend on your library's subscription. Project MUSE offers the full text of more than 450 journals.

These databases offer a convenient starting point for research because you can quickly try out some search terms, browse a list of hits, and read a few promising articles. Abstracts (or summaries) in the detailed records will help you select the most useful and relevant ones. (Click "item information" in JSTOR or "summary" in Project MUSE.) Most articles include notes and bibliographies that will point you to other important sources for your research.

However, these databases include only a small subset of all scholarly journals, and the most recent issues of journals (the past three to five years) are typically not available. So thorough research demands looking further afield.

Using Databases to Find Scholarly Articles

College libraries subscribe to a large number of scholarly journals, including many of the leading journals in the major fields that are taught or researched on campus. Many of these journals are available in electronic format and may be accessible through the library's Web site. But because some journals still publish only in paper and many older issues have yet to be converted into electronic format, researchers must know how to retrieve articles from electronic sources as well as from the shelves of the library.

When a new issue of a journal arrives, librarians record in the catalog only the fact that the issue has been received. They do not enter the titles, subjects, and authors of each separate article. Thus you cannot use the library's catalog to search for these articles: if you were to do a subject search in the library's catalog, you would catch most of the books pertaining to that subject, but you would miss all the relevant scholarly journal articles. (Likewise, if you were to do a search by author in the library's catalog, you would catch the books by that author, but none of the scholarly journal articles.) To find materials in scholarly journals, you need to search a different way.

The best way to locate material in scholarly journals is to use a **bibliographic database**. These contain all the information about the contents of scholarly journals that the library catalog usually lacks: the titles, authors, and subjects of all the essays that appear in scholarly journals, and often a brief summary (or abstract) of the argument of each article. Bibliographic databases do *not* usually contain the articles themselves, though some library catalogs provide links to some articles. Databases are usually created and maintained by private companies, and libraries pay a subscription fee to give faculty and students access to them. At many colleges, you can access these indexes through the college's Web site if you have a college e-mail address, an ID, and a password.

Because so many scholarly journals exist, indexes typically cover just one broad area of study. For example, *America: History and Life* indexes journals pertaining to North American history, the *MLA (Modern Language Association) International Bibliography* indexes journals pertaining to literary studies, and *EconLit* indexes journals in economics. The companies that maintain electronic indexes strive to include information from as many scholarly journals as possible (and many include information about new books in the field as well), so that a search will identify every important article that has been published in recent years on the topic.

You may be able to link from a record in a database to the full text of the article (perhaps in another database). However, in many cases — such as journals that your library holds in paper only, or particular issues of a journal that are unavailable electronically — you will need to enter the library's stacks to retrieve the paper edition. Locating journal articles in print form is typically a three-step process.

Step 1. Conduct a search in a relevant database.

Step 2. Search for journals by title in the library's catalog.

Step 3. Retrieve the volume from the library's stacks.

Let's follow one student, Christina, as she hunts for an article on Davy Crockett's position toward the Indian Removal Act of 1830.

Step 1. Conduct a Search in a Relevant Database

Christina was taking a course in nineteenth-century American history, and one of the essay topics concerned relations between the U.S. government and Native Americans. She decided to work specifically on Davy Crockett's opposition when he served in Congress to the forced removal of Indians from their lands, a fact that had been mentioned only briefly in a lecture but that intrigued her. After finding several books on Crockett's life and politics, she began to look for scholarly articles. Her college library subscribed to several dozen databases, but the *America: History and Life* index seemed the most relevant to her topic.

The index's main search page let her begin with an "all text" search. This allowed her to search every word in every entry in the index — not the full articles, but the abstracts, titles, and descriptor phrases. This approach was thorough, but she quickly learned to avoid terms that were too general. For example, an initial keyword search with the word "Indian" returned more than 16,000 citations — obviously, far too many to browse through.

But a keyword search using the term "Davy Crockett" turned up sixty-two citations — not an impossible number, but still a lot of hits. When she tried "Davy

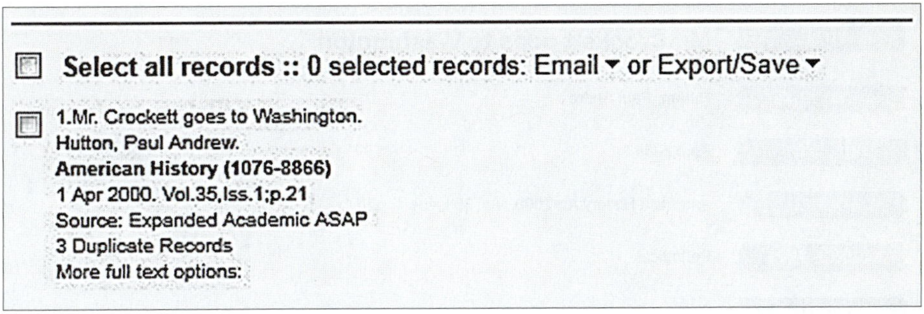

Figure 9.6 **Short Entry in a Database**

Crockett" as a *subject* search, she got eight hits — far more manageable. And when she combined *two* keyword terms, "Davy Crockett" and "Indian," she got just six hits — a good place to start.

A couple of these hits were identified as book reviews, only a few paragraphs in length and not substantial or informative enough to be useful to her at this stage of her research. Christina passed over these.

One of the hits was an article entitled "Mr. Crockett Goes to Washington" by Paul Andrew Hutton. The citation information indicated that it appeared in the journal *American History* in the year 2000, volume 35, issue number 1, page 21 (see Figure 9.6).

Clicking the "Display Full Entry" button took Christina to a longer version of the entry that included an abstract — a summary of the argument (see Figure 9.7). This revealed that the article discusses Crockett's political career. Since it looked useful for her research, she wanted to find out whether her library carried the journal *American History*, and in particular whether it held volume 35.

So Christina copied down the information from the short entry, being especially careful to copy the citation line accurately, and opened a new browser window to search her library's online catalog.

Step 2. Search for Journals by Title in the Library's Catalog

In the library's catalog she conducted a *title* search for *the title of the journal* — not the title of the article, since the library does not catalog articles by title. Christina entered the words "American History" into the textbox on the catalog's main screen

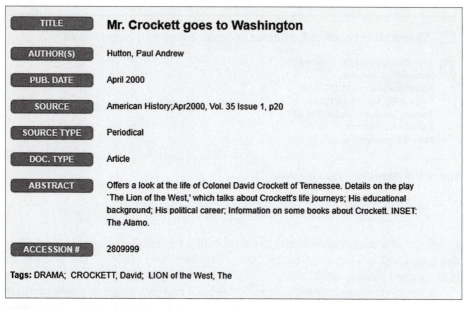

TITLE	**Mr. Crockett goes to Washington**
AUTHOR(S)	Hutton, Paul Andrew
PUB. DATE	April 2000
SOURCE	American History;Apr2000, Vol. 35 Issue 1, p20
SOURCE TYPE	Periodical
DOC. TYPE	Article
ABSTRACT	Offers a look at the life of Colonel David Crockett of Tennessee. Details on the play `The Lion of the West,' which talks about Crockett's life journeys; His educational background; His political career; Information on some books about Crockett. INSET: The Alamo.
ACCESSION #	2809999

Tags: DRAMA; CROCKETT, David; LION of the West, The

Figure 9.7 Long Entry in a Database

and chose "title search" from the menu. The result showed that her library did indeed carry this journal, and it showed a call number for the journal: E171 .A574. (Usually, all volumes of a journal have the same call number. Some libraries shelve journals alphabetically by title.)

Step 3. Retrieve the Volume from the Library's Stacks

Entering the library's stacks, Christina found the "E" call numbers on the fourth floor and soon located E171 and the row of bound volumes with the title "American History" stamped on their spines. (Libraries bind issues of journals together by volume and store them on the shelves in a long row. However, the most recent three or four issues are often kept in a separate location reserved for current periodicals.) Pulling down volume 35, she found the article by Paul Andrew Hutton on page 21 of the first issue in the volume. Since her library does not allow journals to be borrowed, she decided to read part of the article in the library — enough to decide whether to photocopy it.

➔ **Try This**   **Writing an Abstract**

An *abstract* (from the Latin *abstractus*, meaning "drawn off" or "out of") is a summary that presents the essence of the text's argument as briefly and accurately as possible, usually in just a few sentences, at most a few paragraphs. An abstract is strictly objective and impartial; it offers no evaluation or commentary. Writing an abstract can be challenging when the argument is complicated and highly nuanced; the writer must make good decisions about what's *truly* essential to the argument and must choose words carefully to present that essence as clearly and impartially as possible.

Try your hand at writing an abstract.

Option 1. Write an abstract of Frans de Waal's article "Are We in Anthropodenial?" (p. 432).

Option 2. Write an abstract of an article that you find in the library, using *America: History and Life* or another index that provides abstracts. When you have completed your abstract, compare it to the one in the index's "full entry." How does it differ? How would you account for the differences?

Google Scholar

Google Scholar (scholar.google.com) is a specialized search engine that locates scholarly sources. Basic searches are performed in the same way as in regular Google, by typing search terms into a textbox. Though it has been a "beta" (that is, a test) version since November 2004, it is functional and reliable, despite certain limitations.

Google Scholar searches articles and books that have been posted to publicly accessible Web sites; it also searches through some of the subscription-based online indexes and databases of scholarly publications, such as those owned by Elsevier. In addition, it links into library systems so that users can click directly through to the full text of some articles. If you are searching from on-campus via an ".edu" network, you may find that links to items in your library's online holdings appear automatically. If not, you may be able to select your college library in the "Scholar Preferences" pane, as illustrated in Figure 9.8. (Scroll down to "Library Links" and click on "Find Library.")

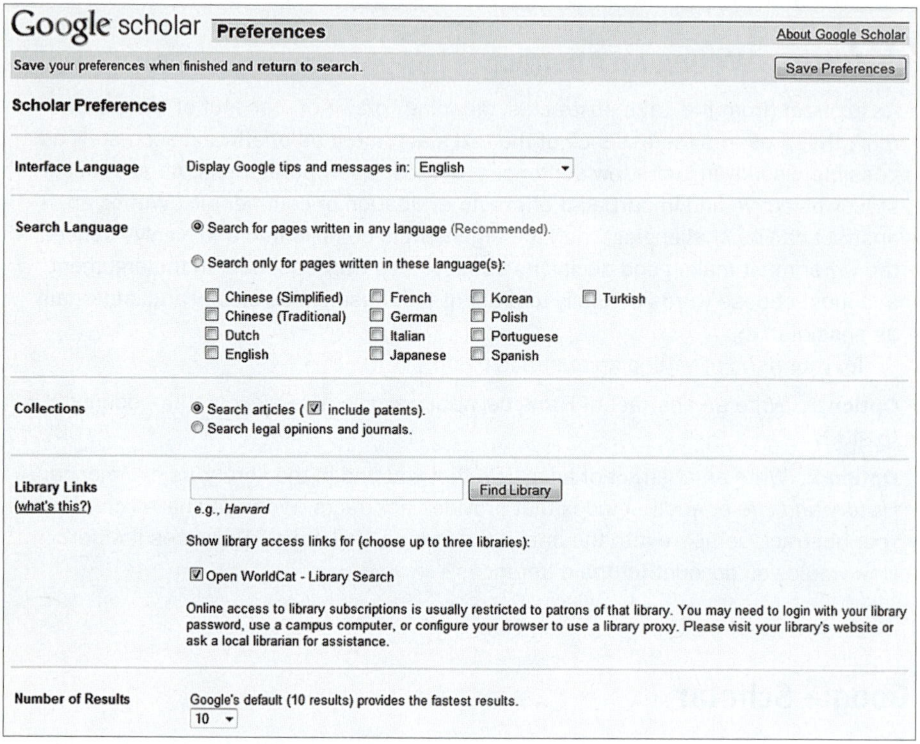

Figure 9.8 "Scholar Preferences" Pane in Google Scholar

Google Scholar also searches through the text of the millions of books that have been scanned into the Google Books database. You can access previews of books under copyright as well as entire texts of books without copyright. If only a few pages of a book discuss your topic, Google Scholar attempts to take you directly to those pages so that you can read them right away. Otherwise, the table of contents and preface can give you a sense of the book's focus and whether you need to hunt it down.

Search results are ranked by their relevance to the search terms (for example, in Figure 9.9, the work that tops the list is the one in which *all* the search terms appear) and by the number of times other writers have cited the work.

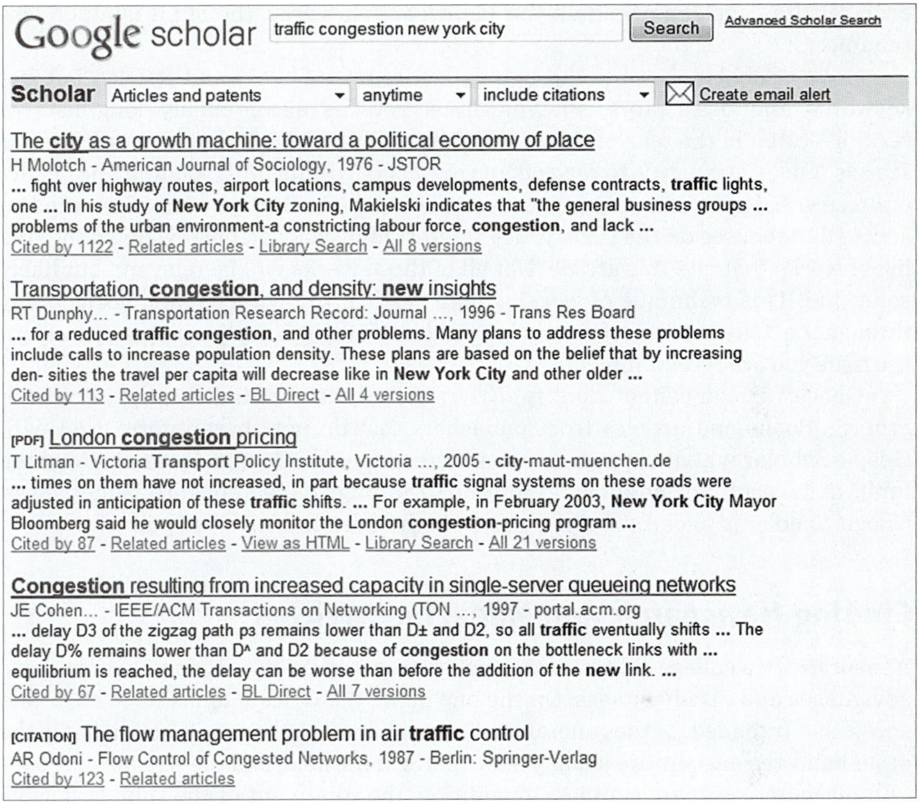
Google scholar traffic congestion new york city Search Advanced Scholar Search

Scholar Articles and patents anytime include citations Create email alert

The city as a growth machine: toward a political economy of place
H Molotch - American Journal of Sociology, 1976 - JSTOR
... fight over highway routes, airport locations, campus developments, defense contracts, **traffic** lights, one ... In his study of **New York City** zoning, Makielski indicates that "the general business groups ... problems of the urban environment-a constricting labour force, **congestion**, and lack ...
Cited by 1122 - Related articles - Library Search - All 8 versions

Transportation, **congestion**, and density: **new** insights
RT Dunphy... - Transportation Research Record: Journal ..., 1996 - Trans Res Board
... for a reduced **traffic congestion**, and other problems. Many plans to address these problems include calls to increase population density. These plans are based on the belief that by increasing den- sities the travel per capita will decrease like in **New York City** and other older ...
Cited by 113 - Related articles - BL Direct - All 4 versions

[PDF] London **congestion** pricing
T Litman - Victoria **Transport** Policy Institute, Victoria ..., 2005 - **city**-maut-muenchen.de
... times on them have not increased, in part because **traffic** signal systems on these roads were adjusted in anticipation of these **traffic** shifts. ... For example, in February 2003, **New York City** Mayor Bloomberg said he would closely monitor the London **congestion**-pricing program ...
Cited by 87 - Related articles - View as HTML - Library Search - All 21 versions

Congestion resulting from increased capacity in single-server queueing networks
JE Cohen... - IEEE/ACM Transactions on Networking (TON ..., 1997 - portal.acm.org
... delay D3 of the zigzag path p3 remains lower than D± and D2, so all **traffic** eventually shifts ... The delay D% remains lower than D^ and D2 because of **congestion** on the bottleneck links with ... equilibrium is reached, the delay can be worse than before the addition of the **new** link. ...
Cited by 67 - Related articles - BL Direct - All 7 versions

[CITATION] The flow management problem in air **traffic** control
AR Odoni - Flow Control of Congested Networks, 1987 - Berlin: Springer-Verlag
Cited by 123 - Related articles

Figure 9.9 **Results Page for a Search Using Google Scholar**

One of the powerful tools of Google Scholar is the "Cited by" feature. For example, in the search results shown in Figure 9.9, the article "Transportation, Congestion, and Density: New Insights" was cited in 113 other works. Clicking on the "Cited by 113" link will take you directly to a list of these 113 items. In turn, each of these items also carries a "Cited by" link.

This daisy chain of citations makes it easier to identify the works that have made a significant contribution to a discussion — the important works that other writers consistently cite. The short list of "key authors" included at the bottom of each results page can also help you identify such works, though it is much less reliable.

Google Scholar searches through the entire text of books and articles, not just keywords and descriptors, so typically it returns exceptionally long lists of results — often in the tens of thousands — many of which will be irrelevant to your search. A good strategy is to read down your list of results until you find one or several items that speak directly to your research question. Once you have identified an article that focuses on the issue you're interested in, you can burrow down into the list of works that cite this article. Not all of those works will be relevant, but likely some will. This technique of working both vertically down a list and horizontally through the "Cited by" pages may help you identify the scholarly conversation about the issue you are researching.

Google Scholar cannot identify *all* the scholarly articles that match your search criteria. Books and articles from publishers that do not share information with Google Scholar will not appear in a search result. Since Google does not reveal the limits of its reach, no one knows exactly how thorough its searches are. Nonetheless, Google Scholar is a good starting point, even though it is not an end point.

Finding Newspaper and Magazine Articles

As sources for a college-level research paper, newspaper and magazine articles have advantages and disadvantages. On the one hand, the writing tends to be clear and accessible, intended for the general reading public rather than for specialists. On the other hand, the authors are usually not experts in the field, and the writing may contain inaccuracies or reflect bias. In addition, the treatment of the subject may be relatively superficial compared with the detailed analysis the subject would receive in a scholarly article. While magazine and newspaper articles can certainly help you become acquainted with a subject, it is usually unwise to depend on them exclusively, unless the assignment requires you to use them. For most assignments, you should eventually move on to more focused and authoritative treatments of your subject.

The Readers' Guide to Periodical Literature This source indexes articles in about 240 general-interest periodicals (magazines and major newspapers) published in the United States and Canada from 1983 to the present. It also includes the full text of about half the periodicals it indexes, starting from 1994. *The Readers'*

Guide Retrospective indexes articles in about 370 general-interest periodicals published in the United States and Canada from 1890 to 1982.

LexisNexis   This database is an archive of more than 45,000 newspapers, magazines, and legal sources. Although it was initially designed for business and law professionals, it can be a valuable resource for scholarly research as well. (Your college might subscribe to several LexisNexis databases; if so, the one named LexisNexis Academic is the most useful for finding newspaper and magazine articles. Despite its name, it does not index a large amount of scholarly material.)

Consulting a Reference Librarian

If you run into problems at any point in the research process, consult a reference librarian (usually to be found at a desk in the reference area of the library). Reference librarians are skilled information specialists who can save you time by steering you toward relevant and reliable sources. They can help you not only with the library's own tools and databases but also with Web search engines and other research tools.

If possible, bring a copy of your assignment with you. Be prepared to answer some questions about your research, such as the following:

- What is your topic area or research question?
- In which academic discipline are you writing?
- How much time can you spend on the project?
- How long will the paper be?

If you have a specific question, you may be able to get a quick answer by phoning the reference desk or by using the chat or text-message services that many libraries offer.

Digging Deeper

Now that you have gathered a few sources (for now, five to ten is probably a good number for a paper of about ten pages), you can use them as a starting point for digging deeper. This process involves (1) narrowing your topic to a specific research question or problem (if you have not already done so) and (2) finding additional sources — ideally, *all* the most important sources that speak directly to your question.

First, peruse your sources and select two or three to read carefully. (You might return to the others later, or reject them entirely.) The best ones for your purpose at this point will be those that are most

- relevant to your topic area
- intelligible
- current
- reliable

Relevant   Depending on your topic, you may not be able to find sources that directly address your topic *exactly*. This is not necessarily fatal — in fact, it can be a good thing if it means that your topic is fresh and original. Sources that may be slightly off your topic may still be highly informative. Moreover, many scholarly articles and even some books have a very narrow, limited focus. If the scope is too narrow, the source may not be useful at this point. Note the page length. A fairly substantial article (more than five pages) will be most useful at this stage. Choose sources that bear on your topic closely enough to deepen your understanding and inspire questions and ideas.

Intelligible   As we have already noted, scholars often write for other specialists in their field, meaning that some scholarly articles and books are too technical for a nonspecialist to comprehend. A source that's merely challenging to read can be extremely helpful, but one that's *impossible* to understand should be ignored, at least for now. You can probably find other sources that will be more helpful to you. Choose sources that you can learn from.

Current   Recently published books and articles are especially helpful at this stage because you will be using these sources as guides to the conversations around your topic. Most scholarly articles and books will reference or discuss the important works that preceded them, because typically their purpose is to make a contribution to a recognized conversation about a problem in the field. Look for sources with the most up-to-date notes and bibliographies.

Reliable   Evaluating sources can be tricky — we will have more to say about this later (p. 308). For your needs at this point, however, prefer scholarly books and articles — ones that include bibliographies or notes that cite sources. If you're unsure whether a work is scholarly or not, do a Web search for the author's name to find out more about his or her qualifications. If the author is a leading scholar in the field, the work is probably reliable. You can also use Google Scholar to find out how often a book or an article has been cited. Works that have been cited many times are usually more influential.

Working with Scholarly Articles

Scholarly articles are typically structured to make it easy to determine whether they are relevant to a particular question or concern. As we have seen, most are accompanied by an abstract (a summary) — a valuable tool for making your selections. You may have already read the abstracts in the database you used. If not, you can often find an abstract at the beginning of the article or in the issue's table of contents.

If you do not find an abstract, read the first two or three paragraphs of the article and the last two paragraphs.

Even if you've already read the abstract, it makes sense to reread it so that you can compare it with those of the other articles you've gathered. This will help you decide which articles bear most closely on your topic and will be most helpful in your search for a specific question or problem.

Articles in the social sciences and natural sciences often use a "finding system," sometimes called "IMRAD" (Introduction, Method, Research, and Discussion). The "Discussion" section often provides a sense of the purpose and significance of the research being presented, so be sure to read that section first.

Working with Books

Because it takes time to read an entire book, you'll need to use some strategies to select the books that are most useful and to get what you need from them.

- Note the book's date of publication (there may be more than one date if the book has appeared in multiple editions). As a general rule, devote more time to more recent books.

- Read the table of contents. Chapter titles and subtitles may not describe the contents exactly, but they will often give you a good sense of what is covered. (A book might contain only one relevant chapter, but that one chapter may be indispensable.)

- To get a sense of the book's overall purpose and focus, read the introduction or preface. It's important to understand the author's position and point of view in the particular chapters you read and use (see p. 315 for more about identifying the writer's position). Often the preface or introduction will also tell you which chapters are most relevant to your topic area and which ones you can skip.

- If the book appears relevant but covers subject matter that lies outside your topic area, use the index to see where your topic is discussed.

Refining Your Research

As you continue your research, you'll want to narrow your search, continue finding relevant material, and keep track of what you find.

Narrow Down Your Topic to a Particular Question or Problem

Perhaps skimming through the sources you've gathered has already helped you identify a specific problem or question for your research. If not, look for one as you read carefully through two or three of your sources. The problem you choose should be appropriate to the assignment you've been given, and it should be sufficiently narrow in scope to be treated within your page or word limit. Moreover, it should be something that interests you, and preferably something you do not already have strong convictions about. (Otherwise, you may be unable to conduct research with an open mind.)

You will probably learn a great deal from reading just two or three sources thoughtfully and attentively, as scholarly works are usually dense with information and ideas. Take notes as you read (include page numbers for any note that refers to a text, so that you can cite the text correctly in your paper). And give yourself time for reflective, informal writing as a way of generating and clarifying ideas (see Chapter 4).

An article or a chapter in a book might spark a new idea that none of your sources directly addresses but that you would like to pursue. If so, it's worth going back to the library catalog and the databases to see what you can find on this new topic, as there's a good chance that a scholar has already discussed it.

If you are not getting much out of the sources that you've found, ask a reference librarian or your instructor for help.

Use Citation Notes and Bibliographies to Point You to Other Sources

Scholarly writers invariably use citations — in-text citations, footnotes, or end-notes — to show readers the source of ideas and to give credit to their authors. Many books and articles also include bibliographies. Once you have narrowed your focus, note any sources that appear to discuss the problem or question you're working with (see the next section, "Keep a Working Bibliography"). Citations often work like a paper trail: one source points you to other sources, which point to still more, and so on. If your research is thorough, you will eventually notice the same sources being cited repeatedly, and you will develop a good sense of the conversation or even the field as a whole — who the important contributors are and how the conversation has unfolded over time.

Once you have a more focused topic, you can also conduct a fresh search for sources in databases and the library catalog.

Keep a Working Bibliography

Even as you begin your research, keep a working bibliography to record all your sources. Keep this bibliography scrupulously organized and up-to-date: add works as you learn about them and fill in complete bibliographical information as soon as you can. Delete entries that you have examined and rejected. Include full publication data, and for each entry include a brief note about its usefulness for your project. If your research involves a large number of sources, record the location of your notes (for example, in a folder on your computer or in a notebook) and/or your printout or photocopy of the item on a separate line. Update this document continually as you work: it will become a crucial component of your research project.

For articles, include the following information:

- Name of the author or authors
- Title of the article
- Title of the periodical
- Year of publication
- Volume number
- Issue number (if the journal is paginated by issue)

- Page range
- Location (name of the database and URL if electronic; library and floor number if print)
- Call number (if print)
- Access date (if electronic)
- Medium (e.g., "Print" or "Web")

For books, include the following information:

- Name of the author or authors
- Title of the book
- Place of publication (city and country)
- Name of the publisher
- Year of publication
- Location (name of the library and floor number)
- Call number
- Medium (e.g., "Print")

For Web sites and other documents found on the Internet, include the following information:

- Brief URL (as much of it as you will need to locate the material again — e.g., loc.gov/rr/program/bib/ourdocs/Louisiana.html)
- Title of the Web page (e.g., "Louisiana Purchase: Primary Documents of American History")
- Author or sponsoring organization (e.g., "Library of Congress")
- Date on which the page was last revised, if available (often found at the bottom of the Web page)
- Access date (the date on which you viewed it)
- Medium (e.g., "Web")

For this working bibliography, you can use a word processing document, a spreadsheet program, a database program, or an online tool such as EasyBib, Noodle Tools, Zotero, or Refworks (see Chapter 10, p. 378).

Sample Working Bibliography

Gara, Larry. *The Presidency of Franklin Pierce*. Lawrence, KS: University Press of
Kansas, 1991. Print.
  Only book I've found so far that focuses just on Pierce's presidency. Scholarly
    and seems pretty objective. Good bibliography.
  E432. G37 1991
  Mugar Library, 4th floor.
Hodder, Frank Heywood. "The Railroad Background of the Kansas-Nebraska Act."
  The Mississippi Valley Historical Review 12.1 (1925): 3-22. Web.
  Old article, but clearly explains how railroads factored into K-N.
  JSTOR: jstor.org/stable/1891782
  Accessed: November 16, 2011
Holt, Michael F. *Franklin Pierce*. New York: Times Books-Henry Holt, 2010. Print.
  Recent bio of Franklin Pierce. Short. Decent bibliography.
  E432. H65 2010
  Mugar Library, 4th floor.
Limerick, Patricia Nelson. *The Legacy of Conquest: The Unbroken Past of the*
  American West. New York: Norton, 1987. Print.
  Debunks myths about the history of the frontier. Chs. 3, 4 look especially useful.
  F591. L56 1987
  Mugar Library, 4th floor.
Nichols, Roy F. "The Kansas-Nebraska Act: A Century of Historiography." *The*
  Mississippi Valley Historical Review 43.2 (1956): 187-212. Web.
  Reviews all the historical studies up to 1956.
  JSTOR: jstor.org/stable/1902683
  Accessed: November 16, 2011

Using Specialized Reference Works

Scholarly articles often treat questions of a very narrow scope, and books may
require a lot of time to read through. So a specialized reference work — an encyclopedia or a dictionary that covers a specific discipline or field of study — can be useful

at this point. Consulting such a reference work is an efficient way to get a clearer sense of the big picture around your research question and to add key sources to your bibliography. Some specialized reference works are available in online versions; others can be found in the reference area of your library. We can list only a few titles here; for a more comprehensive catalog (with more than 16,000 entries), consult Robert Balay's *Guide to Reference Books,* 11th Edition (Chicago: American Library Association, 1996).

Almanacs

American Annual

CIA Factbook

Facts on File Yearbook

World Almanac

Biographical Sources

African American Biographical Database

Biography and Genealogy Master Index

Contemporary Authors

Dictionary of American Biography

Dictionary of National Biography

Who's Who

Specialized Encyclopedias, Databases, and Dictionaries

Contemporary Literary Criticism

Dictionary of Literary Biography

Encyclopedia of Philosophy

Encyclopedia of Sports

The Internet Movie Database

New Grove Dictionary of Music and Musicians

Oxford Dictionary of Art

As you conduct research, you will come across a wide variety of sources. Most of these will belong to a definite type or genre. Each has its own purposes, observes conventions of form and style, and imposes certain expectations on the reader. If you recognize the type of source you are dealing with and understand its conventions, you will be better equipped to use it appropriately in your research.

However, sources do not always make it immediately obvious what type they are, and readers do not always know what to expect from them or why they take a particular form. Table 9.1 on pages 302–03 lists the types of sources that students most frequently encounter in conducting research and identifies some of their pertinent characteristics. It will help you not only identify the type of source you are using but also assess it fairly, weighing one factor against another. A highly selective work, for example, is likely to be more reliable than a nonselective one. But highly selective sources may be difficult to understand. In many situations, a variety of sources will serve your purposes best.

Other Sources

Field Research

Earlier in this chapter, we distinguished between primary research and secondary research (p. 269). In primary research, you are typically producing your own findings by directly investigating the object of study — for example, by studying original manuscripts in an archive or by conducting an online opinion poll. In secondary research, you are working with the findings of other researchers. **Field research** — research conducted outside the library or laboratory — is typically primary research, designed to produce original findings. It is not always appropriate in college writing, but some assignments require it (most frequently in the social sciences and natural sciences), and some allow it as an option.

Observations

A formal observation involves testing a hypothesis by watching and listening to the behaviors of people or things in a particular setting. Formal observations of human beings are used extensively in psychology, sociology, and anthropology and occasionally in some other disciplines. A typical observation might involve attending a meeting or an event to study how a group of individuals behave in that setting.

You usually need to do some preliminary research before designing and arranging an observation so that you become familiar with appropriate research questions associated with the particular group or culture. Before conducting the observation,

Table 9.1 **Types of Sources and Their Characteristics**

Type of Source	Publisher	Author	Purpose
Scholarly books	University or scholarly press	Expert	Review and add to findings in a scholarly field
Scholarly articles	Scholarly journal	Expert	Publish new findings to scholars in the field
Serious books for general readers	Trade publisher	Usually expert, professional writer, or scholar	General interest
Popular magazines	Usually a for-profit company	Professional journalists and guest writers	General interest
Newspapers	Usually a for-profit company	Chiefly professional journalists	General interest
Sponsored Web sites	For-profit or nonprofit company or organization	Professional and amateur writers and contributors	Varies
Personal Web sites	Individual	Anyone. Author may or may not be identified.	Varies
Discussion forums and listservs	Usually a nonprofit organization or group	Anyone. Authors may use pseudonyms.	Varies from entertainment to serious discussion

you might want to make notes concerning your own preconceptions and attitudes about the people you will be observing. Testing these preconceptions can help give your observation purpose and focus.

All research involving human subjects, including observations, must be conducted with an understanding of the rights of these subjects. Some institutions require that all

Selectivity	Accessibility	Interactivity
Highly selective and often peer-reviewed	Varies. Specialized language may be difficult for the general reader to comprehend.	None
Highly selective and often peer-reviewed	Varies. Often difficult for general readers to comprehend.	Minimal. Letters from readers are sometimes published, but the process may take months.
Selective, but not usually peer-reviewed	Medium	None
May be selective, depending on the magazine	Easy	Medium. Many publish letters to the editor and reader feedback columns in every issue.
Somewhat selective, depending on the newspaper	Easy	Medium. Most publish letters and comments from readers in every issue.
Fairly selective	Easy	Strong. Many invite comments and e-mails.
Open; not selective	Easy	Varies. Some personal Web sites invite comments or e-mails; some do not.
Open; not selective	Easy	Strong. Posting a question often gets an immediate response.

research involving human subjects be approved by an Institutional Review Board (IRB) before it proceeds. If your instructor has not already explained your institution's regulations, ask him or her for guidance before making any further arrangements.

If IRB approval is not required, be sure to request permission from the group you plan to observe well in advance of your observation. Use an informed consent

Informed Consent Form

I, [name of participant], give my permission to [your name] to use my written and spoken words in [his/her] research project written for [course] at [your school].

- I understand that I may read and approve the final draft of the material [he/she] uses about me in [his/her] project.
- I understand that I may request that the final draft be kept confidential between [him/her] and the course instructor.

Signature: _____   Date:_____

Address: _____

Telephone Number: _____

E-mail: _____

I prefer to use this pseudonym: _____

Figure 9.10 **Informed Consent Form**

form if you will be observing a situation where privacy might be a concern. (For an example, see Figure 9.10.) If you plan to make an audio or video recording, obtain specific permission to do so.

During the observation, use the double-entry method to take detailed notes. On the left-hand side of a page, note only what you see and hear. On the right-hand side, write down your own reactions, questions, and ideas. Note the date, time, place, and conditions of your observation. Fill out your notes at the first opportunity, while your observations are still fresh in your mind.

Finally, minimize the "observer effect." Avoid interacting with individuals in the group and avoid getting involved in the group's activities. As far as possible, minimize your impact on the group's behaviors.

Interviews

An interview in person, or by phone, e-mail, or chat, can be an excellent way to learn about your research topic and may provide rich insight in a fairly short period of time. Bear in mind, however, that an interviewee — even an expert — can present only one point of view, and it is unlikely to be definitive. Interviews are typically most useful when they form one kind of source in your research, balanced and complemented by others.

Interviews benefit enormously from preliminary background research. Once you have requested and scheduled an interview, prepare your questions carefully. During the interview, however, listen carefully to answers and be ready to improvise new questions.

Use an informed consent form (see Figure 9.10) if any subject matter may be private or sensitive. Obtain permission if you plan to make an audio or video recording. You can add that stipulation to the consent form if you plan to make a recording.

Surveys

Surveys gather data about behaviors or opinions. They are especially useful if your research focuses on a local community, but they may be helpful whenever you need to understand attitudes or opinions on any topic.

The design and implementation of surveys is a science of its own, one we cannot cover in detail here.[4] However, understanding some basic strategies can greatly enhance the credibility and usefulness of your survey or poll.

Surveys work best when their purpose is well defined. Identify the questions you want to ask — and *why* you want to ask these questions: What is the purpose of the survey in your research project as a whole? The more clearly you understand the purpose of your survey, the more effectively you can integrate the results into your writing.

The group you survey is called a "sample" because it represents a small subset of the actual population you hope to learn about. To avoid bias and partiality in your sample, consider the characteristics of the larger group you want to understand, and then build a sample that mirrors these characteristics. The most useful surveys gather data from a *random* sample that is large enough to be representative of the

---

[4] For a comprehensive discussion, see Arleen Fink, *How to Conduct Surveys: A Step-by-Step Guide*, 4th ed. (Los Angeles: Sage, 2009); Floyd Fowler, *Survey Research Methods*, 4th ed. (Los Angeles: Sage, 2008); or Lawrence Orcher, *Conducting a Survey: Techniques for a Term Project* (Glendale, CA: Pyrczak, 2007).

characteristics of the larger group (containing a similar representation of age groups, income levels, genders, and so on).

There will always be some margin of error because the sample is not identical to the target population; the goal is to reduce that margin as much as possible, though it can never be eliminated. Consequently, it is important to understand the limits of your sample. For example, if you wanted to know whether American college students consider economic growth or protection of the environment a higher priority, you might distribute a short survey to some college friends or classmates. But your sample would need to be much more varied to give you credible information about American college students *as a whole*: to be truly reliable, the sample would need to include a significantly large sampling of students from each region in the country and from different types of institutions as well as different types of students within these institutions.

If you cannot conduct a large survey, and if your sample is limited by geographic area or to certain types of respondents, acknowledge these limitations when you present your results in writing, and recognize the survey's limits as evidence. But bear in mind that the larger and more representative your sample group is, the better.

When you use surveys as a source, keep in mind some practical considerations.

- Find out if someone else has already done a survey similar to yours. It may use a larger sample and offer more reliable and meaningful data than you can gather yourself. For opinion polls, check Gallup polls (gallup.com) and the Polling Report (pollingreport.com).

- Keep the survey as short as you can while still obtaining meaningful data. Shorter surveys usually yield higher completion rates than lengthy ones do.

- Construct questions carefully. Questions should be clear, to the point, and impartial. Guard against phrasing that might lead respondents toward one answer over another.

- Test your questions on friends or classmates to make sure they are clear and produce useful results.

- Multiple-choice and true/false questions lend themselves to gathering numerical data; free-response questionnaires provide more nuanced results but require careful interpretation. A **Likert scale**, which asks respondents to rate their level of agreement with a statement on a scale of 1 to 5, can be a good compromise. (For example, respondents might be asked to enter 1 on the answer sheet for "strongly agree," 2 for "agree," 3 for "neutral," 4 for "disagree," and 5 for "strongly disagree.")

- Include a few questions that ask for relevant information about the participants themselves (for example, sex, age, education level, ethnicity). Analyzing this demographic information will help you to understand the representativeness of your sample and the strengths and limitations of your survey as evidence.

- Use an online tool (e.g., SurveyMonkey, Zoomerang, SurveyGizmo, or Yahoo Groups) to construct a Web-based questionnaire to send to potential respondents. These tools automatically tabulate results from the raw data and create reports.

- In your paper, summarize the key findings. Present the complete results in an appendix.

Dynamic Internet Sources

As you know, the Internet is much more than an archive of documents; it is also a forum for the rapid exchange of information and ideas. If you are researching a current event or any topic of ongoing interest, you might find dynamic Internet tools and sources useful, such as Google alerts, RSS feeds, and listservs.

Google Alerts If you are conducting research on a current event or any topic of ongoing discussion, consider setting up a "Google alert" so that you can receive e-mails about new items on the Web that mention your search terms. Go to google .com/alerts, where you can define your alerts and choose how you would like to receive them (as e-mails or a feed).

RSS Feeds If you need to stay current with a particular site or blog that pertains closely to your research, you may be able to subscribe to updates and the latest news in the form of an RSS feed, which will save you the trouble of visiting the site daily. (RSS stands for Really Simple Syndication or Rich Site Summary.) A Web-based feed reader such as My Yahoo or Google Reader will let you subscribe to feeds. Many popular browsers and mail programs also incorporate feed readers, or you can use a special program such as Amphetadesk. Feeds can also be read on many mobile devices, using a Web browser or a designated app.

Listservs Listservs are electronic mailing lists focused on a specific area of interest. They exist on a wide range of topics and concerns, and their subscribers are often knowledgeable. You can subscribe to a listserv (even for just a week or two) and pose questions. (Be diplomatic and considerate. It's best to "listen" for a while before jumping into a discussion.) Although a listserv can put you in touch with experts in your research area, you should use information and ideas from this source cautiously: look for corroboration in reliable sources.

To find a listserv on your research topic, send an e-mail to listserv@listserv.net with a blank subject line and a body that reads "list global [topic]," where [topic] is the general topic of your research. For example, "list global Shakespeare" would return all the listservs dedicated to the discussion of Shakespeare.

Evaluating Sources

An argument cannot succeed if it relies on incorrect information or seriously biased opinion. Yet as a college student, you often have to write papers on unfamiliar subjects, so you have no choice but to rely heavily on the information and arguments offered in secondary sources. This is a difficult position to be in, but not an impossible one. You need not feel at the mercy of your sources as long as you carefully evaluate their trustworthiness and credibility.

Books and Periodicals (Print and Electronic)

Books Scholarly books are often published by an academic press (which usually includes the words "university press" in its name) or a government agency. But trade and mass-market publishers also produce books of a scholarly nature, so the publisher's name is not a sure guide. Scholarly books almost always include a bibliography and references. But so do many books that are not truly scholarly. However, you can take some steps to determine whether the author is an expert and how the book is regarded by other experts.

- Check the preface or introduction for clues about the author's credentials.
- Do a quick Web search for the author's name to find out more about his or her qualifications.
- Find reviews of the book using a database or Google Scholar. Book reviews are usually short and can quickly tell you the book's key findings and its merits and flaws as a work of scholarship.
- Use Google Scholar to check the "Cited by" number (see Figure 9.9). This figure tells you how many times a book or an article has been cited in the works that Google Scholar searches. A high number indicates that the book or article is widely cited and probably influential.

Scholarly Articles Scholarly articles are written by experts in the field and in most cases are published only if other experts affirm that the work merits publication. This does not mean, of course, that every word in such works is *true*, but it does mean that scholarly articles occupy a relatively high position on the reliability scale. Scholarly articles satisfy most or all of the following criteria:

- The author or authors are named, often with their credentials or university affiliation.
- The article includes a bibliography or list of references.
- The article is published in a journal devoted specifically to a field of study.
- The language is somewhat technical, suggesting that the intended audience is other experts in the field of study rather than the general public.
- The journal is peer-reviewed or refereed. Sometimes the database will tell you whether the article is peer-reviewed. If not, your library may subscribe to *Ulrich's Periodicals Directory* or Ulrichsweb, a database that contains information about periodicals. After searching for the journal, click on its title in the results list to see the complete record. Look for the line "refereed."
- The article is cited by other scholars. The "cited by" number in the Google Scholar entry for the article indicates how many times it has been cited in the works that Google Scholar searches. Alternatively, your library may subscribe to the ISI Web of Knowledge database, which includes a "times cited" figure for each entry. (Or use Web of Science for articles in the natural sciences.) High numbers indicate that the book or article is widely cited and probably influential.

Magazine and Newspaper Articles Magazine and newspaper articles are typically written not by experts but by professional writers. They often must develop some degree of expertise fairly quickly for the purpose of writing the article. The writing must be accepted by the magazine's editors, and the better magazines employ fact-checkers; however, these editors and fact-checkers are not themselves experts, and errors and distortions do occur. Also, because magazines and newspapers strive to interest, inform, and entertain the general reader, their articles are typically more superficial (but also more accessible) than is scholarly writing. So this kind of source (usually known as popular or general-interest periodical literature) tends to be less credible than scholarly writing. However, a substantial article in a reputable magazine may be highly informative and useful if you can confirm the information in at least one other reputable source.

Web Sites, Blogs, and Other Internet Sources

The Internet is a vast and constantly changing agglomerate of information and opinion from all over the globe and from every kind of source — individuals, non-profit organizations, for-profit corporations, advocacy groups, special-interest groups, government agencies, charitable associations, clubs, and so on. You can find an amazing amount of valuable and reliable material on the Internet. But you can also find plenty that is biased, one-sided, ill-informed, incorrect, or just plain crazy. After all, the price of admission to Internet publication is practically zero: anyone with access to a computer can contribute to a public forum or set up a site. Sometimes well-designed sites that look perfectly credible are actually full of distortions and fallacies. So how can you tell whether a site is credible or not? In some cases, you will already be familiar with the site or its sponsor, and you can use it confidently (for example, the Library of Congress Web sites or the *New York Times* Web site), but you don't want to restrict yourself only to these. Since there are no censors or filters for truth and fairness on the Internet, *you* have to be the filter. When in doubt, investigate, using the following process to evaluate Web sites.

1. Cross-check Information. Responsible writers — on Web sites and elsewhere — tell readers where the information they provide comes from, whether in the text, in a reference note, or with a link. If the writer fails to do so, and if you cannot find corroboration by conducting your own research, discount the information.

The best test of the reliability of information is to check whether it can be found in multiple sources. If you cannot trace the information to a reliable source, don't use it.

2. Determine Whether the Material Is Current. Start by casting a critical eye over the site itself. Good, well-maintained Web sites date their content to tell readers when items were posted. And active Web sites include items posted within the last six months at least, keeping their readers informed about recent developments in their subject area. To determine the currency of material on the Web, ask yourself the following questions:

- When was this material written?
- When was it last updated?
- Does the site contain more than one or two dead links (nonfunctioning links) to other sites?

3. Test the Site for Signs of Bias.   Many Web sites represent a point of view, but some show no interest in being reasonable or fair and may even distort the truth to make it fit a predetermined conclusion. At worst, a Web site may be little more than a vehicle for propaganda and disinformation.

Be wary of writing that seems emotional — a tirade or rant rather than a carefully reasoned argument — and arguments that seem heavily one-sided and neglect or dismiss counterarguments.

Evidence of bias does not necessarily mean that you should ignore the source altogether. Rather, you should use the source with caution, bearing in mind that it may not be telling the whole story and that you will need to look for other sources that present another side and fill in what's missing.

Note that some items within a Web site may be more trustworthy or objective than others. For example, on a newspaper's Web site, you will find news articles along with opinion columns, reviews, and reader comments.

To test a Web site for signs of bias, ask yourself the following questions:

- Does the site reflect only one point of view?
- Is the tone of the writing emotional instead of logical?
- Does the writer cite sources, and do these sources appear to be reputable and trustworthy?

4. Identify and Research the Author or Owner of the Site.   You should be able to determine who the author or owner of a Web site is; if not, be suspicious. Often the name of the Web site appears in large type at the top of the page, but the name alone may not tell you much. The details — the sponsoring organization's name, address, and contact information — may appear at the very bottom of the page, perhaps in small type. If you cannot find this information anywhere on the site, you should be quite skeptical. Perhaps this isn't a good source for a college research paper.

When you are looking for a site's author or sponsor, bear in mind the following:

- The domain name in the URL (the Web site address) — for example, .gov, .edu, .org, or .com — gives you some idea of whether the sponsoring agency is a government agency, an educational institution, a nonprofit organization, or a for-profit company. These domain names are not, however, a sure guide to the type of organization that sponsors the site. (See "The Principal Internet Domain Types," p. 312.)

The Principal Internet Domain Types

.com, .net, .tv, .fm	Corporate or personal sites (The URL endings ".tv" and ".fm" are actually country codes—for Tuvalu and the Federated States of Micronesia—but these countries license their codes for commercial use.)
.edu	Educational institutions (Personal sites on an educational institution's Web site may also use ".edu.")
.gov	Government agencies
.org	Nonprofit organizations; often sponsors of discussion forums and community blogs (Note, however, that in practice anyone can register a site as a ".org.")

The URLs of Web sites registered in countries other than the United States typically include a country code (such as ".de" for Germany) instead of one of the domain names listed here.

- Don't confuse the author with the webmaster. A webmaster usually maintains the site but does not necessarily create the content.
- Some sites require contributions to be anonymous (for example, Wikipedia and certain news sites or sections of news sites). Nevertheless, the identity of the publisher or sponsor of the site should be clear.

Often a link on a Web page will take you to biographical information about the author or background information about the sponsoring organization. Frequently, the author or sponsoring organization will provide an e-mail address or a phone number. If not, use a general-purpose search engine such as Google or Bing to try to find further information about the author or sponsor.

Try to answer the following questions about the author or sponsor of a site:

- What are the author's credentials or qualifications?
- What is the sponsoring organization's purpose? How is it funded?

➔ Try This Evaluating a Web Site

Choose a news site, a government site, a personal Web page, and a political discussion forum. Using the form on the next page, write a brief evaluation of each.

Web Site Evaluation Form

What is the domain type (e.g., ".com," ".edu," ".gov")?

Is the site current?

- Does material on the site indicate the date it was posted?
- Are the most recent dates within the last two or three months?
- Are all the links active, or do you find dead links?

Does the site show signs of one-sided argument or strong bias?

- Is the site's tone emotional?
- Does the site neglect or dismiss counterarguments or other points of view?

Is the author personal or corporate?

- If corporate, what kind of organization or body is responsible for the site (e.g., nonprofit organization, for-profit corporation, advocacy group, educational institution)?

If corporate, what is the sponsoring organization?

- What is the organization's purpose?
- How is the organization funded?

If corporate, how is the material selected?

- Does the site invite contributions from any user, or does it select material for the site?

If individual, can you determine the author's identity?

- Does the site offer biographical information? (If not, find it using a search engine.)
- What are the author's credentials?

Reading Critically to Develop a Position

Imagine that you join some friends at a café, and they are deep in conversation about the day's big news story, a court ruling about gay marriage. As you listen, you realize that your friends are having a debate, with two on one side, two on the other, and a fifth who asks questions but seems undecided. As you listen to the arguments, you form a position of your own. One participant mentions facts — new to you — concerning constitutional law, and another mentions some statistics. A third makes an impressive philosophical argument. As you continue to listen, you realize that there are really more than two positions — three or four, perhaps even five. Josh supports civil unions but not marriage for same-sex couples; Judy supports neither and doesn't believe in marriage even for heterosexual couples. Sonja feels that individual states should be free to allow same-sex marriage but that other states should not be required to recognize these marriages, whereas Sue feels that same-sex marriages should be treated no differently from opposite-sex marriages. Steve remains undecided on that question. After you have listened long enough to get a good sense of what's at issue and where everyone stands, you feel ready to contribute your own views, explain your reasoning, and offer something new — based on a poll you remember reading about just this morning.

This situation is similar to the one we face as writers of research papers. Just as a newcomer to a conversation first *listens* to find out where the other participants stand and then, after becoming better informed and deciding on a position, makes a *contribution* to the conversation, so a researcher must first listen to what others have said about the issue, must strive to understand the positions that others have taken, and must try to contribute something new to the conversation. Just as the conversation participant would not merely repeat what everyone else has already said, so a researcher should not merely summarize the views of others, but instead should try to work out a particular stand on the question and then explain the reasons for taking that stand.

When conducting any research, the first step is to find out whether others have investigated this matter before and, if so, what they learned and what conclusions they drew. Usually, you will discover that several other researchers have already explored the matter, that they agree on some points and differ on others, and that a conversation among them has developed, unfolding slowly over time as more research is done and old research is approached from fresh angles. Obviously, there's no point in starting an exploration from scratch as though no one had ever thought about the matter before. In thinking carefully about what others have already said, you may find something fresh and interesting to say of your own.

Because research involves entering a conversation, a necessary element in the research process — just as important as gathering the right sources — is careful, patient *reading* of sources. You need to read sources not just for information but for their main point or gist — what they contribute to the conversation.

Read for the Gist: Identify the Writer's Argument and Position

As you read your sources, look for the writer's argument and position.

The argument is the main claim (the thesis) and its support (the reasoning and the evidence for it). Look for a thesis statement (it could be more than one sentence) in the first two or three paragraphs or in the last two or three. If you find the writing in an article or a book chapter unusually difficult or confusing, try this:

- First identify the theme. What subject is mentioned frequently in the first few paragraphs, through repetition of the same terms or closely related terms?

- What is the writer saying *about* this theme? Make a note, and continue through the piece more quickly. Pay special attention to the concluding paragraphs, however, as writers typically return to their central point at the close.

- Now go back to the beginning and read the first three paragraphs again, to confirm and to enhance your sense of the argument.

- The title of the piece is often a good clue to the writer's main purpose: if your sense of the writer's argument is consistent with the title, you're probably getting it right.

The writer's **position** — his or her stand relative to other writers on the subject — is a slightly different aspect of the text from the argument, one that is not always spelled out. It may be that the writer is taking sides in an ongoing debate, or defining a new view of the subject never before adopted, or attempting to define a new problem that has never been investigated previously, or raising questions for further study about the conventional wisdom on the subject. The argument is often a narrower, more specific statement than the position.

Scholars sometimes explain the intellectual context of their argument in the first few paragraphs of an article or in the preface or introduction of a book. Here, they will review what others have said on the subject and sketch out the major positions in order to place their own argument in relation to the work of others. But many writers, and especially scholars who are writing primarily for other scholars in their special-ized field of research, save time and space by leaving some aspects of the argument *implied* rather than fully stated, knowing that their audience will recognize certain well-established ideas and basic assumptions on the basis of a few indications.

Of course, leaving certain ideas unspoken may pose a problem for readers who do not belong to that circle of experts. How can they get access to enough of those unstated ideas so that they can grasp the writer's argument and position? One way is to read reliable and up-to-date reference sources, such as a specialized reference work (see p. 299), or an overview of the kind found in *Congressional Quarterly Researcher*. Another way is to read a substantial article in a reputable newsmagazine or newspaper or on a Web site. But sometimes the full picture will emerge as you put the pieces together from various sources; one source tends to illuminate another.

Once you have identified the writer's argument and position, you will have grasped the writer's overall purpose. This purpose governs the way the writer uses information and ideas from other sources. As we have seen, scholars use two kinds of evidence: primary and secondary. When scholars use secondary evidence, they generally treat it as either a friendly argument or a counterargument. (Counterargu-ments are those that oppose the writer's own argument; friendly arguments are those that support it.) When a writer uses a secondary source, be sure to notice whether it is being used as a counterargument or a friendly argument. A writer may spend several paragraphs or pages summarizing a work that, in the end, will be ques-tioned or refuted. If you ignore the fact that a writer eventually refutes an argument, you could end up misrepresenting your source.

The situation is further complicated by the fact that secondary evidence may function as both argument and counterargument at the same time. For example, a writer (let's call her Smith) might agree with *most* of what another writer (let's call him Jones) has said about an issue but disagree with one part of it. Because Jones has already explained his views in detail in an earlier work, Smith will not bother to repeat in her own work everything she agrees with; she will simply allude to Jones's work briefly and spend most of her time in explaining why she disagrees with the one point that she rejects. A careless reader might get the impression that Smith entirely rejects Jones's views, but this impression would be wrong. A careful reader would see that Smith is greatly indebted to Jones and is paying Jones a kind of com-pliment by following the same general approach to the issue as Jones, even while she aims to improve on one aspect of it. To understand a writer's position and use a writer's work appropriately, you need to recognize these nuances.

Having an understanding of the major voices and positions in a scholarly debate allows you to appreciate the basic convictions and beliefs that underlie a writer's argument. These beliefs are not the same thing as *bias*, if we take that word to mean an unfair prejudice. A bias in this sense is irrational and cannot stand up to scrutiny, and a biased argument is a weak one with weak support for its claims. But a position often expresses a deeply held point of view or set of principles that underpins an argument. For example, if the president of the United States were to address the United Nations General Assembly, listeners could expect him to hold the position that a democratic form of government is preferable to a dictatorship. This is not a bias or prejudice; it's a fundamental conviction that he does not need to spell out explicitly because he can assume his listeners know it. Likewise, Cornel West, in his essay "Malcolm X and Black Rage" (p. 450), holds the position that racist attitudes ought to be eradicated, or at least diminished. He doesn't need to spell it out. But it's not a bias; it's a basic principle or orientation.

Take Notes

Take notes as you read and reread your sources. The strategies that you learned in Chapters 1 through 3, especially the dialectical notebook, will be useful for note-taking. But in addition, make the following practices your habit.

- No matter what kind of source you're using — a text, an interview, a recording, or anything else — be sure to add full bibliographical data to your working bibliography, and place adequate identifiers in your notes, usually the author's last name, the title, and the number of the page you are working with.

- Always distinguish carefully among the following:

  Direct quotations from the text
  Your paraphrases or summaries of the writer's ideas
  Indirect quotations — words the author quotes from another text
  Your own comments and reflections

- Codes such as the following can prevent confusion:

  For direct quotations: use quotation marks plus the page number.
  For paraphrases: use (PP) at the end, plus the page number.

> For indirect quotations: use the original author's name and "qtd. in," plus the
> quoting author's name and the page number.
> For your own comments and reflections: use "(Me)."

Plagiarism is the use of another person's words or ideas without acknowledging the source. It will be discussed in more detail in Chapter 10. If you make scrupulous note-taking of this kind a habit, you will be unlikely to commit unintentional plagiarism.

- Finally, if you use a computer to take notes, take these precautions:

  > Keep all files related to your research in a single folder.
  > Back up the folder to an external drive or server at least daily.

Sample Research Notes   The following example shows a student's research notes and corresponding bibliographical information.

Cirincione, Chapter 8, "Nuclear Solutions"

Cirincione realizes that getting rid of nuclear weapons in Middle East will not be easy. But argues that the alternative is a nuclear arms race "with unresolved territorial, religious, and political disputes." (152)

"The latter is a recipe for nuclear war." (152)

Cirincione believes that Israel can be persuaded to shut down its production reactor at Dimona, and Iran can be persuaded to stop processing its own fuel for nuclear power plants — and step by step a nuclear-free Middle East can become a reality. (PP, 152–3)

Maybe a few years ago, but now? (Me)

Cirincione quotes a 2005 Carnegie Endowment report:

> "The core bargain of the NPT [Nuclear Proliferation Treaty], and of global non-proliferation politics, can neither be ignored or wished away. It underpins the international security system and shapes the expectations of citizens and leaders around the world." (Carnegie Endowment, "Universal Compliance: A Strategy for Nuclear Security, qtd in Cirincione, 153–4.)

Cirincione, Joseph. *Bomb Scare: The History and Future of Nuclear Weapons*. New York: Columbia University Press, 2007.

Drafting and Revising

Establish Your Own Position and Develop a Working Thesis

The strategies for writing that we discussed in Chapters 4 through 8 will be useful as you put together your research paper. But keep in mind certain special considerations as you outline, draft, and revise your research paper.

Students sometimes settle on a thesis early in the research process and then treat sources merely as wells of information to draw on to support their argument. True, books, Web pages, and articles are sources of information, but usually they are more than that: they make arguments with a purpose. If you ignore this purpose, you not only misrepresent that writer's ideas but also miss the opportunity of being challenged by men and women of ideas and of thinking more deeply and critically about your chosen research problem. As a researcher, then, it is your responsibility to follow where the sources lead and also to *sift* the arguments carefully and stake out a position of your own.

Understanding the positions of other writers should help you develop a position of your own. But there's no formula for this: you must work out your position by reading carefully and analytically, identifying key positions in the sources, examining the reasoning in your sources, and assessing the strengths and weaknesses of arguments. At some point, discussing what you've learned with classmates or your instructor can also help you figure out your position.

We suggested earlier that it's important to refine a research topic to a specific question or problem. It may, and probably should, evolve as you conduct research, but try not to lose sight of it while immersed in your sources. At regular intervals during the research process (perhaps every couple of days), restate your understanding of the question or problem in your notes. When you are ready — perhaps a little before you feel *quite* ready — draft your current sense of the answer to the question or solution to the problem. Even if it's incomplete, or only one aspect of the answer or solution, your response to this question or problem will often be the source of your thesis statement.

Sometimes the research you've done may seem like a huge muddle, and you might become overwhelmed by the quantity and complexity of the material. At such times, it can be useful to freewrite your way toward some clarity — that is, write casually and informally in order to sort out what the various writers have to say and how their views relate to one another. This sort of writing can help you understand where you stand and why. If you've been taking double-entry notes, review them periodically and build on your comments on the right-hand side of the page. Pose questions, and develop fragmentary thoughts into full sentences. As your own ideas become clear, you will be able to situate your position in relation to others.

Use freewriting and note-taking to seek clarity about two things:

- Your own argument
- The evidence you will be using to support your argument

Once you have a sense of your argument, do the following:

- List your main claims.
- Figure out the main evidence you need to support these claims. This might include strong arguments made by others as well as data.
- Figure out the main counterarguments. You will need to address these too.

At this point, you can sketch out a rough draft in prose, based on your notes, to give you a "big picture" sense of your argument. Make sure this draft includes a statement of the problem you are addressing and your response to it — a thesis statement — as well as your main claims and the main support for your claims.

When you are ready to expand this preliminary draft into a more complete draft, explain your reasoning more fully and consider the role sources will play. Sources can serve a variety of purposes in your argument. They can provide:

- Evidence for a claim you are making
- A counterargument that you will be refuting
- Background information and context to set up your argument

In this rough draft, it is a good idea to omit quotations altogether. You want your reasoning to be clear, both in your own mind and to the reader. And you need to develop the phrases to express your argument fully in your own words. At this stage of writing, leaving out quotations will help you keep the argument in the foreground.

But do include citations (abbreviated if you like) to all the sources you plan to use. You need to be clear about where and how your sources will be used. Don't risk breaking the thread between an idea that comes from another source and the reference to that source. If you don't include these citations in your draft, you risk wasting time later, when you have to hunt down the source of the idea, and you risk committing unintentional plagiarism.

Foreground Your Voice in Relation to the Other Voices in the Paper

One of the special challenges faced by writers of research papers is the need to keep their argument in the foreground and not allow other "voices" — quotes or paraphrases from sources — to bury it. Your argument can get buried if the reader cannot easily distinguish the primary voice — your voice — from secondary voices. And your argument can get lost if the reader has difficulty holding on to the thread of your argument and has to keep looking back to the introduction to remember what your paper is supposed to be about. Either, or both, of these failings will result in a loss of focus and purpose. So you have to be like a master of ceremonies, making sure that acts come on- and offstage with appropriate introductions, keeping the audience awake and the show moving briskly, and keeping everything under control.

To maintain control, you need to have clarity about your argument and confidence in it. You are most likely to bury your argument when you're not quite sure what it is, or when you don't quite believe in it. (Even if you don't, write as though you do!)

To keep your argument in the foreground, try these techniques.

- Periodically repeat key ideas in fresh phrases, to ensure that your reader remains aware of your argument.

- Relate new ideas to familiar ones. Explain the connection or relationship between new ideas and ones you introduced earlier.

- Remind your reader of your main argument at critical moments, especially after complex or demanding passages in your argument.

Refine Your Writing: Use Quotations Purposefully

As you refine your argument and your use of sources, continue to work closely with your sources. Typically, as you refine your argument, you'll be alternating between writing and rereading a text that you are writing about.

However, *quote sparingly*. Whenever possible, turn quotations into paraphrases that are more smoothly integrated into your argument. When you quote, you are asking your readers to shift from one context — your argument — to a passage that's been extracted from a different context. You cannot rely on your readers to read quotations as carefully as they read your text, and you should never expect readers to see the same thing in a quotation that you see. Never expect a quotation to "speak for itself" — it almost never does.

Avoid using quotations merely to show that a fact or claim is supported by some source. A paraphrase, a brief reference ("As Sacks shows"), or even just a citation is sufficient to show the reader that your statement has support in some other text.

Use quotations when the wording or style of the original is important to your argument or when no paraphrase could express the text's sense adequately.

Integrate Sources Effectively

Whether you quote or paraphrase a source, integrate the source effectively into your own writing. Avoid the "dropped" quotation: a quotation dropped into the text without attribution and without a clear purpose. The following steps will help you integrate sources into your argument.

- Briefly introduce the source with an introductory phrase.
- Include the writer's name and some indication of why the source is credible (such as the writer's credentials).
- The first time you name the author, use the first and last name; thereafter use only the last name.
- Clarify the connection between the quotation or the paraphrase and your own argument.
- Follow up with commentary or analysis that explains the importance of the source's words or ideas for your argument.

The introductory phrase shows the reader clearly where your reliance on a source *begins*. The citation at the end of a quotation or paraphrase usually shows where the debt to your source ends (see Chapter 10). Together, the introductory phrase and the citation "frame" the paraphrase or quotation, indicating clearly where your debt to another writer's thought begins and ends. Such framing also keeps *your own* original thought distinct and clear, helping to foreground your argument.

Use Sentence Templates

Sentence templates are thought structures that can help you keep your own voice in the foreground, use quotations purposefully, and integrate sources effectively.

While sentence templates may seem simple — perhaps even simplistic — they are useful precisely because they are conventional and familiar: they immediately give the reader a clear sense of where you stand in relation to another writer. Once you have tried out templates a few times, you'll begin to internalize the forms and start to use them unconsciously. The exact words used in the following examples are less important than the form of the sentences and the structure of the thought, so you will be able to create your own variations once you get the idea. The templates are powerful tools for incorporating others' views into your work and for making distinctions about parts of arguments.

Presenting What Someone Else Says

In _____, X claims that _____.

X's conclusion is that _____.

On the topic of _____, X contends that _____.

These templates are useful for presenting a brief summary of another writer's views on an issue. Note that the final sample template implies that X has failed to make a convincing argument. (You would then go on to explain why this is the case.)

Incorporating Direct Quotations

In _____, X states, "_____."

X claims that "_____."

After summarizing the topic of _____, X concludes that "_____."

Using quotations is a powerful way to present another writer's views when the language is especially striking, clear, and succinct. These templates help you employ a key skill in making an academic argument: showing the work that others have done on the issue. After you include a quotation, you then need to introduce your own voice to explain its significance. The following templates suggest ways to do that.

Presenting Another Writer's View and Responding to It

In her essay, X writes _____. This is important because

_____.

In his essay _____, X writes that _____. This explains

why _____. However, we still need to consider _____.

With this kind of template, you introduce what the author has to say and then take your turn with your own view.

At times you will agree with some of what a writer says but not all of it; in these instances, you must distinguish between the parts you agree with and those you reject. For such a response, you can use the following templates.

Agreeing in Part

Although much of what X writes about _____ is valid, I reject

X's claim that _____.

X is correct to claim that _____. But because of _____,

I disagree with X's contention that _____.

X argues that _____. While _____ and

_____ are valid points, _____ is not. Instead, I think

that _____.

These sentence templates ask you to identify those parts of the argument that are valid. You will rarely agree with every view expressed by a source. Read the source carefully, and separate out which points are valid and which ones are not. Then respond to the source, explaining why you agree or disagree with certain parts of the source's argument.

At times you'll need to correct a distortion or misstatement of fact. Statistics, for instance, can be manipulated to present a viewpoint in the best light for one side of an argument. You may wish to propose an alternative interpretation or set the statistics in a different context, one more favorable to your own point of view. Of course, be sure that you do not distort statistics. Here are a couple of templates for correcting factual information.

Correcting a Mistake of Fact

While X claims _____, it is actually true that _____.

Although X states _____, a careful examination of

_____ and _____ indicates that _____.

These templates allow you to identify a mistaken claim of fact in an argument and present evidence opposing it.

More often, rather than correcting clear errors of fact, you'll need to refine a writer's argument. You may find that much of the argument makes sense to you but that the writer does not sufficiently anticipate important objections. In those cases, sentence templates such as the following can help you refine the argument to make a stronger conclusion.

Refining an Argument Made by Someone Else

Although it is true, as X shows, that _____, the actual result is

closer to _____ because _____.

While X claims _____ and _____, he fails to consider

the important point _____. Therefore, a more accurate conclusion is

_____.

Such sentence templates allow you to clarify and amplify an argument.

Sometimes you'll need to distinguish between the views of two different writers and then weigh in with your own assessment of the situation. When two authors write on the same topic, they will frequently share similar views on some points but disagree on others. Similarly, you may find that you agree with some parts of what each writer has to say but disagree with other parts. Your job is to identify the points of contrast between the two authors and then explain how your own position differs from the view of one or both authors. In such cases, you may find the following sentence templates helpful.

Explaining Contrasting Views and Adding Your Own Position

X says _____. Y says _____. However, I believe

_____ because _____.

On the topic of _____, X claims that _____. By

contrast, Y argues that _____. However, I believe that

_____ is actually correct for these reasons: _____.

Careful writers make sure that their readers understand fine distinctions. The templates above help make those distinctions clear.

Edit and Polish

When editing a research paper, make sure your voice is in control throughout and that other voices are subordinate to your own.

- Maintain a consistent and credible voice or tone: confident, even-handed, open-minded.
- Craft strong, well-phrased claim sentences for the opening of paragraphs.
- Introduce paraphrases and quotations fully, and explain their relation to your argument.
- To prevent confusion, add metadiscourse where appropriate — signposts to the reader to clarify the direction of the argument.

In addition, pay close attention to stylistic problems that frequently emerge in complex arguments.

- Look out for convoluted or unclear sentences.
- Look out for vague language or faulty diction.
- Cut repetition and needless verbiage.
- Look out for unsupported claims.
- Check the overall flow of your paper, and keep the proportions between sections roughly equal.

Proofread

Once you have finished writing, carefully proofread your paper.

- Take advantage of your word processor's spelling and grammar checkers, but don't rely on them (see p. 223).
- Print your paper. Many writers find that it's much easier to detect errors on a printed copy than on-screen.
- Run your finger or a pen along each line as you read slowly, to help you focus on the actual words on the page rather than what you imagine is there. Or place a blank sheet of paper over the page and move it down as you read one line at a time.
- Read your paper aloud.
- Proofread once for each category of error: once for spelling, once for grammar, once for punctuation, once for formatting (especially notes, page numbers, and lists).

Pay attention to the following:

- Make sure all quotations, paraphrases, and information from other sources have been cited (see Chapter 10).
- Check the spelling of proper nouns, including authors' names and place names.
- Check the spelling of unusual technical terms.

☑ Checklist for Conducting Research

- ☐ Develop a research strategy.
- ☐ Create a project schedule.
- ☐ Choose a topic area.
  - Review course materials.
  - Brainstorm with a classmate.
  - Use an encyclopedia.
- ☐ Develop your sense of the big picture.
  - Find background information on the Internet.
  - Read relevant articles in specialized reference works.
  - Develop a list of search terms.

☐ Gather a starter group of sources.
  - Search the library catalog for books.
  - Search databases and Google Scholar for scholarly articles.
  - Search *Readers' Guide* and LexisNexis for magazine and newspaper articles.
  - Search the Internet for additional material.
  - If necessary, consult a reference librarian.

☐ Select two or three sources to read carefully, those that are most
  - relevant
  - intelligible
  - current
  - reliable

☐ Evaluate Web sites with special care.
  - Cross-check information and trace key information to a reliable source.
  - Determine if material is current.
  - Test the site for signs of bias.
  - Research the author's credentials.

☐ Narrow your focus to a specific research question.

☐ Refine your list of search terms.

☐ Keep a working bibliography.

☐ Find additional sources.

☐ Make interlibrary loan requests as needed.

☐ If appropriate, conduct field research, such as observations, interviews, and surveys.

☐ Read sources and take notes.
  - Keep full bibliographical data in your working bibliography.
  - Include the author's name, the title, and page number references in your notes.
  - Distinguish clearly among direct quotations, indirect quotations, paraphrases, and your own comments.

☐ Use informal writing strategies to develop an argument and a working thesis.

☐ Write a preliminary draft.

☐ Revise and develop; get feedback; revise and develop further.

☐ Edit and polish.

chapter 10

Documentation

Documentation and Scholarship

Documentation — the supplying of information on sources by means of notes and a bibliography — is a hallmark of scholarly writing. Every research paper and most analytical papers must include notes to show the source of all the ideas and information in the paper that are not the writer's own original thoughts or findings.

Scholarly work is fundamentally a collaborative enterprise. Scientists make new discoveries by conducting experiments that have been suggested by the work of other scientists. Historians and literary critics develop new insights by building on, improving upon, or correcting the work of other historians and literary critics. In every discipline, scholars learn from one another and move knowledge forward by sharing their ideas. As Isaac Newton famously put it, not long after the modern scientific method took hold, "If I have seen farther, it is only by standing on the shoulders of giants."[1] This basic truth about scholarly work explains why documentation is so important in academic writing. Indeed, the presence of footnotes

---

[1] Isaac Newton to Robert Hooke, 5 February 1675/6, in David Brewster, *Memoirs of the Life, Writings, and Discoveries of Sir Isaac Newton*, vol. 1 (Edinburgh: Thomas Constable, 1855), 142.

The Function of Citations in a Scholarly Conversation

Citations have a number of functions, including the following:

- Referencing an authority, as in "Here's my expert source for this claim."
- Referencing an argument, as in "This expert makes this claim here. You can examine the evidence and reasoning behind it for yourself if you wish."
- Referencing related material, as in "If you're interested in a full explanation of this topic, consult this source."
- Acknowledging that another individual or group deserves credit for an idea or for quoted material, as in "Here's where to find the source of this idea or quotation."

and a bibliography, or some similar form of citation, almost defines a work as scholarly.

Citations — which might take the form of footnotes, endnotes, or in-text citations — serve several purposes in a scholarly work. First, they allow readers to retrace the writer's steps, verify the claims that the writer is making, and weigh the evidence for themselves. Second, citations make it possible for readers to identify the ideas that are really *new* in the work they are reading and to distinguish these new ideas from ones that have already been published elsewhere. Finally, citations tell readers where to look for a more complete discussion of matters that are perhaps not central to the topic at hand. Thus a good scholarly work, by means of its notes, *invites* the reader into the scholarly conversation, because it will show familiarity with (and cite) the most important books and articles that have already been published on the topic.

•   •   •

This excerpt from an article by business administration professors Praveen K. Kopalle, Donald R. Lehmann, and John U. Farley appeared in the August 2010 *Journal of Consumer Research*. It presents new research on the role that belief in karma plays in the expectations of Indian consumers by lessening their "disconfirmation sensitivity" (that is, satisfaction or dissatisfaction when a product performs better or worse than expected). The authors frequently cite other researchers, even listing multiple works in the same parentheses. Note, however, that the citations can serve different purposes within the argument. (The article uses APA style.)

Praveen K. Kopalle, Donald R. Lehmann, and John U. Farley

Consumer Expectations and Culture: The Effect of Belief in Karma in India

In the customer expectations arena, relatively little attention has been paid to the impact on expectations of variation in cultural variables unique to a country. Here we focus on one country, India, and a major cultural influence there — the extent of belief in karma. Prior research in the United States suggests that disconfirmation sensitivity lowers expectations. Here we examine whether belief in karma and, consequently, having a long-term orientation, counteracts the tendency to lower expectations in two studies that measure and prime respondents' belief in karma. Results show that the extent of belief in karma, operating largely through its impact on long-run orientation, does moderate (decrease) the effect of disconfirmation sensitivity on expectations. These findings suggest that it is important to tailor advertising messages by matching them with customer expectations and their cultural determinants.
1

yena yena śarīreṇa yadyatkarma karoti yaĥ
ten ten śarīeṇa tattatphalamupāśnute

Translated, the epigraph means, "Whatever actions are done by an individual in different embodiments, [s]he reaps the fruit of those actions in those very bodies or embodiments (in future existences)" (Krishan 1997, 97). A belief in karma entails, among other things, a focus on long-run consequences, that is, a long-term orientation. Such an orientation implies that people who believe in karma may be more honest with themselves in general and in setting expectations in particular — a hypothesis we examine here. 2

This research is based on three simple premises. First, because lower expectations often lead to greater satisfaction, individuals in general, and especially those who are sensitive to the gap between performance and expectations, have the incentive to and actually do "strategically" lower their expectations (Kopalle and Lehmann 2001). Second, individuals with a long-term orientation are likely to be less inclined to lower expectations in the hope of temporarily feeling better. Third, long-term orientation and the tendency to lower expectations are at least partially driven by cultural factors. In India, belief in karma, with its emphasis on a longer-term orientation, will therefore to some extent counteract the tendency to lower expectations. The empirical results support our logic; those who believe more strongly in karma are less influenced by disconfirmation sensitivity and therefore have higher expectations. 3

Consumers make choices based on expectations of how alternative options will [4] perform (i.e., expected utility). Expectations about the quality of a product also play a central role in subsequent satisfaction (Anderson and Sullivan 1993; Parasuraman, Zeithaml, and Berry 1994). These expectations may be based on a number of factors, including the quality of a typical brand in a category, advertised quality, and disconfirmation sensitivity (Goering 1985; Kopalle and Lehmann 1995; van Raaij 1991). Recent evidence suggests that consumers who are more disconfirmation sensitive (i.e., consumers who are more satisfied when products perform better than expected or more dissatisfied when products perform worse than expected) have lower expectations (Kopalle and Lehmann 2001; Monga and Houston 2006). However, there is little research concerning the role of culture-specific variables in expectation formation, particularly how they relate to the impact of disconfirmation sensitivity on consumer expectations.

Here we examine how consumer expectation formation is influenced by a fun- [5] damental element in Indian culture — the extent of belief in karma (*Business Week* 2006). Belief in karma has four key aspects (Bernard 1981; Bowes 1978; King 1999; Saksena 1970; Sharma 1991): (i) the spiritual nature of the universe in which we live; (ii) the continuous cycle of the universe; (iii) the consequences of good (bad) actions in the present leading to good (bad) outcomes in the future either in this life or in the hereafter; and (iv) reincarnation or rebirth, where one becomes better due to good actions and worse due to bad actions. According to the concept of karma, although an individual's current experience is determined by what he/she has done in the past, a person is free to choose what to do in the present or the future (Bernard 1981; King 1999). The extent of belief in karma (hereafter simply referred to as belief in karma) has an important influence on many aspects of life in India, including purchase decisions. Importantly, we hypothesize and empirically show that a cultural variable, that is, belief in karma, has implications for consumer expectations as well. Karma's implications for expectations largely stem from statement iii, which suggests that actions have consequences in the future, and statement iv, which suggests that consequences can be long-lasting.

We hypothesize that (1) belief in karma will diminish the impact of disconfir- [6] mation sensitivity in lowering consumer expectations and, hence, lead to generally higher expectations and (2) the effect of belief in karma on expectations is mediated by (operates through) consumers' long-term orientation. The results support our hypotheses and are not explained by potential covariates such as optimism, expertise, and involvement.

We concentrate on India for two reasons. First, the majority of Indian society ⁊
believes in karma. Second, India is an emerging economy that is in the process of
major economic growth. With over 1 billion people, it is interesting in its own right.

Background

Consumer expectations and satisfaction also affect purchase decisions. The relation- ₈
ship between expectations and satisfaction is a central topic in marketing (Anderson
and Sullivan 1993; Bolton and Lemon 1999; Boulding, Kalra, and Staelin 1999; Mittal,
Ross, and Baldasare 1998; Oliver 1997). Expectations are defined as beliefs about a
product's or service's attributes or performance at some time in the future (Rust et al.
1999; Spreng, MacKenzie, and Olshavsky 1996) and are a key determinant of satisfaction (Kumar, Kalwani, and Dada 1997; Oliver and Winer 1987). Research has found a
diminishing effect of the gap between performance and expectations on consumer
satisfaction (Anderson and Sullivan 1993; Mittal et al. 1998).

Consumers at times are "strategic" in their behavior (Wertenbroch 1998). In ₉
the context of consumer expectations, Kopalle and Lehmann (2001) and Monga and
Houston (2006) found that consumers lower expectations to enhance satisfaction
(when a product performs better than expected) or diminish disappointment (when
products perform worse than expected). Moreover, individuals whose satisfaction is
more sensitive to the gap between performance and expectations are more likely to
lower expectations about product quality in order to improve satisfaction or reduce
disappointment. Monga and Houston's (2006) research also suggests that such strategic lowering of expectations occurs as the time to experience a product grows
nearer.

Purchase decisions are also influenced by cultural factors (Aaker and Ma- ₁₀
heswaran 1997; Briley and Aaker 2006; Triandis 1989), and consumer behavior is
often motivated by the fundamental culture in which the consumers operate (Aaker
and Williams 1998; de Mooij 2003). For example, cultural orientation can influence product evaluation through the much-researched country-of-origin effects
(Gurhan-Canli and Maheswaran 2000). In terms of consumer behavior, measurable
aspects of Confucian culture have been shown to vary significantly within a country
(Tan and Farley 1987), affecting evaluation of both products and advertising.

In this research, we focus on the impact of belief in karma on expectations. A ₁₁
central tenet of karma focuses on the "results or consequences of actions or fruits
of action." The doctrine of karma links current conduct to future consequences
either in this life or in the next (Herman 1976, 73, 131). Importantly, actions may not

necessarily lead to immediate consequences but, rather, to consequences that appear sometime in the future.

There are three essential tenets in the doctrine of karma according to Krishan 12 (1997): First is the notion of rebirth, where actions in a particular life may bear fruit either in the current life or the next. More specifically, the consequences of actions taken in this life do not, as a rule, emerge in this life but rather get accumulated, and the results may be seen in a later life or lives. A second tenet is that actions can be broadly classified into appropriate (good) and inappropriate (bad). Finally, good actions in the present lead to good outcomes in the future, and inappropriate current actions lead to bad outcomes in the future.

The extent of belief in karma does not, contrary to some popular conceptions, 13 rely on predestination or on fatalism, where all that happens is preordained due to previous actions. Although a person may be helpless at a point in time in determining their current situation, so far as his/her future is concerned, he/she has complete freedom to regulate his/her actions and hence conduct himself/herself in a manner that leads to a better future. In other words, the philosophy of karma is one of ownership for a person's actions or deeds where each is responsible for his/her actions and he/she alone has to bear the consequences in the future (Bernard 1981; King 1999). A strong belief in karma makes responsibility for one's own behavior in the present more prominent due to its impact in the future in this life or hereafter (due to reincarnation).

In essence, a stronger belief in karma makes one oriented toward the future and 14 leads one to have a longer-term view of life, that is, a long-term orientation (Bearden, Money, and Nevins 2006; Hofstede 2001). The concept of long-term orientation (LTO) has been discussed by Hofstede and Hofstede (2005), who suggest that such an orientation fosters behavior oriented toward future rewards. They argue that long-term orientation is closer to Eastern thinking, where searching for virtue is key. Bearden et al. (2006) suggest that LTO is a salient aspect of national cultural values that influences consumers' decision-making processes. We argue that stronger belief in karma makes a person more long term oriented so that they will be more concerned with the future consequences of their current decisions. "Artificially" lowering expectations is a short-term-oriented action that ignores the truth. Consequently, those with karma-induced long-term orientation will be less prone to decreasing their expectations.

We next present a model of expectation formation and relevant hypotheses. 15 Hypothesis 1 suggests that results on expectations found in the United States will qualitatively replicate in India. Our main interest lies in hypotheses 2 and 3, which suggest that the extent of belief in karma will significantly moderate the effect of disconfirmation sensitivity on consumer expectations in India and that the moderating impact operates largely through long-term orientation.

Expectation Formation

Expectations about the quality of a product or service (E_i) for consumer i may come 16 from a variety of sources, including advertising, "expert" sources such as *Consumer Reports*, the quality of a typical brand in a category (Kopalle and Lehmann 1995, 2001; Meyer and Sathi 1985), or personal experience (Goering 1985). Here we focus on the quality of a typical brand, which leads to the following (fairly obvious) hypothesis:

H1a: The higher the expected quality of a typical brand in a category, the higher expectations will be.

A number of researchers have examined expectation formation (Boulding et al. 17 1999; Meyer and Sathi 1985; Mittal et al. 1998). For example, Boulding et al. (1999) identified two types of expectations: will and should. Here we focus on how will expectations are altered in order to increase future satisfaction (Kopalle and Lehmann 2001). Based on their work, therefore, we hypothesize the following:

H1b: The higher the disconfirmation sensitivity, the lower expectations will be.

The main focus here is to examine the impact of belief in karma, which has par- 18 ticular relevance in India, on expectations. Specifically, we examine the interaction (moderating) effect of belief in karma on expectations. The finding that disconfirmation sensitivity lowers expectations suggests that some individuals take a short-term orientation and artificially deflate their expectations in order to feel happier in the present, without regard to consequences in the future. However, for those who believe in karma, artificially lowering expectations so as to feel better in the present is not appropriate in the long term and therefore could lead to worse outcomes in the future (Chinmayananda 2006; Krishan 1983; Swami 2002). Belief in karma thus should counteract the tendency to artificially lower expectations since it leads one to have a more long-term orientation and hence set more realistic expectations. In other words, a stronger belief in karma should reduce the effect of disconfirmation sensitivity on expectations, thus acting as a moderator.

H2: The effect of disconfirmation sensitivity on expectations will be less negative for those who are higher in belief in karma, that is, belief in karma moderates the impact of disconfirmation sensitivity on expectations.

We capture the hypothesized effects in a model that extends Boulding et al. (1993, 19 1999) and Oliver and Winer (1987). Although not hypothesized, we also estimate the main effect of belief in karma on consumer expectations for completeness....

Finally, having a long-term orientation is fundamental to belief in karma. Such an 20 orientation makes short-run outcomes such as satisfaction with a particular purchase less important. The reduced importance of short-run outcomes, should, in turn, decrease the desirability of establishing artificially low expectations for the purpose of being satisfied in the short run. In other words, belief in karma leads to a long-term orientation which in turn decreases the tendency to set lower expectations, that is, long-term orientation mediates the impact of belief in karma on expectations....

References

Aaker, Jennifer L., and Durairaj Maheswaran (1997), "The Effects of Cultural Orientation on Persuasion," *Journal of Consumer Research*, 24 (December), 315–28.

Aaker, Jennifer L., and Patti Williams (1998), "Empathy versus Pride: The Influence of Emotional Appeals across Cultures," *Journal of Consumer Research*, 25 (December), 241–61.

Anderson, Eugene W., and Mary W. Sullivan (1993), "The Antecedents and Consequences of Customer Satisfaction for Firms," *Marketing Science*, 12 (Spring), 125–43.

Anderson, James C., and David W. Gerbing (1988), "Structural Equation Modeling in Practice: A Review and Recommended Two-Step Approach," *Psychological Bulletin*, 103 (3): 411–23.

Bagozzi, Richard P., Youjae Yi, and Lynn W. Phillips (1991), "Assessing Construct Validity in Organizational Research," *Administrative Science Quarterly*, 36 (3), 421–58.

Baron, Reuben M., and David A. Kenny (1986), "The Moderator-Mediator Variable Distinction in Social Psychological Research: Conceptual, Strategic and Statistical Considerations," *Journal of Personality and Social Psychology*, 51, 1173–82.

Bearden, William O., R. Bruce Money, and Jennifer L. Nevins (2006), "Measure of Long-Term Orientation: Development and Validation," *Journal of the Academy of Marketing Science*, 34 (3), 456–67.

Bernard, Theos (1981), *Hindu Philosophy*, Delhi: M. Banarsidass.

Bolton, Ruth N., and Katherine N. Lemon (1999), "A Dynamic Model of Customers' Usage of Services: Usage as an Antecedent and Consequence of Satisfaction," *Journal of Marketing Research*, 36 (May), 171–86.

Boulding, William, Ajay Kalra, and Richard Staelin (1999), "The Quality Double Whammy," *Marketing Science*, 18 (4), 463–84.

Boulding, William, Ajay Kalra, Richard Staelin, and Valarie A. Zeithaml (1993), "A Dynamic Process Model of Service Quality: From Expectations to Behavioral Intentions," *Journal of Marketing Research*, 30 (February), 7–27.

Bowes, Pratima (1978), *The Hindu Religious Tradition: A Philosophical Approach*, Boston: Routledge.

Briley, Donnel A., and Jennifer L. Aaker (2006), "When Does Culture Matter? Effects of Personal Knowledge on the Correction of Culture-Based Judgments," *Journal of Marketing Research*, 43 (August), 395–408.

Business Week (2006), "Karma Capitalism," October 30, 84–87.

Chinmayananda, Swami (2006), *The Holy Geeta*, Mumbai: Central Chinmaya Mission Trust.

Churchill, Gilbert A., Jr. (1979), "A Paradigm for Developing Better Measures of Marketing Constructs," *Journal of Marketing Research*, 16 (1), 64–73.

Consumers' Research (1991), "What to Know When Shopping for Tires," 74 (July), 16–19.

de Mooij, Marieke (2003), *Consumer Behavior and Culture: Consequences for Global Marketing and Advertising*, Thousand Oaks, CA: Sage.

Fornell, Claes, and David F. Larcker (1981), "Evaluating Structural Equation Models with Unobservable Variables and Measurement Error," *Journal of Marketing Research*, 18 (1), 39–50.

Goering, Patricia A. (1985), "Effects of Product Trial on Consumer Expectations, Demand, and Prices," *Journal of Consumer Research*, 12 (June), 74–82.

Gurhan-Canli, Zeynap, and Durairaj Maheswaran (2000), "Cultural Variations in Country of Origin Effects," *Journal of Marketing Research*, 37 (3), 309–17.

Herman, A. L. (1976), *An Introduction to Indian Thought*, Englewood Cliffs, NJ: Prentice Hall.

Higgins, E. Tory, Ronald Friedman, and James Shah (1997), "Emotional Response to Goal Attainment: Strength of Regulatory Focus as a Moderator," *Journal of Personality and Social Psychology*, 72 (March), 515–25.

Hofstede, Geert (2001), *Culture's Consequences*, 2nd ed., Thousand Oaks, CA: Sage.

Hofstede, Geert, and Gert Jan Hofstede (2005), *Cultures and Organizations*, New York: McGraw-Hill.

Inman, Jeffrey J., Anil C. Peter, and Priya Raghubir (1997), "Framing the Deal: The Role of Restrictions in Accentuating Deal Value," *Journal of Consumer Research*, 24 (June), 68–80.

King, Richard (1999), *Indian Philosophy*, Washington, DC: Georgetown University Press.

Kopalle, Praveen K., and Donald R. Lehmann (1995), "The Effects of Advertised and Observed Quality on Expectations about New Product Quality," *Journal of Marketing Research*, 32 (August), 280–90.

——— (2001), "Strategic Management of Expectations: The Role of Disconfirmation Sensitivity and Perfectionism," *Journal of Marketing Research*, 38 (August), 386–94.

——— (2006), "Setting Quality Expectations When Entering a Market: What Should the Promise Be?" *Marketing Science*, 25 (1), 8–24.

Krishan, Yuvraj (1983), "Karma Vipāka," *Numen*, 30 (December), 199–214.

——— (1997), *The Doctrine of Karma*, Delhi: Motilal Banarsidass.

Kumar, Piyush, Manohar U. Kalwani, and Maqbool Dada (1997), "The Impact of Waiting Time Guarantees on Customers' Waiting Experiences," *Marketing Science*, 16 (4), 295–314.

Meyer, Robert J., and Arvind Sathi (1985), "A Multiattribute Model of Consumer Choice during Product Learning," *Marketing Science*, 4 (Winter), 41–61.

Mittal, Vikas, William T. Ross Jr., and Patrick M. Baldasare (1998), "The Asymmetric Impact of Negative and Positive Attribute-Level Performance on Overall Satisfaction and Repurchase Intentions," *Journal of Marketing*, 62 (January), 33–47.

Monga, Ashwani, and Michael J. Houston (2006), "Fading Optimism in Products: Temporal Changes in Expectations about Performance," *Journal of Marketing Research*, 43 (November), 654–63.

Nunnally, Jum C. (1978), *Psychometric Theory*, 2nd ed., New York: McGraw-Hill.

Oliver, Richard L. (1997), *Satisfaction: A Behavioral Perspective on the Consumer*, New York: McGraw-Hill.

Oliver, Richard L., and Russell S. Winer (1987), "A Framework for the Formation and Structure of Consumer Expectations: Review and Propositions," *Journal of Economic Psychology*, 8 (December), 469–99.

Parasuraman, A., Valarie A. Zeithaml, and Leonard L. Berry (1994), "A Reassessment of Expectations as a Comparative Standard in Measuring Service Quality: Implications for Future Research," *Journal of Marketing*, 58 (January), 111–24.

Roth, David L., and Rick E. Ingram (1985), "Factors in the Self-Deception Questionnaire: Associations with Depression," *Journal of Personality and Social Psychology*, 48 (1), 243–51.

Rotter, Julian B. (1966), "Generalized Expectancies of Internal versus External Control of Reinforcements," *Psychological Monographs*, 80, 1–28.

Rust, Roland T., Jeffrey J. Inman, Jianmin Jia, and Anthony Zahorik (1999), "What You Don't Know about Customer-Perceived Quality: The Role of Customer Expectation Distributions," *Marketing Science*, 18 (1), 77–92.

Saksena, Shri Krishna (1970), *Essays on Indian Philosophy*, Honolulu: University of Hawaii Press.

Sharma, Arvind (1991), *A Hindu Perspective on the Philosophy of Religion*, New York: St. Martin's Press.

Singelis, Theodore M., Harry S. Triandis, Dharm P. S. Bhawuk, and Michele J. Gelfand (1995), "Horizontal and Vertical Dimensions of Individualism and Collectivism: A Theoretical and Measurement Refinement," *Cross-Cultural Research*, 29 (3), 240–75.

Small, Deborah A., Jennifer S. Lerner, and Baruch Fischhoff (2006), "Emotion Priming and Spontaneous Attributions for Terrorism: Americans' Reactions in a National Field Experiment," *Political Psychology*, 27, 289–98.

Spreng, Richard A., Scott B. MacKenzie, and Richard W. Olshavsky (1996), "A Reexamination of the Determinants of Consumer Satisfaction," *Journal of Marketing*, 60 (July), 15–32.

Swami, Vidya Prakasanandagiri S. (2002), *Om Gita Makarandam*, Chittoor, A.P.: Sri Parasarya Press.

Tan, Chin Tiong, and John U. Farley (1987), "The Impact of Cultural Patterns on Cognition and Intention in Singapore," *Journal of Consumer Research*, 13 (March), 540–44.

Triandis, Harry C. (1989), "The Self and Social Behavior in Differing Cultural Contexts," *Psychological Review*, 96 (3), 506–20.

van Raaij, Fred W. (1991), "The Formation and Use of Expectations in Consumer Decision Making," in *Handbook of Consumer Research*, ed. T. S. Robertson and H. H. Kassarjian, Englewood Cliffs, NJ: Prentice Hall, 401–18.

Wertenbroch, Klaus (1998), "Consumption Self-Control by Rationing Purchase Quantities of Virtue and Vice," *Marketing Science*, 17 (4), 317–37.

• • •

In the following selection, the opening of a twenty-one-page article, Gisela Bock introduces her argument and explains the need for her study, situating it within the work of other historians of Nazi Germany and in particular of women in Nazi Germany. The first note is unnumbered, as it pertains to her article as a whole. The numbered footnotes comment and cite sources, sometimes in support of a claim and sometimes as exceptions to a claim. Some of the notes also qualify a statement in the main text, providing detail or explanations that do not fit tidily into her argument.

Gisela Bock

From Racism and Sexism in Nazi Germany: Motherhood, Compulsory Sterilization, and the State

"Alien Races" and the "Other Sex"

By presenting some largely unexplored features of women's lives under National Social- 1
ism in Germany, this essay considers larger questions about the complex connections
between racism and sexism. It does not presume to exhaust the issue or even touch upon
all its aspects. Instead, it approaches the issue through the perspective of one part of
women's lives affected by state policy: reproduction or, as I prefer to call it, the reproduc-
tive aspect of women's unwaged housework. It can be no more than a contribution for
two reasons. First, dealing with racism in Germany during this period involves assessing
an unparalleled mass murder of millions of women and men, an undertaking beyond the
scope of any single essay. Second, this analysis is a first approach, for neither race nor
gender, racism nor sexism — and even less their connection — has been a central theme
in German social historiography.[1] When historians deal with women in modern Germany, they generally do not consider racism or racial discrimination against women,[2]
while the literature dealing with anti-Jewish racism and the Holocaust generally does
not consider either women's specific situation or the added factor of sexism.

The extent to which the racist tradition was concerned with those activities 2
which then and now are considered "women's sphere" — that is, bearing and rearing
children — has also not been recognized. Perhaps we might argue even further that a
large part of this racist tradition remained invisible precisely because the history of

---

This article is a preliminary summary of ongoing research. Space limitations do not permit me to deal
with important aspects of the issues involved, for example, the sterilization procedure, the reactions of
the victims of sterilization and their resistance to it, and the racist and sexist use of state subventions
for marriage and children. They will be dealt with in my forthcoming book on "Zwangssterilisation und
Mutterschaft im Nationalsozialismus."

[1] The more progressive new generation of social historians in Germany since the 1960s has tended to
present racism as a mere ideology, its application as more or less economically/politically "rational" or
"irrational," often as merely instrumental, and mostly as an appendage to more important developments, "political" or "economic." See, e.g., Peter M. Kaiser, "Monopolprofit und Massenmord im Fas-
chismus: Zur ökonomischen Funktion der Konzentrationslager im faschistischen Deutschland,"
Blätter für deutsche und internationale Politik 5 (1975): 552–77.

[2] A rare exception is Marion A. Kaplan, *The Jewish Feminist Movement in Germany: The Campaigns of
the "Jüdischer Frauenbund," 1904–1938* (Westport, Conn.: Greenwood Press, 1979).

women and of their work in the family was not an issue for (mostly male) historians and theoreticians.[3]

To make the issue of motherhood and compulsory sterilization the center of discussion places the focus not so much on anti-Jewish racism, on which we have an extended literature, as on another form of racism: eugenics, or, as it was called before and during the Nazi regime and sometimes also in Anglo-Saxon literature, race hygiene.[4] It comprises a vast field of more or less popular, more or less scientific, traditions, which became the core of population policies throughout the Nazi regime.

Beyond the plain, yet unexplored, fact that at least half of those persecuted on racial grounds were women, there are more subtle reasons for women's historians' interest in the "scientific" or eugenic form of racism. The race hygiene discourse since the end of the nineteenth century deals with women much more than do most other social or political theories, since women have been hailed as "mothers of the race," or, in stark contrast, vilified, as the ones guilty of "racial degeneration." Then, too, definitions of race hygiene made at the time show some conscious links between this field and women's history, describing it, for instance, as *Fortpflanzungshygiene* ("procreation hygiene").[5] In fact, we might consider that most of the scientific and pseudoscientific superstructure of eugenic racism, especially its mythology of hereditary character traits, is concerned with the supposedly "natural" or "biological" domains in

---

[3] However, three conferences of women historians on women's history have taken place: "Women in the Weimar Republic and under National Socialism," Berlin, 1979; "Muttersein und Mutteride-ologie in der bürgerlichen Gesellschaft," Bremen, 1980; and "Frauengeschichte," Bielefeld, 1981. Some of the workshops of the latter are documented in *Beiträge zur feministischen Theorie und Praxis,* vol. 5 (April 1981). Thus, women's history has been exploring this and similar themes in recent years, but much work still needs to be done, and many questions cannot yet be answered in a consistent way.

[4] A good overview on the American and international eugenics movement is Allan Chase, *The Legacy of Malthus: The Social Costs of the New Scientific Racism* (New York: Alfred A. Knopf, Inc., 1977). Although there has been, at the beginning of this century, a debate among experts on distinctions between "eugenics" and "race hygiene," I use these terms interchangeably, as does Chase, for I believe the issue dealt with in this article requires my doing so. On this debate see Georg Lilienthal, "Rassen-hygiene im Dritten Reich: Krise und Wende," *Medizinhistorisches Journal* 14 (1979): 114–34.

[5] See Alfred Grotjahn, *Geburten-Rückgang und Geburten-Regelung im Lichte der individuellen und der sozialen Hygiene* (Berlin: Coblenz., 1914; 2d ed., 1921), p. 153 (hereafter cited as *Geburten-Rückgang*), and the chapter on "Birth Regulation Serving Eugenics and Race Hygiene"; and Agnes Bluhm, *Die ras-senhygienischen Aufgaben des weiblichen Arztes: Schriften zur Erblehre und Rassenhygiene* (Berlin: Metzner, 1936), esp. the chapter on "Woman's Role in the Racial Process in Its Largest Sense."

which women are prominent — body, sexuality, procreation, education — the heretofore "private" sphere.[6]

For a third reason, eugenics and racism in general are significant to women's [5] history. After a long hiatus, the result in part of Nazism, interest in the history of women in Germany has seen a revival during the past half-decade or more. However, this interest has focused almost exclusively on the historical reconstruction and critique of those norms and traditions that underlined women's "natural" destiny as unwaged wives, mothers, and homemakers. Those with this perspective see National Socialism as either a culmination of, or a reactionary return to, belief in women's "traditional" role as mothers and housewives; motherhood and housework become essential factors in a backward, premodern, or precapitalist "role" assigned to women.[7]

Thus most historians seem to agree that under the Nazi regime women counted [6] merely as mothers who should bear and rear as many children as possible, and that Nazi antifeminism tended to promote, protect, and even finance women as childbearers, housewives, and mothers. It seems necessary to challenge various aspects of this widely held opinion, but particularly its neglect of racism.[8] . . .

•   •   •

[6] Good examples are the classic and influential books by Grotjahn, *Geburten-Rückgang* and *Die Hygiene der menschlichen Fortpflanzung* (Berlin and Vienna: Urban & Schwarzenburg, 1926); Erwin Baur, Eugen Fischer, and Fritz Lenz, *Grundriß der menschlichen Erblichkeitslehre und Rassenhygiene,* vol. 2, *Menschliche Auslese und Rassenhygiene* (Munich: Lehmann, 1921). These volumes had many interestingly divergent editions. I have used vol. 1 (1936) and vol. 2 (1931). For a scientific critique of the pseudoscientific theory of character traits see, e.g., Chase, chap. 8.

[7] For a preliminary critique of this view, analyzing housework as no less modern and no less capitalist than employment outside the house, see Gisela Bock and Barbara Duden, "Arbeit aus Liebe — Liebe als Arbeit: Zur Entstehung der Hausarbeit im Kapitalismus," in *Frauen und Wissenschaft: Beiträge zur Berliner Sommeruniversität für Frauen, Juli 1976,* ed. Gruppe Berliner Dozentinnen (Berlin: Courage Verlag, 1977), pp. 118–99. Parts of it have been translated as "Labor of Love — Love as Labor," in *From Feminism to Liberation,* ed. Edith Hoshino Altbach, 2d ed. (Cambridge, Mass.: Schenkman Publishing Co., 1980), pp. 153–92.

[8] Dörte Winkler, *Frauenarbeit im "Dritten Reich"* (Hamburg: Hoffman & Campe, 1977), esp. pp. 42–65, revised this picture by showing that under Nazism employment of lower- and middle-class women was not reduced. This is confirmed by various authors in the anthology edited by Frauengruppe Faschismusforschung, *Mutterkreuz und Arbeitsbuch: Zur Geschichte der Frauen in der Weimarer Republik und im Nationalsozialismus* (Frankfurt a.M.: Fischer, 1981), Leila J. Rupp, *Mobilizing Women for War: German and American Propaganda, 1939–1945* (Princeton, N.J.: Princeton University Press, 1978), esp. pp. 11–50. . . .

➔ **Try This**   Reading Notes

Examine the footnotes in the Bock excerpt. To what purpose does Bock reference other writers in the notes? For each note, identify which of the four functions listed on page 330 corresponds most closely to the footnote's purpose. (If you find that a note has a function other than those listed, explain its purpose.)

A scholarly text does not stand alone but rather exists as a building block in a much larger and more solid structure of knowledge — a structure that continues to expand as insights accumulate and new discoveries are made, but one that would crumble if scholars were to stop linking their own work to others' work. So there are strong practical reasons for carefully documenting sources in scholarly work.

There are also ethical reasons for documenting sources. **Plagiarism** (which comes from the Latin word for "kidnapping") means presenting someone else's words or ideas as your own, without permission or acknowledgment. An act of plagiarism is a triple wrong. It cheats the writer whose work is stolen without credit. It also deceives readers, by misleading them about the true author of the work in front of them. And finally, it robs the plagiarist of an opportunity to think, learn, and create for himself or herself.

➔ **Try This**   Understanding Your School's Code
of Academic Conduct

Many colleges and universities maintain a code of academic conduct or academic integrity and impose penalties on students who infringe it, ranging from grade penalties to expulsion. If your college publishes such a code, read it and consider what it implies about your responsibility to cite your sources and document them accurately.

⊃ **Guidelines**   ## What to Cite

You must cite *any* material that you draw from another work—including facts (other than common knowledge), words, ideas, statistics, and hypotheses. This includes material from texts, multimedia sources, lectures, e-mails, interviews, and even ideas that arise in class discussion if they are attributable to a specific person.

Always cite the following:

- Direct quotations
- Paraphrases or summaries of ideas from another work
- References to another work

You should not cite a thought that is your own or is common knowledge that cannot be attributed to any particular source. Common knowledge is information that most people know, the sort of information you would find in a *basic* dictionary, almanac, or encyclopedia—for example, a famous author's date of birth, a country's capital, or a well-known fact such as the name of the current president of the United States.

Do not cite the following:

- Your own ideas
- Common knowledge

⊃ **Try This**   ## Finding Where Citations Are Needed

All citations have been omitted from the following paper. Place a check mark wherever you believe a citation is needed. Compare your results with your classmates' and explain your decisions.

Soledad Gonzalez

Professor Takacs

Writing 101

5 March 2012

Do High School Students Share

the Right to Free Speech?

In America, the right to free speech is enshrined in the Constitution's First Amendment, which states that "Congress shall make no law . . . abridging the freedom of speech, or of the press. . . . " However, the amendment does not specify whether it applies equally to every American or only to those who have reached the age of majority. An area that remains both unsettled and controversial concerns high school students and their right to question laws and school policies regarding the use of drugs. Should high school students be free to question and even advocate illicit drug use, without restriction? Or do teachers and administrators have the right to limit such speech and to punish students who disregard those limits? Do students have the right to encourage other students to try illegal drugs? In this essay, I will argue that, for better or worse, they do. And high school students' right to free speech should be protected except in rare instances when doing so would create a direct legal conflict for teachers and school administrators.

In 1969, the Supreme Court decided in the case of *Tinker v. Des Moines* that high school students had the right to wear armbands in support of a cease-fire during the Vietnam War. The decision had broad implications. As Justice Abe Fortas wrote for the majority,

Gonzalez 2

It can hardly be argued that either students or teacher shed their constitutional rights to freedom of speech or expression at the schoolhouse gate. . . . In the absence of a specific showing of constitutionally valid reasons to regulate their speech, students are entitled to freedom of expression of their views.

Fortas makes it clear that the decision sought to ensure that high school students should enjoy the same right to free speech as adults.

More recently, however, the Supreme Court has imposed certain limits on high school students' speech. In 2007, it ruled in *Morse v. Frederick* that public schools "can punish students for advocating or promoting illegal drug use." This case concerned a high school principal's decision to impose a ten-day suspension on student Joseph Frederick, who had raised a banner reading "Bong Hits 4 Jesus" at a school event. The Court's 5-4 decision was vehemently opposed by the minority, however. Justice John Paul Stevens wrote in his dissenting opinion that the Court's decision "is deaf to the constitutional imperative to permit unfettered debate, even among high-school students, about the wisdom of the war on drugs or of legalizing marijuana for medical use."

Those who argue in favor of limits on students' speech note that school officials can be held liable for failing to maintain an environment that not only is drug-free but also clearly discourages illicit drug use. As Frederick Hess of the American Enterprise Institute claims, "If there are drugs in school, the public is going to come down hard on the schools for not doing enough to prevent drugs in the schools." However, freedom of speech in every circumstance demands that we keep a clear and firm distinction between words and deeds. To use or possess illicit drugs, to offer them to another student — these are deeds that differ

Gonzalez 3

fundamentally from words. While some kinds of speech, such as obscenity, hate speech, libel, and sedition, are clearly illegal, the freedom to question laws and engage in political debate is as necessary in high schools as in any public forum.

Some worry that freedom of speech means that the loudest students can cause disruptions and distract students and faculty from their principal task: learning the high school curriculum. But this concerns a different kind of discipline, pertaining to the manner in which something is said, not the content.

Avoiding Plagiarism

Most people prefer to be honest and honorable; the chief reason that some students end up plagiarizing is that, for whatever reason, they panic and think they have no other choice. Most frequently, students plagiarize because they fail to manage their time well or they underestimate the size of the project, and so they find themselves forced to produce a paper at the last minute. Under such circumstances, the temptation to plagiarize — maybe just to get a little too much help from a fellow student, maybe to cut corners when paraphrasing an online source — can be strong. So plan ahead. (See the sample schedules for writing a research paper on pp. 273–74.) The second reason that students sometimes plagiarize is that they feel overwhelmed by the difficulty of an assignment and feel incapable of completing it independently. If this happens, speak to your instructor and explain the problems you're having. The vast majority of instructors are eager to help their students get through such difficulties.

By far the most common sort of plagiarism, however, is unintended plagiarism. A student who does not understand the rules of documentation or the difference between a quotation and a paraphrase or the difference between an acceptable and an unacceptable paraphrase may commit an offense without meaning to do so. *But it is an offense nevertheless.* Every student is responsible for understanding the rules of citation and for knowing how to write an acceptable paraphrase.

Writing an Acceptable Paraphrase

A **paraphrase** is a rewording of another person's words — whether written or spoken. A paraphrase might be a summary (shorter than the original) or an explication of the text (longer than the original) or just a close reworking of the text (about the same length as the original). As a rule, direct quotations should be used in academic writing only when necessary, so the art of paraphrase is an essential skill. It requires particular care and attention. Unless you understand and carefully observe the rules for writing acceptable paraphrases, you can easily commit unintended plagiarism. In general, an **unacceptable paraphrase** is either one that is too close to the wording of the original text or one that fails to cite its source properly and completely.

A paraphrase must use your own words to convey the ideas or the information in the original text. Avoid borrowing the original text's distinctive or unusual words or word combinations. Paraphrases can *include* quotations; in fact, quoting brief phrases within a paraphrase is a good way to deal with unique expressions that cannot be reworded or omitted.

But in a paraphrase, not only must the words be your own, so must the sentence structures. Mere "synonym swapping" — replacing the words of the original with close synonyms but keeping the same word order — is unacceptable. A paraphrase in which the grammar and sentence structure of the original remain intact, even though most of the words differ, would be too close to the original. Such a paraphrase would still be plagiarism.

The best way to write a paraphrase is to hide the document by turning off your computer screen or closing the book or journal. Then paraphrase the text in your own words, relying on your memory and doing the best job you can. Then, open up the original again, and correct and improve your draft. Finally, edit carefully to make sure your paraphrase is not only acceptable but accurate and complete.

In practice, however, you will rarely need to write a strict, straight paraphrase; rather, you will want to emphasize some aspect of the original. After all, you will be using the excerpted text for a new purpose — that is, to support a new argument of your own. Since a paraphrase is usually written for a *purpose*, it will stress certain aspects of the original and downplay others. So a paraphrase should be faithful to the original, but it need not be absolutely *complete* in the sense of representing every word and connotation in the original without exception. Most paraphrasing does involve some summary — as some ideas will be more important to your argument than others. (If you truly need all the detail of the original, then it might be better just to quote the original.) Selective paraphrasing does not imply any distortion or misrepresentation of the ideas in the original; it simply means transplanting ideas from one context into a different context.

Finally, remember that paraphrases *must be cited*, just as quotations must be cited. When conducting your research, be careful to label and identify your notes accurately and completely. Place quotation marks around all direct quotations, even single words, and identify the source of all ideas and information that you write down. If you make scrupulous note-taking of this kind a habit, you will be much less likely to plagiarize unintentionally.

Some students write their rough draft without citations, intending to insert all the citations at a later point. But this is a dangerous strategy, as you will find it difficult to distinguish consistently between your own ideas and those of other writers.

Here are examples of unacceptable and acceptable paraphrases.

Original Text

Humans, Tooby and DeVore suggest, entered the "cognitive niche." Remember the definition of intelligence from Chapter 2: using knowledge of how things work to attain goals in the face of obstacles. By learning which manipulations achieve which goals, humans have mastered the art of the surprise attack. They use novel, goal-oriented courses of action to overcome the Maginot Line defenses of other organisms, which can respond only over evolutionary time. The manipulations can be novel because human knowledge is not just couched in concrete instructions like "how to catch a rabbit." Humans analyze the world using intuitive theories of objects, forces, paths, places, manners, states, substances, hidden biochemical essences, and, for other animals and people, beliefs and desires. (These intuitive theories are the topic of Chapter 5.) People compose new knowledge and plans by mentally playing out combinatorial interactions among these laws in their mind's eye.[2]

---

[2] Steven Pinker, *How the Mind Works* (New York: W. W. Norton, 1997), 188.

Unacceptable Paraphrase

Pinker draws on Tooby and DeVore to argue that human beings came to occupy a "cognitive niche" in the evolutionary tree. Pinker defines intelligence as the ability to use knowledge of the way things work in order to overcome obstacles and reach a goal. Humans became proficient in the art of the surprise attack by figuring out which actions and maneuvers achieve which goals. They use inventive, goal-oriented strategies to overcome the formidable defenses of other organisms. But these organisms can only respond over evolutionary time. Their strategies can be novel because human knowledge is not just confined to fixed instructions like "how to catch a boar." Human beings analyze their environments by intuiting ideas concerning objects, forces, paths, places, manners, states, substances, biochemistry, and, for other animals and people, beliefs and desires. Humans create new knowledge and plans by working out in their minds how the laws behind these things will interact. (Pinker 188)

This first paraphrase is not acceptable because the wording is too close to the original. Note how this paraphrase repeats such phrases as "art of the surprise attack"; "defenses of other organisms"; "over evolutionary time"; "can be novel because human knowledge is not just"; and "instructions like 'how to catch'".

Unacceptable Paraphrase

Pinker writes that the human species, as Tooby and DeVore argue, moved into the "cognitive niche." In Chapter 2, he defines intelligence as using understanding of the way things work to achieve objectives in spite of impediments. By figuring out which operations accomplish which objectives, *homo sapiens* became adept at catching their prey unawares. They employ original, purposeful schemes to defeat the most formidable protections of other creatures, which can react only over many generations. The operations can be original because human understanding is not just formulated in fixed directions like "how to trap a hare." Humans explore their milieu using sensed ideas of things, energies, routes, locations, practices, circumstances, material, unseen biochemical substances, and, for other creatures and humans, convictions and aspirations. Humans innovate understanding and strategies by intellectually working out various combinations among these forces in their imaginations. (Pinker 188)

The problem with this second paraphrase is that its sentence structures too closely mirror those of the original. The writer has simply replaced some of the words in Pinker's sentences with synonyms. For instance, the original "objects, forces, paths, places, manners, states, substances, hidden biochemical essences" becomes "things, energies, routes, locations, practices, circumstances, material, unseen biochemical substances."

Acceptable Paraphrase

Steven Pinker explains Tooby and DeVore's theory of the "cognitive niche," which claims that human beings evolved to occupy a unique position among animals: humans are the only creatures to possess an intelligence that enables them to overcome all manner of difficulties to obtain what they want. Only humans can invent ways to penetrate the defenses of other species and organisms; their victims can develop new defenses only through evolutionary processes that take many generations. And humans can improvise new strategies for new situations: their ideas are not restricted to one fixed set of instructions. Rather, they analyze their environments by grasping its laws and thinking out their strategies in their imaginations. This unique ability accounts for the survival of *homo sapiens* over the course of evolution. (Pinker 188)

→ Guidelines   ## When and How to Paraphrase

When to Paraphrase

- Whenever you need to incorporate ideas from another source into your own argument, consider paraphrasing those ideas.
- As a general rule, prefer paraphrase (or summary) to quotation, as quotations tend to disrupt the flow of an argument. If you can express the idea in your own words, and if you do not plan to comment on the particular wording of the original, paraphrase.

How to Paraphrase

- Read the original text several times to make sure that you fully grasp the ideas.
- Express the ideas of the original in your own words and sentence structures.
- Never swap synonyms in order to rewrite the original: find new sentence structures as well as new words.
- If key words or phrases in the original cannot be paraphrased, consider incorporating them as brief quotations within the paraphrase.
- Include an introductory phrase to show where the paraphrase begins.
- Cite the paraphrase or summary. (This indicates where the paraphrase ends.)
- Place your own comments on the writer's ideas *after* the citation.

Writing a Summary or an Abstract

In one sense, a summary is just a paraphrase that is substantially shorter than the original, so many of the same rules apply: use your own words and your own sentence structures to convey faithfully and clearly the sense of the original text; if you must use special words or brief phrases from the original, place them in quotation marks.

But writing a summary or an **abstract** presents special challenges because it must be so condensed, containing nothing but the essentials of the argument (or plot, in the case of fiction and drama). Abstracts rarely exceed one or two paragraphs — about 200 words maximum — and a summary in an essay may need to be even shorter.

The challenge in writing a summary is to distinguish the essential from the inessential: to do this, you need to have a clear sense of the argument. The more complicated the argument, the more difficult this is. However, the more familiar you become with the argument, the easier writing a summary becomes. (Think of how easily you could summarize a story you know very well — perhaps *Romeo and Juliet* or *The Wizard of Oz*.) The first two paragraphs and the last two paragraphs of an essay often provide useful clues, but you cannot rely only on these. The first two paragraphs often do define the *problem or question* that the author is addressing, and they may also present the *solution or answer* (that is, the thesis, even if only a partial one). But the complete thesis statement might occur elsewhere in the essay — at the end or even in the middle.

Read through the essay carefully, taking careful notes on the principal *claims* the author makes (you might use one of the strategies suggested in Chapter 2). After you have identified them, work out how they are logically related to one another — how one claim supports or leads to another — and try to write a skeleton outline of the argument using mostly your own words. Now write a draft of your complete summary, beginning with a statement of the problem and the thesis. Then explain only enough of the argument to make good sense of how the author supports his or her thesis. You may need to include a sentence or two to explain something about the method, context, or purpose of the argument as well. Finally, revise and polish the sum-

➡ **Try This**   **Paraphrasing Texts**

Choose a passage of roughly 100 words from three of the essays included at the end of this book. Write a paraphrase of each. Check that your paraphrase fulfills all the criteria for an acceptable paraphrase.

mary, making sure that you use only your own words, except for brief quotations (never more than a phrase).

Always maintain strict objectivity when writing an abstract, and don't include your subjective reaction or any comments. Even when you write a summary to incorporate into an essay, it is usually wise to avoid confusion by clearly separating the summary from your own comments.

A summary or an abstract includes the following:

- The problem or question that the text addresses
- The solution or answer — the thesis
- The main arguments for that thesis
- If necessary, a brief explanation of the context, method, or purpose
- A citation

An abstract always, and a summary usually, excludes the following:

- Subjective comment, response, or reaction

Documentation in MLA, *Chicago,* and APA Styles

Because they have different needs, academic disciplines have developed distinct formats or styles for document design and citation. The Modern Language Association (MLA) style is widely used in composition and literature courses. *The Chicago Manual of Style* (*Chicago* or *CMS*) is used in many other humanities disciplines as well as in social sciences and in the fine arts. The American Psychological Association (APA) style is used in psychology and other social and behavioral sciences.

What is a citation? A **citation** attributes borrowed material — quoted words or paraphrased ideas or facts — to its source. Often the note is merely an abbreviation, and complete information appears in a bibliography at the end of the text. MLA style uses in-text citations that typically include just a page number and, if necessary, the author's name; the full citation appears in a Works Cited page at the end of the essay. This style does not use footnotes, and endnotes are used only for information, not for citations. *Chicago* style provides complete references in footnotes at the bottom of the page on which the citation occurs or in endnotes at the end of the paper. A bibliography or Works Cited page is optional. Like MLA style, APA style includes a list of references. Footnotes are not used for citations.

MLA Style

Main Features

In-text Citations Abbreviated citations occur in parentheses within the text. Complete bibliographical information appears in a list of Works Cited at the end of the paper. In-text citations may take several forms.

A page number is sufficient if the author's name is clearly given in the text.

> As J. Allan Mitchell observes, "Even this comparison underestimates Griselda, who can actually be said to exhibit the proverbial 'patience of Job' that Job lacks" (22).

If the author's identity is not clear from the text, include the author's last name and a page number in parentheses.

> The serfs "could not plead in court against their lord, no one spoke for them in Parliament, [and] they were bound by duties of servitude which they had no way to break except by forcibly obtaining a change of the rules" (Tuchman 373).

If no page number is available (for example, for material from a Web site), use the author's name or the first significant word or two of the title.

> For some weeks afterward, the revolt would break out here and there, but its back had been broken in a matter of days ("Peasants' Revolt").

Works Cited Page A Works Cited page at the end of the paper contains complete bibliographical information for each citation.

The entry for a book includes the name of the author(s), the title in italics, the city of publication, the publisher, the year of publication, and the medium (such as print or Web).

> Miller, Robert P. *Chaucer Sources and Backgrounds*. New York: Oxford UP, 1977. Print.

The entry for an article includes the name of the author(s), the title of the article in quotation marks, the title of the journal in italics, the volume number, the year, the page range, and the medium.

> Ginsberg, Warren. "'And Speketh So Pleyn': *The Clerk's Tale* and Its Teller." *Criticism* 20 (1978): 307-23. Print.

In addition to the information required for print sources, citations for electronic sources include the sponsor of the site (listed before the publication date). Also include the date you accessed the site. (You do not need to include the URL.)

Aristotle. *Poetics*. Trans. S. H. Butcher. *The Internet Classics Archive*. Web Atomic
and Massachusetts Institute of Technology, 13 Sept. 2007. Web. 15 Feb. 2011.

Entries are listed alphabetically by the first word in the citation, disregarding
"A," "An," and "The." Entries are formatted with a "hanging indent": the first line of
each entry is flush with the margin, and each subsequent line is indented half an
inch.

Format for a Paper No title page is required; give your name, the name of your instructor, the course name, and the date at the top left of the first page. Double-space
throughout — including indented block quotations, endnotes, and the Works Cited
page.

For more details, see the *MLA Handbook for Writers of Research Papers*, 7th
Edition.

Last name and page number ➘

Wynn 1

Name, course,
professor, and date

Charlene Wynn

Professor Hayes

English 318 (Medieval English Literature and Society)

8 April 2011

Title centered

Chaucer's *Clerk's Tale* and the Peasants' Revolt

In *The Clerk's Tale*, the Marquis Walter tests the obedience
and patience of his peasant wife by pretending to arrange the
murder of their children and finally pretending to divorce her.
In the course of telling this tale, the Clerk — a student at
"Oxenford" — questions whether limits should be set on
patience when the master is outrageously cruel. Griselda's
relationship with the Marquis Walter has usually been
discussed in the context of the "marriage debate" in the
Canterbury Tales, but it is also significant that Griselda is a
powerless subject and Walter, the Marquis, is her lord.

Wynn 2

Although the tale is set in a faraway land of apparent social harmony, England's recent history had severely tested the endurance of the common people, provoking the revolt of 1381. Led by John Ball and Wat Tyler, the commoners rose up to protest an intolerable tax burden and the abuses of the clergy and the nobility and to demand reforms that would have effectively ended the feudal system. They succeeded in briefly taking over London, beheaded several of the king's close advisers — including Archbishop of Canterbury Simon Sudbury and Treasurer Richard Hales — and demolished the Savoy palace, the residence of John of Gaunt. However, the commoners' trust in King Richard II (not unlike the simple trust of the people in Marquis Walter), who was at the time only fourteen years old, brought about their downfall, for Richard, while seeming to take their side, quietly plotted with the Lord Mayor and others to kill Wat Tyler and restore order. For some weeks afterward, the revolt would break out here and there, but its back had been broken in a matter of days ("*Peasants'*").[1]

Source: Author is identified; pages in parentheses

Chaucer began writing *The Canterbury Tales* about seven years after the revolt, according to Benson (xxix). These upheavals were therefore not far in the past when Chaucer's Clerk tells the pilgrims about Griselda's patience. The Clerk himself maintains that his tale teaches that Christians should be as patient before God's inscrutable ways as Griselda is with her husband, but that "archewyves" — or women "ready for battle" (Benson 153) — today are far too irreverent to be compared to Griselda (lines 1142-1211). However, the Clerk's actual rendition of the tale makes this

Source: Author and page in parentheses

simple interpretation unsupportable, primarily because the
Clerk himself expresses his horror at Walter's "nedeless" and
"yvele" (evil) cruelty (455-60), so that it becomes impossible
to take him as either God-figure or ideal husband.
Consequently, recent critics have adopted the view that the
tale as told by the Clerk does not lend itself to any
straightforward allegorical reading; instead, the tale seems
richer and more interesting for the fact that it directs our
attention back onto the Clerk himself, to his own
uncertainty about the meaning of this extraordinary fable.[2]
If, as seems clear from the way he chastises women for
failing to resemble Griselda, the Clerk's initial interest in this
particular story would have been as a rebuttal to the Wife of
Bath's heretical views on marriage (1170-72), his plan comes
dangerously close to backfiring. For Walter's cruelty is too
extreme to be tolerated, and Griselda's self-abnegation and
acquiescence are so appalling that the tale begins to work in
the Wife of Bath's favor. Indeed, Petrarch (whose text the
Clerk acknowledges as his source and follows closely)
explicitly disavows a reading that makes Griselda the ideal
wife (138-39). But neither can she function as the model
Christian, since she acquiesces to the murder of her children.

The Clerk gets seduced by his own vivid narration. In
essence, the allegorical promise of the tale is undone by its
dramatic requirements, as character and plot come to life
through the Clerk's powerful and sympathetic imagination.
While Petrarch had preserved the simple allegory by refusing
to pass judgment on Walter (137), the Clerk (perhaps despite
himself) becomes involved in his subject matter and comments

Wynn 4

freely, expressing shock and awe. Whatever may have seemed possible in the abstract, the unsuitability of Griselda and Walter as models of virtue begins to appear as the tale unfolds in a lively flesh-and-blood drama. As it gradually becomes clear that the heartless Walter will not do as a stand-in for God, the spiritual allegory breaks down, and the whole thrust of the tale shifts from simplistic allegory to problematic political fable.

The relatively few, but highly significant, changes that Chaucer's Clerk introduces into Petrarch's tale reveal how this happens. While Petrarch takes no exception to Walter's life of leisure (139-40), Chaucer's Clerk unmistakably expresses his disapproval of Walter's carelessness even as he first presents him:

Block quote indented, double-spaced. Page reference follows period.

> I blame hym thus, that he considered noght
> In tyme comynge what myghte hym bityde,
> But on his lust present was al his thoght,
> As for to hauke and hunte on every syde.
> Wel ny alle othere cures leete he slyde,
> And eek he nolde — and that was worst of alle —
> Wede no wyf, for noght that may bifalle. (73-84)

In the Clerk's version, the Marquis has crossed the line that separates gentlemanly leisure from dissolute self-indulgence. Even before Walter imposes on Griselda the first test, claiming that their daughter must be slain to please his subjects, the Clerk describes the Marquis's desire to tempt her as "yvele." The last four lines of the following passage are Chaucer's addition:

> This markys in his herte longeth so
> To tempte his wyf, hir sadness for to knowe,

> The he ne myghte out of his herte throwe
> This merveillous desir his wyf t'assaye;
> Nedelees, God woot, he thoghte hire for t'affraye.
>
> • • •
>
> He hadde assayed hire ynogh bifore,
> And foond hire evere good; what needed it
> Hire for to tempte, and alwey moore and moore,
> Though som men preise it for a subtil wit?
> But as for me, I seye that yvele it sit
> To assaye a wyf whan that it is no nede,
> And putten hire in angwyssh and in drede. (451-62)

When Walter is about to try Griselda's patience a second time,
now pretending to have their infant son killed, the Clerk's
reproach is even more emphatic:

> O nedeless was she tempted in assay!
> But wedded men ne knowe no mesure,
> Whan that they fynde a pacient creature. (621-23)

Thus the Clerk's departures from Petrarch's text portray a
Marquis who is a dissolute, dishonest, and corrupt despot.

Notes

1. The history of the Peasants' Revolt of 1381 is detailed in Lindsay and Groves; its implications are debated in "The Peasants' Revolt."

2. See Ginsberg, Knapp, Middleton, Morrow, and Morse. An exception is Morgan, who opposes the "application of the dramatic principle to the reading of the Canterbury Tales and of its concomitant preference for tellers over tales" (3). But he himself cites the theological principle that obedience should not be expected when a regime "commands what is wrong" (11). It is exactly this moral principle that creates the complications that the Clerk cannot resolve.

Wynn 7

Works Cited

List of sources in alphabetical order

Benson, Larry, ed. *The Riverside Chaucer*. 3rd ed. Boston:
    Houghton, 1987. Print.

Chaucer, Geoffrey. "The Clerk's Prologue and Tale." *The
    Riverside Chaucer*. 3rd ed. Ed. Larry Benson. Boston:
    Houghton, 1987. 137-52. Print.

Ginsberg, Warren. "'And Speketh So Pleyn': *The Clerk's Tale* and
    Its Teller." *Criticism* 20 (1978): 307-23. Print.

Knapp, Peggy A. "Knowing the Tropes: Literary Exegesis and
    Chaucer's Clerk." *Criticism* 27 (1985): 331-45. Print.

Lindsay, Philip, and Reg Groves. *The Peasants' Revolt 1381*.
    1950. Westport: Greenwood, 1974. Print.

Middleton, Anne. "The Clerk and His Tale." *Studies in the Age
    of Chaucer* 2 (1980): 121-50. Print.

Morgan, Gerald. "The Logic of the Clerk's Tale." *Modern
    Language Review* 104.1 (2009): 1-25. *Academic OneFile*.
    Web. 26 Mar. 2010.

Morrow, Patrick. "The Ambivalence of Truth: Chaucer's 'Clerkes
    Tale.'" *Bucknell Review* 16.3 (1968): 74-90. Print.

Morse, J. Mitchell. "The Philosophy of the Clerk of Oxenford."
    Modern Language Quarterly 19 (1958): 3-20. Print.

"The Peasants' Revolt." Narr. Melvyn Bragg. *In Our Time*. BBC
    Radio 4, 16 Nov. 2006. Web. 23 Mar. 2010.

Petrarch, Francis. Letter to Giovanni Boccaccio. Trans. R. D.
    French. *Chaucer: Sources and Backgrounds*. Ed. Robert P.
    Miller. New York: Oxford UP, 1977. 137-51. Print.

Chicago Style

Main Features

Citations Appear in Footnotes or Endnotes Superscript numbers alert the reader that a note at the bottom of the page accompanies the text.

> Women's earnings have been rising faster than men's, but by 2006 women still earned only 77 percent of what men were earning.[1]

> 1. Carmen DeNavas-Walt et al., "Income, Poverty, and Health Insurance Coverage in the United States: 2006," U.S. Census Bureau, August 2007, p. 8, http://www.census.gov/prod/2007pubs/p60-233.pdf (accessed November 13, 2007).

Other standard practices for preparing *Chicago*-style notes are as follows:

- Notes can include bibliographic citations or other information.
- Notes may be formatted as either footnotes or endnotes. (The choice is usually up to the author or publisher, but check with your instructor.)
- Number notes sequentially throughout the paper; do not use the same number twice, even if you are referring to a work already cited.
- Footnotes appear at the bottom of the page on which the citation reference appears.
- Endnotes appear in a list on a new page at the end of the paper, under the heading "Notes."
- Provide complete bibliographical information in the notes. Publication data (place, name of publisher, and date) appears in parentheses.
- Each note begins with a number and a period, followed by a space. The first line of each note is indented half an inch, while subsequent lines are flush with the margin.
- Include an access date for Internet sources.

Additionally, the Latin abbreviation "Ibid." is used to reference the same source that was cited in the previous note.

Bibliography   Since the notes contain complete bibliographical data, a separate bibliography is optional. However, a bibliography can be helpful to the reader if the paper cites more than five or six sources. In preparing a *Chicago*-style bibliography, do the following:

- List items alphabetically by author's last name or, if no author, by the first word of the title (ignoring "A," "An," and "The").
- Include complete bibliographical data for each entry. Include an access date for Internet sources.
- Omit parentheses around the place and the name of the publisher. The date appears in parentheses only if following a volume number.

Here are a couple of examples. Note that the first example is for a source with one identified author (David Hosansky), and the last name is listed first. The second is for a governmental entity as the author. This entry is alphabetized under "U" in the bibliography (pp. 369–70).

Hosansky, David. "Traffic Congestion: Is the United States Facing Permanent Gridlock?" *Congressional Quarterly Researcher* 9, no. 32 (1999) (accessed January 15, 2012).

U.S. Department of Transportation, Research and Innovative Technology Administration, Bureau of Transportation Statistics. *Transportation Statistics Annual Report 2007*. Washington, DC: printed by author, 2007.

For more details, see chicagomanualofstyle.org and *The Chicago Manual of Style*, 16th Edition.

•   •   •

The following paper is in *Chicago* style. Note that the writer includes full publication information in the footnotes. In the footnotes (unlike the entries in the bibliography), author names are not reversed (see the entry for footnote 1 at the bottom of p. 365 and compare it to its corresponding bibliographic entry on p. 369). In the bibliography, corporate and governmental entities are alphabetized by the first word of their name. Use three dashes to indicate another work by the same source, as with the two entries for "Environmental Defense Fund."

Title centered at
middle of page

Congestion Pricing for New York:
A Solution to the Traffic Problem

Name centered
below title

Serge Morgan

Course, professor,
and date

Rhetoric 101
Professor Sen
February 1, 2012

Morgan 2

Anyone who has sat motionless in rush-hour traffic knows the feeling of helplessness and frustration it brings. But while everyone knows that traffic causes stress, few may realize the economic cost: according to one estimate, "at least $74 billion every year in wasted time and fuel."[1] And in addition to the economic impact, traffic pollution takes a toll on our health and the environment. These are costs we all pay, even if we work at home or use public transport.

And traffic is getting worse. A recent study by the Texas Transportation Institute examined travel times on highways in American cities over a ten-year period; in the vast majority of cities (seventy of eighty-five), times had risen.[2] The number of cars on our roads continues to increase. The obvious fix is to build more roads, but new roads only attract more drivers — and more traffic jams.

One remedy to the traffic problem, already tested with good results in several cities in Asia and Europe, is "congestion pricing," a system of fees for driving in the central business district during rush hours or business hours. Can this work in America? In New York City, Mayor Bloomberg has been a strong supporter, but the plan has run into strong opposition at the state level, where representatives of the boroughs and suburbs of New York saw few benefits for their constituents.[3]

----

1. David Hosansky, "Traffic Congestion," *Congressional Quarterly Researcher* 9, no. 32 (1999): 729.

2. U.S. Department of Transportation, Research and Innovative Technology Administration, Bureau of Transportation Statistics, *Transportation Statistics Annual Report 2007* (Washington, DC: printed by author, 2007), 13.

3. Nicholas Confessore, "$8 Congestion Fee for Manhattan Gets Nowhere," *New York Times*, April 8, 2008, http://www.nytimes.com/2008/04/08/nyregion/08congest.html.

Footnote sources

Full publication information in footnote

Morgan 3

However, as traffic continues to worsen and the ecological crisis becomes more urgent, this may be an idea whose time has come. The New York State legislature should reconsider Mayor Bloomberg's plan for congestion pricing in Manhattan. Congestion pricing will reduce greenhouse gases and make travel within and through Manhattan faster and safer. Tolls can be used to improve public transportation to and from the boroughs, so that everyone will reap benefits, not only Manhattanites.

Of course, no one welcomes new taxes or fees. But since commuters already pay a high price for their congested roads, fees could actually save New Yorkers money in the long run. According to the U.S. Department of Transportation, "In the [ten] most congested areas [of the country], each rush hour traveler 'pays' an annual 'congestion tax' of between $850 and $1,600 in lost time and fuel and spends the equivalent of almost [eight] workdays each year stuck in traffic."[4] Not only does traffic congestion waste time and gas, but it also takes a heavy toll on the environment, as backed-up roads produce more smog than free-flowing ones.[5] And New York's smog can be linked to illnesses that bring about not only medical bills and lost

---

4. U.S. Department of Transportation, Federal Highway Administration, Office of Transportation Management, *Congestion Pricing: A Primer* (Washington, DC: printed by author, 2006), 1.

5. Environmental Defense Fund, "Four Ways New Yorkers Will Benefit from Congestion Pricing," last modified September 17, 2008, http://www.edf.org /page.cfm?tagID=19960.

Morgan 4

work hours but also immeasurable cost to quality of life. The
Environmental Defense Fund reports that asthma rates in
some areas of New York are "more than four times the
average" and that car pollution accounts for "more than 80
percent of New Yorkers' cancer risk."[6]

The plan approved by the New York City Council in March
2008 (and now stalled in the State Assembly) would charge
cars and commercial vehicles $8 and trucks $21 to enter the
central business district between 6 a.m. and 6 p.m. on
weekdays. "EZ Pass" transponders, already used on toll roads,
and license-plate recognition technology would eliminate the
need for barriers. Annual revenue of $491 million would be
used to improve public transit.[7]

According to the Environmental Defense Fund, only
about 5 percent of all commuters take the car to New York's
central business district; for 80 percent of these drivers,
public transportation is available that would allow them to
reach their destination in about the same time. Because so
many more New Yorkers commute by public transit than by
car, the existing transit system could easily handle the
additional burden — about three riders per subway car.[8] Yet
the move to public transport would reduce congestion in the

Use "Ibid." if source
is the same as prior
note.

Short version of
citation for source
already cited.

6. Ibid.
7. New York City Mayor's Office, *PlaNYC* (New York: printed by author,
2007), 89-90, http://www.nyc.gov/html/planyc2030/downloads/pdf/report
_transportation.pdf.
8. Environmental Defense Fund, "Four Ways New Yorkers Will Benefit."

Morgan 5

boroughs too (Bronx, Queens, Brooklyn, and Staten Island), by between 8 and 14 percent. Traffic controls are also good for business because deliveries are faster and more reliable. In London, a vast majority of business owners are "either positive or neutral" about congestion pricing.[9]

A recent survey by the Quinnipiac University Polling Institute found that New Yorkers strongly favor congestion pricing — by a margin of almost two to one — if proceeds are used to improve public transportation.[10]

---

9. Ibid.

10. Quinnipiac University Polling Institute, "Kelly Tops List for New York City Mayor, Quinnipiac University Poll Finds; Voters Back Congestion Pricing, If Funds Go to Transit," last modified March 13, 2008, http://www.quinnipiac.edu /x1302.xml?ReleaseID=1157.

Morgan 6

Bibliography

Atkinson, Robert. "The Role of Road Pricing in Reducing
   Traffic Congestion: Testimony before the Joint Economic
   Committee." *Progressive Policy Institute*. May 6, 2003.
   http://www.ppionline.org/ppi_ci.cfm?knlgAreaID=107&
   subsecID=900034&contentID=251568.

Confessore, Nicholas. "$8 Congestion Fee for Manhattan Gets
   Nowhere." *New York Times*. April 8, 2008. http://www
   .nytimes.com/2008/04/08/nyregion/08congest.html.

Environmental Defense Fund. "Four Ways New Yorkers Will
   Benefit from Congestion Pricing." Last modified
   September 17, 2008. http://www.edf.org/page
   .cfm?tagID=19960.

———. "New York City Faces a Transit Crisis: Why New York
   Needs Congestion Pricing." Last modified September 17,
   2008. http://www.edf.org/page.cfm?tagID=19899.

Hosansky, David. "Traffic Congestion." *Congressional Quarterly
   Researcher* 9, no. 32 (1999): 729-52.

New York City Mayor's Office. *PlaNYC*. New York: printed by
   author, 2007. http://www.nyc.gov/html/planyc2030
   /downloads/pdf/report_transportation.pdf.

Quinnipiac University Polling Institute. "Kelly Tops List for
   New York City Mayor, Quinnipiac University Poll Finds;
   Voters Back Congestion Pricing, If Funds Go to Transit."
   Last modified March 13, 2008. http://www.quinnipiac
   .edu/x1302.xml?Release ID=1157.

Schrank, David, Tim Lomax, and Shawn Turner. *Urban Mobility
   Report 2010*. College Station: Texas Transportation
   Institute, 2010. http://mobility.tamu.edu/ums/report/.

*Full publication
information in
bibliography. Note
that the author's last
name is listed first.*

U.S. Department of Transportation, Federal Highway Administration, Office of Transportation Management. *Congestion Pricing: A Primer*. Washington, DC: printed by author, 2006.

U.S. Department of Transportation, Research and Innovative Technology Administration, Bureau of Transportation Statistics. *Transportation Statistics Annual Report 2007*. Washington, DC: printed by author, 2007.

Vanderbilt, Tom. *Traffic: Why We Drive the Way We Do (and What It Says about Us)*. New York: Knopf, 2008.

Writing
in *Response*

Matthew Parfitt

Resources for Teaching
Writing in Response

Resources for Teaching
Writing in Response

Matthew Parfitt
Boston University, College of General Studies

BEDFORD/ST. MARTIN'S
Boston • New York

Manufactured in the United States of America.

6   5   4   3   2   1
f   e   d   c   b   a

For information, write: Bedford/St. Martin's, 75 Arlington Street, Boston, MA 02116 (617-399-4000)

ISBN: 978–0–312–40395–9

Preface

The chief purpose of this manual is to help you integrate *Writing in Response* into your courses as effectively as possible. The brief overviews of each chapter will give you a quick sense of the book's contents. The sample syllabi are designed to help get you started by suggesting ways to schedule chapters of the book around other readings and assignments, whether you teach a single course in a quarter system, a first-semester composition class, a full-year two-semester sequence, an advanced writing class, or a linked course. Additional activities can help you work effectively with the book over the course of a semester, further connecting reading, in-class work, and writing.

At first glance, it might seem that incorporating a book like this into a writing course is a complicated business: How are you to pace a course that assigns the writing process chapters from *Writing in Response* (Chapters 1 through 8) but also expects students to submit writing throughout the semester, perhaps beginning in the very first week of class?

There are two ways to approach this challenge. In a ten- or thirteen-week course, you might assign roughly a chapter of the book a week and assign an additional reading every two or three weeks. In this case, students would write one or two essays before they reach the end of Chapter 8. In fact, this is unlikely to present a problem. Students come to college already possessing some experience as academic writers, and initially they will still be relying to some extent on high school writing strategies; therefore, we can expect them to integrate what they learn in this book chapter by chapter as they encounter it. In fact, students may be able to reflect more clear-sightedly on their writing process if their most recent writing experience is not very distant.

The alternative approach is to "front-load" the syllabus so that your students are reading relevant chapters while they are working on the stages of a first writing assignment. The chapters are short enough to read in an evening, so students can read two or three a week, getting to Chapter 6 — which completes the discussion of the main stages of the writing process — by the end of the third or fourth week, when a first major writing assignment might be due. This will leave enough time to read and reread one of the essays included in this book, as the text to which students will respond in their formal essays.

Since reading notes and informal writing are a major part of the writing process, you can require students to submit all the material that relates to the composition of the final product in a portfolio, either in a binder or electronically (on a course manage-ment site, on an e-portfolio site, or by e-mail). Requiring students to submit portfolios not only will help you understand the strengths and weaknesses of each of your stu-dents' writing processes but also will encourage the students to take all the stages of the writing process more seriously.

Contents

Resources for Teaching
Writing in Response

SAMPLE SYLLABI

Quarter-System Course (10 weeks)

Course Textbook: Matthew Parfitt, *Writing in Response*

Week 1   Read Introduction and Chapters 1 and 2 (one chapter per class).
Week 2   Read Chapter 3. Take notes on Tompkins.
Week 3   Read Chapters 4–6 (one chapter for each class).
Week 4   Read Schulz. Informal writing toward essay.
Week 5   Draft and revise. **First essay (4–5 pages) due end of this week.**
Week 6   Read Chapters 7 and 8 (in-class work on sentence-crafting and style). Read Gopnik.
Week 7   Reading, note-taking, and informal writing. Read West.
Week 8   Draft and revise. **Second essay (4–5 pages) due midweek.** Read de Waal.
Week 9   Read Chapters 9 and 10. Find scholarly article on animal behavior.
Week 10 **Research assignment (1-page abstract of a scholarly article) due end of this week.**

One-Semester Course (13 weeks)

Course Textbook: Matthew Parfitt, *Writing in Response*

Week 1   Read Introduction and Chapters 1 and 2 (one chapter for each class).
Week 2   Read Chapter 3 and take notes on Tompkins, de Waal.
Week 3   Read Chapters 4–6 (one chapter for each class).
Week 4   Focused exploratory writing toward essay on Tompkins or de Waal.
Week 5   Draft and revise. **First essay (4–5 pages) due end of this week.**
Week 6   Read Chapters 7 and 8 (in-class work on grammar and style).
Week 7   Reading, note-taking, informal writing (Gopnik, Schulz).
Week 8   Draft and revise. **Second essay (4–5 pages) due end of this week.**
Week 9   Read Chapters 9 and 10. Read West.
Week 10 Brainstorm topics.
Week 11 Reading, note-taking, and researched writing.
Week 12 Reading, note-taking, and researched writing. Draft and revise.
Week 13 **Third essay (4–5 pages) due end of this week.**

Two-Semester Writing Sequence with Supplementary Readings

Note: Readings marked with an asterisk (*) are not included in Writing in Response. *These selections represent some personal favorites from various sources. You may of course substitute readings that reflect your interests and the course focus.*

Course Textbook: Matthew Parfitt, *Writing in Response*

Readings

*John Berger, "Why Look at Animals," from *About Looking*
Frans de Waal, "Are We in Anthropodenial?"
Adam Gopnik, "Bumping into Mr. Ravioli"
*Patricia Nelson Limerick, "Denial and Dependence," from *The Legacy of Conquest*
*N. Scott Momaday, "The American West and the Burden of Belief," from
        Geoffrey C. Ward, *The West: An Illustrated History*
*Michael Pollan, "An Animal's Place," from *The New York Times*
Kathryn Schulz, "Two Models of Wrongness"
*Roger Scruton, "A Carnivore's Credo," from *Gourmet*
*Peter Singer, "Down on the Factory Farm," from *Animal Liberation*
*Zadie Smith, "Speaking in Tongues," from *The New York Review of Books*
*John Tirman, "The Future of the American Frontier," from *The American Scholar*
Jane Tompkins, "At the Buffalo Bill Museum, June 1988"
*Frederick Jackson Turner, "The Significance of the Frontier in American History,"
        from *The Frontier in American History*
Cornel West, "Malcolm X and Black Rage"

Composition 101: Introduction to College Writing

Week 1   Read Introduction and Chapters 1 and 2.
Week 2   Read and take notes on Schulz, "Two Models of Wrongness."
Week 3   Read Chapter 3. Read and take notes on Tompkins, "At the Buffalo Bill
        Museum, June 1988."
Week 4   Read Chapter 4. Write informally on Tompkins and Schulz.
Week 5   Read Chapters 5 and 6. Draft and revise. **Expository essay (4–5 pages)
        due end of this week.**

Week 6   Read Chapters 7 and 8 (in-class work on grammar and style).
Week 7   Read and take notes on Gopnik, "Bumping into Mr. Ravioli."
Week 8   Write Informally. Draft.
Week 9   Revise. **Exploratory essay (6–7 pages) due end of this week.**
Week 10 Read and take notes on West, "Malcolm X and Black Rage."
Week 11 Read and take notes on de Waal, "Are We in Anthropodenial?"
Week 12 Write Informally. Draft.
Week 13 Revise. **Final essay (6–7 pages) due end of this week.**

Composition 102: Research and Writing

Note: This syllabus lists readings not included in Writing in Response. *You can of course freely substitute selections based on your own interests.*

Week 1   Read Chapters 9 and 10. Read Berger, "Why Look at Animals."
Week 2   Read de Waal, "Are We in Anthropodenial?"; Singer, "Down on the Factory Farm"; and Scruton, "A Carnivore's Credo." Class in library with research librarian for Q&A about library resources, research strategies.
Week 3   Read Pollan, "An Animal's Place." Do preliminary research. Select topic area.
Week 4   Research. **First research question and working bibliography due.**
Week 5   Read sources. Draft.
Week 6   Revise. **First research paper (7–8 pages) due midweek.** Read Turner, "The Significance of the Frontier in American History."
Week 7   Read Limerick, "Denial and Dependence." Reread Tompkins, "At the Buffalo Bill Museum, June 1988."
Week 8   Read Momaday, "The American West and the Burden of Belief," and Tirman, "The Future of the American Frontier."
Week 9   Brainstorm topics. Do preliminary research.
Week 10 **Second research question and working bibliography due.**
Week 11 Read sources. In-class symposium (two classes).
Week 12 Read sources. Draft. In-class workshops.
Week 13 Revise. **Second research paper (8–10 pages) due end of this week.**

One-Semester Course Linked to Introduction to Sociology

Note: The readings listed below are not included in Writing in Response. *These selections represent some personal favorites from various sources. You may of course substitute readings that reflect your interests and the course focus.*

Course Textbook: Matthew Parfitt, *Writing in Response*

Readings

Peter Berger, "Sociological Perspective — Man in Society" and "Sociological Perspective — Society in Man," from *Invitation to Sociology*

Émile Durkheim, "Anomic Suicide," from *Suicide*

Barbara Ehrenreich, *Nickel and Dimed: On (Not) Getting By in America*

C. Wright Mills, "The Sociological Imagination," from *The Sociological Imagination*, and "The Power Elite," from *The Power Elite*

Max Weber, "The Iron Cage," from *The Protestant Ethic and the Spirit of Capitalism*

Week 1	Read Introduction and Chapters 1 and 2 (one chapter for each class).
Week 2	Read Chapter 3. Read and take notes on Mills, "The Sociological Imagination" and "The Power Elite."
Week 3	Read Chapters 4–6. Read and take notes on Berger, "Sociological Perspective — Man in Society" and "Sociological Perspective — Society in Man."
Week 4	Focused exploratory writing toward essay on Mills and Berger.
Week 5	Draft and revise. **First essay (4–5 pages) due end of this week.**
Week 6	Read Chapters 7 and 8 (in-class work on grammar and style).
Week 7	Read, take notes, and write informally on Durkheim and Weber.
Week 8	Draft and revise. **Second essay (4–5 pages) due end of this week.**
Week 9	Read Chapters 9 and 10. Read Ehrenreich.
Week 10	Brainstorm topics, applying sociological theory to *Nickel and Dimed*.
Week 11	Reading, note-taking, and researched writing. Draft.
Week 12	Reading, note-taking, and researched writing. Revise.
Week 13	**Third essay (4–5 pages) due end of this week.**

One-Semester Course: Advanced Academic Writing

Course Textbook: Matthew Parfitt, *Writing in Response*

Week 1   Read Introduction and Chapters 1 and 2 of *Writing in Response* (one chapter for each class).

Week 2   Read Chapters 3–5. Read and take notes on de Waal, Schulz.

Week 3   Read Chapter 6.

Week 4   Informal writing toward essay.

Week 5   Draft and revise. **Expository essay (4–5 pages) due end of this week.**

Week 6   Read Chapters 7 and 8. Read Tompkins, Gopnik.

Week 7   Read, take notes, and write informally.

Week 8   Draft and revise. **Exploratory essay (4–5 pages) due end of this week.**

Week 9   Read Chapters 9 and 10. Read West.

Week 10   Brainstorm topics. Phase 1 of research process: scouting.

Week 11   Researched writing and reading. Phase 2 of research process: digging deeper. Reading, note-taking.

Week 12   Researched writing and reading. Draft and revise. In-class presentations of research.

Week 13   **Research paper (4–5 pages), incorporating both expository and exploratory elements, due end of this week.**

CHAPTER OVERVIEWS

Introduction: Writing in Response to Reading (p. 1)

The point of the introduction is not so much to acquaint students with the book's contents as it is to orient them to its principal aims by explaining the general expectations of college instructors — which often remain a mystery even to students who have several semesters of college behind them. The introduction emphasizes particularly the differences between a typical high school experience of academic writing and the more varied and complicated writing projects that await undergraduate writers. Even the best-prepared students often find adjustment difficult, because in high school most major writing assignments are usually given in English classes, where the focus is on writing about poetry, fiction, and drama. In college, students suddenly find themselves writing in response to nonfiction texts and must do something very different from literary analysis. Even students who are already familiar with college-level expectations may appreciate some reassurance. The main point of this short chapter is not to explain *how* to meet the expectations of college instructors but simply to give students some sense of where they will be heading.

On occasion, one of my bolder students has ventured to ask, "Why are we doing this?" — meaning not just the task at hand, but the whole course or course sequence, or even the whole liberal arts curriculum! It's a question I welcome because it provides an opportunity to talk to the class about the big picture, the basic purpose of "freshman writing" — a subject we might otherwise never delve into, given all the close work with texts and discussion of writing strategies. I often find it illuminating to hear students reveal their uncensored views about education, writing, the liberal arts, credentializing, and so on, and they seem eager to hear my point of view too. It's not a question of winning them or me over, just one of widening our perspectives. Many students do not understand the importance of research in the life of a college instructor, or the role of research in the institution's mission, or how research shapes expectations for student writing. Some equate "academic writing" primarily with an interdiction against using the word "I." Such a conversation is valuable: in the long run, we will all do better work if we have some understanding of where we're all coming from, whether or not we ever see perfectly eye to eye.

It seemed like a good idea to present this big picture at the beginning. Though your particular circumstances will differ somewhat from mine, of course, this introduction may provide the occasion to talk about the "big picture" with your students and address the questions "Why are we doing this?" and "What really are we doing here, anyway?"

Additional "Try This" Activities for the Introduction

1. The second option for the "Try This: Exploring the Culture of Education" activity in the introduction (p. 4) invites students to look at their institution's Web pages describing its academic programs. You might also invite students to look at how the Web site represents the institution's understanding of its overall mission and its research goals and then discuss them in class. Some institutions include a mission statement on their Web site; some include areas or pages devoted to faculty research projects. Either of these sections on the Web site can help students better understand some of the assumptions behind academic writing.

2. Invite students to conduct a brief face-to-face interview (ten or fifteen minutes will do) with a faculty member other than yourself. In class, guide the students as they create a list of questions for the interview — concerning educational background; research goals; how the faculty member balances teaching, research, and other work; and so on.

PART ONE   Responsive Reading (p. 19)

Writing in Response is unusual in devoting three chapters just to reading. But there are at least two strong reasons for doing so. First, students increasingly find the sort of reading they must do as college students difficult and taxing. Sitting down to concentrate for a long period of time, more or less uninterrupted, to read through a text that was never meant to be "entertaining," and might be complicated or puzzling, is something many students have seldom had to do. Second, reading is an essential part of the process of academic writing. Usually, a good deal of attentive, thoughtful, active reading necessarily precedes the act of writing. But typically, writers also return to reading at every stage of the writing process: it's part of the dialogue or conversation that is the essence of academic writing.

Chapter 1   Reading with a Purpose (p. 21)

Specific strategies for active reading will be introduced in Chapters 2 and 3. In Chapter 1, we lay out some fundamental concepts concerning active reading, rhetorical context, genre, difficulty, argument, and critical reading. Without an understanding of the value of reading "to weigh and consider," in Francis Bacon's phrase, rather than to contradict or believe or take for granted, the strategies in the chapters that follow will make little sense and may even look like mere busy work.

Rather than talk about "active reading" in a general or abstract sense, we focus here on "reading with a purpose" — the specific purpose being coming up with something original to say in response. So we begin by pointing out that in a certain sense *all* reading is active reading: readers must make sense of a text and must make *their own* sense of it. Every reader brings different experiences, different basic assumptions, and a different point of view to the act of reading. This, of course, is partly why reasonable people can differ about matters of interpretation.

Reading scholarly writing with a view to saying something in response is a different kind of reading than many first-year students are used to, especially if much of their reading experience has been with magazines, fiction, or textbooks. For many students, "reading with a purpose" is more demanding, requiring closer attention to the argument — but this is not the only stumbling block. There's also the burden of a responsibility to weigh the words of an expert — and not merely to say "if you say so" or "I disagree," but to explain and defend a thought of their own. So here we stress, as the first requirement, the importance of identifying the writer's argument — looking for the problem and the thesis, and so not missing the main point. But "reading with a purpose" doesn't end there. Students need to understand that rereading will bring the text under their control and also that they inevitably bring something to the text, and hence their reading can legitimately differ from others'. And they can have something fresh and interesting to say.

Additional "Try This" Activities for Chapter 1

1. Devote class time to "close reading" two or three paragraphs from one of the essays in Part Five of the book. Encourage the class to note as many details as possible — for example, diction, style, key terms, rhetorical strategies — and to attempt to understand what these details contribute to the effect of the passage and the author's overall purpose. How does the passage develop the argument? What choices does the writer seem to have made, and why? How does the writer establish a certain tone? The class can also consider why different students might notice different aspects of the text. What might have prepared them to see one thing rather than another?

2. Assign one of the readings from Part Five. Draw students' attention to the checklist at the end of this chapter. Explain that the purpose of the assignment is to

practice "reading with a purpose," and ask students to make brief notes to respond to each of the items in the checklist. In class, compare and discuss the results. On which of the items do student responses differ, how do they differ, and why? Which of the items did students find difficult to respond to, and why?

Chapter 2   Active Reading (p. 44)

This chapter offers the core reading — and rereading — strategies that students can use whenever they must read a text closely in order to write about it. Three basic strategies are discussed: marking up the text, keeping a response journal of some sort, and maintaining an "audit" of their readings in the form of double-entry notes.

At first, students may express dismay when you insist that they employ all three strategies. "It's going to take me hours and hours to get through the reading if I have to do all that!" Yes, it will. But they soon realize that if they come to class with an annotated text, with something to say (or at least the hint of something to say) in the form of a journal response, and with some specific observations and questions, keyed to places in the text, in their double-entry notes — and if every other student in the class does the same — they will be able to participate in a lively discussion that results in a clearer sense of the strengths and weaknesses of their reading, a sense of how their reading differs from that of other students, and, in due time, an exciting "take-away": a sense of purpose and a starting point for their writing. The more thoroughly students do this work, the more satisfying their writing will be. So these three strategies do not involve extra work; rather, they involve "front-loading" some of the work and, in the end, working more efficiently and fruitfully.

It's worth pointing out to students the value of *layering* notes in their dialectical notebooks with each reading and of adding new content to their reading journals. Students who develop a true "audit of meaning" (as Ann E. Berthoff described it) — being able to think about their thinking — will be much more likely to develop an interesting and meaningful response, not just an objective and neutral summary of the reading's content. And it's worth encouraging candor, thoughtfulness, and reflection in all these activities.

Some students may feel that the guidance for keeping a reading journal seems contradictory, in that they are told to follow their own thoughts but are also given some prompts. The main idea here is to keep the writing flexible, informal, and unstructured. Students who *need* some sort of prompt in order to get started can be invited to (1) identify the problem, (2) identify two or three claims, and (3) write down two or three questions. But students who do not need even this much structure should be encouraged to go their own way.

Some students may need help setting up dialectical notebook templates on a laptop. (I find that students can do just as good a job using a computer as using pen and paper, but the former requires some setup time.) One possibility is to create one or two empty templates (in Microsoft Word or whatever word processing tool your students are using) and share it with students via e-mail or a course management site. Alternatively, ask students to bring their laptops to class and to follow along as you spend five minutes figuring it out together. In most word processing programs, the "columns" tool doesn't work well for this purpose. Instead, draw two text boxes next to each other so that text entered side by side remains parallel.

Additional "Try This" Activities for Chapter 2

1. Invite students to write sentences that reflect on, explain or develop the marks they have made in their text (marginalia, underlining, etc.). Give them a prompt something like this: "Why did you make the marks that you made? What questions or thoughts do they suggest? Where might these lead? Develop your marks into full sentences — ones that explain, develop, or reflect on your response to the text. Be sure to link each comment to its corresponding page in the text." A few lines for each page will do, though of course some marks will require or inspire more writing than others. This writing differs from the reading journal because it is more closely tied to the marks students make on the page and to the details of the text.

   Some students may find that this kind of writing provides an alternative to the double-entry notebook method. Done consistently and conscientiously, it serves similar purposes, helping students become more reflective and responsive readers, and bridging the divide between acts of reading and acts of writing.

2. Ask students to write a brief "literacy narrative," reflecting on their experiences as readers. Then discuss these narratives in class. How did students learn to read? What reading experiences challenged them and perhaps markedly developed their skills? What have been their best reading experiences? Their worst? How do they read different materials differently — for example, reading for pleasure, for school, for information?

3. Invite students to write a brief essay on their observations of how technology influences reading. Invite them to share their observations in class. How has technology affected the way they read? How does reading on a screen — such as reading on the Web or on a device such as an iPad or a Kindle or even a phone — differ from reading the printed page? In what ways do technologies facilitate reading, and in what ways do they impede it?

Chapter 3   Further Strategies for Active Reading (p. 63)

This chapter offers additional reading strategies, ones that may be better suited to some needs than to others and are thus presented as options. While the note-taking strategies offered here are certainly worth a try, they represent only a few of the possibilities, and students should be encouraged to experiment with devising their own note-taking strategies.

The first two strategies are adaptations of the basic dialectical notebook described in Chapter 2. One of these focuses on the question being answered by the text; it works well with polemical arguments on debatable issues. The other strategy involves organizing notes into quotation, exegesis, and commentary and works well with particularly complex or dense arguments. The section "Analyzing the Argument" describes some ways of creating an outline or a map of an argument's structure.

The section "Evaluating the Argument" lays out "attitudinal" strategies for reading. The habit of moving continuously back and forth between the writer's point of view and a skeptic's point of view is perhaps the chief trait of a sophisticated reader, and it is one that many undergraduates have not yet fully developed. While it's unrealistic to expect students to develop this habit instantly, it helps to have terms to describe it and activities for practicing it. David Bartholomae and Anthony Petrosky's phrase "reading with and against the grain" (introduction to *Ways of Reading*) and Peter Elbow's "believing and doubting game" (*Writing without Teachers*) offer two well-tested ways of introducing students to this habit.

Next, we suggest some ways of elaborating a response to a reading, in writing or orally. With these, we're approaching the territory of Chapter 4, but they are included here because they have more in common with taking notes than with writing extended reflections, however informal and "writerly." Writing a fictive letter to the author allows for some detachment from the writer's point of view but tends to keep the reader in the orbit of that other point of view. It can be a starting point for developing a response but doesn't require the reader to think through his or her response completely.

Finally, students are encouraged to "talk out" their ideas — in class discussion, with a friend, or with an instructor. This reading strategy has been left for last and is presented as an option in recognition of the fact that the circumstances in which students use this book will vary (for example, some writing classes include few opportunities for discussion, and some discussion sections are too large to give every student a chance to contribute). But in my own experience — and many teachers seem to share this view — this reading strategy is crucial. Students gain immeasurably as readers from learning that their own reading differs from others' readings, and as writers from having the opportunity to verbally explain and justify their ideas in a group. They may begin speaking with only the germ of an idea, but as they speak, their own understanding of what they want to say begins to take shape and gain clarity, and this often becomes the starting point for an essay.

As a participant in these conversations, I feel that I'm most useful to students simply as a sympathetic listener. It's vitally important to avoid explicating the text — and thereby robbing students of the opportunity to develop their own readings. Instead of explicating, I try to pull the class back into the text as necessary, asking questions about relevant or overlooked passages. In this way, I can help students produce their own articulate responses to the text, rather than imposing on them some supposedly "authoritative" reading — which would be fatal.

Additional "Try This" Activities for Chapter 3

1. In class, work together on a radial map of a reading you have assigned. Draw the map on the board as students offer suggestions, but ask students to work on paper at the same time. (Encourage them to use paper rather than laptops, as computers do not lend themselves to creating maps quickly, on the fly.) The work may require some trial and error, and one or two phases of revision. The point, however, is to get students familiar with the process and what it involves. They can complete the work on their own, if necessary.

2. Assign one of the argument essays in this book, such as West, de Waal, or Schulz, and have students role-play believers and doubters. Half the class will play the believers, and half the class will play the doubters. Believers will come up with as many reasons as possible for believing the argument; doubters will come up with as many questions as possible to pose against the argument. Ask students to work alone on their tasks for ten or fifteen minutes; then have them join their group to pool their results. Finally, believers and doubters can come together to share their groups' results. Discuss how playing these roles can help develop a richer reading of the text.

PART TWO   Composing and Revising (p. 91)

Chapters 4, 5, and 6 concern the recursive process of writing, beginning with informal heuristic writing and proceeding to organization strategies. Rather than devoting a special chapter to revision, the book incorporates revision strategies at each stage of the reading and writing process. Indeed, the strategies for rereading in Chapters 1–3 could be considered revision strategies of a sort—assuming that revising one's reading of a text is one kind of revision. The strategies for informal or "writerly" drafts in Chapter 4 presume that revision involves much more than just editing—that ideas take shape through writing and rewriting. Thus an argument might be quite rudimentary at first, but it will grow and develop as the recursive process of rereading, informal writing, and drafting proceeds.

The concept of recursivity is key here. The book does not envision writing as a strict series of "steps" that can be laid out sequentially chapter by chapter and followed like a recipe. Rather, it guides students first through a writerly reading-process and then to the process of argument development. But all the strategies are ones that students can circle back to and draw upon as needed throughout the writing process.

Chapter 4   Writing to Discover and Develop Ideas (p. 93)

This chapter hinges on the distinction between the writerly and the readerly. Some students will have done writing of a purely "writerly" kind before, whether for school or for personal pleasure, but for others it will be an entirely new experience. If they do it with a sense of commitment and adventure, they are likely to find it liberating and exciting.

The central purpose of the chapter is to encourage students to separate their writing process into two distinct phases: a heuristic phase and a revising phase. Many students come to college having rarely written a rough draft: their writing process is merely to "clean up" the first thoughts that they typed on their computer. Such a writing process incorporates no exploratory writing at all and typically leads to superficial and perfunctory results—a performance of academic writing but not its substance. (Word-processing programs—with word counts, on-the-fly spell-checkers, and instant formatting—can have a deceiving effect.) It's important to encourage students to develop a writing process that includes thinking, and especially *questioning*, for themselves.

Exploratory writing is much more than just a way of generating ideas, more than just the messy drafting that has to be done to get a final product out. And although it is the best antidote to writer's block, it is more than just a way of avoiding the frustration of staring at a blank screen with nothing to say. When students truly devote themselves to this work, it leads them to think more deeply and in a more focused fashion about their questions than any other activity can. We educators talk a great deal about "critical thinking," and if that overworked phrase means anything, it refers to the ability to question ideas, including one's own ideas. I know of no better way to do this than to put ideas on paper, look at them objectively, and then subject them to analysis and critique. In that sense, critical thinking and exploratory writing are nearly the same thing — except that the phrase "exploratory writing" suggests how one actually goes about doing it!

To do productive exploratory writing, students need to momentarily forget about the final product. They need to give thinking the time it requires and to do the exploratory writing almost for its own sake. It can be difficult to get students to take the time for this — until they discover that (1) it's fun, perhaps the only *really* fun part of the whole writing process, and (2) it makes an enormous difference to the quality of the final product and its rewards.

Much of this chapter is made up of an argument for the value of exploratory writing and an exhortation to do it. Perhaps the most effective way for instructors to get students interested in exploratory writing is to devote class time simply to writing. Try two consecutive sessions of, say, ten or fifteen minutes each during class time, and ask students to do two more bouts at home. These sessions could involve focused freewriting (using a prompt you give them) or open-ended writing. As the instructor, you too should write along with the students, partly so that you can share in a brief discussion afterward of how it went, partly to contribute to the creative atmosphere.

Additional "Try This" Activities for Chapter 4

1. Review the "Checklist for Exploratory Writing" (p. 100). Then ask students to write on a problem that has emerged in class discussion. (Of course, the best time to do this is immediately after the problem arises.) If possible, devote two in-class sessions of at least ten or fifteen minutes each to this exploratory writing. Encourage students to write continuously, even if they initially feel they have nothing to say: the act of "churning" is often the necessary precursor to writing that takes off in an unexpected and productive direction. At the end of the freewriting sessions, ask students to describe their experiences.

2. Some of your students may have a good deal of experience with freewriting, and some may have kept journals or maintained a practice of writing "morning pages" or something similar. Invite students to describe their experiences to the class, noting the difficulties as well as the benefits.

Chapter 5   Developing an Argument (p. 110)

This chapter has three main parts. The first part lays out basic terms and concepts about argument, including the rhetorical modes of persuasion (*ethos, pathos*, and *logos*) and types of reasoning (deduction and induction); but the main emphasis here is on argument as a *structure* of related claims and support for those claims. The second part concerns drafting — drafting a thesis statement, drafting an argument, drafting paragraphs. And the third part focuses on revising an argument.

The terms and concepts in the first part are needed as tools and vocabulary for analyzing sample arguments (from readings or from student work) in class and for helping students imagine and then analyze arguments of their own. But the second part is where students will find tools of more immediate use: an "argument matrix" that requires them to distinguish among claims, evidence, and discussion; suggestions for addressing counterarguments; and suggestions for composing effective introductory, body, and concluding paragraphs.

In addition to traditional rhetorical concepts such as thesis, claim, support, *ethos, pathos, logos,* and so on, this chapter emphasizes the idea that academic arguments respond to some kind of problem, sometimes a practical problem, but often a "knowledge problem" — a problem that has no immediate practical consequences but that wants to be solved simply because we humans are curious and want to know the answer. Most students find this notion of a problem to be solved easier to grasp and less ambiguous than the term "motive." In fact, some of our students might say, and not insincerely, that their true "motive" for writing is to pass the course or just get the blasted assignment done as painlessly as possible. But it is imperative that students develop a sense that their writing has some purpose beyond mere self-interest. Otherwise, their writing can be little more than perfunctory, a performance that has no bearing on their real intellectual lives and no relation to the real world. In this sense, the problem has priority over the thesis. After all, many good essays have no clear thesis (as we will see in the next chapter when we look at the exploratory essay), but no worthwhile essay lacks a purpose — the sense that it is responding to some kind of problem. If we want college students to join the conversations of the academy, or at least demonstrate an ability to do so, we need to remind them that academic writing responds to problems and that an understanding of the problem must precede the thesis.

The chapter also emphasizes the paragraph as the unit of argument structure (typically built around a significant claim and its support). This emphasis assumes that students have already amassed a good deal of material in the form of notes and informal writing, material that can be shaped into paragraph form once they shift from the writerly state of mind to the readerly and begin to think about structure and organization. Students can start shaping paragraphs before they have a clear sense of their essays' overall organization. In fact, having several paragraphs already drafted will likely make the work of organization easier.

Additional "Try This" Activities for Chapter 5

1. Ask students to find editorials or op-ed articles in newspapers or on the Internet. Have them identify motive, claim, and support in these arguments, as well as how *ethos*, *pathos*, and *logos* function in these articles. If possible, have them identify instances of inductive and deductive reasoning.

2. Invite students to describe a "knowledge problem" that they have encountered in one of their other courses. What is the value of concerning ourselves with such problems? Do some knowledge problems have practical implications?

3. Work together in class on several students' thesis statements. Recognize that these are works in progress and that the statements will probably undergo revision as students further develop the arguments. Are the thesis statements appropriate for the assignment? Appropriate in scope for a relatively brief student paper? Well defined? Do the thesis statements make an original claim that addresses a relevant problem? Can the thesis statements be supported with evidence and reasoning?

4. As a class, look at two or three samples of student writing. (If you use the work of a current student, be sure to ask for permission in advance. Make photocopies of the student's writing or scan to a laptop and project it onto a screen.) Focus the discussion on the components of argument discussed in this chapter: motive, thesis statement, claims (and the placement of claims), support for claims, the use of transitions, the effect of the concluding paragraph, and so on. Invite students to make observations about these matters, noting both strengths and weaknesses.

Chapter 6   Organizing the Essay (p. 150)

This chapter offers advice for organizing two different kinds of essay: an expository (thesis-driven) essay and an exploratory (question-driven) essay. However, the expository essay is given priority because students will be expected to write this type of essay most frequently in college courses. Ultimately, however, students should be encouraged to think of these two approaches not so much as entirely distinct essay types, but as two modes that can be, and often are, combined in the same essay to good effect. But at first, most students will need to focus simply on becoming proficient at organizing arguments.

As a rule, I discourage students from thinking too much about organization until they have something to say and have a certain amount of writing in draft form. There's not much point in writing an outline if you haven't yet decided on the argument you want to make. Otherwise, the outline quickly becomes a straitjacket, distorting and contracting the thought. But students who have been doing the work described in the previous chapters—or even some of it—will be shifting from invention to shaping their argument at a suitable moment. So, after a brief introduction that encourages students to change their point of view and begin to take a reader's perspective on their writing, four main principles for organizing an argument are introduced: (1) keep your argument in the foreground, (2) separate out claims and develop each argument fully, (3) address counterarguments, and (4) establish common ground with the reader. (As the classical rhetorical concept of *dispositio* suggests, principles of organization may also function as principles of persuasion.)

Every argument requires its own particular organization, so one-size-fits-all formulas cannot work, least of all the five-paragraph model (which many students learned in high school and which may continue to serve them well on essay exams, but no longer in full-fledged essay assignments). The approach here is to encourage students to come up with a simple organizational plan that suits the *particular argument* that they want to make. This is often sufficient: if a student gives some careful thought to the best—the simplest and strongest—arrangement for the claims that the argument requires, an organizational plan will often emerge quite clearly out of the argument's logic itself.

As in Chapter 5, here too we begin with *drafting* a rough organizational plan, in the form of a diagram, and then *revising* that organization into a full-sentence outline—first a simple one, then a more elaborate one—that will serve as the skeleton for the complete essay. It's worth insisting on a full-sentence outline, as it foregrounds claims and relationships between claims rather than mere "topics." When topics rather than claims occupy the foreground, there is a danger that the argument will get buried, obscured by matter that may pertain somehow to the *topic* but does not pertain to the core of the *argument*. Moreover, a sentence outline will help students shape their paragraphs effectively as well as arrange them in a logical sequence.

The chapter offers two sample student essays as examples of organization. But students can also benefit from analyzing and critiquing the organization of sample essays—your students' writing or published writing—together in class. The real key is to help students become more aware of structure and organization as an aspect of all good writing, as something that *serves* the expression of ideas but does not limit it.

Finally, toward the end of the chapter, we discuss the structure of the exploratory or "question-driven" essay, a different approach to organization because such an essay normally takes a narrative rather than a polemic structure. (For more about the exploratory essay, see "Appendix: Teaching the Exploratory Essay" in this manual, p. 28.) Some students may find the unfamiliarity of the exploratory mode somewhat daunting. But if they have made a sincere effort at heuristic writing as a writerly invention strategy, they may be able to see how this informal writing, or some part of it, might be reshaped into readerly form without losing its essentially exploratory quality. In addition, the two contrasting sample essays in this chapter will help students see both the differences and some underlying similarities between the expository and the exploratory. And finally, *Writing in Response* includes two exploratory essays by professionals that also reveal how such essays may be organized as narratives of an intellectual quest: Adam Gopnik's "Bumping into Mr. Ravioli" and Jane Tompkins's "At the Buffalo Bill Museum, June 1988." Neither of these is lengthy, and students typically find them engaging. You may find that many of your students are eager to try their hands at this form.

Additional "Try This" Activities for Chapter 6

1. If the class is working on an argument essay, look at some samples of student work-in-progress together as a class. Focus the discussion on the four principles of organizing an argument essay that are explained in the section "Organizing an Argument Essay." How might the writer foreground the argument more effectively? Separate out claims and develop arguments fully? Address counterarguments? Establish common ground with the reader?

2. Using one of the familiar topics listed in "Try This: Developing Arguments" (Chapter 5, p. 128) or another topic that students are likely to have ideas about, ask the class to agree on a position regarding it. Allow ten or fifteen minutes' discussion on the issue so that students have some ideas to work with. Then brainstorm a cluster diagram together in class. (Draw the diagram on the board as students suggest ideas and arguments.) Then invite students to (1) write a thesis statement and (2) transform the class's cluster diagram into a sentence outline.

3. To begin work on an exploratory essay, invite the class to freewrite for fifteen to twenty minutes on a problem that has come up in class discussion, or any problem that cannot easily be solved but can yield insight. Take a short break, and then ask students to read through their freewriting and identify the main "events": Where do they state the problem? Where do insights occur (however small)? Where do useful questions occur? Then ask students to transform their writerly freewriting into a short readerly essay (four or five paragraphs will suffice) that represents "the narrative of an intellectual quest."

PART THREE   Attending to Style (p. 215)

This part includes two chapters discussing sentences and style. They ask students to consider not only meaning and grammar but also stylistic elegance for vigorous and compelling writing.

Chapter 7   Crafting Sentences (p. 217)

The purpose here is not to offer a course in grammar but to give students tools for crafting sentences more deliberately and skillfully. So the chapter necessarily includes certain basics of a "writer's grammar" — a few grammatical terms and concepts that can help writers shape, analyze, and revise sentences. The emphasis is primarily on the clause and secondarily on the phrase. Most college students can identify the most basic elements of the sentence — nouns, verbs, adjectives, adverbs, pronouns, and perhaps prepositions and conjunctions — so there is usually no need to spend a lot of time on these. But many students are less comfortable with the concepts of the clause and the phrase, which are at least equally useful for analyzing and revising sentences. Students need to be able to recognize independent and dependent clauses in order to recognize sentence types.

The chapter offers two different ways of thinking about sentences: grammatical and rhetorical. (Grammatical sentence types include simple, compound, complex, and compound-complex; rhetorical sentence types include loose, periodic, and balanced.) The first helps students more firmly grasp the principles of punctuation (especially the comma, the semicolon, and the colon), while the second helps them make stylistic and rhetorical choices. Sentence-combining was once a staple of composition teaching, and while such exercises should not consume an entire course, students can still find them a helpful way to develop their sentence-level skills. The point is to encourage students to experiment with crafting longer sentences — not that we want students to write long sentences only, of course, but they should be able to craft longer sentences as needed and should be able to introduce some variety into their prose without making too many errors.

Grammar and style shade into each other here, and some strategies for untangling problematic sentences are introduced near the end of the chapter.

Additional "Try This" Activities for Chapter 7

1. Invite students to identify the elements listed in the "Checklist for Crafting Sentences" (clauses, phrases, grammatical and rhetorical sentence types) in their own writing or that of another student. (You can do this collectively as a class, or

students can trade drafts and work with one another's writing.) Invite students to offer examples of clause and phrase types. Ask them to count the frequency of the various sentence types — not as a way of exposing a problem, but simply as a register of stylistic choices.

2. In class, brainstorm a list of twenty to twenty-five attributes of some object (anything will do — but something a little offbeat can elicit some fun ideas). Ask students to construct a single long loose cumulative sentence that incorporates every one of the attributes in the list. Then have students share their work in groups of three or four, to see if they can devise an elegant sentence by incorporating the best ideas. For the purpose of comparison, a representative from each group can write the final results on the board. Finally, ask students to work individually to revise the single long sentence into a short paragraph of sentences, one that exhibits good sentence variety.

Chapter 8   Writing with Style (p. 239)

The subject of style has been reserved for last in Part Three because working on style is a revision strategy. Most student writers are better off not even worrying about style when they compose their drafts.

Some style manuals read like a list of rules, but this chapter presents style more as a matter of choices. Too often, students suppose that style guidelines are rules never to be broken; therefore, they avoid the passive voice no matter how absurd the sentence might be in the active voice, or they pare their prose down to bland dreariness by omitting the necessary words along with the unnecessary ones. So we begin by untangling an ambiguity that confuses many students, between the normative and descriptive senses of the word "style." Students naturally want to develop a style they can call their own; however, they are also told to observe certain principles of "good style," and these may feel like restrictions or impositions. Mature writers have internalized a set of principles that they can choose to apply or not, depending on the circumstances.

Next, we turn to plain style, which we put in historical context but also endorse — at least with two cheers. Most students do find the principles of plain style helpful for the most part, even if some seem aimed at solecisms that student writers today are less likely to commit. The chapter distills these principles to three, so that students can remember them and apply them as they revise: (1) cut excess verbiage, (2) use specific and concrete words, and (3) avoid monotonous sentence patterns. The first principle pertains at the level of the sentence, the second at the level of diction, and the third at the level of larger structures such as the paragraph.

Next, we introduce the Renaissance concept of "copious" style. Rhetorics today often don't treat this topic, but we include it for two reasons: (1) to guard against the excesses of plain style — students, after all, sometimes use *too few* words and fail to explain an idea or a subject sufficiently — and (2) to emphasize that achieving good style is about making appropriate choices, not merely following rules. If students understand that "plainness" is not the only ideal they should aim for, they will be less likely to apply the principles of plain style mechanically and imprudently.

The section "The Roots of English: Simple Words" gives students some sense of how the language has evolved, absorbing words from several other languages, primarily French and Latin.

Finally, we offer a few principles of academic style. Since academic style is hardly uniform, it would be unwise to get too specific, but a few guidelines can help college writers: (1) maintain a scholarly tone, (2) aim to be clear but not simplistic, (3) follow disciplinary conventions in preferring the active or passive voice, (4) use qualifiers to "hedge" claims, and (5) convey impartiality. The emphasis here is on the areas where academic style may differ from both plain style and copious style.

Additional "Try This" Activities for Chapter 8

1. The "Try This: Get Happy" activity (p. 252) invites students to look up the words "cheerful," "happy," "euphoric," and "jolly" and to consider how the meanings and connotations of these words differ. In class, do similar work with other word groups or pairs that are close but distinct in meaning (for example, "endure" and "persist"; "curious" and "weird"). Discuss whether any of the words are more concrete or more abstract. Ask students which of the words (if any) might be considered jargon, neologisms, or "fancy" words.
2. In class, discuss the differences between plain style and copious style. Ask students to find examples of each and to bring them to the next class. Ask them to agree on the clearest example of each style, and invite them to rewrite it in the opposite style. (Students may need to use some creativity to expand plain style into copious style, but that's fine.)

PART FOUR   Research and Documentation (p. 265)

The two chapters in this part provide instruction in conducting academic research and understanding citation. The chapters guide students in finding, evaluating, incorporating, and documenting sources in MLA, APA, and *Chicago* formats.

Chapter 9   Conducting Research (p. 267)

This chapter emphasizes two aspects of conducting research: managing the research process and locating materials in both digital and physical form.

Few students arrive at college having worked in large research libraries before or knowing how to navigate the abundance of library resources. For some, conducting research may have consisted of little more than a Google search. But even those who have done more extensive research in high school may have little sense of how much time a college-level research paper is likely to take and few skills when it comes to time management and project management. Thus the chapter begins by giving students some tools for planning their time and developing a practical research strategy.

As the Internet and search engines evolve, so do the practices of researchers. The description we offer here of the research process is based on the way that skilled undergraduate researchers actually work with currently available tools. Their process typically falls into two phases: (1) preliminary research around some fairly broad topic and (2) focused research on a specific problem or question within that topic area.

These two phases are described here as "Getting Started: Scouting for a Topic" and "Digging Deeper." Students begin scouting for a topic by drawing on lectures, textbooks, search engines, and suggestions given in the assignment; having settled on something that seems promising and appropriate, they then turn to reference sources to get a sense of the big picture around this topic. Next, they will collect and peruse a small number of sources that discuss the topic in enough depth to allow them to identify a *specific* research question or problem. This specific question becomes the focus for the next phase of research, "digging deeper," which involves hunting down and carefully reading the best and most relevant sources.

Methods for using a library's online catalog (and other tools) to find books and for using electronic databases to find scholarly articles are described in some detail. You may want to bring some scholarly journals to class to show students how these periodicals differ from the magazines and newspapers they are more familiar with.

Although more and more scholarly articles are becoming available in full text online, students still need to know how to find articles in paper form in the library stacks. Even in a freshman writing course, a student may find that the one most important source for a topic exists only in paper form.

Students are encouraged to identify the scholarly conversation concerning their research question and to understand their purpose as making some sort of contribution to that conversation. In reading their sources, they are advised to identify not only a work's argument but also its "position." While the argument is internal to the work — a thesis and its support — "position" refers to the place where a writer stands in relation to others in the conversation. An understanding of this, even if it's somewhat vague, will greatly help students integrate sources effectively into their own arguments.

In addition, we advise students to maintain a well-organized working bibliography and show them how to set one up. And fairly detailed advice is offered for evaluating sources and reading critically — not only Internet sources but any source. (Whether we like it or not, students will almost certainly use Wikipedia at some stage of a research project. The section "A Note on Wikipedia" offers a sense of its strengths and weaknesses by explaining how Wikipedia articles get created and edited.)

Even if you cannot assign a full-length research paper in your course, you can still give students an opportunity to practice many of the skills described here by assigning mini–research assignments, asking them to find one scholarly article and write an abstract, or devising some sort of scavenger hunt for several items in the library and online.

Additional "Try This" Activities for Chapter 9

1. Ask students to locate and retrieve one scholarly article and then to write an abstract and a correctly formatted citation. (The article should not be excessively technical. Articles in the humanities and social sciences usually work best.) Students should submit a copy of the article along with their abstract. Invite several students to present to the class the scholarly article each of them chose and to discuss its qualities as academic writing, including the problem or question it addresses, the argument it makes, and the position that the writer takes in relation to others.

2. After reviewing Wikipedia's requirements for editing and writing articles (including "Wikipedia: Your First Article" and "Wikipedia: Neutral Point of View"), invite students to write or edit a Wikipedia article (see the page that lists "needed articles" as a starting point). Students might find an article that's a "stub" and contribute something to it, or they might simply add information to an article. (It's a good idea to work closely with students on their research before they actually edit a Wikipedia page.) If you have access to the Internet and a projector in class, you can edit a Wikipedia article together in class.

Chapter 10   Documentation (p. 329)

This chapter emphasizes fundamental concepts pertaining to documentation, rather than presenting a detailed description of rules for various documentation styles. The chapter includes advice about avoiding plagiarism; the principles of citation in academic writing; and a basic description of MLA, *Chicago*, and APA documentation styles.

Additional "Try This" Activities for Chapter 10

1. When students are ready to submit their first finished essay, work on the details of formatting and citation (in whatever style you choose to use) together in class. That is, ask them to use a pen (if they are submitting paper copies) to add formatting features, such as page numbers in the correct place, formatted personal information on the first page, formatted citations, and so on. In addition, require them to revise their title if it is generic or vague.

2. Distribute or project a single paragraph of text in class, preferably one from a familiar reading. Invite students to read the paragraph two or three times and then to write a paraphrase without looking at it (on the reverse of the sheet or with the projector turned off). Once students have written a first draft, allow them to look again at the original to make corrections and additions. (Short quotations of two or three words may be necessary.) Then ask students to trade their work with a classmate and compare. Give them a few minutes to discuss the differences and reach a conclusion about the merits of one version over another. Finally, ask students to discuss as a group what this activity taught them about the challenges of paraphrasing and what good paraphrasing involves.

PART FIVE   Readings (p. 381)

Five substantial reading selections are included in *Writing in Response*. The book presumes that critical reading of challenging material is an essential component of writing pedagogy; therefore, should you wish to include additional or alternative readings, this section provides suggestions for readings that would work well with a course that includes *Writing in Response*. This list is meant to be generative, not exhaustive. When selections are available online (as of press time), URLs have been listed. Also included are suggestions for thematic groupings, on education, animal rights, and the American frontier.

How to Use Additional Readings

Additional readings need not be "academic writing" in the strictest sense; in fact, it can be difficult (though not impossible) to find scholarly articles published in scholarly journals or books that are accessible and meaningful to college students. However, many readings for a general audience, whether written by academics or by serious journalists, employ scholarly practices and work well to introduce students to the main concepts and conventions of academic discourse. It helps a great deal if the text includes references — if not actual notes and citations, at least references to other works.

Exploratory essays like Jane Tompkins's "At the Buffalo Bill Museum, June 1988" are not the norm in academic writing. But Tompkins's approach is hardly unique. And many scholarly texts include exploratory writing, incorporating open-ended question-driven passages into an essay that is chiefly argument-driven. When we find such moves, it's worth pointing them out to students. Students are often relieved to know that, like them, professional scholars and writers don't have all the answers and are often in doubt.

Students can handle fairly difficult readings if they are given the opportunity to reread and discuss them. Even a text that students find quite bewildering on first reading can become sufficiently clear after three or four readings and two or three class discussions to allow students to begin to work out a response. For a text that students plan to write about, *Writing in Response* supposes that they should read it carefully at least three times.

When discussing a text, whether in class or in a student conference, we need to be careful as instructors not to impose our own reading of the text on students — even though students might want and expect this from us. The temptation to explicate the text can be strong, but it robs students of the opportunity to work out an understanding of the text on their own. It's worth remembering that there can be no absolute reading of a text. You can certainly intervene when students wildly misread a text by drawing their attention to passages that contradict their reading or by raising a question about the contradictions within a misreading; however, when we explicate, we substitute our authority as instructors for the authority of the text — and the text effectively disappears.

Some Suggested Readings

Baum, Dan. "Happiness Is a Worn Gun," from *Harper's*, August 2010.

Griffin, Susan. "Our Secret," from *A Chorus of Stones: The Private Life of War*. Garden City, NY: Doubleday-Anchor, 1992.

Sacks, Oliver. "The Revolution of the Deaf," from *Seeing Voices: A Journey into the World of the Deaf*. New York: Vintage Books, 2000.

Sandel, Michael J. "The Case against Perfection," from *The Atlantic Monthly*, April 2004.

Singer, Peter. "The Singer Approach to Ending World Poverty," from *The Life You Can Save: Acting Now to End World Poverty*. New York: Random House, 2009.

Smith, Zadie. "Speaking in Tongues," from *The New York Review of Books*, February 26, 2009. http://www.nybooks.com/articles/archives/2009/feb/26/speaking-in-tongues-2/.

Wechsler, Lawrence. "Vermeer in Bosnia," from *Vermeer in Bosnia: Cultural Comedies and Political Tragedies*. New York: Pantheon, 2004.

Yoshino, Kenji. "The Pressure to Cover," from *The New York Times*, January 15, 2006. A longer version of his argument can be found in *The Yale Law Journal*, 2002. http://www.yalelawjournal.org/the-yale-law-journal/content-pages/covering/.

Additional Suggestions Grouped into Sequences

Sequence 1: On Learning

Emerson, Ralph Waldo. "The American Scholar," from *Ralph Waldo Emerson: Essays and Poems*. New York: Library of America, 1996.

Gawande, Atul. "The Learning Curve," from *The New Yorker*, January 28, 2002.

Percy, Walker. "The Loss of the Creature," from *The Message in the Bottle: How Queer Man Is, How Queer Language Is, and What One Has to Do with the Other*. New York: Picador, 1954, 1975.

Perry, William. "Examsmanship and the Liberal Arts," from *Examining in Harvard College: A Collection of Essays by Members of the Harvard Faculty*. Edited by Leon Bramson. Cambridge, MA: Harvard University Press, 1963.

Rodriguez, Richard. "The Achievement of Desire," from *Hunger of Memory: The Education of Richard Rodriguez*. New York: Bantam, 1983, 2004.

Sequence 2: Animal Rights

Berger, John. "Looking at Animals," from *Selected Essays of John Berger*. Edited by Geoff Dyer. New York: Pantheon Books, 2001.

Pollan, Michael. "An Animal's Place," from *The New York Times*, November 10, 2002.

Scruton, Roger. "A Carnivore's Credo," from *Harper's*, May 2006.

Singer, Peter. "Down at the Factory Farm," from *Animal Liberation*, 2nd ed. New York: Ecco, 2002.

Sequence 3: The Myth of the American Frontier

Limerick, Patricia Nelson. "Denial and Dependence," from *The Legacy of Conquest: The Unbroken Past of the American West*. New York: W. W. Norton, 1987.

Momaday, N. Scott. "The American West and the Burden of Belief," from *The Man Made of Words: Essays, Stories, Passages*. New York: St. Martin's, 1997.

Tirman, John. "The Future of the American Frontier," from *The American Scholar*, Winter 2009.

Turner, Frederick Jackson. "The Significance of the American Frontier in American History," from *The Frontier in American History*. Whitefish, MT: Kessinger, 2010. http://www.gutenberg.org/ebooks/22994.

APPENDIX

TEACHING THE EXPLORATORY ESSAY

Introduction: How I Came to the Exploratory Essay

I began teaching the exploratory essay several years ago, when I began thinking about the formal differences between what students were reading in my course and what they were writing. Our readings, though scholarly (at least in a broad sense), were engaging and moving in a way that student writing seldom was, less because students were incapable of writing engaging and moving essays than because they had somehow internalized a notion that their school writing ought to be dry and impersonal and constricted. The fascinating essays we were reading were not thesis-driven in that formulaic, linear way of the sample essays and models of student writing that students were seeing in handbooks and on Web sites.

It was partly to close this gap that I originally began to invite students — tentatively and merely as an option at first — to write exploratory, question-driven essays. But after one particular student conference, I began to feel more strongly than ever about the value of such assignments. Clearly, this student was exceptionally bright and inquisitive, but his essays, though readable and "correct," were consistently bland and unremarkable. After probing a little to figure out why he was so disengaged, I learned that for him writing for school was almost too easy. As he put it, "You read or do some research, come up with a thesis, invent some arguments in support, organize them, write it up, and you get a B or better." This was a little depressing, but what really struck me as we talked was the vast gap between his actual intellectual life and the perfunctory work he produced for school. Somewhere along the line, he had learned to rein in his intellect — his curiosity and fascination. He had learned to shoehorn his thinking into the forms of school writing that he had been taught were acceptable.

What Is the Exploratory Essay?

As explained in Chapter 6, the exploratory essay is a question- or problem-driven essay rather than a thesis-driven (expository) one. That is, it begins by defining a difficult problem and moves forward not by making claims and supporting those claims but by seeking answers and then subjecting those claims to rigorous scrutiny. It may or may not end in a solution. Some sort of insight, even if it is only a clearer understanding of the problem, is enough. The expository essay and the exploratory essay do not *really* stand opposed to each other. Many essays, perhaps most of the best ones, contain elements of both. But because students typically come to us having been taught to write rigidly thesis-driven essays for academic purposes, it helps to emphasize the differences at first, and even to insist that students try writing at least one essay that is purely exploratory.

The word "essay" derives from the French *essayer* — an attempt or experiment. The first modern essays, those of Michel de Montaigne, were learned but radically antischolastic, in stark contrast to the academic writing of his time. They were also relatively structureless. When Samuel Johnson came to define the term "essay" for his *Dictionary* as "a loose sally of the mind; irregular undigested piece; not a regular and orderly composition," he may have had Montaigne's archetypes in mind. As the etymology implies, the essay could be considered an inherently exploratory form. Scott Russell Sanders writes:

> The writing of an essay is like finding one's way through a forest without being quite sure what game you are chasing, what landmark you are seeking. You sniff down one path until some heady smell tugs you in a new direction, and then off you go, dodging and circling, lured on by the songs of unfamiliar birds, puzzled by the tracks of strange beasts, leaping from stone to stone across rivers, barking up one tree after another. Much of the pleasure of writing an essay — and when the writing is any good, the pleasure of reading it — comes from this dodging and leaping, this movement of the mind. It must not be idle movement, however, if the essay is to hold up; it must be driven by deep concerns. The surface of a river is alive with lights and reflections, the breaking of foam over rocks, but beneath the dazzle it is going somewhere. We should expect as much from an essay: the shimmer and play of mind on the surface and in the depths a strong current.[1]

However, the exploratory essay is not identical with the personal essay or the familiar essay. While the personal or positioned subject does play a role in exploratory writing (because someone has to be doing the exploring), the main focus is not on the personal but on some question, some knowledge problem — and this is why it should be considered academic writing, even though it may not take the traditional or typical form of academic writing.

---

[1]Scott Russell Sanders, "The Singular First Person," in *Essays on the Essay*, ed. Alexander Butrym (Athens: University of Georgia Press, 1989), 34.

"The Narrative of an Intellectual Quest"

Exploratory essays do have a certain structure, though it's usually looser than that of a thesis-driven essay. Typically, they begin by describing an intellectual problem of some kind and then take the reader along on a quest for a solution — or at least some insight, some illumination. Along the way, the real nature of the problem often becomes clearer or takes a new shape, and this calls for redefinition, but the quest continues. The quick and easy answers are scrutinized; new depths are revealed; we follow the writer into places that we did not expect to go. The essay takes the general shape of a story, with a plot — a beginning, a middle, and an end ("I started with this problem x; I tried this and that; and I discovered y"). There are stories within the story: the narrative proceeds as a series of attempts, considerations, or forward steps. And at the end, we may not have any real answer at all. Perhaps we are left only with questions to think about, but we understand their importance now, and we are left with food for thought. The exploratory essay often seems to leave the ball in the reader's court — at least, to a degree. Yet this is one of its appealing qualities: it is a more dialogical form, one that seems to *invite* participation and response.

Jane Tompkins's essay "At the Buffalo Bill Museum, June 1988" (p. 413) works like this, as does Adam Gopnik's "Bumping into Mr. Ravioli" (p. 384). In class, when we discuss exploratory essays like these for the first time, we note how each one begins with a problem, but not a thesis, and we trace the main stages in the quest for a solution. The reader is taken along, included, in this quest for understanding, and though neither essay leaves us with pat answers, we do not think the less of them for that. They move forward, as many exploratory essays do, by means of a sort of dialectic of *imagination* and *critique*. Imagination throws out hypotheses, possibilities, pathways; critique takes a skeptical, even suspicious view of what imagination produces. To succeed, the exploratory essay must draw on both these faculties.

One of the first questions students may ask when I give this assignment is "Can I use the word 'I'?" The answer, of course, is not just that they can but that they *should*. In the exploratory essay, the subject and the subject's position in time and space fundamentally belong within the narrative. The writer — at least, the writer's mind — is always a character in the story, sometimes the only character (and sometimes not): a *represented* consciousness that not only reasons but also feels, hesitates, questions, objects. To illustrate this notion for students, I sometimes offer the example of Archimedes looking for the solution to the problem of the king's crown. Some of them may already know the story: Archimedes had to figure out a way to determine, without damaging the crown, whether the goldsmith who had made it had substituted some alloy for the pure gold. One day while bathing, he figured out the solution and (according to Vitruvius) was so overjoyed that he ran through the streets of Syracuse naked, yelling "Eureka!"

Now, in principle (I tell them), this insight — or any insight — could be explained to others in one of two ways. One could write it up as a thesis-driven linear argument: "The solution is to weigh the crown in water in order to establish the specific density of gold, and because x and y are true, therefore z." But one could also write it up as the narrative of an intellectual quest: "I needed to know x, so I tried this and then that, and eventually, after much hand-wringing (it's a funny story, really), I hit upon z." And this is true of any insight. The difference between the exploratory and the expository approach is that the former is open-ended and the latter tends to be rather closed off. The exploratory approach does not require a tidy *solution* to get things started — or even ended — and it permits and encourages a relentless questioning that pushes thinking deeper even if the questions disrupt the apparent answers. So it promotes a kind of probing thoughtfulness that, for many students, is not easily accommodated by conventional thesis-driven forms of school writing.

So a certain amount of healthy skepticism on the part of the writer is crucial. The writer must sustain the quest by keeping the questions coming: the real point is not so much to *answer* the question but rather to keep probing deeper, by looking at the question from fresh angles or approaches, by seeking out the weaknesses of hypotheses as they emerge, by reexamining questions and solutions and turning them around in the light. As inquiry, research, and reflection produce further questions, the problem gets amplified rather than reduced.

To illustrate this, I sometimes present to students some reasonably difficult but entertaining puzzle and ask them not just to try to solve it but to keep a record of their attempts (or perhaps "assays"). After they have worked on it for a while — whether they solve it doesn't matter — I ask them to write a page or two describing their "intellectual quest" for a solution. They don't have to include everything that happened; they should focus on just the highlights. Sharing these short pieces and talking about them, comparing them to exploratory essays such as those by Tompkins and Gopnik, helps students understand what the phrase "narrative of an intellectual quest" means and gives them some confidence that they can do it.

The word "narrative" is important here — just as important, ultimately, as the term "quest." The final essay must be a *representation* of the story of the student's quest, and not — like typical heuristic writing — a record of the quest itself. The word "narrative" implies a revision process, one that involves creating a readerly essay out of a writerly quest. Some "emplotment" must take place: a beginning, a middle, and an end must be imposed on the formlessness of actual experience through a process of selection, simplification, and even some fictionalizing (in the sense of employing the techniques of fiction rather than falsification). The problem or question supplies a beginning point, and the insight or resolution, however uncertain and ambiguous, supplies the end point. These two points anchor the story, a sequence of intellectual events that constitutes the "middle."

Hence the revision process for exploratory writing differs considerably from the process for expository writing. The shift from writerly to readerly phases of the writing process involves a refinement of a narrative that already exists, inchoately and perhaps only partially, in the heuristic writing. Revision aims not so much at answering all the questions but at making the questions sharper and stronger. It often means winnowing out canceled questions to bring the unanswered question(s), the true problem, more definitely into the foreground. To understand better how this process works, I find it's helpful for students to look at some examples of student exploratory writing-in-progress together as a class, near the midpoint between receiving the assignment and the deadline. We look in particular for moments when the narrative moves well and those when it seems to bog down or turn in circles.

We compositionists have tended to draw a rather heavy line between thesis-driven academic writing and personal essayistic writing. But the academic exploratory essay *is* academic writing, though writing that incorporates reflection on the subject position of the writer and acknowledges that subject position matters. In principle, the narrative of an intellectual quest can meet the requirements of academic discourse in any discipline; it just takes a different approach to communicating insight. And arguably this alternative might even be considered the more epistemologically tenable of the two, as a narrative approach requires an "I," an inquirer situated in time and space — in history — and so subject position must be much more explicit. (Jane Tompkins's well-known essay "Me and My Shadow" explores the importance of subject position to academic writing.[2]) So although the end result may be more tentative than the argument of an expository essay, it is also likely to be less abstract, "thicker" with context and the concreteness of experience. (Thus *ethos* and *pathos* play a more prominent role in this kind of writing.) And as students begin to see that their narratives differ quite a bit depending on various factors such as personality, personal history, personal aptitudes, and mood — even though they're all working on the same puzzle or similar

[2]Jane Tompkins, "Me and My Shadow," *New Literary History* 19, no. 1 (1987): 169–78. http://www.jstor.org/stable/469310.

puzzles — they begin to understand what the term "subject position" means, both in theory and in practice.

The exploratory academic essay represents a new writing challenge for most students, but a deeply engaging one that expands their sense of what's possible in academic writing. But the chief virtue of the exploratory form is that it doesn't *need* to end in a monumental insight like that of Archimedes. Students don't need to feel they must find something new to say about *Hamlet*. As Scott Russell Sanders writes in the essay quoted earlier, "essays . . . are experiments in making sense of things." The quest itself is enough, as long as it takes us somewhere. I tell my students that the exploratory essay sustains the quest by resisting answers that bring closure: it requires that, every time they think they've found an answer, they need to figure out what *further* questions can be asked. Thus the thinking that comes out of an exploratory essay is often much more sophisticated and complicated than that which emerges from thesis statements that are too often superficial and ill considered.

APA Style

Papers in APA style typically employ the standard structure of scientific papers, in which an abstract (or a summary) is followed by distinct sections entitled "Introduction," "Method," "Results," and "Discussion." The list of references (bibliography) and, if necessary, appendices follow.

Main Features

"Author-Date" In-text Citations Parenthetical references in the main text refer the reader to full bibliographic information in the list of references at the end of the text.

In-text citations may take several forms. Provide the author and date in parentheses (McMahon, 2009) if neither is mentioned in the text.

> One study looked specifically at the effectiveness of music therapy in reducing undesirable behaviors (McMahon, 2009).

If the author is mentioned in the text, provide only the date in parentheses.

> Toth and Aikens (2001) studied the effect of music therapy on patients' moods, as measured by the frequency of responses such as smiling, laughing, and singing along with the music.

No parenthetical reference is needed if both the author and date are mentioned in the text. Full bibliographical information appears in the list of references.

> Mary Ellen Geist's 2008 memoir, *Measure of the Heart: A Father's Alzheimer's, A Daughter's Return*, describes her father's remarkable memory for music even after he had lost virtually all other memories.

Include a page number when quoting text or citing a specific passage in a text. If page numbers are unavailable (for example, on a Web page), cite the paragraph number, using the abbreviation "para." (para. 6).

> Curiously, people with dementia are often able to recognize and enjoy familiar music, and perhaps even play an instrument or sing flawlessly, long after they have lost other brain functions (Sacks, 2008, pp. 379-380).

If the reference list contains several works published in the same year by the same author, distinguish between them in the text by using a letter following the year of publication (2003a, 2003b, and so on).

The List of References   A references page at the end of the paper contains complete bibliographical information for each citation. Items in the list of references appear alphabetically, under the heading "References."

For a book, list the author(s), the year of publication (in parentheses), the title (italicized), the city of publication, and the publisher.

> Aldridge, D. (1996). *Music therapy research and practice in medicine: From out of the silence*. London, England: Jessica Kingsley.

For an article, list the author(s), the year of publication (in parentheses), the title of the article, the title of the journal (italicized), the volume number (italicized), and the page range. If a journal is paginated by issue, place the issue number in parentheses.

> Koger, S. M., Chapin, K., & Brotons, M. (1999). Is music therapy an effective intervention for dementia? A meta-analytic review of literature. *Journal of Music Therapy, 36*(1), 2-15.

If the item is a chapter from a book, place the page range in parentheses following the title of the book.

Endnotes   Endnotes may be used for informational material that does not fit well into the body of the text, but not for bibliographical citations.

For more details, see apastyle.org and the *Publication Manual of the American Psychological Association*, 6th Edition.

•   •   •

The following paper uses APA style. A short version of the title of the paper ("Music Therapy") is listed in the upper right corner of each page, followed by the page number. Note that instead of labeling the first page of citations "Bibliography," as is done in *Chicago* style, APA style use the term "References" (see p. 377). Entries in the references invert the author's name and use initials for first and middle names. In the APA style, only the first words in titles and subtitles of sources are capitalized; other words are not.

Short title and page number at top right ➤ Music Therapy   1

Full title, student's name, and name of college are centered halfway down the page.

The Effectiveness of Music Therapy
in the Treatment of Disease
Ellen Kang
Boston University, College of General Studies

An author note lists the name of the course and the professor.

Author Note
This paper was prepared for Sociology 108, Section C,
taught by Professor Moore.

Sources cited in parentheses with year of publication

The American Music Therapy Association (AMTA, 1999) has defined therapy as "the clinical and evidence-based use of music interventions to accomplish individualized goals within a therapeutic relationship by a credentialed professional who has completed an approved music therapy program" ("What Is Music Therapy," para. 1). Thus music therapy is not simply a matter of playing music to soothe suffering patients. Therapies are tailored to the needs of the individual and to the particular disease and its symptoms. Therapists are typically trained in a graduate degree program and certified by the Certification Board of Music Therapists (AMTA, 1999, "Who Is Qualified," para. 1). A few universities offer PhD programs in music therapy.

Music has been used as a healing practice since at least the 1940s, and in one form or another music therapy dates as far back as ancient Greece (AMTA, 1999, "What Is the History," para. 1). But until recently, few scientific studies had convincingly demonstrated the effectiveness of music therapy or produced data to indicate just *how* effective music therapy can be, and under what circumstances (Raglio et al., 2008). In the last twenty years, however, several studies have shown that music therapy is effective in treating a number of diseases (Aldridge, 1996), and evidence is continuing to mount.

Music therapy has been shown to be effective in accelerating full recovery in a variety of diseases, including stroke and head injury, when used alongside traditional therapy (Aldridge, 1996). But it is also being used to improve the quality of life, and reduce the symptoms, of patients with incurable diseases such as Alzheimer's and other forms of dementia (Aldridge, 1996). Curiously, people with dementia are often able to recognize and enjoy familiar music, and perhaps even play an instrument or sing flawlessly, long after they have lost other brain functions (Sacks, 2008, pp. 379–380). And in fact, music seems to have an especially powerful effect on many patients with dementia: while it cannot "cure" them, it is able to "reach" and move them as no other stimulus can do. Sacks (2008) has written that

> the therapeutic role of music in dementia is quite different from what it is in patients with motor or speech disorders. . . . The aim of music therapy in people with dementia is far broader . . . it seeks to address the emotions, cognitive powers, thoughts, and memories, the surviving "self" of the patient, to stimulate these and bring them to the fore. It aims to enrich and enlarge existence, to give freedom, stability, organization, and focus. (pp. 372-373)

Sacks offered a number of moving and compelling anecdotes that show the extraordinary power of music for these particular individuals (Chapter 29). But can such effects be empirically measured or quantified? Do we have anything approaching scientific proof that, for people with dementia, music therapy works?

A "meta-analytic" review of 21 studies published between 1985 and 1999 found that, although the methods and size of the studies varied too widely to draw precise conclusions, the effect of music therapy on the symptoms of dementia was "highly significant" (Koger, Chapin, & Brotons, 1999). The type of music used and the way it was used as therapy varied widely but were selected based on the particular needs of the patient.

Music Therapy   4

A more recent study by Raglio et al. (2008) concluded that music therapy can diminish the symptoms of patients with severe dementia. The study involved 59 patients and measured the reduction in symptoms using a number of objective criteria. Half the patients were placed in a control group and half in an experimental group. Patients in the experimental group were given 30-minute music therapy sessions, while patients in the control group were given other educational or entertainment activities (such as a bath or playing cards). Music therapy sessions were videotaped, and the patients' responses were measured by observing behaviors. At the end of the 16-week experimental period, and even four weeks after that, dementia symptoms, as measured by the Barthel Index (a scale that measures the ability to perform 10 "Activities of Daily Living"), had diminished significantly (pp. 160-161).

References

Aldridge, D. (1996). *Music therapy research and practice in medicine: From out of the silence*. London, England: Jessica Kingsley.

American Music Therapy Association. (1999). Frequently asked questions. Retrieved from http://www.musictherapy.org/faqs.html#WHAT_IS_MUSIC_THERAPY

Koger, S. M., Chapin, K., & Brotons, M. (1999). Is music therapy an effective intervention for dementia? A meta-analytic review of literature. *Journal of Music Therapy, 36*(1), 2-15.

Raglio, A., Bellelli, G., Traficante, D., Gianotti, M., Ubezio, M. C., Villani, D., & Trabucchi, M. (2008). Efficacy of music therapy in the treatment of behavioral and psychiatric symptoms of dementia. *Alzheimer Disease and Associated Disorders, 22*(2), 158-162.

Sacks, O. (2008). *Musicophilia: Tales of music and the brain* (Rev. ed.). New York, NY: Vintage Books.

List of sources on a separate page

Latin Documentation Terms

You may encounter a variety of Latin abbreviations in the notes of scholarly texts. Here's an explanation of the most common Latin documentation terms, followed by an example of "ibid." used in footnotes.

et al.	An abbreviation of *et alii* (or, if feminine, *et aliae*), Latin for "and others." Used in footnotes and endnotes to shorten a series of authors' names. (For example, "John Adams, Joan Bentley, Susan Critchley, and Linda Smatter" might be abbreviated "John Adams et al.")
op. cit.	An abbreviation of *opere citato*, Latin for "in the work cited." Used in footnotes or endnotes to indicate that the reference is to a work already cited; now obsolete. When "op. cit." is used, a short form of the full citation is given, including only the author's name and the page reference. If more than one work by the author has been cited, a short title is also included.
loc. cit.	An abbreviation of *loco citato*, Latin for "in the place cited." It was used in the same way as "op. cit." and has also become obsolete.
ibid.	An abbreviation of *ibidem*, Latin for "in the same place." Used in footnotes or endnotes to indicate that the reference is to the work cited in the immediately preceding note. A page reference is still necessary if different from the page number in the preceding note.

> 1. David Hosansky, "Traffic Congestion: Is the United States Facing Permanent Gridlock?" *Congressional Quarterly Researcher* 9, no. 32 (1999): 733.
> 2. Ibid.
> 3. Ibid., 740.

Tools to Help with Citation

Web-based or desktop bibliography managers, such as Refworks, Zotero, Endnote, JabRef, Scholar's Aid, EasyBib, or NoodleTools, can help you build your own database of sources and can automatically generate a bibliography from that database in the style you choose. If your college library subscribes to a Web-based citation manager, you may be able to upload references from your library's catalog, from electronic databases, and from Google Scholar directly into your own online database of sources. In some cases, you can attach the source itself, as a PDF file, to the reference information, and you can add notes about each source.

While these tools are certainly a convenience, you must check their output carefully, as the formatting is not always correct and key information may be missing.

 Checklist for Documentation

Keep these guidelines in mind as you document your sources.

☐ Always cite
- Direct quotations
- Paraphrases or summaries of someone else's words
- References to another work

☐ Do not cite
- Your own ideas
- Common knowledge

☐ Avoid plagiarism.
- Start your project early and manage your time.
- In order to write appropriate paraphrases, avoid using the language of the original text, and avoid using the original text's sentence structures.

☐ Observe the assignment's formatting style (e.g., MLA, *Chicago*, and APA).

☐ If using a bibliography management tool, check the output carefully for formatting errors.

part 5

Readings

Adam Gopnik

Adam Gopnik (b. 1956) is a staff writer for *The New Yorker* magazine and the author of five books. He has earned a reputation as a master of the familiar essay, the kind of essay that, in the manner of Charles Lamb (1775–1834) or E. B. White (1899–1985), conveys observations about contemporary life in a warm, companionable voice. Much of the charm of these essays comes from the sense of a genuine personality speaking directly to the reader. But Gopnik is a learned as well as an entertaining writer, and though he wears his learning lightly, the remarkable range of historical and cultural reference in his essays is essential to their interest. In a 2001 interview with Robert Birnbaum, he remarked, "I'm an addicted reader. My wife teases me because I read in the shower, when I'm shaving. I read incessantly. I need to be reading a lot. A lot of what I write — I hope it's not too bookish — comes from other books."

Gopnik was born in Philadelphia and grew up in Montreal, Canada, where his parents taught at McGill University. After earning a BA at McGill, Gopnik moved to New York to study art history at the Institute of Fine Arts, New York University. Without completing his doctorate, he began working as a writer and an editor, first at *GQ Magazine* and later at Knopf publishing house. In 1986, he began contributing to *The New Yorker* with the essay "Quattrocento Baseball," which reflected on the connections between professional baseball and Italian Renaissance painting. The magazine soon hired him as a staff writer, and his essays began to appear frequently.

In 1995, *The New Yorker* sent him, with his wife and young son, to Paris, France, to contribute a regular column, "Paris Journal." A number of these essays were eventually published as *Paris to the Moon* (2000). After five years abroad, Gopnik and his family returned to New York (now with a second child, Olivia), where he continued to contribute regularly to *The New Yorker*, often focusing on his experience as a father and on life in New York, now seen through fresh eyes. A number of these pieces were collected as *Through the Children's Gate* (2006). The following essay, "Bumping into Mr. Ravioli," first appeared in *The New Yorker* in September 2002.

Like many of Gopnik's essays, "Bumping into Mr. Ravioli" does not announce a clear argument in its opening paragraphs but rather begins with a puzzle or minor problem of sorts that occasions an informal research project, one that eventually takes in child psychology, social history, the history of technology, the social milieu of New York, and other themes. At the end, the essay takes an unexpected turn; whether this represents a "conclusion" may be up for discussion, but certainly Gopnik has shed new light on the problem of his daughter's too-busy friends.

Bumping into Mr. Ravioli

My daughter, Olivia, who just turned three, has an imaginary friend whose name is 1
Charlie Ravioli. Olivia is growing up in Manhattan, and so Charlie Ravioli has a lot of
local traits: he lives in an apartment "on Madison and Lexington," he dines on grilled
chicken, fruit, and water, and, having reached the age of seven and a half, he feels, or is
thought, "old." But the most peculiarly local thing about Olivia's imaginary playmate is
this: he is always too busy to play with her. She holds her toy cell phone up to her ear,
and we hear her talk into it: "Ravioli? It's Olivia . . . It's Olivia. Come and play? OK. Call
me. Bye." Then she snaps it shut and shakes her head. "I always get his machine," she
says. Or she will say, "I spoke to Ravioli today." "Did you have fun?" my wife and I ask.
"No. He was busy working. On a television" (leaving it up in the air if he repairs electronic devices or has his own talk show).

On a good day, she "bumps into" her invisible friend and they go to a coffee shop. 2
"I bumped into Charlie Ravioli," she announces at dinner (after a day when, of
course, she stayed home, played, had a nap, had lunch, paid a visit to the Central Park
Zoo, and then had another nap). "We had coffee, but then he had to run." She sighs,
sometimes, at her inability to make their schedules mesh, but she accepts it as inevitable, just the way life is. "I bumped into Charlie Ravioli today," she says. "He was
working." Then she adds brightly, "But we hopped into a taxi." What happened then?
we ask. "We grabbed lunch," she says.

It seemed obvious that Ravioli was a romantic figure of the big exotic life that 3
went on outside her little limited life of parks and playgrounds — drawn, in particular, from a nearly perfect, mynah bird–like imitation of the words she hears her
mother use when she talks about *her* day with *her* friends. ("How was your day?"
Sighing: "Oh, you know. I tried to make a date with Meg, but I couldn't find her, so I
left a message on her machine. Then I bumped into Emily after that meeting I had in
SoHo, and we had coffee and then she had to run, but by then Meg had reached me on
my cell and we arranged . . .") I was concerned, though, that Charlie Ravioli might
also be the sign of some "trauma," some loneliness in Olivia's life reflected in imaginary form. "It seems odd to have an imaginary playmate who's always too busy to
play with you," Martha, my wife, said to me. "Shouldn't your imaginary playmate be
someone you tell secrets to and, I don't know, sing songs with? It shouldn't be someone who's always *hopping* into taxis."

We thought, at first, that her older brother, Luke, might be the original of Charlie 4
Ravioli. (For one thing, he is also seven and a half, though we were fairly sure that

this age was merely Olivia's marker for As Old as Man Can Be.) He *is* too busy to play with her much anymore. He has become a true New York child, with the schedule of a cabinet secretary: chess club on Monday, T-ball on Tuesday, tournament on Saturday, play dates and after-school conferences to fill in the gaps. But Olivia, though she counts days, does not yet really *have* days. She has *a* day, and into this day she has introduced the figure of Charlie Ravioli — in order, it dawned on us, to insist that she does have days, because she is too harried to share them, that she does have an independent social life, by virtue of being too busy to have one.

Yet Charlie Ravioli was becoming so constant and oddly discouraging a com- 5 panion — "He canceled lunch. Again," Olivia would say — that we thought we ought to look into it. One of my sisters is a developmental psychologist who specializes in close scientific studies of what goes on inside the heads of one- and two- and three-year-olds. Though she grew up in the nervy East, she lives in California now, where she grows basil in her garden and jars her own organic marmalades. I e-mailed this sister for help with the Ravioli issue — how concerned should we be? — and she sent me back an e-mail, along with an attachment, and, after several failed cell-phone connections, we at last spoke on a land line.

It turned out that there is a recent book on this very subject by the psychologist 6 Marjorie Taylor, called *Imaginary Companions and the Children Who Create Them*, and my sister had just written a review of it. She insisted that Charlie Ravioli was nothing to be worried about. Olivia was right on target, in fact. Most under-sevens (sixty-three percent, to be scientific) have an invisible friend, and children create their imaginary playmates not out of trauma but out of a serene sense of the possibilities of fiction — sometimes as figures of pure fantasy, sometimes, as Olivia had done, as observations of grownup manners assembled in tranquility and given a name. I learned about the invisible companions Taylor studied: Baintor, who is invisible because he lives in the light; Station Pheta, who hunts sea anemones on the beach. Charlie Ravioli seemed pavement-bound by comparison.

"An imaginary playmate isn't any kind of trauma marker," my sister said. "It's 7 just the opposite: it's a sign that the child is now confident enough to begin to understand how to organize her experience into stories." The significant thing about imaginary friends, she went on, is that the kids know they're fictional. In an instant message on AOL, she summed it up: "The children with invisible friends often interrupted the interviewer to remind her, with a certain note of concern for her sanity, that these characters were, after all, just pretend."

I also learned that some children, as they get older, turn out to possess what 8 child psychologists call a "paracosm." A paracosm is a society thought up by a child — an invented universe with a distinctive language, geography, and history. (The Brontës invented a couple of paracosms when they were children.) Not all children who have an imaginary friend invent a paracosm, but the two might, I think, be related. Like a lonely ambassador from Alpha Centauri in a fifties sci-fi movie who, misunderstood by paranoid Earth scientists, cannot bring the life-saving news from his planet, perhaps the invisible friend also gets an indifferent or hostile response, and then we never find out about the beautiful paracosm he comes from.

> *"Don't worry about it,' my sister said in a late-night phone call. "*

"Don't worry about it," my sister said in a late-night phone call. "Knowing something's made up while thinking that it matters is what all fiction insists on. She's putting a name on a series of manners." 9

"But he seems so real to her," I objected. 10

"Of course he is. I mean, who's more real to you, Becky Sharp or Gandalf or the guy down the hall? Giving a manner a name makes it real." 11

I paused. "I grasp that it's normal for her to have an imaginary friend," I said, "but have you ever heard of an imaginary friend who's too busy to play with you?" 12

She thought about it. "No," she said. "I'm sure that doesn't occur anywhere in the research literature. That sounds *completely* New York." And then she hung up. 13

The real question, I saw, was not "Why this friend?" but "Why this fiction?" Why, as Olivia had seen so clearly, are grownups in New York so busy, and so obsessed with the language of busyness that it dominates their conversation? Why are New Yorkers always bumping into Charlie Ravioli and grabbing lunch, instead of sitting down with him and exchanging intimacies, as friends should, as people do in Paris and Rome? Why is busyness the stuff our children make their invisible friends from, as country children make theirs from light and sand? 14

This seems like an odd question. New Yorkers are busy for obvious reasons: they have husbands and wives and careers and children, they have the Gauguin show to see and their personal trainers and accountants to visit. But the more I think about this, the more I think it is — well, a lot of Ravioli. We are instructed to believe that we are busier because we have to work harder to be more productive, but everybody knows that busyness and productivity have a dubious, arm's-length relationship. Most of our struggle in New York, in fact, is to be less busy in order to do more work. 15

Constant, exhausting, no-time-to-meet-your-friends Charlie Ravioli–style busyness arrived as an affliction in modern life long after the other parts of bour- 16 geois city manners did. Business long predates busyness. In the seventeenth and eighteenth centuries, when bourgeois people were building the institutions of bourgeois life, they seem never to have complained that they were too busy — or, if they did, they left no record of it. Samuel Pepys, who had a navy to refloat and a burned London to rebuild, often uses the word "busy" but never complains of busyness. For him, the word "busy" is a synonym for "happy," not for "stressed." Not once in his diary does Pepys cancel lunch or struggle to fit someone in for coffee at four-thirty. Pepys works, makes love, and goes to bed, but he does not bump and he does not have to run. Ben Franklin, a half century later, boasts of his industriousness, but he, too, never complains about being busy, and always has time to publish a newspaper or come up with a maxim or swim the ocean or invent the lightning rod.

Until sometime in the middle of the nineteenth century, in fact, the normal 17 affliction of the bourgeois was not busyness at all but its apparent opposite: boredom. It has even been argued that the grid of streets and cafés and small engagements in the nineteenth-century city — the whole of social life — was designed self-consciously as an escape from that numbing boredom. (Working people weren't bored, of course, but they were engaged in labor, not work. They were too busy to be busy.) Baudelaire, basically, was so bored that he had to get drunk and run out onto the boulevard in the hope of bumping into somebody.

Turn to the last third of the nineteenth century and the beginning of the twen- 18 tieth, though, and suddenly everybody is busy, and everybody is complaining about it. Pepys, master of His Majesty's Navy, may never have complained of busyness, but Virginia Woolf, mistress of motionless lull, is continually complaining about how she spends her days racing across London from square to square, just like — well, like Charlie Ravioli. Ronald Firbank is wrung out by his social obligations; Proust is constantly rescheduling rendezvous and apologizing for being overstretched. Henry James, with nothing particular to do save live, complains of being too busy all the time. He could not shake the world of obligation, he said, and he wrote a strange and beautiful story, "The Great Good Place," which begins with an exhausting flood of correspondence, telegrams, and manuscripts that drive the protagonist nearly mad.

What changed? That James story helps supply the key. It was trains and tele- 19 grams. The railroads ended isolation, and packed the metropolis with people whose work was defined by a complicated network of social obligations. Pepys's network in 1669 London was, despite his official position, relatively small compared even with that of a minor aesthete like Firbank, two centuries later. Pepys had more time to make love because he had fewer friends to answer.

If the train crowded our streets, the telegram crowded our minds. It introduced 20
something into the world which remains with us today: a whole new class of communications that are defined as incomplete in advance of their delivery. A letter,
though it may enjoin a response, is meant to be complete in itself. Neither the Apos-
tle Paul nor Horace Walpole ever ends an epistle with "Give me a call and let's discuss." By contrast, it is in the nature of the telegram to be a skeletal version of another
thing — a communication that opens more than it closes. The nineteenth-century
telegram came with those busy threatening words "Letter follows."

Every device that has evolved from the telegram shares the same character. 21
E-mails end with a suggestion for a phone call ("Anyway, let's meet and/or talk
soon"), faxes with a request for an e-mail, answering-machine messages with a
request for a fax. All are devices of perpetually suspended communication. My wife
recalls a moment last fall when she got a telephone message from a friend asking her
to check her e-mail apropos a phone call she needed to make vis-à-vis a fax they had
both received asking for more information about a bed they were thinking of buying
from Ireland online and having sent to America by Federal Express — a grand slam of
incomplete communication.

In most of the Western world outside New York, the press of trains and of tele- 22
graphic communication was alleviated by those other two great transformers: the car
and the television. While the train and the telegram (and their love children, subways
and commuter trains and e-mail) pushed people together, the car and the television
pulled people apart — taking them out to the suburbs and sitting them down in front of
a solo spectacle. New York, though, almost uniquely,

"Busyness is felt so intently here because we are both crowded and overloaded."

got hit by a double dose of the first two technologies,
and a very limited dose of the second two. Car life — car
obsessions, car-defined habits — is more absent here
than almost anywhere else in the country, while television, though obviously present, is less fatally prevalent
here. New York is still a subject of television, and we
compare *Sex and the City* to sex and the city; they are
not yet quite the same. Here two grids of busyness
remain dominant: the nineteenth- and early-twentieth-century grid of bump and run,
and the late-twentieth- and early-twenty-first-century postmodern grid of virtual call
and echo. Busyness is felt so intently here because we are both crowded and overloaded. We exit the apartment into a still dense nineteenth-century grid of street corners and restaurants full of people, and come home to the late-twentieth-century grid
of faxes and e-mails and overwhelming incompleteness.

We walk across the Park on a Sunday morning and bump into our friend the baker   23
and our old acquaintance from graduate school (what the hell is she doing now?) and
someone we have been avoiding for three weeks. They all invite us for brunch, and we
would love to, but we are too ... busy. We bump into Charlie Ravioli, and grab a coffee
with him — and come home to find three e-mails and a message on our cell phone from
him, wondering where we are. The crowding of our space has been reinforced by a
crowding of our time, and the only way to protect ourselves is to build structures of perpetual deferral: I'll see you next week, let's talk soon. We build rhetorical baffles around
our lives to keep the crowding out, only to find that we have let nobody we love in.

Like Charlie Ravioli, we hop into taxis and leave messages on answering machines   24
to avoid our acquaintances, and find that we keep missing our friends. I have one intimate who lives just across the Park from me, whom I e-mail often, and whom I am fortunate to see two or three times a year. We are always ... busy. He has become my Charlie
Ravioli, my invisible friend. I am sure that he misses me — just as Charlie Ravioli, I realized, must tell his other friends that he is sorry he does not see Olivia more often.

Once I sensed the nature of his predicament, I began to feel more sympathetic toward   25
Charlie Ravioli. I got to know him better, too. We learned more about what Ravioli did in
the brief breathing spaces in his busy life when he could sit down with Olivia and dish.
"Ravioli read your book," Olivia announced, for instance, one night at dinner. "He didn't
like it much." We also found out that Ravioli had joined a gym, that he was going to the
beach in the summer, but he was too busy, and that he was working on a "show." ("It isn't
a very good show," she added candidly.) Charlie Ravioli, in other words, was just another
New Yorker: fit, opinionated, and trying to break into show business.

I think we would have learned to live happily with Charlie Ravioli had it not   26
been for the appearance of Laurie. She threw us badly. At dinner, Olivia had been
mentioning a new personage almost as often as she mentioned Ravioli. "I talked to
Laurie today," she would begin. "She says Ravioli is busy." Or she would be closeted
with her play phone. "Who are you talking to, darling?" I would ask. "Laurie," she
would say. "We're talking about Ravioli." We surmised that Laurie was, so to speak,
the Linda Tripp[1] of the Ravioli operation — the person you spoke to for consolation
when the big creep was ignoring you.

---

[1] Linda Tripp was a confidante of Monica Lewinsky, the White House intern whose sexual relationship
with President Bill Clinton caused a scandal and led to his impeachment by the House of Representatives
in 1998. Tripp illegally recorded her telephone conversations with Lewinsky and, in exchange for immu-
nity from prosecution, turned the tapes over to Independent Counsel Kenneth Starr. [Editor's note]

But a little while later a more ominous side of Laurie's role began to appear. 27
"Laurie, tell Ravioli I'm calling," I heard Olivia say. I pressed her about who, exactly,
Laurie was. Olivia shook her head. "She works for Ravioli," she said.

And then it came to us, with sickening clarity: Laurie was not the patient friend 28
who consoled you for Charlie's absence. Laurie was the bright-toned person who
answered Ravioli's phone and told you that unfortunately Mr. Ravioli was in a meeting.
"Laurie says Ravioli is too busy to play," Olivia announced sadly one morning. Things
seemed to be deteriorating; now Ravioli was too busy even to say he was too busy.

I got back on the phone with my sister. "Have you ever heard of an imaginary 29
friend with an assistant?" I asked.

She paused. "Imaginary friends don't have assistants," she said. "That's not only 30
not in the literature. That's just ... I mean — in California they don't have assistants."

"You think we should look into it?" 31

"I think you should move," she said flatly. 32

Martha was of the same mind. "An imaginary playmate shouldn't have an assis- 33
tant," she said miserably. "An imaginary playmate shouldn't have an agent. An imaginary playmate shouldn't have a publicist or a personal trainer or a caterer — an
imaginary playmate shouldn't have . . . *people*. An imaginary playmate should just
play. With the child who imagined it." She started leaving on my pillow real-estate
brochures picturing quaint houses in New Jersey and Connecticut, unhaunted by
busy invisible friends and their entourages.

Not long after the appearance of Laurie, though, something remarkable happened. 34
Olivia would begin to tell us tales of her frustrations with Charlie Ravioli, and, after
telling us, again, that he was too busy to play, she would tell us what she had done
instead. Astounding and paracosmic tall tales poured out of her: she had been to a
chess tournament and brought home a trophy; she had gone to a circus and told jokes.
Searching for Charlie Ravioli, she had "saved all the animals in the zoo"; heading home
in a taxi after a quick coffee with Ravioli, she took over the steering wheel and "got all
the moneys." From the stalemate of daily life emerged the fantasy of victory. She had
dreamed of a normal life with a few close friends, and had to settle for worldwide fame
and the front page of the tabloids. The existence of an imaginary friend had liberated
her into a paracosm, but it was a curiously New York paracosm — it was the unobtain-
able world outside her window. Charlie Ravioli, prince of busyness, was not an end but
a means: a way out onto the street in her head, a declaration of potential independence.

Busyness is our art form, our civic ritual, our way of being us. Many friends have 35
said to me that they love New York now in a way they never did before, and their love,

I've noticed, takes for its object all the things that used to exasperate them — the curious combination of freedom, self-made fences, and paralyzing preoccupation that the city provides. "How did you spend the day?" Martha and I now ask each other, and then, instead of listing her incidents, she says merely, "Oh, you know . . . just . . . bumping into Charlie Ravioli," meaning, just bouncing from obligation to electronic entreaty, just spotting a friend and snatching a sandwich, just being busy, just living in New York. If everything we've learned in the past year could be summed up in a phrase, it's that we want to go on bumping into Charlie Ravioli for as long as we can.

Olivia still hopes to have him to herself someday. As I work late at night in the 36 "study" (an old hallway, an Aalto screen) I keep near the "nursery" (an ancient pantry, a glass-brick wall), I can hear her shift into pre-sleep, still muttering to herself. She is still trying to reach her closest friend. "Ravioli? Ravioli?" she moans as she turns over into her pillow and clutches her blanket, and then she whispers, almost to herself, "Tell him call me. Tell him call me when he comes home."

Questions for Discussion and Writing

1. How would you describe the problem that Gopnik faces at the beginning of the essay? How does his understanding of the problem change as the essay proceeds? Does the essay offer any sort of solution to the problem? If so, what sort of solution is it? How would you describe the results of Gopnik's inquiry?

2. How does this inquiry, this research project, proceed? What are the stages in the exploration, and how do Gopnik's questions push it forward? At what points does Gopnik turn to some new source? Where does he turn, and why? What are the major turning points in the exploration? (Notice the breaks between sections of the essay.) What lesser twists and turns do you notice?

3. We often hear that technology is changing our way of life, but Gopnik approaches the issue from the standpoint of particularly precious and intimate relationships — childhood and the world of imaginary friends. Gopnik wrote this essay in 2002; since then, of course, communication technologies have continued to make rapid strides. How do you experience and understand the ways that communication technologies — including social networking and texting — are affecting your own life and the lives of others? How do you think these new technologies make your life different from the experiences of previous generations? How do these technologies define life for your generation? What do you imagine the future will bring? And what is the value of looking back to the past for insight, as Gopnik does?

Kathryn Schulz

Kathryn Schulz (b. 1973) is a freelance journalist and editor whose writing has appeared in *Rolling Stone, Foreign Policy, The New York Times Magazine*, and elsewhere. *Being Wrong: Adventures in the Margin of Error* (2010) is her first book and is the source of the following selection. Although she half seriously coined the term "wrongology" to underscore the fact that her subject does not quite fall within any existing academic field, her book is not a rigorous study of error but rather a survey of wrongness—a "Wrongness 101" perhaps. In the book, she discusses how "being wrong" happens, how it feels, and why it may deserve more attention than we have realized. Her theme perhaps strikes a chord at a time when "being wrong" seems to have so profoundly shaped America's political and economic realities, from the intelligence that launched the Iraq War to the Federal Reserve's reassurances before the financial collapse of 2008. But for Schulz, being wrong is not simply an embarrassment to flee from or a condition to cure. We can learn from error itself (not just from our own errors) and even embrace error as intrinsic to human nature and essential to our creativity. Her style is often informal, but her range of reference is deep and wide, and her insights are often surprising.

Schulz is a graduate of Brown University (where she studied history), and she was a 2004 recipient of the Pew Fellowship in International Journalism. She lectures frequently and was a speaker at the 2011 TED (Technology Entertainment and Design) Conference. Her blog, "The Wrong Stuff," appears regularly in the online magazine *Slate*.

Two Models of Wrongness

Our errors are surely not such awfully solemn things. In a world where we are so certain to incur them in spite of all our caution, a certain lightness of heart seems healthier than this excessive nervousness on their behalf.[1]　　**WILLIAM JAMES, "THE WILL TO BELIEVE"**

Ross Gelbspan is a colleague of mine, a fellow journalist who has been writing about environmental issues for forty-odd years. Back in 1972, when he was working for the *Village Voice,* he covered a press conference about *The Limits to Growth,* a study of the impact of economic development and population pressures on natural resources. *The Limits to Growth* made headlines all over the world when it was published, and is still the best-selling environmental book of all time.[2]

"It was very interesting, very frightening stuff," Ross recalled. "The press con-   2
ference was about how all these various factors — increasing population, increasing
pollution, diminishing resources — were going to hit a point of exponential takeoff."
One of the speakers at the conference was Donella Meadows, a coauthor of the book
and a pioneering environmental scientist. Sitting in the audience during her presen-
tation, Ross was struck by the contrast between the grim predictions she was
describing and the fact that she was pregnant — that, as he put it, "she had somehow
found personal hopefulness in the midst of this really massive gloom and doom." He
saw it as a small grace note, a reminder about the possibility of optimism and renewal
in even the hardest of times, and he used it as the kicker to his story. The *Voice*
printed the article on the front page. That would have been nice for Ross — except
that Donella Meadows wasn't pregnant.

Certain mistakes can actually kill us, but many, many more of them just make us   3
want to die. That's why the word "mortify" comes up so often when people talk about
their errors. Here is Ross, verbatim: "I was mortified. I mean, *mortified* mortified. I
was not a rookie. I'd been a reporter since 1961. I'd worked for the *Philadelphia Bulletin,* I'd worked for the *Washington Post.* But I'd never made an error like that, and I cannot begin to describe the embarrassment. Truth is, I'm still mortified when I talk about
it." Nearly forty years have elapsed since Ross's article was published. The world has,
in varying degrees, ignored, learned from, and defied the predictions in *The Limits to
Growth*. Donella Meadows died in 2001. Even journalism as we know it is on its way
out. Ross's embarrassment has outlived it all. When I told him the expected publication date for this book, he said, "Good — with luck I'll be dead by then."

> *"Indeed, one of our
> recurrent responses
> to error is to wish
> ourselves out of
> existence."*

Granted, Ross's mistake was particularly awk-   4
ward. But it was not particularly consequential — not
for Meadows, who was gracious about it; not for Ross;
not even for Ross's career. So wasn't wanting to die
something of an extreme reaction? Maybe. But if so, it
is an extreme reaction to which we all sometimes succumb. Indeed, one of our recurrent responses to error
is to wish ourselves out of existence. Describing the
moment of realizing certain mistakes, we say that we
wanted to crawl into a cave, or fall through a hole in the floor, or simply disappear.
And we talk about "losing face," as if our mistakes really *did* cause us to disappear — as if our identity was rubbed out by the experience of being wrong.

In addition to this death-wish response to error, we have another reaction that is   5
less drastic. But more gastric: sometimes, instead of wanting to die, we just want to

vomit. Or so one might assume from the strangely culinary vocabulary we use to talk about being wrong. In the aftermath of our mistakes, we eat crow, eat humble pie, eat our hat, or, at the other end of the sartorial menu, eat our shoe. And, of course, we eat our words. These sayings differ in their origins, but the overall implication is clear: error is both extremely unappetizing and very tough to digest. If being right is succulent, being wrong runs a narrow, unhappy gamut from nauseating to worse than death.

This is the received wisdom about error: that it is dangerous, humiliating, dis- 6
tasteful, and, all told, un-fun in the extreme. This view of error — let's call it the pessimistic model — has some merit. . . . As everyone knows, our mistakes really can be irritating or humiliating or harmful, to ourselves as well as to others. To dismiss that fact would be disingenuous, but as an overall outlook on wrongness, the pessimistic one is radically incomplete. To begin with, it obscures the fact that whatever damage can arise from erring pales in comparison to the damage that arises from our fear, dislike, and denial of erring. This fear acts as a kind of omnipurpose coagulant, hardening heart and mind, chilling our relationships with other people, and cooling our curiosity about the world.

Like many fears, the fear of being wrong stems partly from a lack of understand- 7
ing. The pessimistic model of error tells us *that* wrongness is unpleasant, but it doesn't tell us *why*, and it has nothing at all to say about errors that don't turn out to be disagreeable. To account for the breadth of our real-life experiences with wrongness, we need to pair the pessimistic outlook with another one. In this second, optimistic model of error, the experience of being wrong isn't limited to humiliation and defeat. Actually, in this model, the experience of being wrong is hardly limited at all. Surprise, bafflement, fascination, excitement, hilarity, delight: all these and more are a part of the optimistic understanding of error. This model is harder to recognize around us, since it is forever being crowded out by the noisier notion that error is dangerous, demoralizing, and shameful. But it exists nonetheless, and it exerts a subtle yet important pull both on our ideas about error and on our ideas about ourselves.

These two models of error, optimistic and pessimistic, are in perpetual tension 8
with each other. We could try to study them in isolation — the discomforts and dangers of being wrong over here, its delights and dividends over there — and we could try to adjudicate between them. But it is when we take these two models together, not when we take them apart, that we begin to understand the forces that shape how we think and feel about being wrong.

"Our errors are surely not such awfully solemn things." That cheery quote, which 9
heads this chapter, could be the motto of the optimistic model of wrongness; and its

author, the nineteenth-century philosopher and psychologist William James, could serve as its foremost spokesperson. For a representative of the pessimistic model, we might [turn] to Thomas Aquinas, the medieval monk who . . . associated error with original sin. "The mind being the faculty of truth," wrote the philosopher Leo Keeler, both summarizing and quoting Aquinas, "error cannot be its normal fruit, but will necessarily have the character of a defective byproduct, an accidental disorder, a miscarriage comparable to 'monstrous births' in nature."[3]

Defective, accidental, monstrous, a miscarriage: the message is clear enough. For Aquinas, error was not merely abhorrent but also abnormal, a perversion of the prescribed order of things. William James, had he been around, would have had none of it — none of the revulsion (this was a man whose prescription for error was "a certain lightness of heart"), and none of the business about abnormality, either. Given that all of us get things wrong again and again, how abnormal, he might have asked, can error possibly be? 10

This debate over whether error is normal or abnormal is central to the history of how we think about wrongness. What's most interesting about the debate isn't what it tells us about wrongness per se, but what it tells us about the kind of creatures we think we are and the kind of world we think we live in. Take Aquinas and James: they fundamentally disagreed, but their disagreement was only secondarily about error. The real issue was Aquinas's claim about "the mind being the faculty of truth." If you believe, as he did, that there is a truth and that (to borrow James's formulation) "our minds and it are made for each other," then error is both deplorable and difficult to explain. On the other hand, if you believe that truth is not necessarily fixed or knowable, and that the human mind, while a dazzling entity in its own right (in fact, *because* it is a dazzling entity in its own right), is not reality's looking glass — if you believe all of that, as James did, then error is both explicable and acceptable. 11

These competing ideas of error crop up in efforts to define the term, as we saw when we tried to do so ourselves. In the 1600s, France's *Larousse* dictionary defined error, rather beautifully, as "a vagabondage of the imagination, of the mind that is not subject to any rule."[4] Scarcely a hundred years later, in the same country, Denis Diderot's famed *Encyclopédie* defined it, instead, as endemic to *every* human mind, that "magic mirror" in which the real world is distorted into "shadows and monsters." These two definitions suggest two markedly different understandings of human nature. As error goes from being a hallmark of the lawless mind to our native condition, people cease to be fundamentally perfectible and become fundamentally imperfect. Meanwhile, truth goes from being a prize that can be achieved through spiritual or intellectual discipline to a fugitive that forever eludes the human mind. 12

The history of error is not an account of the shift from one of these frameworks   13
to the other. Instead, it is an ongoing, millennia-long argument between the two.
Over that time, this argument has come to be defined by several other questions, in
addition and closely related to whether screwing up is basically aberrant or basically
normal. One of these questions is whether error is with us to stay or if it can somehow be eradicated. James Sully, a British psychologist whose 1881 *Illusions* constitutes perhaps the most thoroughgoing early investigation of human error, thought
that most forms of it would eventually be overcome. Observing that "the power of
introspection is a comparatively new acquisition of the human race," Sully concluded that "as it improves, the amount of error connected with its operation may
reasonably be expected to become infinitesimal."[5]

A similar sentiment was expressed a half-century later by Joseph Jastrow, an   14
American psychologist who conceived and edited an anthology of folly across the
ages that he titled *The Story of Human Error*. A story, it might be observed, traditionally has a beginning, a middle, and an end, and Jas-
trow clearly thought we were approaching the final
chapter in the history of wrongness. Praising "the
present peak of scientific achievement," he predicted
that "such advances in the uses of mind . . . mark the
decisive stages in the elimination of error."[6] Jastrow
was inspired to write his book by a visit to the 1933
World's Fair, which was appropriate since such
events are themselves often paeans to the perfectibil-
ity of the human race. At the 1939 fair in New York, for
example, the literature at the "World of Tomorrow"
exhibit reproved its visitors for "still grant[ing] to belief or opinion the loyalty which   15
should go only to fact," while prophesying that in the future, "we will behave as the
trained scientist behaves today. We will welcome the new, test it thoroughly, and
accept it joyously, in truly scientific fashion."[7]

> *"But the idea that we can eradicate error . . . has a timeless hold on the human imagination."*

Inevitably, from the present vantage point, these rosy predictions sound hopelessly dated and naive. But the idea that we can eradicate error — through evolutionary advancement, technological innovation, establishing an ideal society, or
spreading the word of God — has a timeless hold on the human imagination.
Implicit in this idea is the belief that we should *want* to eradicate error. And, sometimes, we should: we'd all be happy to see mistakes permanently disappear from,
say, the nuclear power industry. But eradicating the entirety of error is another
matter. Practicality aside, such an objective presents three problems. The first is

that, to believe we can eradicate error, we must also believe that we can consistently distinguish between it and the truth — a faith squarely at odds with remembering that we ourselves could be wrong. Thus the catch-22 of wrongology: in order to get rid of error, we would already need to be infallible.

The second problem with this goal is that virtually all efforts at eradica-   16
tion — even genuinely well-intentioned ones — succumb to the law of unintended consequences. Take the pests out of their ecological niche, and pretty soon you won't have any hummingbirds or marmots or mountain lions, either. Even if you can't be brought to believe that error itself is a good thing, I hope to convince you . . . that it is inseparably linked to other good things, things we definitely do not want to eliminate — like, say, our intelligence.

The final problem with seeking to eradicate error is that many such efforts are   17
not well intentioned — or if they are, they tend in the direction for which good intentions are infamous. Here, for instance, is Sully, averring that error's "grosser forms manifest themselves most conspicuously in the undisciplined mind of the savage and the rustic."[8] And here is the anthropologist Ralph Linton, a contributor to Jastrow's anthology, observing (critically) that at one time, "all heathen cultures were [regarded as] at best examples of human error, while at worst they were devices of Satan, devised to keep damned souls securely in his net. In either case it was the duty of Christians to destroy them."[9] As these quotations make clear, it is alarmingly easy to impute error to those whose beliefs and backgrounds differ from our own. And, as they also show, there is a slippery slope between advocating the elimination of putatively erroneous beliefs, and advocating the elimination of the institutions, cultures, and — most alarmingly — people who hold them.

The idea that error can be eradicated, then, contains within it a frighteningly   18
reactionary impulse. And yet, at heart, it is an idea about progress: a belief that there is an apex of human achievement, and that the way to reach it is through the steady reduction and eventual elimination of mistakes. But we have another, competing idea of progress as well — one that rests not on the elimination of error but, surprisingly, on its perpetuation. This idea began to emerge during the Scientific Revolution, through that era's hallmark development, the scientific method.[10] It is a measure of the method's success (and its simplicity, in theory if not in practice) that, some 400 years later, virtually every reader of this book will have learned it in junior high school. The gist of the scientific method is that observations lead to hypotheses (which must be testable), which are then subjected to experiments (whose results must be reproducible). If all goes well, the outcome is a theory, a logically consistent, empirically tested explanation for a natural phenomenon.

As an ideal of intellectual inquiry and a strategy for the advancement of   19
knowledge, the scientific method is essentially a monument to the utility of error.
Most of us gravitate toward trying to verify our beliefs, to the extent that we bother
investigating their validity at all. But scientists gravitate toward falsification; as a
community if not as individuals, they seek to dis-
prove their beliefs. Thus, the defining feature of a
hypothesis is that it has the potential to be proven
wrong (which is why it must be both testable and
tested), and the defining feature of a theory is that it
hasn't been proven wrong yet. But the important
part is that it can be — no matter how much evidence
appears to confirm it, no matter how many experts
endorse it, no matter how much popular support it

> *"The advancement of knowledge depends on current theories collapsing."*

enjoys. In fact, not only *can* any given theory be proven wrong; . . . sooner or later, it
probably will be. And when it is, the occasion will mark the success of science, not
its failure. This was the pivotal insight of the Scientific Revolution: that the
advancement of knowledge depends on current theories collapsing in the face of
new insights and discoveries. In this model of progress, errors do not lead us away
from the truth. Instead, they edge us incrementally toward it.

During and after the Scientific Revolution, the leading minds of Western   20
Europe took this principle and generalized it. As they saw it, not only scientific theories but also political, social, and even aesthetic ideas were subject to this same pattern of collapse, replacement, and advancement. In essence, these thinkers
identified the problem of error-blindness on a generational and communal scale. We
can no more spot the collective errors of our culture than we can spot our own private ones, but we can be sure that they are lurking somewhere.

The thinkers responsible for this insight came by it honestly. They lived at a   21
time when fifteen centuries of foundational truths had lately been disproved or
displaced by a staggering influx of new information: about previously unknown
plants and animals, about geology and geography, about the structure of the universe, about the breadth and diversity of human culture. In our own globally intimate, Google-mapped era, it is almost impossible to fathom the degree of
intellectual and emotional disruption all that new information must have occa-
sioned. I suppose that if tomorrow a UFO landed in Pittsburgh, I might experience a comparable combination of stunning error and thrilling possibility.
Certainly I would have to rebuild my understanding of the cosmos from the
ground up.

Faced with that task, many of these thinkers concluded that the best and safest 22 tool for this sweeping intellectual reconstruction was doubt: deep, systematic, abiding, all-encompassing doubt. Thus Michel de Montaigne, the great Renaissance philosopher and essayist, inscribed above the door of his study *que sais-je?* — what do I know? And thus Descartes set himself the task of doubting *everything*, up to and including his own existence. . . . These thinkers weren't nihilists, not even skeptics. They believed in truth, and they wanted to discover it. But they were chastened by the still-palpable possibility of drastic error, and they understood that, from a sufficiently distant vantage point, even their most cherished convictions might come to look like mistakes.

What was new and radical about this perspective wasn't the recognition of how 23 difficult it is to distinguish error from truth. That idea is at least as old as Plato. It appears in the Bible as well — for instance, as the question of how to tell false prophets from true. ("For Satan himself masquerades as an angel of light," we read in 2 Corinthians.[11]) Renaissance and Enlightenment thinkers would also have been familiar with this idea from the work of their medieval counterparts, who often characterized errors as *ignes fatui* — literally fool's fires, although often translated as false or phantom fires.[12] Today we know these false fires as will o' the wisps: mysterious wandering lights that, in folklore, lead unwary travelers astray, typically into the depths of a swamp or over the edge of a cliff. Less romantically, false fires also referred to the ones lit by bandits to fool travelers into thinking they were approaching an inn or town. In either case, the metaphor says it all: error, disguised as the light of truth, leads directly into trouble. But Enlightenment thinkers mined a previously unnoticed aspect of this image. Error, they observed, wasn't simply darkness, the absolute absence of the light of truth. Instead, it shed a light of its own. True, that light might be flickering or phantasmagoric, but it was still a source of illumination. In this model, error is not the opposite of truth so much as asymptotic to it — a kind of human approximation of truth, a truth-for-now.

This is another important dispute in the history of how we think about being 24 wrong: whether error represents an obstacle in the path toward truth, or the path itself. The former idea is the conventional one. The latter, as we have seen, emerged during the Scientific Revolution and continued to evolve throughout the Enlightenment. But it didn't really reach its zenith until the early nineteenth century, when the French mathematician and astronomer Pierre-Simon Laplace refined the theory of the distribution of errors, illustrated by the now-familiar bell curve. Also known as the error curve or the normal distribution, the bell curve is a way of aggregating individually meaningless, idiosyncratic, or inaccurate data points in order to generate a meaningful and accurate big picture.[13]

Laplace, for instance, used the bell curve to determine the precise orbit of the 25
planets. Such movements had been recorded since virtually the beginning of history,
but those records were unreliable, afflicted by the distortion intrinsic to all human
observation. By using the normal distribution to graph these individually imperfect
data points, Laplace was able to generate a far more precise picture of the galaxy.
Unlike earlier thinkers, who had sought to improve their accuracy by getting rid of
error, Laplace realized that you should try to get *more* error: aggregate enough flawed
data, and you get a glimpse of the truth. "The genius of statistics, as Laplace defined
it, was that it did not ignore errors; it quantified them," the writer Louis Menand
observed. "... The right answer is, in a sense, a function of the mistakes."[14] For thinkers of that particular historical moment, who believed in the existence of an ordained
truth while simultaneously recognizing the omnipresence of error, the bell curve
represented a kind of holy grail: wrongness contained, curtailed, and coaxed into
revealing its opposite.[15]

A century later, the idea that errors reveal rather than obscure the truth gained a 26
powerful new proponent in Freud. But while earlier thinkers had been interested
primarily in external truths — in the facts of the world as ordained by nature or
God — Freud's domain was the internal. The truths he cared about are the ones we
stash away in our unconscious. By definition, those truths are inaccessible to the
reasoning mind — but, Freud argued in *The Psychopathology of Everyday Life*, we
can catch occasional glimpses of them, and one way we do so is through error. Today,
we know these truth-revealing errors as Freudian slips — as the old saw goes, saying
one thing and meaning your mother. According to Freud, these seemingly trivial
mistakes are neither trivial nor even, in any standard sense, mistakes. That is, they
aren't the result of accident or absentmindedness or the misfiring of a stray neuron
or any such mundane cause. Instead, they arise from — and therefore illuminate —
a submerged but significant psychic truth. In this view, such errors are envoys from
our own innermost universe; and, however garbled their messages may be, they contain valuable information about what's really going on in there.

In addition to these slips, Freud also thought there were a few other avenues by 27
which the secret truths of the unconscious could seep out. One of these, dreams, is
relevant to us all. Another, relevant only to the unfortunate few, is insanity. At first,
dreams and madness might not seem terribly germane. . . . But what these two conditions have in common with each other is the misperception of reality — which, you'll
recall, is also one definition (indeed, the earliest and most pervasive one) of being
wrong. To better understand our mundane misperceptions, it pays to look closely at
our extreme ones. So that is where I want to turn now — to dreams, drug trips, hallu-

cinations, and madness; and, by way of those examples, to a closer look at the notion that, through error, we perceive the truth.

However far-fetched this connection between wrongness and whacked-outness 28 might seem, you yourself invoke it routinely. I say this with some confidence, because our everyday ways of thinking and talking about error borrow heavily from the argot of altered states. For starters, we commonly (if crudely) com-

> *"We commonly (if crudely) compare being wrong to being high."*

pare being wrong to being high. Try saying something patently erroneous to a member of my generation, and you'd better be prepared to hear "what are you smoking?" or "are you on crack?" Likewise, we seldom hesitate to impute insanity to people who strongly hold beliefs that we strongly reject. (Witness all the mudslinging about "liberal lunatics" and "right-wing wingnuts.") Finally, we talk about snapping out of our false beliefs as if they were trances and waking up from them as if they were dreams.

Of all these analogies, the association between erring and dreaming is the most 29 persistent and explicit. "Do you not see," asked the eleventh-century Islamic philosopher and theologian Abu Hamid Muhammad al-Ghazali, "that while asleep you assume your dreams to be indisputably real? Once awake, you recognize them for what they are — baseless chimeras."[16] The same could be said, he observed, of our waking beliefs. "In relation to your present state they may be real; but it is possible also that you may enter upon another state of being" — and from the vantage point of that future state, he continued, your present one will seem as self-evidently false as your dreams do when you awake.

Although we treat errors and altered states as analogous in certain ways, there is 30 one important respect in which we treat them very differently. As I began . . . by noting, mistakes, even minor ones, often make us feel like we're going to be sick, or like we want to die. But altered states — some of which really *can* sicken or kill us — frequently enthrall us. We keep journals of our dreams and recount them to our friends and family (to say nothing of our therapists). We feel that our lives are illuminated and enriched by them, and we regard those who seldom remember theirs as, in some small but important way, impoverished. We are highly motivated to seek out the reality-altering power of drugs, despite the danger of overdose, addiction, or arrest. The delirium of extreme illness is arguably even riskier, not to mention harder to come by and all-around less desirable. Yet I will say this: once, while running a very high fever in a tropical rainforest, I carried on a long conversation with the poet Samuel Taylor Coleridge, who was sitting on the end of my bed, knitting. Coleridge, of course, was long dead, and as for me, I've never been sicker. But I've almost never been so mesmerized or elated, either — and, since then, I haven't once taken medicine to reduce a fever. If, on those occasions when I'm already sick anyway, I could take a pill to *increase* my temperature instead, to nudge it up just into the zone of hallucination, I would seriously consider doing so. Granted, it's not what the doctor ordered — in fact, it's plainly idiotic — but that's the point. Altered states are so compelling that we often do what we can, wisely or otherwise, to produce, reproduce, and prolong them.

The attraction of an altered state is not, as one might initially imagine, just its 31 pure weirdness — how far it diverges from everyday life. Instead, it is the combination of this weirdness and its *proximity* to everyday life. What is altered, in an altered state, are the elements of the world, the relations among them, and the rules that govern them. But the way we experience these states remains essentially unchanged. The tools we use to gauge and understand the sober world — our reason, our emotions, and above all our senses — are largely unimpaired and sometimes even enhanced in the trippy one. As a result, these false worlds have all the intimacy, intensity, and physicality — in short, all the indicators of reality — of the true one.

What does it mean about the realness of reality if it is so susceptible to altera- 32 tion — by a dream, a drug, a difference of just a few degrees in body temperature? And, conversely, what does it mean about the supposedly unreal if it is so easy to conjure and so intensely convincing? These questions have haunted our collective imagination from *A Midsummer Night's Dream* to *The Matrix* (both of which, incidentally, hinge on drug trips). One of the most consistent answers — and the crucial one, for my purposes — is that the false and the true are reversed: that the unreal is, so to speak, the real real. Freud, as I've already noted, believed that the false worlds of our dreams reveal deep and hidden truths about ourselves. So did the writer Artemidorus Daldianus, who, almost two thousand years earlier, penned the *Oneirocritica* — a Greek *Interpretation of Dreams*. And they weren't alone. Virtually every culture in every era has believed that dreams express otherwise inaccessible truths about the dreamer: about her forgotten or unknown past, her secret beliefs and desires, her destiny. In the same vein, virtually every culture in every era (with the halfway exception of the industrialized West) has regarded visions and hallucinations as revealing the otherwise inaccessible truths of the universe. From Siberian shamans to Aztec priests to the Merry Pranksters to spiritually inclined potheads the world over (ancient Christians, early Jews, Scythians, Sikhs, Sufis, and Rastafarians, to name just a few), we have regarded our drugs as entheogens — substances that can lay bare the truth of the cosmos and show us the face of God.

If dreams and drug states create acute but temporary alterations in our under- 33 standing of reality, the acute and ongoing version is insanity. You might think (and hope) that insanity would take us even further away from everyday error, but instead it brings us full circle. Diderot's *Encyclopédie* defined madness as the act of depart- ing from reason "with confidence and in the firm conviction that one is following it."[17] Maybe so, but if that's how we go crazy, it is also how we go wrong. The more recent French philosopher and historian Michel Foucault called insanity "the pur- est and most complete form of *quid pro quo*" — of taking one thing for another. To take something for something it is not: If that's not error, what is?

Ultimately, only three factors seem to distinguish the false reality of madness 34 from the false reality of wrongness. The first is purity, as in Foucault's "purest form": insanity is error undiluted. The second is consistency: one noted early classifier of dis- ease, the eighteenth-century physician François Boissier de Sauvages, described the insane as those "who persist in some notable error." The third factor concerns sub- stance: which *quid* you take for which *quo*. We can be wrong about all manner of things, even persistently and purely wrong about them, while still retaining our claim to san- ity — just so long as enough other people are wrong about them, too. This point is made by the medical definition of delusion ("a false belief *not shared by others*"),[18] but not nearly as well as it was made by the Renaissance scholar Desiderius Erasmus in *The Praise of Folly*. "The reason a person who believes he sees a woman when in reality he is looking at a gourd is called crazy is because this is something beyond usual experi- ence," he wrote.[19] "However, when a person thinks his wife, who is enjoyed by many, to be an ever-faithful Penelope, he is not called insane at all" — although he *is* called wrong — "because people know that this is a common thing in marriage." In other words, error in extremis — extremely pure, extremely persistent, or extremely pecu- liar — becomes insanity. Madness is radical wrongness.

Like all equations, this one is reversible. If madness is radical wrongness, being 35 wrong is minor madness. Thus Sully, the author of *Illusions*, conceived of error as a "border-land between perfectly sane and vigorous mental life and dementia."[20] Something of the same attitude is reflected in the Romance languages, in which being right is rendered as being sane: in French, *j'ai raison*; in Spanish, *tengo razon*. Translation: I have reason on my side, I'm in possession of my senses — whereas you, my errant friend, are straying near the borders of crazy. Minor madness can also be an apt description of how being wrong actually *feels*. . . .

We already saw that hallucinations and dreams are widely regarded as revealing 36 greater truths. So too with madness. Societies throughout the ages have nurtured the belief that the insane among us illuminate things as they truly are, despite their own ostensibly deranged relationship to reality. That's why, in literature, it is always the fools (those who never had any sense in the first place) and the madmen (those who lost it) who speak truth to power. (Children — i.e., those who have not yet reached the age of reason — sometimes play this role as well.) This narrative of wrongness as rightness might have achieved its apotheosis in *King Lear*, a play that features a real madman (Lear, after he loses it), a sane man disguised as a madman (Edgar), a blind man (Gloucester), and a fool (the Fool). I don't know where else so many characters have been set in orbit around the idea of truth, or where else truth itself has been so set on its head. Here, wisdom is folly ("for wise men are grown foppish," observes the Fool),[21] and folly is wisdom ("This [Fool] is not altogether fool, my lord," the king's courtier dryly notes). Blindness is insight: "I stumbled when I saw," says Gloucester, who perceives the truth only after he has lost his eyes. And insanity is intellectual and moral clarity: it is only after Lear loses his daughters and his senses that he understands what he has done and can feel both loss and love.

This idea — that from error springs insight — is a hallmark of the optimistic 37 model of wrongness. It holds even for mundane mistakes, which is why proponents of this model (myself included) see erring as vital to any process of invention and creation. The example of altered states simply throws this faith into relief: make the error extreme enough, depart not a little way but all the way from agreed-upon reality, and suddenly the humdrum of human fallibility gives way to an ecstasy of understanding. In place of humiliation and falsehood, we find fulfillment and illumination. We hear this strangely intimate relationship between error and truth in the double meaning of the word "vision," which conveys both delusion and revelation.

Unfortunately, as proponents of the pessimistic model of wrongness will be 38 quick to point out, the reassuring notion that error yields insight does not always comport with experience. Sometimes, being wrong feels like the *death* of insight — the moment when a great idea or a grounding belief collapses out from under us. And sometimes, too, our mistakes take too great a toll to be redeemed by easy assurances of lessons learned. Here, as everywhere, the pessimistic and optimistic models part ways on the fundamental meaning of wrongness. Our errors expose the real nature of the universe — or they obscure it. They lead us toward the truth, or they lead us astray. They are the opposite of reality, or its almost indistinguishable approximation — certainly as close as we mere mortals can ever hope to get. They are abnormalities we should work to eliminate, or inevitabilities we should strive to accept. They are essentially "monstrous." They are quintessentially human.

Together, these two conflicting models form the backbone of our understanding 39 of error. Even if we've never contemplated them before, they account for the contradictions in how we think about being wrong, and for the varying ways we experience it. . . . I want to introduce two figures who vividly embody these different models of wrongness. . . . These figures do not actually exist. They are creatures of mythology, and they do not so much err as animate — and illuminate — the ways we think about error.

In ancient Indo-European, the ancestral language of nearly half of today's global population, the word *er* meant "to move," "to set in motion," or simply "to go."[22] (Spanish speakers will recognize it as *ir*.) That root gave rise to the Latin verb *errare*, meaning to wander or, more rakishly, to roam. The Latin, in turn, gave us the English word "erratic," used to describe movement that is unpredictable or aimless. And, of course, it gave us "error." From the beginning, then, the idea of error has contained a sense of motion: of wandering, seeking, going astray. Implicitly, what we are seeking — and what we have strayed from — is the truth.[23]

In the two archetypal wanderers of Western culture, we see clearly the contrasting ideas that shape our understanding of error. One of these is the knight errant and the other is the *juif errant* — the wandering Jew.[24] The latter figure, a staple of anti-Semitic propaganda, derives from a medieval Christian legend in which a Jew, encountering Jesus on the road to the crucifixion, taunts him for moving so slowly under the weight of the cross. In response, Jesus condemns the man to roam the earth until the end of time. As the historian David Bates has observed, the wandering Jew "literally embodied, for Christian Europeans, the individual separated from the truth." In this model, erring is inextricably linked to both sin and exile. To err is to experience estrangement from God and alienation among men.

The knight errant is also a staple of medieval legend, but otherwise he could scarcely be more different. Where the wandering Jew is defined by his sin, the knight errant is distinguished by his virtue; he is explicitly and unfailingly on the side of good. His most famous representatives include Galahad, Gawain, and Lancelot, those most burnished of knights in shining armor. (A bit further afield, they also include Don Quixote, who, as both knight errant and utter lunatic, deserves his own special place in the pantheon of wrongology.) Although far from home, the knight is hardly in exile, and still less in disgrace. Unlike the *juif errant*, who is commanded to wander and does so aimlessly and in misery, the knight errant is on a quest: he wanders on purpose and with purpose, as well as with pleasure. He is driven, like all travelers, by curiosity, by the desire to experience something more of the world.

It will be clear, I hope, that I am not invoking these archetypes to endorse their obvious prejudices. Instead, I'm interested in the way those prejudices lend meaning to our two main models of wrongness. As embodied by the wandering Jew, erring is both loathsome and agonizing — a deviation from the true and the good, a public spectacle, and a private misery. This image of wrongness is disturbing, especially given the all-too-frequent fate of the non-mythological Jews: abhorred, exiled, very nearly eradicated. Yet it far more closely resembles our everyday understanding of wrongness than do the virtue and heroism of the knight errant. If this bleak idea of error speaks to us, it is because we recognize in the wandering Jew something of our own soul when we have erred. Sometimes, being wrong really does feel like being exiled: from our community, from our God, even — and perhaps most painfully — from our own best-known self.

> *"Sometimes, being wrong really does feel like being exiled."*

So we should acknowledge the figure of the wandering Jew as a good description 44 of how it can feel to be wrong. But that doesn't mean we need to accept it as the final word on error's essential meaning and moral status. For one thing, it's hard to claim *any* fixed meaning or moral status for error when we have such radically competing ideas about it. In light of that, why cleave any more closely than necessary to the most disagreeable vision of wrongness around? We have, after all, a better alternative. In fact, the idea of erring embodied by the wandering knight is not just preferable to the one embodied by the wandering Jew. It is also, and somewhat remarkably, preferable to not erring at all. To err is to wander, and wandering is the way we discover the world; and, lost in thought, it is also the way we discover ourselves. Being right might be gratifying, but in the end it is static, a mere statement. Being wrong is hard and humbling, and sometimes even dangerous, but in the end it is a journey, and a story. Who really wants to stay home and be right when you can don your armor, spring up on your steed, and go forth to explore the world? True, you might get lost along the way, get stranded in a swamp, have a scare at the edge of a cliff; thieves might steal your gold, brigands might imprison you in a cave, sorcerers might turn you into a toad — but what of that? To fuck up is to find adventure: it is in that spirit that this . . . is written.

Notes

1. This and all the quotations from William James are from his "Will to Believe," a lecture he delivered at the Philosophical Clubs of Yale and Brown Universities in 1896. The page citations . . . are from William James, *The Will to Believe and Other Essays in Popular Philosophy* (Longmans, Green and Company, 1921). The above quotation appears on p. 19.

2. Ross initially shared his story with me via email. The quotations here are from a subsequent phone interview.

3. Leo W. Keeler, *The Problem of Error from Plato to Kant: A Historical and Critical Study* (Apud Aedes Pontificiae Universitatis Gregorianae, 1934), 87.

4. I found both this definition and the one from Diderot's *Encyclopédie* in David Bates's *Enlightenment Aberrations: Error and Revolution in France* (Cornell University Press, 2002), an immensely useful intellectual history of error. The first definition appears on p. 20, the second on p. 25.

5. James Sully, *Illusions: A Psychological Study* (IndyPublish, undated), 116. Sully goes on to make a much more extensive case that error is on the decline in the human species, an argument he bases in large part on the then-nascent field of evolutionary theory. "All correspondence, [the evolutionist] tells us, means fitness to external conditions and practical efficiency, all want of correspondence practical incompetence. Consequently, those individuals in whom the correspondence was more complete and exact would have an advantage in the struggle for existence and so tend to be preserved. . . . It may be argued, the forces at work in the action of man on man, of society on the individual, in the way of assimilating belief, must tend, in the long run, to bring about a coincidence between representations and facts. Thus, in another way, natural selection would help to adjust our ideas to realities, and to exclude the possibility of anything like a permanent common error." Then there's just the sheer matter of practice: "The exercise of a function tends to the development of that function. Thus, our acts of perception must become more exact by mere repetition. . . . For external relations which are permanent will, in the long run, stamp themselves on our nervous and mental structure more deeply and indelibly than relations which are variable and accidental." See pp. 192–193.

6. Joseph Jastrow, *The Story of Human Error: False Leads in the Stages of Science* (D. Appleton–Century Company, Inc., 1936), 11. The book is behemoth in scope — Jastrow takes "science" to include anthropology, sociology, psychology, and psychiatry, in addition to the more obvious suspects — but his introduction is both short and charming. He conceives of his work "as a project in errorology," which sounds akin to my own, but he is interested largely in errors that remained unknown to their makers and were revealed only to posterity.

7. Roland Barker, ed., *Official Guide Book: New York World's Fair 1939: The World of Tomorrow* (Exposition Publications, 1939), 2.

8. Sully, 186.

9. Ralph Linton, "Error in Anthropology," in Jastrow, ed., 298.

10. Systematic methods for inquiring into the natural world have been around for ages: ancient Greek naturalists practiced a form of empiricism, and medieval Muslim scientists developed a method of inquiry that relied on experimentation to weigh competing hypotheses. But the scientific method as we understand it today was introduced to the world through the work of Francis Bacon in his 1620 *Novum Organum*, and René Descartes in his 1637 *Discourse on the Method*. Whether or not this method has ever been practiced as such (that is, to what extent scientists, especially as individuals, seek to replicate experiments and falsify hypotheses) is an open question, as Thomas Kuhn made abundantly clear in *The Structure of Scientific Revolutions*. But my point here concerns the method as an intellectual ideal more than an actual practice.

11. *The Bible, New International Version* (HarperTorch, 1993), 2 Corinthians 11:14–15.

12. Bates, 46.

13. Bates touches on this development toward the end of *Enlightenment Aberrations* (248), but my primary source here was Steven M. Stigler's *History of Statistics: The Measurement of Uncertainty Before 1900* (Harvard University Press, 1990), especially 31–38 and 109–148.

14. Louis Menand, *The Metaphysical Club: A Story of Ideas in America* (Farrar, Straus and Giroux, 2002), 182.

15. If Laplace helped catapult the bell curve into fame, another astronomer, the Belgian Adolphe Quetelet, helped it achieve something closer to infamy. Quetelet gathered data about people — about our heights and criminal records and number of children and age at death — and graphed them the way Laplace had graphed the stars. In the theory of the distribution of errors, he realized, the particular quirks and characteristics of any given human represented the errors: deviations from a norm that only became visible when all those quirks were aggregated. This innovation solidified an association, implicit since antiquity, between being deviant and being wrong — and, conversely, between being normal and being right. (It was Quetelet who came up with that stock character of statistics, the "average man.")

Many observers have been troubled by the application of the bell curve to the social sciences, since plotting people on a curve like so many data points tends to create an idea of an average or optimal version of a given human characteristic — with correspondingly unwelcome consequences for those who find themselves on the tail end of the curve. In the worst-case scenario, those consequences include stigmatizing variation, equating difference with deviance, and seeking to eradicate anything that diverges from the ideal: in short, all the classic signs of fascism. That's why dystopian literature is full of societies consisting entirely of "average men," clonelike copies of eerily bland, interchangeable people. Nor is this problem limited to literature; history bears tragic witness to the urge to bring these ostensibly ideal societies into being.

This capacity to treat human beings as potentially erroneous data points is why some thinkers blame the intellectual legacy of the Enlightenment for the genocidal horrors of the twentieth century. In more conventional historical accounts, the Enlightenment represents the high-water mark of Western culture, and all subsequent outbreaks of barbarism stem from the abdication of its central values. But other thinkers hold that Enlightenment values are the *source* of that barbarism. They argue that, by elevating cold rationality above all other virtues, esteeming abstract and supposedly universal truths over individual lives, and imposing the values and methods of science on all of human activity, the Enlightenment created the motive, the means, and the justification for systemic violence. This criticism was first articulated during the French Revolution, whose stunning brutality was justified as necessary to the establishment of a perfect government. Since there can be no rational objection to a perfect government (the argument went), all political opposition was dangerously wrong and could — indeed must — be eliminated. This criticism of the Enlightenment was revived (most famously by the German philosopher Theodor Adorno and the associated Frankfurt School of philosophers) in the wake of the twentieth century's spasms of ideologically motivated, mechanically enabled, perfection-minded violence. Incidentally, David Bates, whom I cite above, locates the intellectual roots of such violence later, with the rise of positivism in the nineteenth century.

16. Translations of al-Ghazali vary widely, down to the titles of his works and the spelling of his name. I have used two different translations . . . : Abu Hamid Muhammad Al Ghazzali, *The Confessions of Al Ghazzali*, Claud Field, trans. (Cosimo, Inc., 2007) and Abu Hamid Muhammad Al-Ghazali, *Al-Ghazali's Path to Sufism: His Deliverance from Error*, R. J. McCarthy, trans. (Fons Vitae, 2006). This quotation is from the first one and appears on p. 17. For comparison's sake, the same passage in the other translation is rendered as follows: "Don't you see that when you are asleep you believe certain things and imagine certain circumstances and believe that they are fixed and lasting and entertain no doubts about that being their status? Then you wake up and know that all your imaginings and beliefs were groundless and unsubstantial. So . . . what assurance have you that you may not suddenly experience a state which would have the same relation to your waking state as the latter has to your dreaming, and your waking state would be dreaming in relation to that new and further state?" (p. 22).

17. Both this definition and the quotation from François Boissier de Sauvages in the next paragraph appear in Michel Foucault's *Madness and Civilization: A History of Insanity in the Age of Reason*, Richard Howard, trans. (Vintage Books, 1965), 104. The quotation from Foucault in this same paragraph appears on p. 33.

18. See for instance Caroline Bunker Rosdahl and Mary T. Kowalski, *Textbook of Basic Nursing* (Lippincott Williams & Wilkins; Ninth Edition, 2007), 1469. The italics are mine.

19. Desiderius Erasmus, *The Praise of Folly*, in *The Essential Erasmus*, John P. Dolan, trans. (The New American Library, 1964), 128.

20. Sully, 3.

21. William Shakespeare, *King Lear*, Russell Fraser, ed. (Signet Classics, 1998). The quotations in this paragraph appear on pp. 30 and 29, respectively.

22. See for instance the entry on "to move" at the Center for Indo-European Language and Culture of the University of Texas at Austin's Linguistics Research Center (http://www.utexas.edu/cola/centers/lrc/iedocctr/ie-ling/ie-sem/MO/MO_MO.html), and their chart of Proto-Indo-European root words (http://www.utexas.edu/cola/centers/lrc/ielex/PokornyMaster-X.html).

23. Here, too, we can detect the intertwined histories of wrongness and madness. The word "hallucinate" comes from the Latin meaning to wander mentally, while "raving" comes from "roving."

24. I am indebted to David Bates for this insight. His discussion of the etymology of "error" and of these two wanderers appears on pp. 19–21. The quote appears on p. 21.

Questions for Discussion and Writing

1. Schulz alludes to and quotes from so many sources that a reader could lose sight of Schulz's own argument. What is the positive value and what are the uses of error, in Schulz's own view? What, according to her, might be worth celebrating about error?

2. It's a cliché, but it's true: we all make mistakes. Recall an instance in your experience when you were wrong. As best you can, describe how the error came about and how you felt about it. Which of the two models of wrongness that Schulz describes comes closest to describing how you felt? Would the other model of wrongness, had you known about it, have caused you to feel differently?

3. Schulz identifies two broad models of wrongness—one that seeks chiefly to eradicate error and one that, at least in some sense, embraces error. Schulz extrapolates the two models from a wide array of sources that (as she sees it)

embody or exhibit one model or the other. So several different versions of each model are described in the essay; for example, the scientific method is one model that embraces error, and the skepticism of Michel de Montaigne is another approach that also embraces error.

Consider the four other essays included in this part of the book. What "model of wrongness" might each be said to embody? Does Schulz offer a specific example of a model of wrongness that comes closest to the approach or method taken by the essay? Next, consider your own nonfiction writing—academic and nonacademic. (For simplicity, you might choose two examples that you recall clearly.) Which model of wrongness do your own works exhibit?

Jane Tompkins

Jane Tompkins (b. 1940) completed her undergraduate degree at Bryn Mawr University and earned a PhD in English from Yale University in 1966. She has taught English at Temple, Columbia, and Duke universities, among other institutions. She is currently retired from teaching and lives in Florida and New York.

Her writing in the 1980s—articles, edited collections, and the book *Sensational Designs: The Cultural Work of American Fiction, 1790–1860* (1985)—quickly established her reputation as a literary critic and theorist. But as she explained in a pivotal and influential 1987 essay, "Me and My Shadow," she eventually became attracted to a different kind of scholarly writing, one that allowed greater freedom and reflected the genuine connection she felt between the several dimensions of her life—as a teacher, as a critic and theorist, and as a private individual. In "Me and My Shadow," she announced, "The public-private dichotomy, which is to say the public-private *hierarchy*, is a founding condition of female oppression. I say to hell with it. The reason I feel embarrassed at my own attempts to speak personally in a professional context is that I have been conditioned to feel that way. That's all there is to it." While some have criticized this work for lacking the rigor of her earlier scholarship, others see it as achieving a degree of integrity and authenticity not always evident in academic writing.

Tompkins's memoir *A Life in School: What the Teacher Learned* (1996) recounts her experiences in the classroom from kindergarten to full professorship at Duke University, and along the way she challenges academic conventions as she searches for more humane approaches to both teaching and scholarship. It might be considered a book-length reflection on the questions she first raised in "Me and My Shadow."

This essay, from her 1992 book *West of Everything: The Inner Life of Westerns* (nominated for a Pulitzer Prize for nonfiction), explores her responses to the exhibits at the Buffalo Bill Historical Center in Cody, Wyoming, and to her subsequent reading about Buffalo Bill that her visit inspired. While she does not hesitate to express strong views, the essay is less concerned with making an argument than with raising questions, and it seems to invite readers to think the issues through for themselves—much as Tompkins strove to do as a teacher.

At the Buffalo Bill Museum, June 1988

The video at the entrance to the Buffalo Bill Historical Center says that Buffalo Bill 1 was the most famous American of his time, that by 1900 more than a billion words had been written about him, and that he had a progressive vision of the West. Buffalo Bill had worked as a cattle driver, a wagoneer, a Pony Express rider, a buffalo hunter for the railroad, a hunting guide, an army scout and sometime Indian fighter; he wrote dime novels about himself and an autobiography by the age of thirty-four, by which time he was already famous; and then he began another set of careers, first as an actor, performing on the urban stage in wintertime melodramatic representations of what he actually earned a living at in the summer (scouting and leading hunting expeditions), and finally becoming the impresario of his great Wild West show, a form of entertainment he invented and carried on as actor, director, and all-around idea man for thirty years. Toward the end of his life he founded the town of Cody, Wyoming, to which he gave, among other things, two hundred thousand dollars. Strangely enough, it was as a progressive civic leader that Bill Cody wanted to be remembered. "I don't want to die," the video at the entrance quotes him as saying, "and have people say — oh, there goes another old showman. . . . I would like people to say — this is the man who opened Wyoming to the best of civilization."

"The best of civilization." This was the phrase that rang in my head as I moved 2 through the museum, which is one of the most disturbing places I have ever visited. It is also a wonderful place. It is four museums in one: the Whitney Gallery of Western Art, which houses artworks on Western subjects; the Buffalo Bill Museum proper, which memorializes Cody's life; the Plains Indian Museum, which exhibits artifacts of American Indian civilization; and the Winchester Arms Museum, a collection of firearms historically considered.

The whole operation is extremely well designed and well run, from the video 3 program at the entrance that gives an overview of all four museums, to the fresh-faced young attendants wearing badges that say "Ask Me," to the museum shop stacked with books on Western Americana, to the ladies room — a haven of satiny marble, shining mirrors, and flattering light. Among other things, the museum is admirable for its effort to combat prevailing stereotypes about the "winning of the West," a phrase it self-consciously places in quotation marks. There are placards declaring that all history is a matter of interpretation, and that the American West is a source of myth. Everywhere, except perhaps in the Winchester Arms Museum, where the rhetoric is different, you feel the effort of the museum staff to reach out to the public, to be clear, to be accurate, to be fair, not to condescend — in short, to educate in the best sense of the term.

On the day I went, the museum was featuring an exhibition of Frederic 4
Remington's works. Two facts about Remington make his work different from that of artists usually encountered in museums. The first is that Remington's paintings and statues function as a historical record. Their chief attraction has always been that they transcribe scenes and events that have vanished from the earth. The second fact, related to this, is the brutality of their subject matter. Remington's work makes you pay attention to what is happening in the painting or the piece of statuary. When you look at his work you cannot escape from the subject.

Consequently, as I moved through the exhibit, the wild contortions of the buck- 5
ing broncos, the sinister expression invariably worn by the Indians, and the killing of animals and men made the placards discussing Remington's use of the "lost wax" process seem strangely disconnected. In the face of unusual violence, or implied violence, their message was: what is important here is technique. Except in the case of paintings showing the battle of San Juan Hill, where white Americans were being killed, the material accompanying Remington's works did not refer to the subject matter of the paintings and statues themselves. Nevertheless, an undertone of disquiet ran beneath the explanations; at least I thought I detected one. Someone had taken the trouble to ferret out Remington's statement of horror at the slaughter on San Juan Hill; someone had also excerpted the judgment of art critics commending Remington for the lyricism, interiority, and mystery of his later canvasses — pointing obliquely to the fascination with bloodshed that preoccupied his earlier work.

The uneasiness of the commentary, and my uneasiness with it, were nothing com- 6
pared to the blatant contradictions in the paintings themselves. A pastel palette, a sunlit stop-action haze, murderous movement arrested under a lazy sky, flattened onto canvas and fixed in azure and ochre — two opposed impulses nestle here momentarily. The tension that keeps them from splitting apart is what holds the viewer's gaze.

The most excruciating example of what I mean occurs in the first painting in the 7
exhibit. Entitled *His First Lesson*, it shows a horse standing saddled but riderless, the white of the horse's eye signaling his fear. A man using an instrument to tighten the horse's girth, at arm's length, backs away from the reaction he clearly anticipates, while the man who holds the horse's halter is doing the same. But what can they be

afraid of? For the horse's right rear leg is tied a foot off the ground by a rope that is also tied around his neck. He can't move. That is the whole point.

His First Lesson. Whose? And what lesson, exactly? How to stand still when terrified? How not to break away when they come at you with strange instruments? How to be obedient? How to behave? It is impossible not to imagine that Remington's obsession with physical cruelty had roots somewhere in his own experience. Why else, in statue after statue, is the horse rebelling? The bucking bronco, symbol of the state of Wyoming, on every license plate, on every sign for every bar, on every belt buckle, mug, and decal — this image Remington cast in bronze over and over again. There is a wild diabolism in the bronzes; the horse and rider seem one thing, not so much rider and ridden as a single bolt of energy gone crazy and caught somehow, complicatedly, in a piece of metal.

8

His First Lesson, by Frederic Remington, 1903. Oil on canvas.

In the paintings, it is different — more subtle and bizarre. The cavalry on its way 9
to a massacre, sweetly limned, softly tinted, poetically seized in mid-career, and
gently laid on the two-dimensional surface. There is about these paintings of military men in the course of performing their deadly duty an almost maternal tenderness. The idealization of the cavalrymen in their dusty uniforms on their gallant
horses has nothing to do with patriotism; it is pure love.

Remington's paintings and statues, as shown in this exhibition, embody everything 10
that was objectionable about his era in American history. They are imperialist and racist;
they glorify war and the torture and killing of animals;
there are no women in them anywhere. Never the West
as garden, never as pastoral, never as home. But in their
aestheticization of violent life, Remington's pictures
speak (to me, at least) of some other desire. The maternal tenderness is not an accident, nor is the beauty of the
afternoons or the warmth of the desert sun. In them
Remington plays the part of the preserver, as if by catching the figures in color and line he could save their lives
and absorb some of that life into himself.

> *"Remington's paintings and statues . . . embody everything that was objectionable about his era in American history."*

In one painting that particularly repulsed and 11
drew me, a moose is outlined against the evening sky
at the brink of a lake. He looks expectantly into the distance. Behind him and to one
side, hidden from his view and only just revealed to ours, for it is dark there, is a
hunter poised in the back of a canoe, rifle perfectly aimed. We look closer; the title of
the picture is *Coming to the Call.* Ah, now we see. This is a sadistic scene. The hunter
has lured the moose to his death. But wait a moment. Isn't the sadism really directed
at us? First we see the glory of the animal; Remington has made it as noble as he
knows how. Then we see what is going to happen. The hunter is one up on the moose,
but Remington is one up on us. He makes us feel the pain of the anticipated killing,
and makes us want to hold it off, to preserve the moose, just as he has done. Which
way does the painting cut? Does it go against the hunter — who represents us, after
all — or does it go against the moose who came to the call? Who came, to what call?
Did Remington come to the West in response to it — to whatever the moose represents or to whatever the desire to kill the moose represents? But he hasn't killed it;
he has only preserved an image of a white man about to kill it. And what call do we
answer when we look at this painting? Who is calling whom? What is being preserved here?

That last question is the one that for me hung over the whole museum. 12

The Whitney Gallery is an art museum proper. Its allegiance is to art as aca- 13
demic tradition has defined it. In this tradition, we come to understand a painting by
having in our possession various bits of information. Something about the technical
process used to produce it (pastels, watercolors, woodblock prints, etc.); something
about the elements of composition (line and color and movement); something about
the artist's life (where born, how educated, by whom influenced, which school
belonged to or revolted against); something about the artist's relation to this particular subject, such as how many times the artist painted it or whether it contains a
favorite model. Occasionally there will be some philosophizing about the themes or
ideas the paintings are said to represent.

The problem is, when you're faced with a painter like Remington, these bits of 14
information, while nice to have, don't explain what is there in front of you. They
don't begin to give you an account of why a person should have depicted such things.
The experience of a lack of fit between the explanatory material and what is there on
the wall is one I've had before in museums, when, standing in front of a painting or a
piece of statuary, I've felt a huge gap between the information on the little placard
and what it is I'm seeing. I realize that works of art, so-called, all have a subject matter, are all engaged with life, with some piece of life no less significant, no less compelling than Remington's subjects are, if we could only see its force. The idea that art
is somehow separate from history, that it somehow occupies a space that is not the
same as the space of life, seems out of whack here.

I wandered through the gallery thinking these things because right next to it, 15
indeed all around it, in the Buffalo Bill Museum proper and in the Plains Indian
Museum, are artifacts that stand not for someone's expertise or skill in manipulat-
ing the elements of an artistic medium, but for life itself; they are the residue of life.

The Buffalo Bill Museum is a wonderful array of textures, colors, shapes, sizes, forms. 16
The fuzzy brown bulk of a buffalo's hump, the sparkling diamonds in a stickpin, the
brilliant colors of the posters — the mixture makes you want to walk in and be sur-
rounded by it, as if you were going into a child's adventure story. For a moment you can
pretend you're a cowboy too; it's a museum where fantasy can take over. For a while.

As I moved through the exhibition, with the phrase "the best of civilization" 17
ringing in my head, I came upon certain objects displayed in a section that recreates
rooms from Cody's house. Ostrich feather fans, peacock feather fans, antler furniture — a chair and a table made entirely of antlers — a bearskin rug. And then I saw
the heads on the wall: Alaska Yukon Moose, Wapiti American Elk, Muskox (the
"Whitney," the "DeRham"), Mountain Caribou (the "Hyland"), Quebec Labrador

Caribou (the "Elbow"), Rocky Mountain Goat (the "Haase," the "Kilto"), Woodland Caribou (world's record, "DeRham"), the "Rogers" freak Wapiti, the "Whitney" bison, the "Lord Rundlesham" bison. The names that appear after the animals are the names of the men who killed them. Each of the animals is scored according to measurements devised by the Boone and Crockett Club, a big-game hunters' organization. The Lord Rundlesham bison, for example, scores 124⁶/₈, making it number 25 in the world for bison trophies. The "Reed" Alaska Yukon Moose scores 247. The "Witherbee" Canada moose holds the world's record.

Next to the wall of trophies is a small enclosure where jewelry is displayed. A 18 buffalo head stickpin and two buffalo head rings, the heads made entirely of diamonds, with ruby eyes, the gifts of the Russian crown prince. A gold and diamond stickpin from Edward VII; a gold, diamond, and garnet locket from Queen Victoria. The two kinds of trophies — animals and jewels — form an incongruous set; the relationship between them compelling but obscure.

If the rest of the items in the museum — the dime novels with their outrageous 19 covers, the marvelous posters, the furniture, his wife's dress, his daughter's oil painting — have faded from my mind it is because I cannot forget the heads of the animals as they stared down, each with an individual expression on its face. When I think about it I realize that I don't know why these animal heads are there. Buffalo Bill didn't kill them; perhaps they were gifts from the famous people he took on hunts. A different kind of jewelry.

After the heads, I began to notice something about the whole exhibition. In one 20 display, doghide chaps, calfskin chaps, angora goathide chaps, and horsehide chaps. Next to these a rawhide lariat and a horsehair quirt. Behind me, boots and saddles, all of leather. Everywhere I looked there was tooth or bone, skin or fur, hide or hair, or the animal itself entire — two full-size buffalo (a main feature of the exhibition) and a magnificent stone sheep (a mountain sheep with beautiful curving horns). This one was another world's record. The best of civilization.

In the literature about Buffalo Bill you read that he was a conservationist, that if 21 it were not for the buffalo in his Wild West shows the species would probably have become extinct. (In the seventeenth century 40 million buffalo roamed North America; by 1900 all the wild buffalo had been killed except for one herd in northern Alberta.) That the man who gained fame first as a buffalo hunter should have been an advocate for conservation of the buffalo is not an anomaly but typical of the period. The men who did the most to preserve America's natural wilderness and its wildlife were big-game hunters. The Boone and Crockett Club, founded by Theodore Roosevelt, George Bird Grinnell, and Owen Wister, turns out to have been one of the earliest organizations to devote itself to environmental protection in the United States. *The Reader's Encyclopedia of the American West* says that the club "supported the national park and forest reserve movement, helped create a system of national wildlife refuges, and lobbied for the protection of threatened species, such as the buffalo and antelope." At the same time, the prerequisites for membership in the club were "the highest caliber of sportsmanship and the achievement of killing 'in fair chase' trophy specimens [which had to be adult males] from several species of North American big game."

The combination big-game hunter and conservationist suggests that these men had no interest in preserving the animals for the animals' sake but simply wanted to ensure the chance to exercise their sporting pleasure. But I think this view is too simple; something further is involved here. The men who hunted game animals had a kind of love for them and a kind of love for nature that led them to want to preserve the animals they also desired to kill. That is, the desire to kill the animals was in some way related to a desire to see them live. It is not an accident, in this connection, that Roosevelt, Wister, and Remington all went west originally for their health. Their devotion to the West, their connection to it, their love for it are rooted in their need to reanimate their own lives. The preservation of nature, in other words, becomes for them symbolic of their own survival.

> *"That is, the desire to kill the animals was in some way related to a desire to see them live."*

In a sense, then, there is a relationship between the Remington exhibition in the Whitney Gallery and the animal memorabilia in the Buffalo Bill Museum. The moose in *Coming to the Call* and the mooseheads on the wall are not so different as they might appear. The heads on the wall serve an aesthetic purpose; they are decorative objects, pleasing to the eye, which call forth certain associations. In this sense they are like visual works of art. The painting, on the other hand, has something of the trophy about it. The moose as Remington painted it is about to become a trophy, yet in another sense it already is one. Remington has simply captured the moose in another form. In both cases the subject matter, the life of a wild animal, symbolizes the life of the observer. It is the preservation of that life that both the painting and the taxidermy serve.

What are museums keeping safe for us, after all? What is it that we wish so much to preserve? The things we put in safekeeping, in our safe-deposit boxes under lock and key, are always in some way intended finally as safeguards of our own existence. The money and jewelry and stock certificates are meant for a time when we can no longer earn a living by the sweat of our brows. Similarly, the objects in museums pre-serve for us a source of life from which we need to nourish ourselves when the resources that would normally supply us have run dry.

The Buffalo Bill Historical Center, full as it is of dead bones, lets us see more   25 clearly than we normally can what it is that museums are for. It is a kind of charnel house that houses images of living things that have passed away but whose life force still lingers around their remains and so passes itself on to us. We go and look at the objects in the glass cases and at the paintings on the wall, as if by standing there we could absorb into ourselves some of the energy that flowed once through the bodies of the live things represented. A museum, rather than being, as we normally think of it, the most civilized of places, a place most distant from our savage selves, actually caters to the urge to absorb the life of another into one's own life.

If we see the Buffalo Bill Museum in this way, it is no longer possible to sepa-   26 rate ourselves from the hunters responsible for the trophies with their wonder-ing eyes or from the curators who put them there. We are not, in essence, different from Roosevelt or Remington or Buffalo Bill, who killed animals when they were abundant in the Wild West of the 1880s. If in doing so those men were practicing the ancient art of absorbing the life of an animal into their own through the act of killing it, realizing themselves through the destruction of another life, then we are not so different from them, as visitors to the museum, we stand beside the bones and skins and nails of beings that were once alive, or stare fixedly at their painted images. Indeed our visit is only a safer form of the same enterprise as theirs.

So I did not get out of the Buffalo Bill Museum unscathed, unimplicated in the   27 acts of rapine and carnage that these remains represent. And I did not get out with-out having had a good time, either, because however many dire thoughts I may have had, the exhibits were interesting and fun to see. I was even able to touch a piece of buffalo hide displayed especially for that purpose (it was coarse and springy). Every-one else had touched it too. The hair was worn down, where people's hands had been, to a fraction of its original length.

After this, the Plains Indian Museum was a terrible letdown. I went from one exhibit   28 to another expecting to become absorbed, but nothing worked. What was the mat-ter? I was interested in Indians, had read about them, taught some Indian literature, felt drawn by accounts of native religions. I had been prepared to enter this museum as if I were going into another children's story, only this time I would be an Indian instead of a cowboy or a cowgirl. But the objects on display, most of them behind glass, seemed paltry and insignificant. They lacked visual presence. The bits of leather and sticks of wood triggered no fantasies in me.

At the same time, I noticed with some discomfort that almost everything in 29 those glass cases was made of feathers and claws and hide, just like the men's chaps and ladies' fans in the Buffalo Bill Museum, only there was no luxury here. Plains Indian culture, it seemed, was made entirely from animals. Their mode of life had been even more completely dedicated to carnage than Buffalo Bill's, dependent as it was on animals for food, clothing, shelter, equipment, everything. In the Buffalo Bill Museum I was able to say to myself, well, if these men had been more sensitive, if they had had a right relation to their environment and to life itself, the atrocities that produced these trophies would never have occurred. They never would have exterminated the Indians and killed off the buffalo. But the spectacle before me made it impossible to say that. I had expected that the Plains Indian Museum would show me how life in nature ought to be lived: not the mindless destruction of nineteenth-century America but an ideal form of communion with animals and the land. What the museum seemed to say instead was that cannibalism was universal. Both colonizer and colonized had had their hands imbrued with blood. The Indians had lived off animals and had made war against one another. Violence was simply a necessary and inevitable part of life. And a person who, like me, was horrified at the extent of the destruction was just the kind of romantic idealist my husband sometimes accused me of being. There was no such thing as the life lived in harmony with nature. It was all bloodshed and killing, an unending cycle, over and over again, and no one could escape.

But perhaps there was a way to understand the violence that made it less ter- 30 rible. Perhaps if violence was necessary, a part of nature, intended by the universe, then it could be seen as sacramental. Perhaps it was true, what Calvin Martin had said in *Keepers of the Game*: that the Indians had a sacred contract with the animals they killed, that they respected them as equals and treated their remains with honor and punctilio. If so, the remains of animals in the Plains Indian Museum weren't the same as those left by Buffalo Bill and his friends. They certainly didn't look the same. Perhaps. All I knew for certain was that these artifacts, lifeless and shrunken, spoke to me of nothing I could understand. No more did the life-size models of Indians, with strange featureless faces, draped in costumes that didn't look like clothing. The figures, posed awkwardly in front of tepees too white to seem real, carried no sense of a life actually lived, any more than the objects in the glass cases had.

The more I read the placards on the wall, the more disaffected I became. Plains 31 Indian life apparently had been not only bloody but exceedingly tedious. All those porcupine quills painstakingly softened, flattened, dyed, then appliqued through even more laborious methods of stitching or weaving. Four methods of attaching porcupine quills, six design groups, population statistics, patterns of migration. There wasn't any glamour here at all. No glamour in the lives the placards told about, no glamour in the objects themselves, no glamour in the experience of looking at them. Just a lot of shriveled things accompanied by some even drier information.

Could it be, then, that the problem with the exhibitions was that Plains Indian 32 culture, if representable at all, was simply not readable by someone like me? Their stick figures and abstract designs could convey very little to an untrained Euro-American eye. One display in particular illustrated this. It was a piece of cloth, behind glass, depicting a buffalo skin with some marks on it. The placard read: "Winter Count, Sioux ca. 1910, after Lone Dog's, Fort Peck, Montana, 1877." The hide with its markings had been a calendar, each year represented by one image, which showed the most significant event in the life of the tribe. A thick pamphlet to one side of the glass case explained each image year by year: 1800–1801, the attack of the Uncapoo on a Crow Indian Fort; 1802–1803, a total eclipse of the sun. The images, once you knew what they represented, made sense, and seemed poetic interpretations of the experiences they stood for. But without explanation they were incomprehensible.

The Plains Indian Museum stopped me in my tracks. It was written in a lan- 33 guage I had never learned. I didn't have the key. Maybe someone did, but I wasn't too sure. For it may not have been just cultural difference that made the text unreadable. I began to suspect that the text itself was corrupt, that the architects of this museum were going through motions whose purpose was, even to themselves, obscure. Knowing what event a figure stands for in the calendar doesn't mean you understand an Indian year. The deeper purpose of the museum began to puzzle me. Wasn't there an air of bad faith about preserving the vestiges of a culture one had effectively extinguished? Did the museum exist to assuage our guilt and not for any real educational reason? I do not have an answer to these questions. All I know is that I felt I was in the presence of something pious and a little insincere. It had the aura of a failed attempt at virtue, as though the curators were trying to present as interesting objects whose purpose and meaning even they could not fully imagine.

> *"The Plains Indian Museum stopped me in my tracks."*

In a last-ditch attempt to salvage something, I went up to one of the guards and 34 asked where the movie was showing which the video had advertised, the movie about Plains Indian life. "Oh, the slide show, you mean," he said. "It's been discontinued." When I asked why, he said he didn't know. It occurred to me then that that was the message the museum was sending, if I could read it, that that was the bottom line. Discontinued, no reason given.

The movie in the Winchester Arms Museum, *Lock, Stock, and Barrel*, was going 35 strong. The film began with the introduction of cannon into European warfare in the Middle Ages, and was working its way slowly toward the nineteenth century when I left. I was in a hurry. Soon my husband would be waiting for me in the lobby. I went from room to room, trying to get a quick sense impression of the objects on display. They were all the same: guns. Some large drawings and photographs on the walls tried to give a sense of the context in which the arms had been used, but the effect was nil. It was case after case of rifles and pistols, repeating themselves over and over, and even when some slight variation caught my eye the differences meant nothing to me.

But the statistics did. In a large case of commemorative rifles, I saw the Antlered 36 Game Commemorative Carbine. Date of manufacture: 1978. Number produced: 19,999. I wondered how many antlered animals each carbine had killed. I saw the Canadian Centennial (1962): 90,000; the Legendary Lawman (1978): 19,999; the John Wayne (1980–81): 51,600. Like the titles of the various sections of the museum, these names had a message. The message was: guns are patriotic. Associated with national celebrations, law enforcement, and cultural heroes. The idea that firearms were inseparable from the march of American history came through even more strongly in the titles given to the various exhibits: Firearms in Colonial America; Born in America: The Kentucky Rifle; The Era of Expansion and Invention; The Civil War: Firearms of the Conflict; The Golden Age of Hunting; Winning the West. The guns embodied phases of the history they had helped to make. There were no quotation marks here to indicate that expansion and conquest might not have been all they were cracked up to be. The fact that firearms had had a history seemed to consecrate them; the fact that they had existed at the time when certain famous events had occurred seemed to make them not only worth preserving but worth studying and revering. In addition to the exhibition rooms, the museum housed three "study galleries": one for hand arms, one for shoulder arms, one for U.S. military firearms.

As I think back on the rows and rows of guns, I wonder if I should have looked at 37 them more closely, tried harder to appreciate the workmanship that went into them, the ingenuity, the attention. Awe and admiration are the attitudes the museum invites. You hear the ghostly march of military music in the background; you imagine flags waving and sense the implicit reference to feats of courage in battle and glorious death. The place had the air of an expensive and well-kept reliquary, or of the room off the transept of a cathedral where the vestments are stored. These guns were not there merely to be seen or even studied; they were there to be venerated.

But I did not try to appreciate the guns. They were too technical, too foreign. I 38 didn't have their language, and, besides, I didn't want to learn. I rejoined my husband in the lobby. The Plains Indian Museum had been incomprehensible, but in the Winchester Arms Museum I could hardly see the objects at all, for I did not see the point. Or, rather, I did see it and rejected it. Here in the basement the instruments that had turned live animals into hides and horns, had massacred the Indians and the buffalo, were being lovingly displayed. And we were still making them: 51,600 John Waynes in 1980–81. Arms were going strong.

As I bought my books and postcards in the gift shop, I noticed a sign that read 39 "Rodeo Tickets Sold Here," and something clicked into place. So that was it. *Everything* was still going strong. The whole museum was just another rodeo, only with the riders and their props stuffed, painted, sculpted, immobilized and put under glass. Like the rodeo, the entire museum witnessed a desire to bring back the United States of the 1880s and 1890s. The American people did not want to let go of the winning of the West. They wanted to win it all over again, in imagination. It was the ecstasy of the kill, as much as the life of the hunted, that we fed off here. The Buffalo Bill Historical Center did not repudiate the carnage that had taken place in the nineteenth century. It celebrated it. With its gleaming rest rooms, cute snack bar, opulent museum shop, wooden Indians, thousand rifles, and scores of animal trophies, it helped us all reenact the dream of excitement, adventure, and conquest that was what the Wild West meant to most people in this country.

This is where my visit ended, but it had a sequel. When I left the Buffalo Bill His- 40 torical Center, I was full of moral outrage, an indignation so intense it made me almost sick, though it was pleasurable too, as such emotions usually are. But the outrage was undermined by the knowledge that I knew nothing about Buffalo Bill, nothing of his life, nothing of the circumstances that led him to be involved in such violent events. And I began to wonder if my reaction wasn't in some way an image, however small, of the violence I had been objecting to. So when I got home I began to read about Buffalo Bill, and a whole new world opened up. I came to love Buffalo Bill.

"I have seen him the very personification of grace and beauty . . . dashing over the 41 free wild prairie and riding his horse as though he and the noble animal were bounding with one life and one motion." That is the sort of thing people wrote about

Buffalo Bill. They said "he was the handsomest man I ever saw." They said "there was never another man lived as popular as he was." They said "there wasn't a man woman or child that he knew or ever met that he didn't speak to." They said "he was handsome as a god, a good rider and a crack shot." They said "he gave lots of money away. Nobody ever went hungry around him." They said "he was way above the average, physically and every other way."

These are quotes from people who knew Cody, collected by one of his two most 42 responsible biographers, Nellie Snyder Yost. She puts them in the last chapter, and by the time you get there they all ring true. Buffalo Bill was incredibly handsome. He was extremely brave and did things no other scout would do. He would carry messages over rugged territory swarming with hostile Indians, riding all night in bad weather, and get through, and then take off again the next day to ride sixty miles through a blizzard. He was not a proud man. He didn't boast of his exploits. But he did do incredible things, not just once in a while but on a fairly regular basis. He had a great deal of courage; he believed in himself, in his abilities, in his strength and endurance and knowledge. He was very skilled at what he did — hunting and scouting — but he wasn't afraid to try other things. He wrote some dime novels, he wrote his autobiography by age thirty-four, without very much schooling; he wasn't afraid to try acting, even though the stage terrified him and he knew so little about it that, according to his wife, he didn't even know you had to memorize lines.

Maybe it was because he grew up on the frontier, maybe it was just the kind of 43 person he was, but he was constantly finding himself in situations that required resourcefulness and courage, quick decisions and decisive action and rising to the occasion. He wasn't afraid to improvise.

He liked people, drank a lot, gave big parties, gave lots of presents, and is reputed to 44 have been a womanizer (Cody, 16). When people came to see him in his office tent on the show grounds, to shake his hand or have their pictures taken with him, he never turned anyone away. "He kept a uniformed doorman at the tent opening to announce visitors," writes a biographer. "No matter who was outside, from a mayor to a shabby woman with a baby, the Colonel would smooth his mustache, stand tall and straight, and tell the doorman to 'show 'em in.' He greeted everyone the same" (Yost, 436).

As a showman, he was a genius. People don't say much about *why* he was so suc- 45 cessful; mostly they describe the wonderful goings-on. But I get the feeling that Cody was one of those people who was connected to his time in an uncanny way. He knew what people wanted, he knew how to entertain them, because he *liked* them, was open to them, felt his kinship with them, or was so much in touch with himself at some level that he was thereby in touch with almost everybody else.

He liked to dress up and had a great sense of costume (of humor, too, they say).   46
Once he came to a fancy dress ball, his first, in New York, wearing white tie and tails
and a large Stetson. He knew what people wanted. He let his hair grow long and wore
a mustache and beard, because, he said, he wouldn't be believable as a scout otherwise. Hence his Indian name, Pahaska, meaning "long hair," which people loved to
use. Another kind of costume. He invented the ten-gallon hat, which the Stetson
company made to his specifications. Afterward, they made a fortune from it. In the
scores of pictures reproduced in the many books about him, he most often wears
scout's clothes — usually generously fringed buckskin, sometimes a modified caval-
ryman's outfit — though often he's impeccably turned out in a natty-looking three-
piece business suit (sometimes with overcoat, sometimes not). The photographs
show him in a tuxedo, in something called a "Mexican suit" which looks like a cowboy outfit, and once he appears in Indian dress. In almost every case he is wearing
some kind of hat, usually the Stetson, at exactly the right angle. He poses deliberately, and with dignity, for the picture. Cody didn't take himself so seriously that he
had to pretend to be less than he was.

What made Buffalo Bill so irresistible? Why is he still so appealing, even now,   47
when we've lost, supposedly, all the illusions that once supported his popularity?
There's a poster for one of his shows when he was

> *"What made
> Buffalo Bill so
> irresistible?"*

traveling in France that gives a clue to what it is that
makes him so profoundly attractive a figure. The
poster consists of a huge buffalo galloping across the
plains, and against the buffalo's hump, in the center of
his hump, is a cutout circle that shows the head of
Buffalo Bill, white-mustachioed and bearded now, in his famous hat, and beneath, in
large red letters, are the words ["I am coming"].

"I am coming" are the words of a savior. The announcement is an annunciation.   48
Buffalo Bill is a religious figure of a kind who makes sense within a specifically
Christian tradition. That is, he comes in the guise of a redeemer, of someone who
will save us, who will through his own actions do something for us that we ourselves
cannot do. He will lift us above our lives, out of the daily grind, into something larger
than we are.

His appeal on the surface is to childish desires, the desire for glamour, fame, big-   49
ness, adventure, romance. But these desires are also the sign of something more profound, and it is to something more profound in us that he also appeals. Buffalo Bill
comes to the child in us, understood not as that part of ourselves that we have outgrown but as the part that got left behind, of necessity, a long time ago, having been

I Am Coming, ca. 1900. Color lithograph.

starved, bound, punished, disciplined out of existence. He promises that that part of the self can live again. He has the power to promise these things because he represents the West, that geographical space of the globe that was still the realm of exploration and discovery, that was still open, that had not yet quite been tamed, when he began to play himself on the stage. He not only represented it, he *was* it. He brought the West itself with him when he came. The very Indians, the very buffalo, the very cowboys, the very cattle, the very stagecoach itself which had been memorialized in story. He performed in front of the audience the feats that had made him famous. He shot glass balls and clay pigeons out of the air with amazing rapidity. He rode his watersmooth silver stallion at full gallop. "Jesus he was a handsome man," wrote e. e. cummings in "Buffalo Bill 's Defunct."

"I am coming." This appearance of Buffalo Bill, in the flesh, was akin to the apparition of a saint or of the Virgin Mary to believers. He was the incarnation of an ideal. He came to show people that what they had only imagined was really true. The West really did exist. There really were heroes who rode white horses and performed amazing feats. e. e. cummings was right to invoke the name of Jesus in his poem. Buffalo Bill was a secular messiah.

He was a messiah because people believed in him. When he died, he is reputed to   51 have said, "Let my show go on." But he had no show at the time, so he probably didn't say that. Still, the words are prophetic because the desire for what Buffalo Bill had done had not only not died but would call forth the countless reenactments of the Wild West, from the rodeo — a direct descendant of his show — to the thousands of Western novels, movies, and television programs that comprise the Western genre in the twentieth century, a genre that came into existence as a separate category right about the time that Cody died. Don Russell maintains that the way the West exists in our minds today is largely the result of the way Cody presented it in his show. That was where people got their ideas of what the characters looked like. Though many Indian tribes wore no feathers and fought on foot, you will never see a featherless, horseless Indian warrior in the movies, because Bill employed only Sioux and other Plains tribes which had horses and traditionally wore feathered headdresses. "Similarly," he adds, "cowboys wear ten-gallon Stetsons, not because such a hat was worn in early range days, but because it was part of the costume adopted by Buffalo Bill for his show" (Russell, 470).

But the deeper legacy is elsewhere. Buffalo Bill was a person who inspired other   52 people. What they saw in him was an aspect of themselves. It really doesn't matter whether Cody was as great as people thought him or not, because what they were responding to when he rode into the arena, erect and resplendent on his charger, was something intangible, not the man himself, but a possible way of being. William F. Cody and the Wild West triggered the emotions that had fueled the imaginative lives of people who flocked to see him, especially men and boys, who made up the larger portion of the audience. He and his cowboys played to an inward territory; a Wild West of the psyche that hungered for exercise sprang into activity when the show appeared. [*I am coming*] was a promise to redeem that territory, momentarily at least, from exile and oblivion. The lost parts of the self symbolized by buffalo and horses and wild men would live again for an hour while the show went on.

People adored it. Queen Victoria, who broke her custom by going to see it at all   53 (she never went to the theater, and on the rare occasions when she wanted to see a play she had it brought to her), is supposed to have been lifted out of a twenty-five-year depression caused by the death of her husband after she saw Buffalo Bill. She liked the show so much that she saw it again, arranging for a command performance to be given at Windsor Castle the day before her Diamond Jubilee. This was the occasion when four kings rode in the Deadwood stagecoach with the Prince of Wales on top next to Buffalo Bill, who drove. No one was proof against the appeal. Ralph Blumenfeld, the London correspondent for the New York *Herald*, wrote in his diary while the show was in London that he'd had two boyhood heroes, Robin Hood and Buffalo Bill, and had delighted in Cody's stories of the Pony Express and Yellow Hand:

> Everything was done to make Cody conceited and unbearable, but he remained the simple, unassuming child of the plains who thought lords and ladies belonged in the picture books and that the story of Little Red Riding Hood was true. I rode in the Deadwood coach. It was a great evening in which I realized a good many of my boyhood dreams, for there was Buffalo Bill on his white rocking horse charger, and Annie Oakley behind him. (Weybright, 172)

Victor Weybright and Henry Blackman Sell, from whose book on the Wild West 54 some of the foregoing information has come, dedicated their book to Buffalo Bill. It was published in 1955. Nellie Snyder Yost, whose 1979 biography is one of the two scholarly accounts of Cody's life, dedicates her book "to all those good people, living or dead, who knew and liked Buffalo Bill." Don Russell's *The Lives and Legends of Buffalo Bill* (1960), the most fact-filled scholarly biography, does not have a dedication, but in the final chapter, where he steps back to assess Cody and his influence, Russell ends by exclaiming, "What more could possibly be asked of a hero? If he was not one, who was?" (Russell, 480).

Let me now pose a few questions of my own. Must we throw out all the wonder- 55 ful qualities that Cody had, the spirit of hope and emulation that he aroused in millions of people, because of the terrible judgment history has passed on the epoch of which he was part? The kinds of things he stands for — courage, daring, strength, endurance, generosity, openness to other people, love of drama, love of life, the possibility of living a life that does not deny the body and the desires of the body — are these to be declared dangerous and delusional although he manifested some of them while fighting Indians and others while representing his victories to the world? And the feelings he aroused in his audiences, the idealism, the enthusiasm, the excitement, the belief that dreams could become real — must these be declared misguided or a sham because they are associated with the imperialistic conquest of a continent, with the wholesale extermination of animals and men?

It is not so much that we cannot learn from history as that we cannot teach his- 56 tory how things should have been. When I set out to discover how Cody had become involved in the killing of Indians and the slaughter of buffalo, I found myself unable to sustain the outrage I had felt on leaving the museum. From his first job as an eleven-year-old herder for an army supply outfit, sole wage earner for his ailing widowed mother who had a new baby and other children to support, to his death in Colorado at the age of seventy-one, there was never a time when it was possible to say, there, there you went wrong, Buffalo Bill, you should not have killed that Indian. You should have held your fire and made your living some other way and quit the army and gone to work in the nineteenth-century equivalent of the Peace Corps. You should have known how it would end. My reading made me see that you cannot prescribe for someone in Buffalo Bill's position what he should have done, and it made me reflect on how eager I had been to get off on being angry at the museum. The thirst for moral outrage, for self-vindication, lay pretty close to the surface.

I cannot resolve the contradiction between my experience at the Buffalo Bill 57 Historical Center with its celebration of violent conquest and my response to the shining figure of Buffalo Bill as it emerged from the pages of books — on the one hand, a history of shame; on the other, an image of the heart's desire. But I have reached one conclusion that for a while will have to serve.

Major historical events like genocide and major acts of destruction are not sim- 58 ply produced by impersonal historical processes or economic imperatives or ecological blunders; human intentionality is involved and human knowledge of the self. Therefore, if you're really, truly interested in not having any more genocide or killing of animals, no matter what else you might do, if you don't first, or also, come to recognize the violence in yourself and your own anger and your own destructiveness, whatever else you do won't work. It isn't that genocide doesn't matter. Genocide matters, and it starts at home.

Works Cited

Cody, Iron Eyes. *Iron Eyes: My Life as a Hollywood Indian,* as told to Collin Perry. New York, Everest House, 1982.

Lamar, Howard R., ed. *The Reader's Encyclopedia of the American West.* New York: Crowell, 1977.

Russell, Donald B. *The Lives and Legends of Buffalo Bill.* Norman, Okla.: University of Oklahoma Press, 1960.

Weybright, Victor, and Henry Blackman Sell. *Buffalo Bill and the Wild West.* New York: Oxford University Press, 1955.

Yost, Nellie Snyder. *Buffalo Bill, His Family, Friends, Fame, Failure, and Fortunes.* Chicago: Sage Books, 1979.

Questions for Discussion and Writing

1. Near the beginning of the essay, Tompkins remarks that she can feel the effort of the Buffalo Bill Historical Center "to educate in the best sense of the term." One might say that Tompkins approaches the exhibits as a kind of student. What kind of student is she? How would you describe her attitude, approach, and aims?

2. How do the sections of Tompkins's essay represent stages in an intellectual journey? What happens in each stage? What are the key "events" in each stage — intellectual or other?

3. Why do you think Tompkins includes the section at the end of the essay on the biography and appeal of Buffalo Bill Cody? How does Tompkins's reading about Buffalo Bill affect the ways she thinks and feels about her experience at the Buffalo Bill Historical Center?

Frans de Waal

Frans B. M. de Waal (b. 1948) is C. H. Candler Professor of Primate Behavior in the Psychology Department at Emory University in Atlanta, Georgia. He is also director of "Living Links" at the Yerkes National Primate Research Center, an institute committed to learning about human evolution by studying the behavior of great apes. De Waal's research has long focused on the political, emotional, and, most controversially, moral lives of primates. His discovery of moral behavior among apes challenges one of the very last barriers that was presumed to separate human beings from other animals. It also challenges the conventional view that moral sentiments are a relatively recent development in human evolution. At the same time, it raises far-reaching questions about the basis of moral behavior among humans.

De Waal rejects the notion that scientists who write for a general audience as well as for fellow specialists risk being taken less than seriously. His books look at human behavior through the lens of animal behavior; they have helped to change the way we understand what it means to be human and how we both resemble and differ from other great apes.

De Waal was born in the Netherlands and earned a PhD from Utrecht University in 1977. After completing a postdoctoral study of political behaviors among chimpanzees in 1981, he moved to the United States. In addition to numerous articles and book chapters, he has written nine books, including *Chimpanzee Politics: Power and Sex among Apes* (1982), *Primates and Philosophers: How Morality Evolved* (2006), and *The Age of Empathy: Nature's Lessons for a Kinder Society* (2009). The following essay is from *The Ape and the Sushi Master* (2001) and concerns some of the reasons that his ideas about morality among primates originally met considerable resistance. In 2007, de Waal was named one of the World's One Hundred Most Influential People by *Time* magazine. In 2010, he was knighted to the Order of the Netherlands Lion.

Are We in Anthropodenial?

The human hunter anticipates the moves of his prey by attributing intentions and tak-   1
ing an anthropomorphic stance when it comes to what animals feel, think, or want. Somehow, this stance is highly effective in getting to know and predict animals. The reason it is in disrepute in certain scientific circles has a lot to do with the theme of [my] book, which is how we see ourselves in relation to nature. It is not, I will argue,

because anthropomorphism interferes with science, but because it acknowledges continuity between humans and animals. In the Western tradition, this attitude is okay for children, but not for grown-ups.

In one of my explorations of this issue, I ended up in Greece with a distinguished group of philosophers, biologists, and psychologists.[1] The ancient Greeks believed that the center of the universe was right where they lived. On a sun-drenched tour of the temple ruins in the foothills of Mount Parnassus, near Delphi, we saw the *omphalos* (navel) of the world — a large stone in the shape of a beehive — which I couldn't resist patting like a long-lost friend. What better location to ponder humanity's position in the cosmos? We debated concepts such as the anthropic principle, according to which the presence of human life on earth explains why the universe is uniform in all of its directions. Next to this idea, the Greek illusion of being at the navel of the world looks almost innocent. The theme of our meeting, the problem of anthropomorphism, related very much to the self-absorbed attitude that has spawned such theories.

Anthropomorphism and anthropocentrism are never far apart: the first is partly a "problem" due to the second. This is evident if one considers which descriptions of animal behavior tend to get dismissed. Complaints about anthropomorphism are common, for example, when we say that an animal acts intentionally, that is, that it deliberately strives toward a goal. Granted, intentionality is a tricky concept, but it is so equally for humans and animals. Its presence is as about as hard to prove as its absence; hence, caution in relation to animals would be entirely acceptable if human behavior were held to the same standard. But, of course, this is not the case: cries of anthropomorphism are heard mainly when a ray of light hits a species other than our own.

Let me illustrate the problem with an everyday example. When guests arrive at the Field Station of the Yerkes Primate Center, near Atlanta, where I work, they usually pay a visit to my chimpanzees. Often our favorite troublemaker, a female named Georgia, hurries to the spigot to collect a mouthful of water before they arrive. She then casually mingles with the rest of the colony behind the mesh fence of their compound, and not even the sharpest observer will notice anything unusual. If necessary, Georgia will wait minutes with closed lips until the visitors come near. Then there will be shrieks, laughs, jumps, and sometimes falls when she suddenly sprays them.

Georgia performs this trick predictably, and I have known quite a few other apes that were good at surprising people, naive and otherwise. Heini Hediger, the great Swiss zoo biologist, recounts how even when he was fully prepared to meet the challenge, paying attention to the ape's every move, he nevertheless got drenched by an experienced old chimpanzee. I once found myself in a similar situation with Georgia. She had taken a drink from the spigot and was sneaking up to me. I looked straight into her eyes and pointed my finger at her, warning, in Dutch, "I have seen you!" She immediately stepped back, let some of the water fall from her mouth, and swallowed the rest. I certainly do not wish to claim that she understands Dutch, but she must have sensed that I knew what she was up to, and that I was not going to be an easy target.

Georgia's actions are most easily described in terms of human qualities such as   6 intentions, awareness, and a taste for mischief. Yet some scientists feel that such language is to be avoided. Animals don't make decisions or have intentions; they respond on the basis of reward and punishment. In their view, Georgia was not "up to" anything when she spouted water on her victims. Far from planning and executing a naughty plot, she merely fell for the irresistible reward of human surprise and annoyance. Thus, whereas any person acting like her would be scolded, arrested, or held accountable, some scientists would declare Georgia innocent.

Such knee-jerk rejections of anthropomorphism usually rest on lack of reflec-   7 tion on how we humans go about understanding the world. Inevitably, we ourselves are both the beginning and end of such understanding. Anthropomorphism — the term is derived from the Greek for "human form" — has enjoyed a negative reputation ever since Xenophanes objected to Homer's poetry in 570 B.C. because it treated the gods as if they were people. How could we be so arrogant as to think that they should look like us? If horses could draw pictures, Xenophanes joked, they would no doubt make their gods look like horses. Hence the original meaning of anthropomorphism is that of misattribution of human qualities to nonhumans, or at least overestimation of the similarities between humans and nonhumans. Since nobody wants to be accused of any kind of misattribution or overestimation, this makes it sound as if anthropomorphism is to be avoided under all circumstances.

Modern opposition to anthropomorphism can be traced to Lloyd Morgan, a   8 British psychologist, who dampened enthusiasm for liberal interpretations of animal behavior by formulating, in 1894, the perhaps most quoted statement in all of psychology: "In no case may we interpret an action as the outcome of the exercise of a higher psychical faculty, if it can be interpreted as the outcome of the exercise of one which stands lower on the psychological scale."[2] Generations of psychologists have repeated Morgan's Canon, taking it to mean that the safest assumption about animals is that they are blind actors in a play that only we understand. Yet Morgan himself never meant it this way: he didn't believe that animals are necessarily simpleminded. Taken aback by the one-sided appeals to his canon, he later added a rider according to which there is really nothing wrong with complex interpretations if an animal species has provided independent signs of high intelligence. Morgan thus encouraged scientists to consider a wide array of hypotheses in the case of mentally more advanced animals.[3]

Unfortunately, the rider is not nearly as well known as the canon itself. In a recent assault on the "delusions" of anthropomorphism in the behavioral sciences, John Kennedy proudly holds up the behaviorist tradition as the permanent victor over naive anthropomorphism. He confidently claims in *The New Anthropomorphism*: "Once a live issue, a butt for behaviorists, it [anthropomorphism] now gets little more than an occasional word of consensual disapproval." In almost the same breath, however, the author informs us that "anthropomorphic thinking about animal behaviour is built into us. We could not abandon it even if we wished to. Besides, we do not wish to."[4]

This seems illogical. On the one hand, anthropomorphism is part and parcel of the way the human mind works. On the other hand, we have all but won the battle against it. But how did we overcome an irresistible mode of thinking? Did we really manage to do so, or is this a behaviorist delusion?

> *"But how did we overcome an irresistible mode of thinking?"*

Is it even desirable to suppress thoughts that come naturally to us? Why is it that we, in Kennedy's own words, "do not wish to" abandon anthropomorphism? Isn't it partly because, even though anthropomorphism carries the risk that we overestimate animal mental complexity, we are not entirely comfortable with the opposite either, which is to deliberately create a gap between ourselves and other animals? Since we feel a clear connection, we cannot in good conscience sweep the similarities under the rug. In other words, if anthropomorphism carries a risk, its opposite carries a risk, too. To give it a name, I propose *anthropodenial* for the a priori rejection of shared characteristics between humans and animals when in fact they may exist.

Those who are in anthropodenial try to build a brick wall between themselves and other animals. They carry on the tradition of French philosopher René Descartes, who declared that while humans possessed souls, animals were mere machines. Inspired by the pervasive human-animal dualism of the Judeo-Christian tradition, this view has no parallel in other religions or cultures. It also raises the question why, if we descended from automatons, we aren't automatons ourselves. How did we get to be different? Each time we must ask such a question, another brick is pulled out of the dividing wall. To me, this wall is beginning to look like a slice of Swiss cheese. I work on a daily basis with animals from which it is about as hard to distance oneself as from Lucy, the Australopithecus fossil. All indications are that the main difference between Lucy and modern apes resided in her hips rather than her cranium. Surely we all owe Lucy the respect due an ancestor — and if so, does not this force a different look at the apes?

If Georgia the chimpanzee acts in a way that in any human would be considered 13 deliberately deceitful, we need compelling evidence to the contrary before we say that, in fact, she was guided by different intentions, or worse, that apes have no intentions, and that Georgia was a mere water-spitting robot. Such a judgment would be possible only if behavior that in its finest details reminds us of our own — and that, moreover, is shown by an organism extremely close to us in anatomy and brain organization — somehow fundamentally differs from ours. It would mean that in the short evolutionary time that separates humans from chimpanzees, different motives and cognition have come to underlie similar behavior. What an awkward assumption, and how unparsimonious!

Isn't it far more economical to assume that if two closely related species act in a 14 similar way, the underlying mental processes are similar, too? If wolves and coyotes have behavior patterns in common, the logical assumption is that these patterns mean the same thing, inasmuch as they derive from the common ancestor of both species. Applied to humans and their closest relatives, this rationale makes cognitive similarity the default position. In other words, given that the split between the ancestors of humans and chimpanzees is assumed to have occurred a mere five to six million years ago, anthropomorphism should be less of an issue than anthropodenial.[5]

This radical-sounding position — according to which, in the case of monkeys and 15 apes, the burden of proof should be shifted from those who recognize similarity to those who deny it — is not exactly new. One of the strongest advocates of a unitary explanation was the philosopher David Hume. More than a century before both Lloyd Morgan and Darwin, Hume formulated the following touchstone in *A Treatise of Human Nature*:

> 'Tis from the resemblance of the external actions of animals to those we
> ourselves perform, that we judge their internal likewise to resemble ours;
> and the same principle of reasoning, carry'd one step farther, will make us
> conclude that since our internal actions resemble each other, the causes,
> from which they are deriv'd, must also be resembling. When any hypothesis,
> therefore, is advanc'd to explain a mental operation, which is common to
> men and beasts, we must apply the same hypothesis to both.[6]

Bambification

As soon as we admit that animals are not machines, that they are more like us than like automatons, then anthropodenial becomes impossible and anthropomorphism inevitable. Nor is anthropomorphism necessarily unscientific, unless it takes one of the unscientific forms that popular culture bombards us with. I was once struck by an advertisement for clean fuel in which a grizzly bear had his arm around his mate's shoulders while both enjoyed a beautiful landscape. Since bears are nearsighted and do not form pair-bonds, the image was nothing but our own behavior projected onto these animals.

Walt Disney made us forget that Mickey is a mouse and Donald a duck. Sesame Street, the Muppet Show, Barney: television is populated with talking and singing animal representations with little relation to their actual counterparts. Popular depictions are often pedomorphic, that is, they follow ethology's *Kindchenschema* (baby-appeal) by endowing animals with enlarged eyes and rounded infantile features designed to evoke endearment and protectiveness.

> *"Walt Disney made us forget that Mickey is a mouse and Donald a duck."*

I've had firsthand experience with another form that I refer to as satirical anthropomorphism, which exploits the reputation of certain animals as stupid, stubborn, or funny in order to mock people. When my book *Chimpanzee Politics* came out in France in 1987, the publisher decided, unbeknownst to me, to put François Mitterrand and Jacques Chirac on the cover with a grinning chimpanzee between them. I can only assume that he wanted to imply that these politicians acted like "mere" apes. Yet by doing so he went completely against the whole point of my book, which was not to ridicule people but to show that chimpanzees live in complex societies full of alliances and jockeying for power, societies that in some ways mirror our own.

You can hear similar attempts at anthropomorphic humor at the monkey rock of most zoos. Isn't it interesting that antelopes, lions, and giraffes rarely elicit hilarity, but that people who watch primates often end up hooting and yelling, scratching themselves in an exaggerated manner, and pointing at the animals while shouting things like "I had to look twice, Larry, I thought it was you"? In my mind, the laughter reflects anthropodenial: it is a nervous reaction caused by an uncomfortable resemblance.

The most common anthropomorphism, however, is the naive kind that attributes human feelings and thoughts to animals based on insufficient information or wishful thinking. I recall an interview with a woman in Wisconsin who claimed that

the squirrels in her backyard loved her to an extraordinary degree. The rodents visited her every day, came indoors, and accepted food directly from her hand. She
spent over a thousand dollars per year on nuts. When the interviewer discreetly suggested that perhaps the abundant goodies explained the animals' fondness of her,
the woman denied any connection.

Naive anthropomorphism makes us exclaim "He must be the daddy!" when an 21
adult male animal gently plays with a youngster. We are the only animals, however,
with the concept of paternity as a basis of fatherhood. Other animals can be
fathers — and fathers may treat juveniles differently than non-fathers — but this is
never based on an explicit understanding of the link between sex and reproduction.
Similarly, when Elizabeth Marshall Thomas tells us in *The Hidden Life of Dogs* that
virgin bitches "save" themselves for future "husbands," she assumes Victorian values in an animal not particularly known for its sexual fidelity.

All such instances of anthropomorphism are profoundly anthropocentric. The 22
talking animals on television, the satirical depiction of public figures, and the naive
attribution of human qualities to animals have little to do with what we know
about the animals themselves. In a tradition going back to the folktales, Aesop, and
La Fontaine, this kind of anthropomorphism serves human purposes: to mock, educate,
moralize, and entertain. Most of it further satisfies the picture, cherished by many, of
the animal kingdom as a peaceable and cozy paradise. The fact that, in reality, animals
kill and devour each other, die of starvation and disease, or are indifferent to each other,
does not fit the idealized image. The entertainment industry's massive attempt to strip
animals of their nasty side has been aptly labeled their "Bambification."[7]

The general public is less and less aware of the discrepancy with the real world 23
as fewer people grow up on farms or otherwise close to nature. Even though having a
pet provides a reality check (dogs are generally nice, but neither to their prey nor to
invaders of their territory), the full picture of nature in all its glory and horror
escapes the modern city dweller.

What Is It Like to Be a Bat?

The goal of the student of animal behavior is rarely a mere projection of human 24
experiences onto the animal. Instead, the goal is to interpret behavior within the
wider context of a species' habits and natural history.

Without experience with primates, one might think that a grinning rhesus 25
monkey must be delighted, or that a chimpanzee running toward another with
loud grunts must be in an aggressive mood. But primatologists know from hours of

watching that rhesus bare their teeth when intimidated and that chimpanzees often grunt when they meet and embrace. In other words, a grinning rhesus monkey signals submission, and grunting by a chimpanzee serves as a greeting. In this way the careful observer arrives at an informed anthropomorphism that is often at odds with extrapolations from human behavior.

When Sofie, a six-month-old kitten, bounces toward me sideways, with wide eyes, 26 arched back, and fluffy tail, I recognize this as playful bluff. This judgment is not based on knowing any people who act this way. I just know how Sofie's behavior fits with all the other things cats do. By the same token, when an animal keeper says "Yummy!" while feeding mealworms to a squirrel monkey, she is speaking for the animal, not for herself.

Or take an example that reached the best-sellers list. In *The Man Who Listens to* 27 *Horses*, animal trainer Monty Roberts freely employs what appears to be hopelessly anthropomorphic language to describe his animals' reactions. When the horses make licking and chewing movements, for example, they are said to be negotiating with their trainer: "I am a herbivore; I am a grazer, and I'm making this eating action with my mouth now because I'm considering whether or not to trust you. Help me out with that decision, can you, please?"[8]

Rather than attributing human tendencies to his animals, however, Roberts's 28 interpretations are from the animal's perspective. His extraordinary success as a trainer rests on the fact that he treats the horse as a flight animal in need of trusting relations. A horse has a fear-based psychology totally different from that of a predator.

While the goal of understanding animals from the inside out may be considered 29 naive, it certainly is not anthropocentric. Ideally, we understand animals based on what we know about their *Umwelt* — a German term introduced in 1909 by Jacob von Uexküll for the environment as perceived by the animal. In the same way that parents learn to see through their children's eyes, the empathic observer learns what is important to his or her animals, what frightens them, under which circumstances they feel at ease, and so on.

Is it really anthropomorphic to look at the world from the animal's viewpoint, 30 taking its Umwelt, intelligence, and natural tendencies into account? If anthropomorphism is defined as the attribution of human mental experiences to animals, then, strictly speaking, Roberts is not anthropomorphizing; he explicitly postulates major differences in the psychological makeup of horses and people. Although he does put human words in the horse's mouth, this seems done for the sake of reaching an audience, not because of any confusion between the species.

The animalcentric approach is not easy to apply to every animal: some are more 31 like us than others. The problem of sharing the experiences of organisms that rely on different senses was expressed most famously by the philosopher Thomas Nagel when he asked, "What is it like to be a bat?"[9] A bat perceives its world in pulses of reflected sound, something that we creatures of vision have a hard time imagining. Still, Nagel's answer to his own question — that we will never know — may have been overly pessimistic. Some blind persons manage to avoid collisions with objects by means of a crude form of echolocation.[10]

Perhaps even more alien would be the experience of an animal such as the star- 32 nosed mole. With its twenty-two pink, writhing tentacles around its nostrils, it is able to feel microscopic textures on small objects in the mud with the keenest sense of touch of any animal on earth. Humans can barely imagine this creature's Umwelt. Obviously, the closer a species is to us, the easier it is to do so. This is why anthropomorphism is not only tempting in the case of apes, but also hard to reject on the grounds that we cannot know how they perceive the world. Their sensory systems are essentially the same as ours.

Animalcentric anthropomorphism must be sharply distinguished from anthro- 33 pocentric anthropomorphism (see diagram). The first takes the animal's perspective, the second takes ours. It is a bit like people we all know, who buy us presents

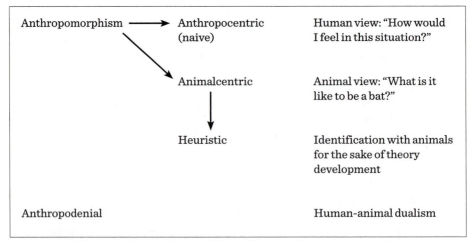

Anthropomorphism comes in many shapes and forms. The type to be treated with caution is the naive, humanizing (anthropocentric) type. Most students of animal behavior, however, try to understand animals on their own terms. Animalcentric anthropomorphism is a common heuristic tool: it generates testable ideas. The opposite of anthropomorphism is anthropodenial, which is based on the assumption that it is safer to err on the side of difference than continuity.

"To make proper use of anthropomorphism we must view it as a means rather than an end."

that they think *we* like versus people who buy us presents that *they* like. The latter have not yet reached a mature form of empathy, and perhaps never will.[11]

To make proper use of anthropomorphism 34 we must view it as a means rather than an end. It should not be our goal to find some quality in an animal that is precisely equivalent to some aspect of our own inner lives. Rather, we should use the fact that we are animals to develop ideas we can put to a test. This heuristic use of anthropomorphism is very similar to the role of intuition in all of science. It inspires us to make predictions, and to ask ourselves how they can be tested, how we can demonstrate what we think is going on. In this way, a speculation is turned into a challenge.[12]

Gorilla Saves Boy

On August 16, 1996, an ape saved a three-year-old boy. The child, who had fallen six 35 meters into the primate exhibit at Chicago's Brookfield Zoo, was scooped up and carried to safety by Binti Jua, an eight-year-old western lowland gorilla. The gorilla sat down on a log in a stream, cradling the boy in her lap, giving him a gentle back-pat before continuing on her way. Her act of sympathy touched many hearts, making Binti a celebrity overnight. It must have been the first time in U.S. history that a gorilla figured in the speeches of leading politicians, who held her up as an example of much-needed compassion. *Time* elected her one of the "best people" of 1996.

Some scientists were not as lyrical. They cautioned that Binti's motives might 36 have been less noble than they seemed, pointing out that she had been raised by people, and had been taught parental skills with a stuffed animal. The whole affair, they suggested, might be explained by a confused maternal instinct. Other speculations included that Binti might have acted the same way with a sack of flour, or that she presented the child to the keepers with the same "pride" with which a house cat presents a dead mouse to her owner.

The intriguing thing about this flurry of creative explanations was that nobody 37 thinks of raising similar doubts when a person saves a dog hit by a car. The rescuer might have grown up around a kennel, have been praised for being kind to animals, and have a nurturing personality, yet we would still see his behavior as an act of caring. Why, then, was Binti's background held against her?[13]

I am not saying that I can look into Binti's heart, but I do know that no one had ³⁸ prepared her for this specific, unique emergency, and that it is highly unlikely that she, with her own seventeen-month-old infant riding on her back, was "maternally confused." How in the world could such a highly intelligent animal mistake a blond boy in sneakers and a red T-shirt for a juvenile of her species? Actually, the biggest surprise was how surprised most people were. Students of ape behavior did not feel that Binti had done anything unusual. Jürg Hess, a Swiss gorilla expert, put it most bluntly in an interview in *Stern*: "The incident can be sensational only for people who don't know a thing about gorillas."

What Hess meant — and I fully agree — is that Binti's action made a deep impres- ³⁹ sion only because it benefited a member of our own species. To take care of a hurt juvenile is perfectly normal behavior for an ape, but of course it typically is directed at the ape's own kind. Instances of such caretaking behavior never reach the media, but they are well known and in line with Binti's assistance to the unfortunate boy. The idea that apes have a capacity for empathy is further supported by how they embrace and caress recent victims of aggression, a reaction thus far not observed in other primates.[14]

The incident at the Brookfield Zoo illustrates how hard it is to avoid both ⁴⁰ anthropodenial and anthropomorphism at the same time: in shying away from anthropomorphism one runs straight into the problem that Binti's actions hardly make any sense if one refuses to assume intentions and emotions. All one can come up with then is a confused instinct.

The larger question behind all of this is what kind of risk we are willing to take: ⁴¹ the risk of underestimating animal mental life or the risk of overestimating it? There is no simple answer, but from an evolutionary perspective, Binti's kindness, like Georgia's mischievousness, is most parsimoniously explained in the same way that we explain our own behavior.

Darwistotle

The debate about anthropomorphism exposes old fault lines in Occidental thought, ⁴² going back to the united view of Aristotle and the dualistic position of the Christian religion. Aristotle saw human social and political life as flowing from natural impulses, such as the reliance on cooperation and need for parental care that we share with many other animals. These views agree so well with current evolutionary biology that in the writings of at least one American political scientist, Larry

Arnhart, Darwin and Aristotle have begun to blend into a single person, perhaps to be called Darwistotle.[15]

The Catholic Church, on the other hand, saw the universe as vertically arranged between heaven and earth. From this perspective, it made sense to speak of "higher" and "lower" forms of life, with humans being closest to the deity. Via philosophy, this way of thinking permeated all of the social sciences and humanities, where it still lingers even though biology has made it absolutely clear that the idea of a linear progression among life forms is mistaken. Every organism fits on the phylogenetic tree without being above or below anything else. Biologists make distinctions between organisms that do well or are extinct, that are specialized or generalized, or that multiply slowly or rapidly, but they never look at one organism as a model that others strive for or that is inherently superior.

These distinct strands of thought have made the West's relation with nature fundamentally schizophrenic: the dominant religion tells us that we are separate, yet science puts us squarely inside nature. This bears on the issue of anthropomorphism and explains why I attribute opposition to it to a desire to keep animals at arm's length rather than concerns about scientific objectivity. The latter is largely a rationalization by behaviorists.

Of course, picking on behaviorists is nothing new for an ethologist such as myself. Given the historical background of the contrasting views of humans' relationships to animals, there is nothing more logical than that an approach to animal behavior coming out of biology should collide with one coming out of psychology.[16] Behaviorists and ethologists have been at each other's throats ever since Daniel Lehrman wrote his stinging attack on Lorenz's instinct theory, in 1953. The ill feelings were mutual, and the stage seemed set for a disastrous split. That this didn't happen is due to both camps discovering in time that they shared a fascination with animals. Gerard Baerends, a Dutch ethologist, described his meeting with the enemy in Montreal, in 1954:

> Jan van Iersel and I were the first ethologists to meet Danny Lehrman after his critique had appeared. After a few minutes of irrelevant behavior, we happened to discover that bird-watching was our common interest. This greatly facilitated our further exchange of ideas, which — as we soon found out — were far more compatible than earlier thought.[17]

Since then, both ethology and behaviorism have been transformed from within and now go largely by different names. The most effective criticism of behaviorist

43

44

45

46

positions was delivered in-house by psychologists who questioned the ladder-like *Scala Naturae* view of evolution and objected to reliance on the albino rat as the animal of choice. Behaviorism still exists, but the old type has been relegated to history as "radical."[18]

The descendants of behaviorists call themselves comparative psychologists, a 47 school that has grown considerably closer to ethology since Robert Hinde's grand synthesis, *Animal Behavior*, was published in 1966. The *Journal of Comparative Psychology* has become a meeting ground of students of animal behavior from backgrounds as diverse as traditional learning psychology, cognitive psychology, anthropology, behavioral ecology, and ethology. Thus, a recent handbook entitled *Comparative Psychology* lists Darwin, Lorenz, and Tinbergen among the discipline's pioneers even though all three were biologists.[19] The evolutionary approach and its attention to species diversity are clearly gaining ground, whereas opposition to mentalistic interpretations of animal behavior is more and more a rear-guard movement.

In the meantime, ethology, with its methodology of careful description and 48 observation, has been absorbed into fields as diverse as child behavior and sociobiology. Even though early sociobiologists were quick to distance themselves from ethology as a way of showing that they were on to some new ideas (which was indeed the case), they were heavily inspired by it, especially by the Tinbergian school and its work on behavioral adaptation. Later, the term "sociobiology" fell into disrepute, leading to further name changes such as "behavioral ecology" and "evolutionary psychology," but without corresponding changes in outlook or research agenda.[20]

Whatever names we choose, students of animal behavior are still being trained 49 largely in either biology or psychology, and the two have learned from each other, and have grown closer as a result. With increasing awareness of the flexibility of animal behavior, "instinct" is a term hardly used anymore, and the current interest in animal culture could be regarded as a triumph of those who have insisted all along on the importance of learning. In order to develop the study of behavior into a mature science we now need to find our inspiration in the Aristotelian view and organize our study along topic areas (such as cognition, evolutionary adaptation, culture, and genetics) rather than basing the structure of our discipline on whether we're dealing with a single bipedal primate or any other animal. Removal of this artificial split will go a long way toward calming the excessive fear of anthropomorphism, which fear was born from it.

Notes

1. The Athens-Pittsburgh Symposium in the History & Philosophy of Science & Technology, entitled The Problem of Anthropomorphism in Science and Philosophy, was held in May, 1996, in Delphi, Greece.
2. Morgan (1894).
3. Lloyd Morgan's rider went as follows: "To this, however, it should be added, lest the range of the principle be misunderstood, that the canon by no means excludes the interpretation of a particular activity in terms of the higher processes if we already have independent evidence of the occurrences of these higher processes in the animal under observation" (Morgan 1903). For the view that Morgan in fact had nothing against anthropomorphism, see Thomas (1998) and Sober (1998).
4. Kennedy (1992). For an antidote see the volume by Mitchell et al. (1997).
5. This position draws upon the familiar homology argument. Cross-specific similarities in behavior are either "analogies" (independently derived) or "homologies" (owing to shared descent), and the latter is more likely the more closely related the species are. De Waal (1991) discusses evolutionary (as opposed to cognitive) parsimony.
6. Hume (1739, p. 226).
7. Vicchio (1986).
8. Quotes are from Roberts (1996). The author's idea that the horse's chewing movements refer to grazing is not far removed from the ethological concept of ritualization. Evolution has turned many an instrumental act (such as preening or feeding) into a communication signal through exaggeration and increased stereotypy.
9. Nagel (1974).
10. Vermeij (1996), a blind biologist, writes: "If I had difficulty adjusting to blindness, the memory has faded. Almost immediately . . . I discovered the value of echoes for telling me where I was. Sounds bouncing off obstructions provided cues to the size of the room, the position of a tree, the speed of a car, the presence of a person, whether a door was open or closed, and much more." Atkins (1996) exposes the limitations of Nagel's (1974) question.
11. Similarly, Batson et al. (1990) investigated human response patterns associated with two kinds of empathy: one based on imagining how you would feel in the other person's situation, the other based on imagining how the other feels.
12. Burghardt (1985).

13. A videotape of the incident (and a series of stills in *Stern*, September 5, 1996) shows Binti sitting down upright on a log in a stream while correctly positioning the unconscious boy, cradling him in her lap. It seems as if she is trying to put him on his feet. The Brookfield gorillas might not have reacted the same to an adult person (i.e., they probably recognized the boy as a youngster), and they certainly would not have reacted this way to a sack of flour. They would probably have been afraid of the sack at first, but then have opened it, causing a mess (Jay Peterson, curator at the Brookfield Zoo, personal communication).

14. Systematic data on the consolation of distressed individuals by chimpanzees has been provided by de Waal and Aureli (1996). For other accounts of empathy by apes, see de Waal (1996). For example, in the Arnhem chimpanzee colony a mother put the normal preference for her younger offspring aside when her older offspring was seriously hurt in a scuffle. Ignoring the noisy protests of her infant, she took tender care of this juvenile for weeks until his injuries had healed.

15. Arnhart (1998) explains that Aristotle knew about apes — he had dissected primates and believed that they represented an intermediate form between man and the quadrupeds. One prominent biologist, J. A. Moore (1993), has declared all of biology a footnote to Aristotle.

16. The distinction goes back to the old one between *Naturwissenschaften* (natural sciences) and *Geisteswissenschaften* (sciences of the mind and human spirit), with psychology increasingly adopting the methods and rigor of the first but tracing its intellectual history to the second.

17. Van Iersel was another Dutch ethologist. What Baerends calls "irrelevant behavior" is a humorous reference to so-called displacement activities (such as scratching one's head), which ethologists interpret as a sign of contradictory motivations. The quotation is from Baerends' unpublished lecture at the 1989 International Ethological Conference in Utrecht, the Netherlands.

18. Hodos and Campbell (1969) and Beach (1950).

19. Greenberg and Haraway (1998).

20. Hence Wilson's (1998) offhand comment: "Sociobiology (or Darwinian anthropology, or evolutionary psychology, or whatever more politically acceptable term one chooses to call it) offers a key link in the attempt to explain the biological foundation of human nature." The reason I stubbornly keep calling myself an ethologist/zoologist despite the many name changes is that I consider the groundbreaking theoretical developments of the 1960s and 1970s a logical continuation of the original ethological agenda, spelled out in Tinbergen's (1963) four research aims: causation, ontogeny, adaptive value, and evolution.

Bibliography

Arnhart, L. (1998). *Darwinian Natural Right: The Biological Ethics of Human Nature.* Albany, NY: SUNY Press.

Atkins, K. A. (1996). A bat without qualities? In M. Bekoff and D. Jamieson (eds.), *Readings in Animal Cognition,* pp. 345–58. Cambridge, MA: MIT Press.

Batson, C. D., Early, S., and Salvarani, G. (1990). Perspective taking: Imagining how another feels versus imagining how you would feel. *Personality and Social Psychology Bulletin* 23: 751–58.

Beach, F. A. (1950). The snark was a boojum. *American Psychologist* 5: 115–24.

Burghardt, G. M. (1985). Animal awareness: Current perceptions and historical perspective. *American Psychologist* 40: 905–19.

Greenberg, G., and Haraway, M. M. (1998). *Comparative Psychology: A Handbook.* New York: Garland.

Hodos, W., and Campbell, C. B. (1969). *Scala Naturae:* Why there is no theory in comparative psychology. *Psychological Review* 76: 337–50.

Hume, D. (1985 [1739]). *A Treatise of Human Nature.* Harmondsworth, UK: Penguin.

Kennedy, J. S. (1992). *The New Anthropomorphism.* Cambridge: Cambridge University Press.

Mitchell, R. W., Thompson, N. S., and Miles, H. L. (1997). *Anthropomorphism, Anecdotes, and Animals.* Albany, NY: SUNY Press.

Moore, J. A. (1993). *Science as a Way of Knowing: The Foundations of Modern Biology.* Cambridge, MA: Harvard University Press.

Morgan, C. L. (1894). *An Introduction to Comparative Psychology.* London: Scott.

Nagel, T. (1974). What is it like to be a bat? *Philosophical Review* 83: 435–50.

Roberts, M. (1996). *The Man Who Listens to Horses.* New York: Random House.

Sober, E. (1998). Morgan's Canon. In D. D. Cummins and C. Allen (eds.), *The Evolution of Mind,* pp. 224–42. Oxford: Oxford University Press.

Thomas, R. K. (1998). Lloyd Morgan's canon. In G. Greenberg and M. M. Haraway (eds.), *Comparative Psychology: A Handbook,* pp. 156–63. New York: Garland.

Tinbergen, T. (1963). On aims and methods of ethology. *Zeitschrift für Tierpsychologie* 20: 410–33.

Vermeij, G. 1996. The touch of a shell. *Discover* 17(8): 76–81.

Vicchio, S. J. (1986). From Aristotle to Descartes: Making animals anthropomorphic. In R. J. Hoage and L. Goldman (eds.), *Animal Intelligence: Insights into the Animal Mind,* pp. 187–207. Washington, DC: Smithsonian Institution Press.

de Waal, F. B. M. (1991). Complementary methods and convergent evidence in the study of primate social cognition. *Behaviour* 118: 297–320.

de Waal, F. B. M. (1996). *Good Natured*. Cambridge, MA: Harvard University Press.
de Waal, F. B. M., and Aureli, F. (1996). Consolation, reconciliation, and a possible cognitive difference between macaque and chimpanzee. In A. E. Russon, K. A. Bard, and S. T. Parker (eds.), *Reaching into Thought: The Minds of the Great Apes*, pp. 80–110. Cambridge: Cambridge University Press.
Wilson, E. O. (1998). *Consilience: The Unity of Knowledge*. New York: Knopf.

Questions for Discussion and Writing

1. De Waal draws on a number of other writers—René Descartes, David Hume, Lloyd Morgan, John Kennedy (author of *The New Anthropomorphism*), and others—to build his argument. (Note the publication dates of the works de Waal references.) Which of these writers does de Waal side with, and which does he disagree with? How does each author help him refine his argument about the value of "heuristic anthropomorphism"? How does he stake out his own position within a long-running conversation about the study of animal behavior?

2. Take the case of Binti, the gorilla who "saved" the boy at the Brookfield Zoo. (You can find video of this incident on YouTube.) Use the diagram on page 440 to imagine various explanations for Binti's behavior, one for each of the positions that de Waal identifies: naive anthropomorphism, animalcentric anthropomorphism, heuristic anthropomorphism, and anthropodenial. (Alternatively, you can work with another animal behavior—perhaps that of a pet or any animal that you have observed carefully.)

3. De Waal writes that anthropomorphism "acknowledges continuity between humans and animals" (p. 433). How do de Waal's views reflect a certain understanding of what it means to be human, of the place of human beings in relation to animals? De Waal wrote his book *The Ape and the Sushi Master* (from which this essay is taken) for a general audience. In your view, what point or meaning does de Waal's argument have for nonscientists?

Cornel West

Cornel West (b. 1953) is a philosopher and theologian who teaches in the Department of Religion and the Center for African American Studies at Princeton University. He is the author of nineteen books and numerous articles and the editor of another thirteen books. Although his scholarly writing can be daunting for nonspecialists (*The American Evasion of Philosophy: A Genealogy of Pragmatism* [1989] and *Keeping Faith* [1994], for example), he also produces accessible and provocative works for a general audience. He has always been politically active, and he has steadily risen to prominence as a public intellectual and even something of a pop culture icon. He first attracted the attention of a broad reading public with his 1993 book *Race Matters* (the essay that follows is the final chapter in that book). *Democracy Matters: Winning the Fight against Imperialism* (2004) offered a censorious and controversial reflection on the condition of America's democracy. He has released two music albums, *Street Knowledge* (2005) and *Never Forget: A Journey of Revelations* (2007, with BMWMB: Black Men Who Mean Business), as well as collaborations with the hip-hop group the Cornel West Theory. In the films *The Matrix Reloaded* (2003) and *The Matrix Revolutions* (2003), he played the part of Councillor West. He appears regularly on politically oriented talk shows such as Bill Maher's *Real Time* and *The Tavis Smiley Show*.

Born in Tulsa, Oklahoma, and raised in Sacramento, California, West grew up a Christian Baptist. A precocious student, an athlete, and a violinist, he entered Harvard at sixteen, graduated magna cum laude after three years, and went on to earn a PhD from Princeton in 1980. His interest in liberation theology, a social justice movement that draws on Marxist principles, led him to accept his first teaching position at Union Theological Seminary. He published his first book, *Prophesy Deliverance! An Afro-American Revolutionary Christianity*, in 1982. Since then, West has taught at a number of institutions, including the Université de Paris, Yale, Harvard, and Princeton.

While his views sometimes strike readers as politically radical, they are often so tightly argued and so firmly founded in philosophical and ethical traditions that they can be difficult to resist. His energy and strong convictions—both political and ethical—are renowned. While teaching at Yale in 1987, he was arrested during a protest against the university's investments in South Africa and was consequently denied a leave of absence to teach at the Université de Paris VIII. Having already agreed to offer courses there, he decided to commute between Paris and New Haven, Connecticut, every week for the semester and thus fulfill his teaching obligations to both schools. In 2001–2002, an unusually public disagreement with Harvard University's then-president, Larry Summers, led to his leaving Harvard for Princeton.

Though active on many fronts, West's influence still comes chiefly from his writing. His wide range is evident in *The Cornel West Reader* (1999), which includes essays and excerpts on politics, music, religion, history, and other topics. He has recently published a memoir, *Brother West: Living and Loving Out Loud* (2010).

Malcolm X and Black Rage

If ever America undergoes great revolutions, they will be brought about by the presence of the black race on the soil of the United States, — that is to say, they will owe their origin, not to the equality, but to the inequality, of conditions.

ALEXIS ∎TOCQUEVILLE, DEMOCRACY IN AMERICA (1840)

I do not imagine that the white and black races will ever live in any country upon an equal footing. But I believe the difficulty to be still greater in the United States than elsewhere. An isolated individual may surmount the prejudices of religion, of his country, or of his race, and if this individual is a king he may effect surprising changes in society; but a whole people cannot rise, as it were, above itself. A despot who should subject the Americans and their former slaves to the same yoke, might perhaps succeed in commingling their races; but as long as the American democracy remains at the head of affairs, no one will undertake so difficult a task; and it may be foreseen that the freer the white population of the United States becomes, the more isolated will it remain.

ALEXIS ∎TOCQUEVILLE, DEMOCRACY IN AMERICA (1835)

Malcolm X articulated black rage in a manner unprecedented in American history. His style of communicating this rage bespoke a boiling urgency and an audacious sincerity. The substance of what he said highlighted the chronic refusal of most Americans to acknowledge the sheer absurdity that confronts human beings of African descent in this country — the incessant assaults on black intelligence, beauty, character, and possibility. His profound commitment to affirm black humanity at any cost and his tremendous courage to accent the hypocrisy of American society made Malcolm X the prophet of black rage — then and now.

Malcolm X was the prophet of black rage primarily because of his great love for   2
black people. His love was neither abstract nor ephemeral. Rather, it was a concrete
connection with a degraded and devalued people in need of psychic conversion. This
is why Malcolm X's articulation of black rage was not directed first and foremost at
white America. Rather, Malcolm believed that if black people felt the love that motivated that rage the love would produce a psychic conversion in black people; they
would affirm themselves as human beings, no longer viewing their bodies, minds,
and souls through white lenses, and believing themselves capable of taking control
of their own destinies.

In American society — especially during Malcolm X's life in the 1950s and early   3
1960s — such a psychic conversion could easily result in death. A proud, self-
affirming black person who truly believed in the capacity of black people to throw off
the yoke of white racist oppression and control their own destiny usually ended up
as one of those strange fruit that Southern trees bore, about which the great Billie
Holiday poignantly sang. So when Malcolm X articulated black rage, he knew he also
had to exemplify in his own life the courage and sacrifice that any truly self-loving
black person needs in order to confront the frightening consequences of being self-
loving in American society. In other words, Malcolm X sharply crystallized the relation of black affirmation of self, black desire for freedom, black rage against
American society, and the likelihood of early black death.

Malcolm X's notion of psychic conversion holds that black people must no   4
longer view themselves through white lenses. He claims black people will never
value themselves as long as they subscribe to a standard of valuation that devalues
them. For example, Michael Jackson may rightly wish to be viewed as a person, not a
color (neither black nor white), but his facial revisions reveal a self-measurement
based on a white yardstick. Hence, despite the fact that he is one of the greatest
entertainers who has ever lived, he still views himself, at least in part, through white
aesthetic lenses that devalue some of his African characteristics. Needless to say,
Michael Jackson's example is but the more honest and visible instance of a rather
pervasive self-loathing among many of the black professional class. Malcolm X's call
for psychic conversion often strikes horror into this privileged group because so
much of who they are and what they do is evaluated in terms of their wealth, status,
and prestige in American society. On the other hand, this group often understands
Malcolm X's claim more than others precisely because they have lived so intimately
in a white world in which the devaluation of black people is so often taken for granted
or unconsciously assumed. It is no accident that the black middle class has always

had an ambivalent relation to Malcolm X — an open rejection of his militant strategy of wholesale defiance of American society and a secret embrace of his bold truth-telling about the depths of racism in American society. One rarely encounters a picture of Malcolm X (as one does of Martin Luther King, Jr.) in the office of a black professional, but there is no doubt that Malcolm X dangles as the skeleton in the closet lodged in the racial memory of most black professionals.

In short, Malcolm X's notion of psychic conversion is an implicit critique of 5 W. E. B. Du Bois's idea of "double-consciousness." Du Bois wrote:

> The Negro is a sort of seventh son, born with a veil, and gifted with second-sight in this American world, — a world which yields him no true self-consciousness, but only lets him see himself through the revelation of the other world. It is a peculiar sensation, this double-consciousness, this sense of always looking at one's self through the eyes of others, of measuring one's soul by the tape of a world that looks on in amused contempt and pity.[1]

For Malcolm X this "double-consciousness" pertains more to those black people who live "betwixt and between" the black and white worlds — traversing the borders between them yet never settled in either. Hence, they crave peer acceptance in both, receive genuine approval from neither, yet persist in viewing themselves through the lenses of the dominant white society. For Malcolm X, this "double-consciousness" is less a description of a necessary black mode of being in America than a particular kind of colonized mind-set of a special group in black America. Du Bois's "double-consciousness" seems to lock black people into the quest for white approval and disappointment owing mainly to white racist assessment, whereas Malcolm X suggests that this tragic syndrome can be broken through psychic conversion. But how?

"Malcolm X suggests that this tragic syndrome can be broken through psychic conversion. But how?"

Malcolm X does not put forward a direct answer to this question. First, his well-known distinction 6 between "house negroes" (who love and protect the white master) and "field negroes" (who hate and resist the white master) suggests that the masses of black people are more likely to acquire decolonized sensibilities and hence less likely to be "co-opted" by the white status quo. Yet this rhetorical device, though insightful in highlighting different perspectives

---

[1] West is quoting from Du Bois's seminal work, *The Souls of Black Folk* (1903). For a recent version, see the volume edited by Henry Louis Gates Jr. (New York: Oxford UP, 2007), 3. [Editor's note]

among black people, fails as a persuasive description of the behavior of "well-to-do" black folk and "poor" black folk. In other words, there are numerous instances of "field negroes" with "house negro" mentalities and "house negroes" with "field negro" mentalities. Malcolm X's often-quoted distinction rightly highlights the propensity among highly assimilated black professionals to put "whiteness" (in all its various forms) on a pedestal, but it also tends to depict "poor" black peoples' notions and enactments of "blackness" in an uncritical manner. Hence his implicit critique of Du Bois's idea of "double-consciousness" contains some truth yet offers an inadequate alternative.

Second, Malcolm X's black nationalist viewpoint claims that the only legiti- 7 mate response to white supremacist ideology and practice is black self-love and black self-determination free of the tension generated by "double-consciousness." This claim is both subtle and problematic. It is subtle in that every black freedom movement is predicated on an affirmation of African humanity and a quest for black control over the destinies of black people. Yet not every form of black self-love affirms African humanity. Furthermore not every project of black self-determination consists of a serious quest for black control over the destinies of black people. Malcolm's claim is problematic in that it tends to assume that black nationalisms have a monopoly on black self-love and black self-determination. This fallacious assumption confuses the issues highlighted by black nationalisms with the various ways in which black nationalists and others understand these issues. 8

For example, the grand legacy of Marcus Garvey forces us never to forget that black self-love and black self-respect sit at the center of any possible black freedom movement. Yet this does not mean that we must talk about black self-love and black self-respect in the way in which Garvey did, that is, on an imperial model in which black armies and navies signify black power. Similarly, the tradition of Elijah Muhammad compels us to acknowledge the centrality of black self-regard and black self-esteem, yet that does not entail an acceptance of how Elijah Muhammad talked about achieving this aim, that is, by playing a game of black supremacy that awakens us from our captivity to white supremacy. My point here is that a focus on the issues rightly targeted by black nationalists and an openness to the insights of black nationalists does not necessarily result in an acceptance of black nationalist ideology. Malcolm X tended to make such an unwarranted move — despite his legitimate focus on black self-love, his rich insights on black captivity to white supremacy, and his profound notion of psychic conversion.

• • •

Malcolm X's notion of psychic conversion depends on the idea that black spaces, in 9 which black community, humanity, love, care, concern, and support flourish, will emerge from a boiling black rage. At this point, however, Malcolm X's project falters. How can the boiling black rage be contained and channeled in the black spaces such that destructive and self-destructive consequences are abated? The greatness of Malcolm X is, in part, that he raises this fundamental challenge with a sharpness and urgency never before posed in black America, yet he never had a chance in his short life to grapple with it, nor solve it in idea and deed.

The project of black separatism — to which Malcolm X was beholden for most of 10 his life after his first psychic conversion to the Nation of Islam — suffered from deep intellectual and organizational problems. Unlike Malcolm X's notion of psychic conversion, Elijah Muhammad's idea of religious conversion was predicated on an obsession with white supremacy. The basic aim of black Muslim theology — with its distinct black supremacist account of the origins of white people — was to counter white supremacy. Yet this preoccupation with white supremacy still allowed white people to serve as the principal point of reference. That which fundamentally motivates one still dictates the terms of what one thinks and does — so the motivation of a black supremacist doctrine reveals how obsessed one is with white supremacy. This is understandable in a white racist society — but it is crippling for a despised people struggling for freedom, in that one's eyes should be on the prize, not on the perpetuator of one's oppression. In short, Elijah Muhammad's project remained captive to the supremacy game — a game mastered by the white racists he opposed and imitated with his black supremacy doctrine.

Malcolm X's notion of psychic conversion can be understood and used such that 11 it does not necessarily *entail* black supremacy; it simply rejects black captivity to white supremacist ideology and practice. Hence, as the major black Muslim spokesperson, he had many sympathizers but many fewer Muslim members. Why did Malcolm X permit his notion of psychic conversion to result in black supremacist claims of the Nation of Islam — claims that undermine much of the best of his call for psychic conversion? Malcolm X remained a devoted follower of Elijah Muhammad until 1964 partly because he believed the other major constructive channels of black rage in America — the black church and black music — were less effective in producing and sustaining psychic conversion than the Nation of Islam. He knew that the electoral political system could never address the existential dimension of black rage — hence he, like Elijah, shunned it. Malcolm X also recognized, as do too few black leaders today, that the black encounter with the absurd in racist American society yields a profound spiritual need for human affirmation and recognition.

Hence, the centrality of religion and music — those most spiritual of human activities — in black life.

Yet, for Malcolm, much of black religion and black music had misdirected black rage away from white racism and toward another world of heaven and sentimental romance. Needless to say, Malcolm's conception of black Christianity as a white man's religion of pie-in-the-sky and black music as soupy "I Love You B-a-b-y" romance is wrong. While it may be true that most — but not all — of the black music of Malcolm's day shunned black rage, the case of the church-based civil rights movement would seem to counter his charge that black Christianity serves as a sedative to put people to sleep rather than to ignite them to action. Like Elijah Muhammad (and unlike Malcolm X), Martin Luther King, Jr., concluded that black rage was so destructive and self-destructive that without a broad moral vision and political organization, black rage would wreak havoc on black America. His project of nonviolent resistance to white racism was an attempt to channel black rage in political directions that preserved black dignity and changed American society. And his despair at the sight of Watts in 1965 or Detroit and Newark in 1967 left him more and more pessimistic about the moral channeling of black rage in America. To King it looked as if cycles of chaos and destruction loomed on the horizon if these moral channels were ineffective or unappealing to the coming generation. For Malcolm, however, the civil rights movement was not militant enough. It failed to speak clearly and directly to and about black rage.

Malcolm X also seems to have had almost no intellectual interest in dealing with what is distinctive about black religion and black music: *their cultural hybrid character in which the complex mixture of African, European, and Amerindian elements are constitutive of something that is new and black in the modern world.* Like most black nationalists, Malcolm X feared the culturally hybrid character of black life. This fear rested upon the need for Manichean[2] (black/white or male/female) channels for the direction of black rage — forms characterized by charismatic leaders, patriarchal structures, and dogmatic pronouncements. To be sure, these forms are similar to those of other religious organizations around the world, yet the fear of black cultural hybridity among the Nation of Islam is significant for its distinctive form of Manichean theology and authoritarian arrangements. The Manichean theology kept the white world at bay even as it heralded dominant modern European

[2] Manichaeism was a dualistic religious movement founded by Mani (216–276 CE) in Persia. Flourishing from the third to the sixth century, it taught that the human soul is caught in a cosmic struggle between spirit, good, and light on one side and matter, evil, and darkness on the other. [Editor's note]

notions like racial supremacy and nationalism. The authoritarian arrangements imposed a top-down disciplined corps of devoted followers who contained their rage in an atmosphere of cultural repression (regulation of clothing worn, books and records consumed, sexual desire, etc.) and paternalistic protection of women.

This complex relation of cultural hybridity and critical sensibility (or jazz and democracy) raises interesting questions. If Malcolm X feared cultural hybridity, to what degree or in what sense was he a serious democrat? Did he believe that the cure to the egregious ills of a racist American "democracy" was more democracy that included black people? Did his relative silence regarding the monarchies he visited in the Middle East bespeak a downplaying of the role of democratic practices in empowering oppressed peoples? Was his fear of cultural hybridity partly rooted in his own reluctance to come to terms with his own personal hybridity, for example, his "redness," light skin, close white friends, etc.? 14

Malcolm X's fear of cultural hybridity rests upon two political concerns: that cultural hybridity downplayed the vicious character of white supremacy and that cultural hybridity intimately linked the destinies of black and white people such that the possibility of black freedom was farfetched. His fundamental focus on the varieties, subtleties, and cruelties of white racism made him suspicious of any discourse about cultural hybridity. Furthermore, those figures who were most eloquent and illuminating about black cultural hybridity in the 1950s and early 1960s, for example, Ralph Ellison and Albert Murray, were political integrationists. Such a position seemed to pass over too quickly the physical terror and psychic horror of being black in America. To put it bluntly, Malcolm X identified much more with the mind-set of Richard Wright's Bigger Thomas in *Native Son* than with that of Ralph Ellison's protagonist in *Invisible Man*. 15

> *"This deep pessimism also rendered Malcolm X ambivalent about American democracy."*

16

Malcolm X's deep pessimism about the capacity and possibility of white Americans to shed their racism led him, ironically, to downplay the past and present bonds between blacks and whites. For if the two groups were, as Martin Luther King, Jr., put it, locked into "one garment of destiny," then the very chances for black freedom were nil. This deep pessimism also rendered Malcolm X ambivalent about American democracy — for if the majority were racist how could the black minority ever be free? Malcolm X's definition of a "nigger" was "a victim of American democracy" — had not the *Herrenvolk* democracy of the United States made black people noncitizens or anticitizens of the Republic? Of course, the aim of a constitutional democracy is to safeguard the rights of the minority and avoid the tyranny of the majority. Yet the concrete practice of the U.S. legal system from 1883 to 1964 promoted a tyranny of the white majority much more than a safeguarding of the rights of black Americans. In fact, these tragic facts drove Malcolm X to look elsewhere for the promotion and protection of black people's rights — to institutions such as the United Nations or the Organization of African Unity. One impulse behind his internationalization of the black freedom struggle in the United States was a deep pessimism about America's will to racial justice, no matter how democratic America was or is.

In addition, Malcolm X's fear of cultural hybridity was linked to his own personal hybridity (he was the grandson of a white man), which blurred the very boundaries so rigidly policed by white supremacist authorities. For Malcolm X, the distinctive feature of American culture was not its cross-cultural syncretism but rather the enforcement of a racial caste system that defined any product of this syncretism as abnormal, alien, and other to both black and white communities. Like Garvey, Malcolm X saw such hybridity, for example, mulattoes, as symbols of weakness and confusion. The very idea of not "fitting in" the U.S. discourse of positively valued whiteness and negatively debased blackness meant one was subject to exclusion and marginalization by whites and blacks. For Malcolm X, in a racist society, this was a form of social death. 17

One would think that Malcolm X's second conversion, in 1964, to Orthodox Islam might have allayed his fear of cultural hybridity. Yet there seems to be little evidence that he revised his understanding of the radically culturally hybrid character of black life. Furthermore, his deep pessimism toward American democracy continued after his second conversion — though it was no longer based on mythological grounds but solely on the historical experience of Africans in the modern world. It is no accident that the nonblack persons Malcolm X encountered who helped change his mind about the capacity of white people to be human were outside of America and Europe, Muslims in the Middle East. Needless to say, for him, the most striking feature of these Islamic regimes was not their undemocratic practices but rather their acceptance of his black humanity. This great prophet of black rage — with all his brilliance, courage, and conviction — remained blind to basic structures of domination based on class, gender, and sexual orientation in the Middle East. 18

The contemporary focus on Malcolm X, especially among black youth, can be understood as both the open articulation of black rage (as in film videos and on tapes targeted at whites, Jews, Koreans, black women, black men, and others) and as a 19

> *"The young black generation are up against forces of death, destruction, and disease. "*

desperate attempt to channel this rage into something more than a marketable commodity for the culture industry. The young black generation are up against forces of death, destruction, and disease unprecedented in the everyday life of black urban people. The raw reality of drugs and guns, despair and decrepitude, generates a raw rage that, among past black spokespersons, only Malcolm X's speech approximates. Yet the issue of psychic conversion, cultural hybridity, black supremacy, authoritarian organization, borders and boundaries in sexuality, and other matters all loom large at present— the same issues Malcolm X left dangling at the end of his short life spent articulating black rage and affirming black humanity.

If we are to build on the best of Malcolm X, we must preserve and expand his 20 notion of psychic conversion that cements networks and groups in which black community, humanity, love, care, and concern can take root and grow (the work of bell hooks is the best example). These spaces — beyond the best of black music and black religion — reject Manichean ideologies and authoritarian arrangements in the name of moral visions, subtle analyses of wealth and power, and concrete strategies of principled coalitions and democratic alliances. These visions, analyses, and strategies never lose sight of black rage, yet they focus this rage where it belongs: on any form of racism, sexism, homophobia, or economic injustice that impedes the opportunities of "everyday people" (to use the memorable phrase of Sly and the Family Stone and Arrested Development) to live lives of dignity and decency. For example, poverty can be as much a target of rage as degraded identity.

Furthermore, the cultural hybrid character of black life leads us to highlight a 21 metaphor alien to Malcolm X's perspective — yet consonant with his performances to audiences — namely, the metaphor of jazz. I use the term "jazz" here not so much as a term for a musical art form, as for a mode of being in the world, an improvisational mode of protean, fluid, and flexible dispositions toward reality suspicious of "either/or" viewpoints, dogmatic pronouncements, or supremacist ideologies. To be a jazz freedom fighter is to attempt to galvanize and energize world-weary people into forms of organization with accountable leadership that promote critical exchange and broad reflection. The interplay of individuality and unity is not one of uniformity and unanimity imposed from above but rather of conflict among diverse groupings that reach a dynamic consensus subject to questioning and criticism. As with a soloist in a jazz quartet, quintet or band, individuality is promoted in order to sustain and increase the *creative* tension with the group — a tension that yields higher levels of performance to achieve the aim of the collective project. This kind of critical and democratic sensibility flies in the face of any policing of borders and boundaries of "blackness," "maleness," "femaleness," or "whiteness." Black people's rage ought to target white supremacy, but also ought to realize that blackness *per se* can encompass feminists like Frederick Douglass or W. E. B. Du Bois. Black people's rage should not overlook homophobia, yet also should acknowledge that heterosexuality *per se* can be associated with so-called "straight" anti-homophobes — just as the struggle against black poverty can be supported by progressive elements of any race, gender, or sexual orientation.

Malcolm X was the first great black spokesperson who looked ferocious white 22 racism in the eye, didn't blink, and lived long enough to tell America the truth about this glaring hypocrisy in a bold and defiant manner. Unlike Elijah Muhammad and Martin Luther King, Jr., he did not live long enough to forge his own distinctive ideas and ways of channeling black rage in constructive channels to change American society. Only if we are as willing as Malcolm X to grow and confront the new challenges posed by the black rage of our day will we take the black freedom struggle to a new and higher level. The future of this country may well depend on it.

Questions for Discussion and Writing

1. West offers both an analysis and a critique of Malcolm X's core views, trying to save those aspects he believes to be of enduring value while also bringing to light those he believes to be problematic. As you reread, create two lists — a list of the elements in Malcolm X's thinking that West wants to retain and a list of the elements that he rejects. Explain (as best you can) *why* West wants to retain or reject each of these elements. Drawing on your two lists, describe the alternative that West offers to Malcolm X's "Manichean ideologies."

2. How would you explain the relationship between the two epigraphs from Alexis de Tocqueville's *Democracy in America* (1840 and 1835) and the argument that West makes in this chapter?

3. How does the concept of "psychic conversion" differ from W. E. B. Du Bois's concept of "double-consciousness"? In your view, how might other minorities, or other groups with a history of discrimination or oppression, employ the concept of "psychic conversion"? What value would it have for them? Might the concepts of cultural hybridity and what West calls "jazz" also be applied to these groups? What do you suppose this would mean in practice?

Glossary

abstract (1) *noun:* A summary of an argument. (2) *adjective:* Denoting a thought, an idea, or a quality rather than a concrete thing.

academic discourse The characteristic language use, or conventions of speaking and writing, practiced by members of institutions of higher education.

academic literacy A familiarity with academic discourse that enables a person to understand it and speak it.

active reading A kind of reading that brings all of one's mental faculties to bear, including questioning, analyzing, weighing, drawing inferences, and more.

active verb A verb form in which the subject performs the action: "Stephen King wrote this book." Sentences constructed in this way are in the "active voice." (See PASSIVE VERB.)

annotate To add a note to a text or graphic, usually as a comment or an explanation.

appositive phrase A phrase that expands on the term that immediately precedes it. For example, "Barack Obama, the first African American president, was born in Honolulu." Here, "the first African American president" is an appositive phrase.

argument A logical structure made up of a claim and support for the claim.

argument matrix A device for developing arguments that consists of a document divided into three columns for noting claims, the evidence that supports the claim, and the discussion that links and explains the two.

audit of meaning A reader's active assessment of the sense of a text. The term is a definition of "dialectic," offered by the critic I. A. Richards (*How to Read a Page* [New York: W. W. Norton and Co., 1942], 240) and employed by professor of English Ann E. Berthoff to explain how readers and writers must continually review and revise their understanding of meaning as it emerges. In *Forming/Thinking/Writing,* Second Edition (Portsmouth, NH: Heinemann–Boynton/Cook, 1988), Berthoff writes, "Just as a bookkeeper has to account for income and expenditures in order to balance credits and debits, an audit of meanings would have to balance what one sentence seems to say against what others seem to say; how one way of saying something compares with another; what one word seems to refer to in a certain context with what it seems to refer to in another" (240).

balanced sentence A sentence that uses parallel sentence structures, usually two or more independent clauses joined together. For example, "He liked to like people, therefore people liked him" (Mark Twain, *Joan of Arc*).

bibliographic database An electronic index to journal, magazine, or newspaper articles, usually including citations. It may also include abstracts, full text, and links to full text.

call number A number or combination of numbers and letters used to arrange and locate items on a library's shelves.

citation A note that attributes referenced, paraphrased, or quoted material to its source.

claim An assertion that something is true or valid.

clause A group of words that contains a subject and a predicate.

close reading A careful, detailed analysis or interpretation of a text (or other artifact such as a visual or piece of music). Such a reading attends to diction, syntax, imagery, structure, voice, and other features.

complete predicate A predicate's verb plus its complements, objects, and modifiers.

complete subject The noun or pronoun that performs the action of a clause's main verb together with its modifying words. Also known as the "whole subject."

complex sentence A sentence that contains one independent clause and at least one subordinate clause.

compound-complex sentence A sentence that contains more than one independent clause and at least one subordinate clause.

compound predicate A predicate that contains more than one main verb.

compound sentence A sentence that contains more than one independent clause.

concept An idea or a general notion, usually one that is widely held and drawn from many instances or examples.

concrete Existing in a material form or as an actual reality, or pertaining to such things (as opposed to ABSTRACT).

conjunction A word used to join words, phrases, or clauses (for example, "and," "if," "or," "yet").

connotation The associations, ideas, or feelings that a word conjures, as distinct from its literal meaning.

coordination Connecting two or more ideas or clauses of roughly equal weight or emphasis in a sentence, usually with a semicolon or a coordinating conjunction. For example, "She loved Barcelona, but she could not visit often." (See SUBORDINATION.)

copious style A style of writing described by Erasmus in *De Copia* (1512), characterized by its abundant embellishments, amplifications, and descriptive details.

counterargument An argument or a line of reasoning in opposition to another argument or line of reasoning.

critical thinking The process of skillfully applying, analyzing, evaluating, and synthesizing ideas and information in order to solve problems and answer questions.

culture The customs, arts, way of life, and social practices of a people, society, period, or social group.

cumulative loose sentence A loose sentence in which words and phrases that develop or qualify the main idea appear after the independent clause. (See LOOSE SENTENCE.)

current belief An idea or a set of ideas that is widely accepted based on available evidence in a given historical period, though new evidence might negate it.

database In general, a set of data stored in a computer. Often used as shorthand for BIBLIO-GRAPHIC DATABASE.

deduction The inference of particular instances from a general truth, or of one general truth from another. (See INDUCTION.)

denotation The literal dictionary definition of a word.

descriptive Serving to portray the characteristic qualities of a thing (or person or place).

dialectic A method of arriving at insights or truths through the back-and-forth of debate, discussion, or an exchange of ideas.

dialectical notebook A type of double-entry notebook, developed by Ann E. Berthoff, that uses a divided page to allow direct observation, transcription, or quotation on one side of the page and reflection or commentary on the other. "The point of this double-entry system is that it encourages you to think about your thinking and to carry out an audit of the meanings you are making" (in Berthoff, *Forming/Thinking/Writing*, 2nd ed. [Portsmouth, NH: Heinemann–Boynton/Cook, 1988], 26). (See AUDIT OF MEANING.)

diction The choice of words and phrases in a text or speech.

documentation The supplying of information on sources by means of notes and a bibliography.

drafting The act of making a preliminary, rough version of a text.

editing The act of correcting and improving a text, or preparing it for submission or publication.

enthymeme An argument in which one premise is unstated.

epitome A brief summary.

evidence Facts or information that support a claim, showing it to be valid.

exegesis (*plural:* exegeses) An interpretation, an explanation, or a paraphrase.

expletive A phrase that fills out a sentence without adding to the sense, often using the word "there" or "it" and a form of the verb "to be," as in "There are nine muses who are celebrated in Greek mythology."

fact A well-established item of information or knowledge, usually based on actual observation or trusted testimony.

fallacy A failure of reasoning or an error in logic.

field research Studies conducted outside the library or laboratory, producing original data. Common types of field research include observations, interviews, surveys, and opinion polls.

genre A category or type of work, usually defined by similarities in form or purpose.

gerund A word form derived from a verb that functions as a noun — for example, the word "writing" in the sentence "Writing is one of my favorite activities."

grammar The structure of a language; the study of relations between words in a sentence; the rules for using language in accordance with accepted usage.

induction The inference of a general truth from particular instances. (See DEDUCTION.)

informal writing Free, casual, relaxed writing, normally performed to generate and clarify ideas rather than to present ideas to a reader.

intellectual property The right of individuals and organizations to own their original ideas or data.

keyword Any significant word in a database or catalog record.

knowledge problem The question that remains unanswered, the mystery that remains unsolved, or the need that remains unfilled.

Likert scale A type of multiple-choice survey or questionnaire in which respondents indicate their level of agreement with a series of statements. Named for the twentieth-century psychologist Rensis Likert.

logic Systematic reasoning conducted according to strict rules of validity.

loose sentence A sentence in which the independent clause appears first, followed by any modifying clauses and phrases.

main argument A work's major claims and the reasons given in support of these claims.

malapropism An incorrect use of a word or phrase that sounds similar to the correct one.

marginalia Notes in the margins of a text.

metadiscourse Words that explain or discuss the text (or speech) of which they are a part.

monograph A written study of a single specialized subject.

nominalization A noun formed from a verb.

normative Relating to a norm or standard.

nucleus (of an argument) The core ideas that make up an argument.

opinion A view, belief, or judgment that rests on grounds insufficient for certainty.

paraphrase A rewording of a text. An acceptable paraphrase does not use the same words or the same grammatical structures as the original.

passive verb A verb form in which the subject is acted upon rather than performing the action. The actor may or may not be stated — for example, "The book was beautifully written" or "The book was beautifully written by Stephen King." Sentences constructed in this way are in the "passive voice." (See ACTIVE VERB.)

peer-reviewed Evaluated for publication by other experts in the same field.

periodical A journal, magazine, or newspaper published at regular intervals.

periodic sentence A sentence in which the independent clause appears at or near the end, preceded by modifying phrases and clauses.

periphrasis (*adjective:* periphrastic) A roundabout, indirect, or wordy expression or style.

phrase Any group of words that makes sense as a unit but lacks a predicate.

plagiarism Taking another person's words or ideas and presenting them as one's own.

plain style A style of writing characterized by economy, clarity, simplicity, and directness.

position A writer's stand or point of view relative to that of other writers on the subject.

predicate A group of words that says something about the subject and includes a main verb.

premise A proposition that supports a conclusion. In logic, a statement from which another follows as a conclusion. Either of the first two statements in a syllogism, from which a conclusion is drawn.

prepositional phrase A group of words beginning with a preposition and ending with a noun, pronoun, gerund, or clause — for example, "at home," "before noon," "by force."

primary research Research in which the researcher gathers or produces the data himself or herself, as distinct from secondary research, in which data and ideas are gathered from other sources.

principle of charity The proposition that readers should give an author's views fair consideration before making criticisms and raising questions.

proof Evidence or argument that establishes the fact, certainty, or truth of a statement.

proposition A statement that asserts or denies something, or a statement offered for consideration.

qualifier A modifier; a word or phrase that limits or attributes a quality to another word or phrase.

qualify To modify, limit, or add reservations (to a statement).

readerly Concerning the reader, or with attention to the reader's needs and enjoyment (as opposed to WRITERLY).

reading with a purpose Reading in order to generate ideas of your own, with the aim of responding, rather than reading simply to understand the writer's ideas or to expand your own knowledge. It is reading as a means to an end, rather than as an end in itself.

reasoning A sequence of logically connected statements.

recursive A process that repeats the same functions, but produces advances with each repetition.

refereed Evaluated for publication by other experts in the same field.

relevant (support) Connected to, and appropriate for, an argument.

research Systematic investigation aiming to contribute to knowledge; a systematic investigation conducted to gather material for an original essay, article, report, or other document.

research paper A composition that presents the results of a systematic investigation.

research report A composition that summarizes the research conducted by other scholars on a topic or question.

response A verbal or written reply to, or comment on, a statement or an idea.

revising Altering and improving a text; one of the two principal phases of the writing process (the other being INFORMAL WRITING).

rhetoric The art of argument or persuasion.

rhetorical structure The arrangement of the elements of an argument, especially the relationship between claims and their support.

scholarship Learning or erudition, the attainments and methods of a scholar.

scope The range or extent of an argument, topic, or theme. To "broaden the scope" of a topic is to make it more general; to "narrow the scope" is to make it more specific.

secondary research Research in which data and ideas are gathered from other sources, as distinct from primary research, in which the researcher gathers or produces the data himself or herself.

sentence structure The arrangement of words, phrases, or grammatical elements in a sentence.

simple predicate The verb (including auxiliary verbs) of a predicate.

simple sentence A sentence that contains only one independent clause and no subordinate clauses.

simple subject The noun or pronoun (without its modifiers) that performs the action of the clause's main verb.

stadium (*plural: stadia*) Another word for a STAGE in an argument.

stage A major segment of an argument, a group of related arguments that together form part of a larger argument.

strategy A technique or plan of action designed to achieve a significant aim.

subject The part of a sentence that performs an action. It may be a noun, a pronoun, a noun phrase, or a clause that functions as a noun.

subordination Connecting an idea of lesser weight or emphasis in a sentence by turning it into a phrase or dependent clause. For example, "Although she loved Barcelona, she knew she would never visit it again." ("Although she loved Barcelona" is the dependent clause.) (See COORDINATION.)

support In rhetoric, the evidence and reasoning that back up a claim.

syllogism A form of logical argument frequently used in deductive reasoning in which a conclusion is drawn from two premises — for example, "All men are mortal. Aristotle is a man. Therefore, Aristotle is mortal." (See ENTHYMEME.)

thesis The main argument of an essay or a longer text.

thesis statement A statement of the author's main argument; the "master claim" for the argument as a whole. It may be one sentence or several.

tone A quality in writing that expresses or suggests a particular voice, inflection, character, or mood.

topic The subject matter or theme of a text or discourse.

topic sentence A sentence that declares the main concern, theme, or point of a paragraph.

turning point In a text, a place where a significant change of direction occurs, from one topic to another or from one approach or method to another.

unacceptable paraphrase A version of a text that is too close to the wording or the grammatical structure of the original, or one that fails to cite its source properly and completely. (See PARAPHRASE.)

unity In paragraphs, the quality of consistency of purpose, wholeness, and cohesion.

valid (support) Logically sound and to the point; grounded in logic, fact, or truth.

whole subject See COMPLETE SUBJECT.

working thesis statement A provisional thesis statement that will be developed or improved later. (See THESIS STATEMENT.)

writerly Concerning the writer, or with attention to the writer's own needs (as opposed to READERLY).

writing to communicate A kind of writing, or phase in the writing process, that emphasizes sharing ideas with a reader or conveying ideas clearly and effectively.

writing to learn A kind of writing, or phase in the writing process, that emphasizes discovery, invention, and the generation of ideas (as opposed to their communication).

Acknowledgments

Gisela Bock. Excerpt from "Racism and Sexism in Nazi Germany," in *Signs: Journal of Women in Culture and Society* 1983, vol. 8, no. 3. Copyright © 1983 by University of Chicago Press. Reproduced by permission.

Joan Didion. Excerpt from "On Keeping a Notebook." From *Slouching Towards Bethlehem*, pp. 133–36. Copyright © 1966, 1968. Renewed 1996 by Joan Didion. Reprinted by permission of Farrar, Straus and Giroux, LLC.

Adam Gopnik. "Bumping into Mr. Ravioli," in *The New Yorker*, September 30, 2002. Copyright © 2002 by Adam Gopnik. Reproduced by permission.

Temple Grandin. Excerpt from *Animals in Translation*, pp. 148–49. Scribner, 2004. Copyright © 2004 by Temple Grandin. Reprinted by permission from the author.

Martin Luther King, Jr. Excerpt from "Letter from Birmingham Jail." Copyright © 1963 Dr. Martin Luther King, Jr.; copyright renewed 1991 Coretta Scott King. Reprinted by arrangement with The Heirs to the Estate of Martin Luther King, Jr., c/o Writers House as agent for the proprietor, New York, NY.

Praveen K. Kopalle, Donald R. Lehmann, John U. Farley. "Consumer Expectations and Culture: The Effect of Belief in Karma in India." From *The Journal of Consumer Research*, Vol. 37, No. 2 (August 2010), pp. 251–53. The University of Chicago Press, 2010. Copyright © 2010 by University of Chicago Press. Reproduced by permission.

Kathryn Schulz. "Two Models of Wrongness." From *Being Wrong*, pp. 25–43. HarperCollins, 2010. Copyright © 2010 by Kathryn Schulz. Reprinted by permission of HarperCollins Publishers.

James Surowiecki. Excerpts from "A Drug on the Market." From *The New Yorker*, June 25, 2007. Reprinted by permission of SLL/Sterling Lord Literistic, Inc. Copyright by James Surowiecki.

Lewis Thomas. "To Err Is Human." Originally appeared in the *New England Journal of Medicine*, v. 294, January 8, 1976, pp. 99–100. Copyright © 1976 by The New England Journal of Medicine. Reproduced by permission.

Jane Tompkins. "At the Buffalo Bill Museum, June 1988." From *West of Everything: The Inner Life of Westerns*, pp. 179–203. Oxford University Press, 1992. Copyright © 1992 by Jane Tompkins.

Frans de Waal. "Are We in Anthropodenial?" From *The Ape and the Sushi Master* by Frans de Waal, pp. 63–84. Basic Books, 2001. Copyright © 2001 Frans de Waal. Reprinted by permission of Basic Books, a member of the Perseus Books Group.

Cornel West. "Malcolm X and Black Rage." From *Race Matters* by Cornel West, pp. 95–105. Copyright 1993, 2001 by Cornel West. Reprinted by permission of Beacon Press, Boston.

Image Credits

Page 36: Ad Council advertisement, *Start Talking Before They Start Drinking*. Kaplan Thaler Group.

Page 37: Thomas Ball, *The Freedmen's Memorial*. Library of Congress.

Page 47: Martin Luther, page from *Colloquia Mensalia*. © The British Library Board. Ashley 4773 Chapter 13 pg 212.

Index